High IQ Kids

Collected Insights, Information, and Personal Stories from the Experts

Edited by
Kiesa Kay, Deborah Robson, and Judy Fort Brenneman

free spirit
PUBLiSHiNG®

Meeting kids'
social & emotional
needs since 1983

Cataloging-in-Publication Data
High IQ kids : collected insights, information, and personal stories from the experts / edited by Kiesa Kay, Deborah Robson, and Judy Fort Brenneman.
    p. cm.
    Includes index.
    ISBN-13: 978-1-57542-261-9
    ISBN-10: 1-57542-261-1
    1. Gifted children—Education—United States. 2. Gifted children—United States—Identification. I. Kay, Kiesa. II. Robson, Deborah. III. Brenneman, Judy Fort.
    LC3993.9.H54 2008
    371.95—dc22

                                                                                2007014327

At the time of this book's publication, all facts and figures cited are the most current available. All telephone numbers, addresses, and Web site URLs are accurate and active; all publications, organizations, Web sites, and other resources exist as described in this book; and all have been verified as of April 2007. The editors and Free Spirit Publishing make no warranty or guarantee concerning the information and materials given out by organizations or content found at Web sites, and we are not responsible for any changes that occur after this book's publication. If you find an error or believe that a resource listed here is not as described, please contact Free Spirit Publishing. Parents, teachers, and other adults: We strongly urge you to monitor children's use of the Internet.

Reprint with Permission; FRAZZ: © Jef Mallett/Distributed by United Feature Syndicate, Inc.

Cover and interior design by Percolator

10 9 8 7 6 5 4 3 2 1
Printed in the United States of America

Free Spirit Publishing Inc.
217 Fifth Avenue North, Suite 200
Minneapolis, MN 55401-1299
(612) 338-2068
help4kids@freespirit.com
www.freespirit.com

For Michelle Bierstedt, with love and admiration.
—K.K.

For my daughter, who made me learn about all this stuff, and for both of my parents, each for a different reason.
—D.R.

For Kyle, who guarantees that I will never be bored, and for Ted, who listens, believes, and asks the right questions.
—J.F.B.

Contents

PART 1: What's in a Number?

PART 2: Take a Number

PART 3: More Than a Number

APPENDIX: Resources and More Information

Foreword

BY ANNETTE REVEL SHEELY

School Counselor of the Rocky Mountain School
for the Gifted and Creative

There are no MapQuest directions for you on this journey. You are traveling down a path few have taken and fewer have charted. You are helping a very gifted child grow and mature and find a place in this world.

You are not alone. Others have come before you and some of their wisdom is contained in these pages. I hope the personal stories bring the comfort of recognition.

Parents and guardians may find the chapters from experts in the field especially useful when working with schools and professionals who want to help but have no training about children in this IQ range. In my experience, most teachers and administrators are caring but overworked, and they appreciate succinct pieces of practical information. Educators working in the classroom may be most interested in the research findings and the suggestions (and encouragement) for implementing them on a daily basis, as well as the parents' and students' perspectives to which they may not otherwise have such ready access.

Perhaps you will pass on the wisdom you gain to those who are following behind you. When something works for your child, or you find a school or professional who really "gets" PG (profoundly gifted), post a note on an online bulletin board for other PG families to find.

Be an adult whom this child can trust and depend on. Being highly gifted can be highly stressful; provide sanctuary for your child when necessary.

Parenting and educating the highly gifted can be exceptionally stressful. These children have high energy, demanding curiosity, and unrelenting intensity. Take good care of yourself. If that sounds selfish to you, think of it in terms of modeling a healthy life for this very observant child.

Parents, trust your good instincts. You know this child better than anyone on earth. Approach teachers as the caring, hardworking professionals you hope they are.

Teachers, ask the parents about the child. They can help you keep the child engaged in learning, which is easier to manage in the classroom than his or her boredom and acting out.

And finally, repeat this phrase as needed: We'll do fine.

Preface

BY KIESA KAY

My profoundly gifted (PG) children are grown now. My daughter has graduated from high school three years early and hasn't decided what comes next. My son has launched himself into college. Many years and miles since my parenting journey began, I'm exhaling into a clear stretch of empty air in the space where my children's childhoods used to be. As the sun sets, sending a golden glow across the pasture, my soul soars into that space, and one regret flies back to me: if only I'd known then what it's taken me their whole lifetimes to learn.

In the hope of making similar journeys easier for other parents—as well as for educators, counselors, and all adults who work with or care about high-IQ kids—this book contains the resources I needed. It includes personal stories, hard data, and many perspectives in between those extremes.

Although every kid differs, each gifted family bumps into the question of what to do with unmet needs. High-IQ children don't live in isolation. They grow up within families and communities. Their needs differ radically depending on the resources available to them. Most of all, these kids need support for learning passionately and deeply. That's hard to arrange. My children have tried public, private, home, alternative, online, and charter schools.

A child's environment can change even if a family stays in one place. Many high-IQ children now negotiate invisible highways as well as regular roads. With the advent of the Internet, children can take college courses online and receive mentorships from across the globe while they actively pursue other activities within their hometowns. Kids who can surf the airwaves have a distinct advantage, but a danger exists if electronic connections replace face-to-face friendships and interactions.

In my opinion, we need to create an entirely new paradigm for what constitutes an appropriate learning environment, not only for high-IQ kids but for all kids. At the same time, I've learned that education constitutes only the smallest part of what matters most to high-IQ kids. Good decisions about how to raise a highly gifted child take the whole child and the entire family's needs into consideration; my own biggest bloopers as a parent resulted from looking at one set of needs out of context.

I hope this book will help parents, teachers, and counselors define the important questions in advance so they can quickly devise creative, individual answers for the high-IQ children who depend on them. We have such a short time to reach these kids, and so much is at stake in our ability to do so.

This book is a gift from those of us who had to learn these things the hard way to those of you who we hope will be able to raise your children with fewer struggles and more joy.

Acknowledgments

||||||||||||||||||||||||||||||||||||||||||||||||||||||||||||||||||||||||||||||||||||||||||||||||||||||||||||||||||||||||||||||||||||||||||||||||||||||

My children, Benjamin and Ameli Kat, inspired the creation of this book. Their strong spirits lift me every day as they teach me to live with the questions.

When Michelle Bierstedt, past president of the Denver Association for the Gifted and Talented, and I met at our first conference on giftedness, we looked at each other and asked, "What are we going to do with our kids?!" Her four children, Alicia, Christopher, Zachary, and Adam, and her husband, Eric, have created a wonderful home environment for loving and learning. Michelle is my role model.

Special appreciation goes to Cindy Kalman, Kristin Sanne-Gunderson, and Robin Carrington, for friendship and comfort, and to W. Bradley Chance, who shared everything. Annette Revel Sheely contributed intense professionalism.

Deborah Robson made something useful and beautiful of the disparate elements. Judy Fort Brenneman kept us going when we surely would have faltered, and she found the perfect publication home in Free Spirit Publishing, where Eric Braun took us swiftly over the finish line.

The Davidson Institute for Talent Development has been supportive of my work and I am grateful to all of the staff and the Davidson families. Jan Davidson exemplifies profound kindness.

This book would not have been possible without the ongoing support of many amazing people. Thanks to Terry Ray, Charlie Carrington, Leia Schultz, Camryn Schultz, Vic Contoski, Suzy Stevenson Ryan, Tom Hall, Laura Lewis, Evelyn Bassoff, Garnet MacPhee, Evelyn MacPhee, Patricia Killpack, Sachiko Imamura, Eva Wojcik-Obert, Meredith Warshaw, Bernadette Gimpel, Colleen Harsin, Rosanne Daryl Thomas, Linda Silverman, Barbara Gilman, the Ward family, the Daldorph family, the Kalman-Marx family, and the Gunderson-Libouban family. The Hedgebrook Retreat for Women Writers provided support and encouragement.

Thanks to Clark R. Cyr for sharing the resources that gave me the time to create this book, and to Judy LaBuda, Stuart Kingsbery, and Cara Malen for making those resources accessible. I also want to thank everyone who has responded to *Uniquely Gifted: Identifying and Meeting the Needs of the Twice-Exceptional Student*. The outpouring of love provided by those readers has kept me going.

Special thanks to the contributors to this volume, who have generously offered their knowledge and time for the benefit of high-IQ kids and their families and their teachers and who have been so patient with the long editing process required to bring this resource into existence: Amanda Avallone, Kathryn (Kit) Finn, Laura Freese, Tarek Grantham, Miraca Gross, Shaun Hately, Courtney James, Ilona von Károlyi-Ross, Carolyn Kottmeyer, Linda Long, Elizabeth Lovance, Deirdre Lovecky, Richard Maddox, Trindel Maine, Cathy Marciniak, Elizabeth Meckstroth, Christine (Tee) Neville, Sally Reis, Annemarie Roeper, Karen Rogers, Annette Sheely, Linda Silverman, Lee Singer, Annamarie Summers, Stephanie Tolan, Joyce VanTassel-Baska, Marilyn Walker, and John Wasserman.

# Introduction

This book is an invitation.

To parents. To teachers, counselors, and therapists. To anyone who ever wondered about or cared for high-IQ kids.

Most people—especially those with little experience raising or working with these kids—view above-average intelligence as an unqualified blessing that must make life easier. The smarter you are, the reasoning goes, the more successful you'll be, and the faster you'll reach that success. Being a genius must be like winning the lottery.

If you're the parent of a high-IQ kid, you already know it isn't that easy. High-IQ kids present unique challenges to their parents and teachers. They are at unique risk, too: exceptional IQ often walks hand-in-hand with exceptional vulnerability.

We three editors know about those challenges and risks first-hand. Our now-grown children are all uncommonly intelligent. That seemingly small fact shook up our lives more than it should have.

Developmental stages were never the same as the ones in the baby books. Sure-fire behavioral strategies backfired. Parent-teacher conferences began with "such a smart child *but*" and ended with lists of problem behaviors and unmet expectations. It didn't take us long to realize that our children really were different—not wrong, bad, or broken, but different.

Figuring out what to do took longer.

This book is a promise.

You are not alone in this process.

There are experts out there—other parents who have found their way. Other teachers and caring adults who have guided high-IQ kids and their families through education and life. Researchers who have explored everything from the meaning and measurement of intelligence to the social and emotional landscape of the profoundly gifted.

1

These experts are in this book, too, sharing their stories, experiences, discoveries, and expertise. In these pages are deep, wise, sorrowful, silly, and helpful voices who understand what it's like to care for these extraordinary and often misunderstood children. They know you, because they've been there already, and they are here to help.

This book is a guide.

But it is not a how-to manual. You won't find step-by-step instructions on how to raise and teach high-IQ kids. That's because there is no step-by-step method that works for all (or even most) of them. They aren't just radically different from their age-peers; they're radically different from each other. The needs of a specific high-IQ child are a reflection of the whole individual, and they encompass personality, thinking and learning styles, emotional development, and more.

For many parents, one of the most helpful things is to hear someone else say, "Yes, you are right, your kid is different, and different is amazing and wonderful. You are not crazy or pushy to be trying so hard to figure out what's best for your child."

For example, Judy recently met with a fellow independent business owner whose services she was considering. As they were wrapping up their meeting, the owner mentioned something about her five-year-old daughter, and by the time they left the coffee shop—an hour later—the woman had a list of resources that Judy could recall off the top of her head. Creating the list took maybe two minutes. The rest of the time, Judy listened to the woman talk about how challenging it was to keep up with her daughter and how tired she was. Although Judy offered some encouragement and suggestions about how to talk to the daughter's teachers, she suspects what the other mom most appreciated was the reassurance that her exhaustion was legitimate—and the confirmation that she's going to be this tired for another fifteen years or so. The woman already suspected that; what she needed was someone to validate her experience and point her in the right direction.

In large part, that's what we hope to do through this book. So although we can't offer you a canned approach that's consistent, linear, and generally applicable, we can reassure you that the emotional upheaval parents experience, the risks kids face, and the constant need for persistence, creativity, and vision are all part of everyday life in the high-IQ world.

The question of raising and educating high-IQ kids produces a lot of right answers. The trick is deciding which is the best right answer for a particular child at a particular time. In the pages ahead, you'll find practical advice and research-based recommendations. You'll find ideas and examples of how individual parents in individual situations followed those ideas in real life. And you'll find lots of empathy.

This book is practical inspiration.

We believe all children, including the extra-bright ones, deserve to thrive—to enjoy living, learning, working, playing, and just being in the world. (And no, they can't "figure it out for themselves because they're so smart." That's what they count on you for.)

Whether you're connected to a high-IQ kid as a parent, teacher, counselor, or other caring adult, you have a tough job ahead of you. Regardless if you live in a small community and yours is the only high-IQ kid or if you're in a huge metropolitan area with several high-IQ kids within the city limits, services for high-IQ kids are few and far between.

So how do you help your high-IQ kid thrive?

The short answer: become an advocate for your child.

Explore resources, including those online. Learn and keep learning, from books, people, Web sites, and rumors. Trust your instincts, even when it's hard to believe the evidence that shows your child is far out of step with the expectations of other kids and environments. Refuse to take "no" for an answer. Hunt for champions locally and go wherever you can to get the services and programs that meet the needs of your child.

The diverse body of knowledge contained in this book can help in your quest. It contains personal essays, academic research papers, and the collected wisdom of people who have lived with and studied high-IQ kids for decades.

It's divided into three sections:

Part 1: What's in a Number? explores what "high-IQ" means, from numbers and labels to family life and thinking styles.

Part 2: Take a Number tackles the problems and challenges of educating high-IQ kids.

Part 3: More Than a Number expands the concept of high-IQ and addresses the social and emotional lives of these children.

Just because the sections are numbered one, two, and three doesn't mean you have to read them in that order! The kind of information you need depends on the challenge of the moment, so dive in wherever you want to. Some days, you'll need the sanity-saving laughter and acceptance of "Normal Kids Don't Quack." Other days, you may need information on assessment and identification to challenge the school's program (or lack thereof) (Chapters 1 and 4, for example). Sometimes, you'll need ideas for educational and parenting approaches. Sometimes, you'll simply need the comfort of knowing that you and your child aren't the only ones dealing with high-IQ issues.

Each section begins with a short introduction describing what you'll find, and each chapter in turn begins with a brief overview. You'll know as soon as you begin to read whether the chapter is the right one for right now. If not, flip to another.

You'll also find a list of resources at the end of the book. New programs and research arise constantly; Internet searches, beginning with some of the sites listed, can be invaluable.

This book is, most of all, a hope—

That through its stories, advice, and information, it eases the burdens and increases the wonder and joy of raising, teaching, and nurturing high-IQ kids.

We'd love to hear how this book has helped you care for the high-IQ kid or kids in your life. You can email us at help4kids@freespirit.com or send us a letter at:

Free Spirit Publishing
217 Fifth Avenue North, Suite 200
Minneapolis, MN 55401-1299

Kiesa Kay, Deborah Robson, and Judy Fort Brenneman

PART: 1

What's in a Number?

Who's high-IQ? What's high-IQ?

From the outside, it's easy to think that IQ points are what it's all about. You'll discover in this book, and especially in this section, that IQ is much more than a test score. The entire neurological makeup of high-IQ kids is different.

High-IQ kids come in all colors, shapes, and sizes, from all cultural backgrounds and socioeconomic levels. They're not just a "sped up, farther ahead" version of average-IQ children; the way they think is fundamentally different. Their extra IQ points may give them an intellectual edge that shines every day, or not. Many are hypersensitive to their environments. They're passionately concerned about topics that their age-peers don't give two figs for. High-IQ kids are never what we assume or suppose, and they surprise us daily.

From the urchin in the high chair to the statistical analysis of IQ assessments, this section explores what we know about high-IQ kids from personal experience, clinical practice, and research. Within these pages, you'll learn about testing and what the numbers and labels mean. You'll discover how high-IQ kids are alike and the many more ways in which they are different, both from their age-mates and from each other. You'll get a peek into how they think and some of the challenges they face.

Defining the Few

What Educators and Parents Need to Know About Exceptionally and Profoundly Gifted Children

BY ANNETTE REVEL SHEELY
& LINDA KREGER SILVERMAN

Annette Revel Sheely is the counselor of the Rocky Mountain School for the Gifted and Creative in Boulder, Colorado. Prior to that, she assessed and counseled gifted people of all ages at the Gifted Development Center in Denver, Colorado, and directed the Center in Boulder.

Linda Kreger Silverman is a licensed psychologist and director of the Gifted Development Center in Denver, Colorado, which has assessed and assisted over 5,200 children in the last twenty-eight years. The Center is a subsidiary of the Institute for the Study of Advanced Development, which Linda founded and directs. Linda provides support for the gifted community through her work as an author, editor, researcher, clinician, and lecturer on all aspects of giftedness.

This chapter answers the fundamental questions about children in the exceptionally and profoundly gifted range. What makes them different from other people? Why do parents and educators both need to identify children who fall into this realm, and what tests can help them do this? Why is it so important to understand these children's unusual needs?

- "Can I raise him properly?"

- "This is going to cost a lot of money."

- "Is she smarter than we are?"

- Guilt.

- Shock.

- Denial.

- New respect for the child.

These are real reactions from parents after learning that their child is exceptionally gifted.[1]

Who Are the Exceptionally and Profoundly Gifted?

People who are exceptionally gifted are as different from moderately gifted individuals as the moderately gifted differ from the average. Test results can be interpreted in standard deviations (SD) from the norm, a way of talking about "how far from average" an individual's responses are. Traditionally, each standard deviation from the norm represents a different group to be served. While in the past there was no consistency in delineating the highly gifted ranges, a new nomenclature is developing that takes into account the burgeoning number of children found who score in the upper regions. Until recently, the term *profoundly gifted* denoted scores of 160 or above. However, it is now being reserved for individuals who score above 174, at the fifth SD above the norm on standardized intelligence tests. Current terminology thus reflects the following levels of giftedness:

Levels of Giftedness[2]

Level	IQ Range	Standard Deviations
Profoundly Gifted	above 175	+5 SD
Exceptionally Gifted	160–174	+4 SD
Highly Gifted	145–159	+3 SD
Moderately Gifted	130–144	+2 SD
Mildly Gifted	115–129	+1 SD

According to the normal curve of probability, theoretically there should be only one person in ten thousand with an IQ of 160, and only one in a million with an IQ of 180. However, in the last two decades we have been finding many more children who score at these levels than we would anticipate if intelligence followed the normal curve. As of January 20, 2007, the Gifted Development Center had identified 933 children with IQ scores of 160 and above, out of 5,200 tested.

What do we know empirically about these children? In a study of 241 exceptionally and profoundly gifted children, with IQs ranging from 160 to 237+, researchers Karen Rogers and Linda Silverman found the following patterns:

- Boys and girls in the group had the same mean IQ.

- More than 99 percent of parents reported that their children learned rapidly, had extensive vocabularies and excellent memories, and reasoned well.

- 97.9 percent of parents reported that their children were curious.

- 96.1 percent of parents stated that their children were at times mature for their ages.

- 95.9 percent of parents said that their children had excellent senses of humor.

- 94 percent of these children were described as having long attention spans and being alert as infants or toddlers.

- 90 percent of parents described their children as "sensitive."

- 79 percent of parents stated that their children had high energy or activity levels.[3]

From our clinical experience, we know that in families with exceptionally gifted children we find deep and complex people. These exceptionally gifted people tend to have heightened capacities for experiencing not only extreme highs and lows of life, but also extraordinary awareness of details and subtleties. For people in this range, life tends to be rich with sensations and awareness.

At times the sensations and heightened awareness can be too much. Often described as "highly sensitive," many exceptionally gifted children experience physical sensations to a much greater degree than other children. Forty-four percent of the children in Rogers and Silverman's study had a heightened sensitivity to clothing tags and other tactile sensations.[4] Many parents of exceptionally gifted children report having to locate socks without seams. Their children are so conscious of feeling the seam with their toes that they can't concentrate in school. While not all exceptionally gifted children experience tactile sensitivity, many do have problems with light, sound, or smells.

Children in this range may not understand what makes them different from other children their age, but they know they are different. Other children are often intimidated by their mature vocabulary. Other children don't laugh at their sophisticated jokes. Other children don't share their interest in advanced and complex pursuits. Karen Rogers and Linda Silverman found that exceptionally gifted children had social self-concepts significantly lower than their confidence in their academic ability on the Harter Self-Perception Inventory.[5] It can be very difficult for these children to find true peers. They tend to be more comfortable with children who are much older than they are, or with adults.

Academically, exceptionally gifted children react to school in a variety of ways. Some thrive when radically accelerated. One nine-year-old child we know spends part of his day at an elementary school and part taking advanced placement courses at a high school. He is very happy with this arrangement. A large percentage need to be homeschooled, because few public school systems are able to meet the needs of these unusual children. Fortunately, there are more resources now for homeschooling exceptionally gifted children than ever before, especially with the increase in distance learning on the Internet. Young children can now take high school and college courses online. Many exceptionally gifted students do well in private schools for the gifted, especially schools that are willing to create individual education programs for their students.

Some children in this category no one would suspect of being exceptionally gifted. They have found such an inadequate fit in school that they receive poor grades and display behavior problems.[6] We know of one exceptionally gifted student who nearly dropped out of high school, even though his ACT score was the highest his school had ever seen. Author and counselor Elizabeth Meckstroth observed that "[t]hese students may find little meaning in classroom activities and resist waiting for classmates to catch up. . . . Sometimes they may counter unstimulating environments by disruptive acting out, passive withdrawal or psychosomatic stomachaches, headaches, etc."[7]

Why Is It Important to Identify Exceptionally and Profoundly Gifted Children?

Differences exist at both ends of the IQ continuum. Educators who work with children of subnormal intelligence find that knowing a child's IQ range helps with placement decisions. Children who are mildly developmentally delayed (IQs between 50 and 75) are able to be educated in public schools with special modifications, i.e., special education programs. Children with IQs between 25 and 50 can be trained in specific tasks.[8] And children with IQs below 25 typically need custodial care.

At the other end of the bell curve, mildly, moderately, highly, exceptionally, and profoundly gifted children also have special identifiable needs and differences. The higher the IQ, the greater the need for differentiated services.[9] Children who are mildly gifted may be able to do well in a regular school, taking honors classes and enrichment courses. Moderately gifted children may do well with a one-year grade acceleration. But children who are exceptionally gifted will likely have a difficult time in school and will need special support to maintain their academic motivation.[10] These students may also need preventive counseling to help them cope with being so different from their age peers. They and their families will certainly need academic guidance to know what options are available to them, such as early college entrance.

In addition, when a child is found to test in the exceptionally gifted range, a variety of unique opportunities become available. For example, one organization, the Davidson Institute for Talent Development, provides its Young Scholars with comprehensive, ongoing support in academic, social, and emotional areas. The handful of organizations like this are blessings to families struggling to meet the extraordinary needs of these children.

Difficulties in Identifying Exceptionally and Profoundly Gifted Children

Imagine that your child's school is going to measure her height against a yardstick that is nailed to a wall in the nurse's office, with its base against the floor. Children shorter than one yard can be accurately measured. But if your child is taller than thirty-six inches and the school has no other way to measure your child, the school may be able to tell you only that she is thirty-six inches tall or "at least thirty-six inches."

This example may seem absurd, but IQ tests follow this Procrustean methodology. They are not designed to capture the full range of abilities among the most intellectually advanced children. Wechsler tests, such as the WPPSI™-III (for ages 3 to 7¼)[11] and the WISC®-IV (for ages 6 through 16)[12] as well as the Stanford-Binet Intelligence Scales, Fifth Edition,[13] only go up to a score of 160. These limitations are called the tests' *ceilings*—their highest measurable points.

Even those who design these tests admit that they are not intended for use with children at the highest levels of intelligence. Elizabeth Hagen, one of the authors of the Stanford-Binet Intelligence Scales, Fourth Edition, said that "the upper one percent of individuals is not usually well differentiated by our present tests."[14]

Assessment of the Exceptionally and Profoundly Gifted

So how are exceptionally and profoundly gifted children identified? To locate children beyond the norms of the current tests, it is necessary to think outside the box, and the Talent Searches provide an excellent model. In Talent Search programs, middle school students take an achievement test that compares their performance to their age peers. If they reach a certain criterion (95th or 97th percentile on mathematics and reading), they are allowed to take an out-of-level test—a college board examination—designed for college-bound juniors and seniors. Testers of exceptionally gifted children employ a similar two-stage process. They begin with a recently normed test of intelligence. Children who achieve at the 99th percentile or above on two or more subtests are allowed to take the Stanford-Binet Intelligence Scales, Form L-M

(SB L-M), as a supplemental, out-of-level test, comparing their performance with considerably older children. Children who score in the moderately or highly gifted ranges on current IQ tests sometimes score as many as forty, fifty, or even one hundred points higher on the SB L-M.[15]

It is permissible to use the SB L-M as a supplemental test, as long as examiners acknowledge that the scores are on a different metric and, therefore, not comparable to deviation IQs.[16] The SB L-M is an excellent measure of abstract verbal reasoning with a ceiling at the Superior Adult III level, whereas the fifth edition of the Stanford-Binet scales (SB5) is a better instrument for measuring mathematical and spatial abilities.[17] The publisher prefers that the SB L-M be co-administered with the SB5, as they measure different abilities and the scores can be contrasted.[18]

Achievement tests perform a different type of assessment. They measure academic skills. Finding an achievement test to use with exceptionally gifted children can also be an arduous task. The Gifted Development Center usually administers the Woodcock-Johnson III Tests of Achievement because of their ceiling of at least 200 standard score, roughly equivalent to an IQ score.

If parents suspect that their child may be unusually gifted, it is highly advisable that the child be tested by professionals with experience in assessing exceptionally gifted children. Few test administrators fit this category, but they can be found by inquiring within the gifted-education community; a place to start is the Hoagies' Gifted Education Page, www.hoagiesgifted.org. Test administrators who have little or no experience with children in the higher ranges may misunderstand the child or misinterpret the test results.

These children may be, as Elizabeth Meckstroth puts it, "statistically insignificant," but they do exist, and there seem to be more of them than we would expect.[19] Their needs are different from those of the moderately gifted. It is not always easy to identify exceptionally and profoundly gifted children, but it is important to try. With the right support, they can realize their extraordinary potential and can thrive.

Notes

1. Edwards, "POGO Parents' Reactions."

2. Adapted from Wasserman, "Assessment of Intellectual Functioning," 435.

3. Rogers and Silverman, "Factors in 160+ IQ Children."

4. Ibid.

5. Ibid.

6. Dickinson, "Caring for the Gifted."

7. Meckstroth, "Statistically Insignificant," 1, 5.

8. Maloney and Ward, *Mental Retardation and Modern Society.*

9. Silverman, "Highly Gifted Children."

10. Gilman and Revel, "Current Use of the Stanford-Binet, Form L-M."

11. Wechsler, *WPPSI-III.*

12. Wechsler, *WISC®-IV.*

13. Roid, *Stanford-Binet Intelligence Scales.*

14. Silverman, "An Interview with Elizabeth Hagen," 171.

15. Silverman, "The Measurement of Giftedness."

16. Carson and Roid, "Acceptable Use of the Stanford-Binet Form L-M."

17. Silverman, "The Measurement of Giftedness."

18. Carson and Roid, "Acceptable Use of the Stanford-Binet Form L-M."

19. Meckstroth, "Statistically Insignificant."

References

Carson, Andrew D., and Gale H. Roid. "Acceptable Use of the Stanford-Binet Form L-M: Guidelines for the Professional Use of the Stanford-Binet Intelligence Scale, Third Edition (Form L-M)." Itasca, IL: Riverside Publishing, 2004. http://www.educationaloptions.com/Statement%20Form%20L-M%2012-14-04.pdf (accessed March 23, 2007).

Dickinson, Rita Minton. *Caring for the Gifted.* North Quincy, MA: Christopher, 1970.

Edwards, S. "POGO Parents' Reactions to Identification of Their Gifted Kids." Denver: Gifted Development Center, 1987. Unpublished manuscript available from the Gifted Development Center, 1452 Marion Street, Denver, CO 80218.

Gilman, Barbara, and Annette Revel. "Current Use of the Stanford-Binet, Form L-M." *Highly Gifted Children* 12, no. 4 (1999): 10–12.

Maloney, Michael P., and Michael P. Ward. *Mental Retardation and Modern Society.* New York: Oxford University Press, 1979.

Meckstroth, Elizabeth. "Statistically Insignificant." *Counseling and Guidance* 5, no. 3 (Fall 1995): 1, 5.

Riverside Publishing. "Stanford-Binet Intelligence Scale, Form L-M." *Assessment Catalog* 19. Chicago: Riverside Publishing, 1999.

Rogers, Karen, and Linda Kreger Silverman. "Personal, Social, Medical, and Psychological Factors in 160+ IQ Children." Paper presented at the annual convention of the National Association for Gifted Children, Little Rock, Arkansas, November 1997.

Roid, G. H. *Stanford-Binet Intelligence Scales, Fifth Edition*. Itasca, IL: Riverside Publishing, 2003.

Silverman, Linda Kreger. "Highly Gifted Children." *Serving Gifted and Talented Students: A Resource for School Personnel*, edited by Judy L. Genshaft, Marlene Bireley, and Constance L. Hollinger: 217–240. Austin, TX: Pro-Ed, 1995.

———. "An Interview with Elizabeth Hagen: Giftedness, Intelligence, and the New Stanford-Binet." *Roeper Review* 8 (1986): 168–171.

———. "The Measurement of Giftedness." *The International Handbook on Giftedness*, edited by Larisa V. Shavinina, in press. Amsterdam: Springer Science, 2008.

Wasserman, John. "Assessment of Intellectual Functioning." *Assessment Psychology*, edited by John R. Graham and Jack A. Naglieri: 417–442. Vol. 6 of *Handbook of Psychology*, edited by Irving B. Weiner. Hoboken, NJ: Wiley, 2003.

Wechsler, David. *WISC®-IV: Wechsler Intelligence Scale for Children: Manual*. San Antonio: Psychological Corporation, Harcourt Brace Jovanovich, 2003.

———. *WPPSI-III: Wechsler Preschool and Primary Scale of Intelligence, Revised*. San Antonio: Psychological Corporation, Harcourt Brace Jovanovich, 2002.

2 Normal Kids Don't Quack

BY CATHY MARCINIAK

Cathy Marciniak, mother, survivor, and poet, lives with her family in San Antonio, Texas, where currently she is writing, among other works, *A Survival Guide for Civilians on Barthgenol.*

From the beginning, profoundly gifted children set the family style and define their own milestones. The parents who will come through raising these kids unscathed must, like Cathy Marciniak, learn to step outside everyone's expectations, including their own. And remember to laugh.

Adam quacks.

He is busy, pounding the Cheerios on his high-chair tray into dust. "Quack!" he exclaims.

Well, this is unexpected. None of the baby books mention quacking. None of the Sears kids or the Brazelton grandkids ever quacked. Penelope Leach hasn't researched quacking and there are no quack debates on the online parenting boards.

Adam wrinkles up his tiny face, pondering some unknown problem. "Duck!" he announces when he's solved it. "Quack! Quackquackquackquack!"

Where did this come from? He's never seen a duck and he's too young to have learned about them from Big Bird or Mr. Greenjeans. (Is Mr. Greenjeans even on any more? Was there ever a Mrs. Greenjeans? Why can't I quit asking myself things like this?) Unless this is some cute baby mispronunciation of the f-word, I certainly don't quack. We don't own barnyard-sound toys. I gave all of those instruments of the devil away as soon as their batteries died or they began to make my head vibrate, whichever came first.

"Quack," Adam says again, and I don't think this is quite normal. I've seen normal. Thomas Michael and Diana Rose, for example—both of whom were birthed more naturally than my son and breastfed for longer, both of whom sleep through the night and don't quack—are amazingly, admirably normal. Fiftieth percentiles all around. I hate their mothers. They're my best friends. I'll think that through, later.

I eye my nine-year-old suspiciously. "Kim," I ask, "Have you been teaching Adam to quack?"

She shrugs. "He just does that. All the time. Meredith and Katie and me have been calling him Duckman from the planet Barthgenol."

"Meredith and Katie and I," my husband corrects from behind his newspaper. "Tell your friends it isn't nice to call your baby brother a Barthgenolian."

"Duck quack, quack duck, quack," Adam tells me, leaning forward as if he is divulging some important secret.

Oh, face it, I think: he is a Barthgenolian. Or at least some kind of alien. It's a little unreasonable for me to have expected otherwise. I'm not precisely from the center of the distribution, and I'm married to a person who right now is reading the science section of the paper and no doubt mentally composing his grant proposal while wearing a Snoopy necktie. What made me think either of our kids would be strictly planet-Earth?

Not that this mutation is necessarily bad, as these things go. I have worse ones, myself. It's kind of cute, actually. Just . . . not what I expected.

Not what I expected. That, again. If there is any one phrase that describes the parenting of children like mine, wouldn't that be just it?

It is too early in the day, too early with this child, for me to be confronting the weight and tangles of my expectations again. Maybe I should have some chocolate.

Maybe I should cut myself some slack. Parenting any child is not what we expected. This sentiment is so common (and so devastating to the uninitiated) that a popular, seminal work on the subject of postpartum depression is entitled *This Isn't What I Expected.*

Which really means—doesn't it?—that I am not what I expected, not the person I believed motherhood would magically transform me into. I'm just as sensitive to criticism, just as sarcastic, just as quick to anger over perceived injustices that do not directly affect me, just as prone to daydreams and the telling of pointless lies called poetry, as I was before my children were born. I'm not the unexcitable, objective, commercially and socially acceptable cross between Mother Teresa and Martha Stewart that my kids deserve. I'm still me, only ten pounds heavier and bone-tired. If I ever met the person I thought having children would make me, I'd probably run over her with my car.

"Duck, quack," Adam tells me, his face covered with Cheerio-goo, and that finalizes it. There is, definitely, a one-of-a-kind "Adam" inside that outwardly normal, brand-X baby, and it is asserting itself for the first time. Nothing for it but to brace myself and welcome the challenge.

I run my hand over his smooth, bald head (and that's another thing: where are those golden ringlets I imagined?) and wonder: what else is in there? What else will you teach me that I don't imagine, because I don't know that it can be imagined? What else do you have for me, what marvels and frustrations, that my vision is too limited to anticipate?

This was supposed to be easier the second time around. Normal mothers of normal children know what to expect, more or less, with their second child. They don't wonder which new curve will be thrown at them, or which heretofore incomprehensible events they will encounter along with the hand-me-downs and the sibling rivalry. They don't have to make it up as they go along, all over again. They may wonder what the first word will be, when the first steps will take place, but they do not look into the future and see only the unknowable. There is no page in the second child's baby album for "first completely inexplicable expression of personhood."

Normal parents of normal first children do not wonder when, or why, they first will see that look from other adults in response to their second child. They've never seen the look at all—that annoyed, helpless expression of disapproval and confusion that is so familiar to me now that I can hardly pinpoint the first time it was aimed in my direction. I believe it was on kindergarten's "D Day," when every other kid in the class took in a toy drum or a plastic doggie or a rubber duck to illustrate an understanding of the fourth letter of the alphabet. My child ambled in fifteen minutes late with her frantically late-for-work mother in tow, to explain that "D is for dawdle." I'm pretty sure that normal mothers of normal kids wouldn't understand what a harrying, fun-filled reaction we got to that.

My life is full of things that other parents can't relate to. No normal mother of normal kids has ever ended an administrative conference with the straight-faced conclusion, "The worksheet was ambiguous and the answer is correct. Both of those words do start with M. And anyway, a mandrill is a monkey, you can look it up." Normal moms of normal kids just don't say things like that to other grown-ups. They don't have to. They don't have to grit their teeth through discussions with indifferent parochial-school teachers or scream at uncompassionate pediatricians. They don't have to go through the theological adventures of determining how prayer resembles the Vulcan mind-meld, whether the devil ever has to go to the bathroom, and whether roadkill goes to heaven so the pet dogs up there can have fun chasing it.

Normal mothers of normal kids can make vague threats without being asked for specifics. They can make promises like, "If you clean your room I'll take you for ice cream," and not be asked to sign a contract more complicated than the Marshall Plan. ("Clause Three: Six or more pieces of dirt and/or articles of clothing on the dresser and under the bed combined preclude the chocolate sprinkles.") Normal moms yell things like, "If I have to get off this phone and come in there, it isn't going to be pretty!" all the time. I bet that never once, in the history of momdom, has one of those mothers heard in response, "No offense, Mom, but you're not exactly Mary Poppins now."

The only thing normal mothers have to do with their kid's Beanie Baby collection is keep the dust-collecting nuisance off the family-room carpet. When they tell a seven-year-old to pick up the darned things and put them in order, past experience does not cause them to automatically add, "Sequential, chronological, or alphabetical; it doesn't matter—to me!" Normal mothers don't keep every single one of the fifty Beanie Babies' names, personalities, and food preferences straight in their heads, or know how Beanie Babies demonstrate the economic principles of supply, demand, and monopoly power. Normal moms may even think Beanie Babies are cute.

On the other hand, normal kids don't know what a thrill it is to do an imitation of an adult's mother-in-law that is so funny, so wittily perfect, that it causes the adult in question to urinate on herself. Normal kids will never have that kind of power. They will never experience the willing distraction, the fierce protectiveness, the deliberate patience and forethought, the flights of fancy and inquiry, the precision of thought, that I've developed in self-defense with Adam's sister, and that he's now claiming as his own birthright. Normal kids don't realize how far a mother's love can take an otherwise sane and rational person. How could they? I barely believe it myself sometimes.

Maybe other mothers would, if necessary, quash their almost overwhelming natural impulses and Not, Not, NOT Strangle The Nun!, or spend two hours re-analyzing the Cobb-Douglas production function as it relates to Stripes and Freckles. But how many children have seen their very own personal mothers actually do those things, just for them? If my children have a gift, it is the privilege of knowing how uniquely appreciated they are, how special and worthwhile, as evidenced by their ability to completely derange me and drive me to such weird heroics.

"Aaaaaadam," my daughter singsongs. "Adam. Lookit me. Yo, Adam, what's a duck say?"

He glances at his father, at me, and grins. "MOOOO!" he shouts, and they both dissolve into peals of laughter.

If I had normal children, I wouldn't know why that is so funny. I wouldn't get to witness or feel the passions and rages and joys that these children, these particular people with their own oddities and peculiar needs, inspire on such a regular basis.

My own mother, who loves me deeply and has given up hope of ever being able to understand me, lamented once that she had too many generic, personality-lacking photographs of her decidedly non-generic children. "All those stupid blue Sears backgrounds and Christmas trees," she sniffed. "What I ought to have is a picture of that time you told your grandmother you were changing your religion. That cowboy hat you wore to Sunday School every single week for a year. That time you clanked your sister with the pipe to the vacuum cleaner and she flew six feet. Now that was the damnedest thing I ever saw. That kid was airborne. Shoot, everybody's kids lose teeth and get haircuts and have Christmases."

"What are you doing now?" My husband has put down his newspaper. "Don't tell me you're looking for chocolate already?"

"Getting out the camcorder," I tell him. "I want to get some footage of the Duckman's first quacks."

Hang what the baby album pages say. I'll call the Kodak moments as I see 'em.

3

Young Gifted Children as Natural Philosophers

BY DEIRDRE V. LOVECKY

Deirdre V. Lovecky, a clinical child psychologist with the Gifted Resource Center of New England, in Providence, Rhode Island, specializes in gifted children, offering clinical, assessment, and consultation services. She is particularly interested in exceptionally gifted children and those with ADHD, Asperger Syndrome, learning disabilities, and emotional problems. She is the author of *Different Minds: Gifted Children with AD/HD, Asperger Syndrome and Other Learning Deficits*, Jessica Kingsley Publishers, 2005. Her Web site is www.GRCNE.com.

Deirdre Lovecky takes a special professional and personal interest in profoundly gifted children's remarkable fascination with, and ability to form theories about, life's biggest and most puzzling questions. She has observed through both research and life study that the way these children think is even more remarkable than the speed with which they learn, and that this way of thinking is evident early on. Parents and teachers who recognize this qualitative difference are better prepared to understand and nurture these remarkable and complex children.

In some cases, the children described are composites of several individuals; in other cases, parents have given permission to include the description of a specific child. In order to protect confidentiality, names and identifying details have been changed.

"The philosophy which is so important in each of us . . . is our individual way of just seeing and feeling the total push and pressure of the cosmos."

—William James

When Danny was four years and one month old, he lived in an older house with pine board floors that had slanted with the settling of the house. One day, he said to his mother, "This is called the inspiration about a golf ball sliding down the hill. It's the curve that's making the golf ball slide down the hill. In the hallway, one side is bent down to here, and one side is bent down to here." He gestured accordingly with his right and left hands. "The middle is up. That means the house is curving with the Earth. That is why my golf ball rolls down the side."

Exceptionally and profoundly gifted children are, in many ways, natural philosophers. They ask questions about big issues—the meaning of life; what death is; the origins and destinies of people, things, and the universe. They make interesting observations about how things work and why things are certain ways; they even develop hypotheses about their observations. Some derive general rules based on observations of numbers or natural phenomena. These young gifted children may also ask themselves questions, and then set about finding out a way to think about the answer, a sort of paradigm or thought experiment. Not all exceptionally and profoundly gifted children ask original questions, but most show precocity in the types of questions asked, and the ages at which these questions are first asked.[1] These gifted children also may show advanced development in how they think about subjects of interest to them.

Young gifted children ask many interesting questions about the big issues of life and death. Four-year-old Danny also asked his parents, "How did the first baby get here before there were adults?" and "Was God ever a baby?" In addition, he made observations, such as, "I think I get infinity. It's always more, forever." Emmanuel, at three and a half, asked how far outer space went on, and where it came from. When his mother explained about the Big Bang theory, he asked where the Big Bang came from, and then where God came from. At seven, he was more interested in how the brain is connected to the soul, and how we think. He was also fascinated by who people are, and how they become individuals.

When gifted children ask questions about the big issues, these questions reflect an ability to analyze and synthesize material. Gifted children develop their observations into questions which show an underlying complexity of reasoning ability. It is not that these gifted children only ask questions that are complex and precocious; they also ask many of the questions that are typical of average children. However, just the fact that they ask any complex questions at all illustrates their difference from more typical average children, because such questions are not expected from children of their age.

The Cognitive Development of Young Gifted Children

One of the difficulties in discussing the cognitive development of young gifted children is the assumption that they are just precocious. That is, we assume that how they think is older thinking done at an earlier age. This is somewhat true, if one uses criteria such as the age at which Piagetian tasks are passed—for example, conservation of volume. However, if it were true that gifted children's advancement was only one of speed, then eventually everyone else would catch up. But if the *way* gifted children think about concepts is different as well as precocious, they are not only more mature in various cognitive abilities. They may also manifest these abilities differently than average people, perhaps even differently than more moderately gifted children.[2]

Leta Hollingworth, who studied high-IQ children in the 1930s, discussed the need for logically coherent answers to questions when children reach a mental age of twelve to thirteen years.[3] For profoundly gifted children, this need may occur as early as age five. Indeed, some children show the beginnings of an ability to understand and build coherent logic systems even earlier. For example, some profoundly gifted children seem inordinately interested in time, both its passage and its meaning. Thus, an average child of seven might become interested in how we measure time, but will primarily conceptualize time as that which is measured by a clock, since this is what they experience in the world. Asked if time would exist if there were no clocks, the average child would likely say, "No." The concept of time's independent existence is beyond their comprehension. The profoundly gifted child, at a younger age, might ask what time is and when time started, as if time were a separate entity. At age six, Ian wondered if there was anti-time before the Big Bang. At age three, Benjamin asked whether time would run backward if the Earth revolved in the opposite direction. The levels of knowledge, conceptual complexity, and reasoning ability required to ask these questions differ qualitatively from those needed to form the type of question asked by a more average six-year-old, Jeff: "Where did clocks come from?"

Exceptionally and profoundly gifted children not only form more complex questions, they demand more complex responses. A simple explanation cannot satisfy—it doesn't allow the child to add to the developing concept that was in place when the question was asked. These children require complex answers both to questions of complexity, and to questions that are more typical of their age-peers. A more average child might ask where heaven is located and would be satisfied with an answer that provides a physical location (for example, above the clouds). A young gifted child, asking the same question and receiving the same answer, might argue that "above the clouds" consists of the rest of the atmosphere and then outer space, so heaven could not really be located there. Because the young gifted child knows so much more information about the universe, and because a much greater level of complexity is needed to answer this child's question satisfactorily, young gifted children tend not to accept easy answers.

The Forming of Hypotheses

Many gifted children, from an early age, develop hypotheses about where things come from, why certain things happen as they do, and how things work. They seek explanations for observations they have made or for ideas they have heard. These explanations are not always correct. For example, many young gifted children appear to hypothesize that after one grows up, there comes a time when one then grows down again and becomes a baby. Bobby, a profoundly gifted child, explored the idea of "growing down again" when he was just two years old. In contrast, Melissa, a more moderately gifted child, asked similar questions when she was seven. Bobby also formed other hypotheses that provided interesting windows on his thought processes. At four years and eleven months, he asked his mother if he would turn white if he ate too much calcium. His mother told him no. He explained that he knew that he'd turn orange if he ate too much carotene. He had learned about turning orange from Miss Frizzle, the fictional teacher in the Magic School Bus series of books and programming.

Danny, at age three years and seven months, was working on a large block structure and became frustrated. Calling to his mother, he said, "Mom, come in here, please. I can't do it. I need a hypothesis."

"That may be," his mother replied. "What is a hypothesis?"

Danny answered, "It gives you clues to solve your problems. It makes your problem smaller."

At five, Elise developed a hypothesis about evolution. She thought that if people became extinct then other living things might find fossils of us and wonder what we were like, just like we do about the dinosaurs. In fact, if we were gone, maybe the dinosaurs would come back, then the asteroid, then the Ice Age again, then us as we are now. Maybe, she thought, all life is just a cycle.

As gifted children get older, their hypotheses become more sophisticated.

At age eight, John Matthews described to his father an idea that had been puzzling him: "Daddy, why don't I see you double, because I have two eyes, and I can see you with each one by itself?" Over time, John developed a theory of binocular vision. While not accurate, it did enable him to follow the path of light through the eye into the brain.[4]

In junior high school, Kate undertook a science-fair project in which she studied whether there were inherent differences in how boys and girls of different grades viewed girls' abilities in math and science. In effect, she replicated the work of several adult researchers. The following year, she developed an attitude questionnaire to research affinities for these subjects among students in different grades. She compared the self-perceptions of girls in co-educational environments to those of girls in single-sex environments. Her results were highly significant and suggested that both boys and girls viewed girls as less talented in science and math. Kate is typical of many gifted young adolescents, able to do impressive work to answer questions that rise from her own interests.

The Derivation of Rules and Algorithms

Many exceptionally and profoundly gifted children are fascinated with numbers. Some derive relationships between numerical entities from an early age. They literally invent math for themselves. Researcher Miraca Gross described Richard, who at four could do mental arithmetic in binary, octal, hexadecimal, and decimal systems.[5] Eric, age nine, derived an original mathematical formula. His teacher told him that he had developed a new theorem, but Eric corrected him, saying that it was only a hypothesis, because he hadn't yet tested it with all possible sets of numbers.[6]

The derivation of rules also occurs for subjects other than mathematics. Lydia, a highly verbal eleven-year-old, explored how different works by one author developed particular metaphoric themes.[7]

The construction of themes, rules, and algorithms allows exceptionally and profoundly gifted children to determine relationships and interactions among variables, and they do this much earlier than their age-peers. This can lead to further development of knowledge in a field, as well as to new work when the child develops variations on the rules, or looks for exceptions and tries to explain them.

A number of researchers have concluded that gifted children move through Jean Piaget's developmental stages (described in his theory of cognitive development) faster than average children. At age thirteen, they may be at the stage of formal operations (deductive and inductive reasoning ability), when average children would not reach this stage for several more years (how many more years is debatable). In addition, there appear to be many alternative developmental roads to the same outcome. For one thing, prodigies who excel (in one or multiple areas) are not accounted for by Piaget's stages.[8] Also, children who are exceptionally or profoundly gifted may reach the end point of a particular stage more quickly, or differently than more average children.[9] That is, when they are given a few examples and presented with feedback, young gifted children may try to construct patterns and derive general principles that apply to all similar tasks. Their approaches to problem-solving differ both from those of age-peers, and from those of other gifted children. These gifted children start to order their thinking into hierarchies and to find relationships among the parts.[10]

The Development of Paradigms

The observations of young gifted children can be developed into a type of paradigm, a thought experiment that the child then tries to answer for him- or herself (as Danny did with his ideas about the golf ball following the curve of the Earth in their slanted house). Gareth B. Matthews, a professor at the University of Massachusetts at Amherst who has a special interest in philosophy for children, developed the idea of the paradigm as the model or the pattern the child uses to explore a concept.[11] The child develops a model and then uses it as a basis for comparison. Other examples or cases are held up to the pattern made by the paradigm to see if they also fit. Not all questions asked by the modeling paradigm require words; often young children show us only by their actions what they have discovered. For example, Matthews described himself at age six, puzzling over the beginning of the world. His inquiry took the form of a question: "Supposing that God created the world at some particular time, how is it that the world looks as if it had been going on forever?"[12] Receiving no helpful response from his mother, he later explained to her an analogy he had conceived that answered his question. He had thought of a circle. If one was there when it was drawn, one knew where the artist had started; but if one only saw the completed circle, it would appear to have no beginning. Matthews grew up to become a philosopher.

The literature also describes paradigms used by young gifted children. Leta Hollingworth discussed Child A, who, after being read the Eugene Fields poem about the gingham dog and calico cat who fought and ate each other up, protested that this was a logical impossibility.[13] A child who makes this observation at three has already developed a paradigm about what *logical* means.

Four-year-old Jenny, concerned about why people die and the circumstances under which they do, ended up feeling that there was no answer because even children could die. She was exploring a paradigm about what causes death and what might be done to prevent it. Each attempt to reassure Jenny was measured against her standard of sureness and rejected, until she concluded that there was no way to predict death.[14]

Five-year-old Peter, a profoundly gifted boy, discovered and read Steven Hawking's *A Brief History of Time* around Christmas time. At about the same time, he saw a television special in which Big Bird worried about how Santa Claus could get down so many chimneys in one night. Peter applied what he had learned from Hawking's book and came up with a solution—scientifically correct—based on the idea of being able to control the forces generated within a black hole. By using these forces, Santa could become long and thin, and time would slow down, thereby allowing him to both fit in and visit all those chimneys on Christmas Eve.[15]

"What would happen if . . ." is another paradigm young gifted children try to explore. In general, the questions asked by gifted young children show very high levels of abstract reasoning ability, as well as the ability to articulate a problem and to understand a complex response. Often their questions are well in advance of the concepts that developmental predictions suggest they might be considering. For example, six-year-old Ian pondered who would win a potential battle between Godzilla and a black hole. This paradigm was developed at a level of abstraction well above what would be predicted for his age.

Cognitive Reasoning and Asynchrony

These early questions constitute a form of problem-finding, a most unusual type of thinking for young children. Indeed, problem-finding requires abstract reasoning ability. Before being able to formulate a paradigm about how something works, one has to be able to think in concepts. Nevertheless, these conceptualizations do not consist of pure reason. They are also formed from the emotions and beliefs of the child. When reasoning and emotion are not at the same level of development, these two human capacities are considered to be *asynchronous*.[16] Another type of asynchrony occurs when gifted children exhibit differing levels of abstraction depending on the type of task and the level of interest in it.

Asynchrony means that exceptionally and profoundly gifted children may be capable of dealing with a high degree of abstraction *at the same time* that they do not yet question the existence of Santa Claus, as in Peter's vignette. A child does not have to determine the "realness" of a concept in order to solve a problem using a high level of abstraction. Thus, Peter used Stephen Hawking's book to solve a puzzle about Santa's visit without needing to know that Santa wasn't real. Ian can use knowledge about nuclear power to decide the energy value of Godzilla without having to decide if Godzilla is real or not. This type of asynchrony may mislead parents or teachers into thinking the child is more cognitively advanced in all areas than he or she is. Parents might presume that the child realizes that Santa or Godzilla is fantasy.

One good example of asynchrony occurred when Ian was five. He was discussing why day and night get longer and shorter over the course of the year. His aunt, teasing him, told him that sun demons need to eat the sun to keep warm. She elaborated by saying that each night they eat the sun, and then, as they get too hot, they release the sun again in order to cool down. The period of sun-release is our day. In the cold of winter, the sun demons need more warmth and keep the sun longer before they get too hot, so the length of the day decreases.

Ian's aunt was sure that Ian knew she was kidding, but he looked so perturbed that she asked him. It turned out that he had believed her, and was trying reconcile this version with his own explanation, one that involved the Earth tilting on its axis toward and away from the sun.

These abilities—to ask high-level questions, to wonder about the world, and to formulate interesting and original ideas about things—differentiate gifted children from the average in more ways than just the speed at which they learn. Older average children do not advance to the level where they spontaneously ask these questions. The gifted child indeed has a *qualitatively* different mind.

The Moral Philosopher

Young gifted children make observations, form hypotheses, derive rules, and form paradigms not only about the natural world around them but also about abstract ideals, such as justice, fairness, honesty, truth, and freedom. The literature suggests that many exceptionally and profoundly gifted children show evidence of sensitivity about moral concerns from an early age. They display exceptional awareness about moral issues, as well as advanced understanding and judgment of moral problems.[17] Advanced sensitivity to moral issues was noted in gifted children as far back as the time when psychologist Lewis Terman was studying gifted children in the 1920s.[18] Terman's early studies described gifted children as advanced in trustworthiness and moral stability. Leta Hollingworth, working in the 1930s, described many examples of early moral awareness, including a boy of nine who "wept bitterly at how the North taxed the South after the Civil War."[19] She saw this as indicative of how good and evil, in the abstract, may become troublesome for exceptionally and profoundly gifted children. Hollingworth also mentioned specific traits of character related to early moral development. For example, she noted that Child D showed a "refusal to lie, loyalty to standards once adopted, readiness to admit to just criticisms, unselfishness and amiability."[20]

Following Hollingworth, a number of contemporary writers have also mentioned concern about moral issues as important to exceptionally and profoundly gifted children.[21] Miraca Gross's studies of children with IQs over 160, published in 1993, found them far in advance of age-peers in conceptualization of fairness, justice, responsibility for self, and responsibility toward others.[22] In 1994, Linda Silverman suggested that advanced moral sensitivity may be an essential feature of being gifted.[23] She described a number of unusually compassionate children who were intensely aware of world issues and the feelings of others.

A number of researchers who study how children make moral judgments have shown advanced development in gifted children when compared to age-peers. Paul Janos and Nancy Robinson compared radically accelerated college students (ages 11 to 18) and two groups of nonaccelerated highly gifted high school students with a group of typical undergraduate college students. To test moral reasoning, they used the Defining Issues Test (DIT), which is based on Lawrence Kohlberg's premises about moral judgment.[24] Janos and Robinson found that the three groups of highly gifted students scored higher on the DIT, thus exhibiting higher levels of moral reasoning and judgment. In 1994, Mary Howard-Hamilton found that gifted high school students scored well above the norm for age-peers on the DIT.[25] Miraca Gross found that two of the exceptionally gifted students she studied scored, at age twelve, above the levels of typical college students.[26]

Theories of Moral Development

Two of the main modern theories of moral development, constructed by psychologists Lawrence Kohlberg and Carol Gilligan, are based on long-standing, underlying, philosophical differences about the basis of moral development.[27]

For Kohlberg, moral development is seen principally as *moral judgment*, the ability to reason about universal principles of justice and fairness. For Gilligan, it is *compassion*, the ability to empathize with and act to alleviate others' suffering. Both reasoning and compassion are necessary before a person can formulate moral actions; nevertheless, it is the relative importance of each that distinguishes different theories.

Kohlberg's theory focuses on the use of reason to decide what ought to be done to achieve justice and fairness. In his theory, altruism, compassion, and empathy are less important than are principles of justice, and thus are not the main way in which moral decisions are made. The moral reasoner is one who knows that a moral decision is required, understands that principles need to be applied universally, thinks of the greatest good for the most people, and then makes a decision based on abstract principles of justice and fairness. Kohlberg's theory follows Jean Piaget and Bärbel Inhelder's theories about stages of mental development,[28] and is based on the ability to reason abstractly. Young children are not seen as being able to reason about moral issues; they are considered pre-moral because they cannot yet be abstract.[29]

The second major avenue of exploration of moral issues is based on altruism. Modern philosophers such as Lawrence Blum, at the University of Massachusetts in Boston, and Gareth Matthews, at the University of Massachusetts in Amherst, have suggested that childhood responsiveness to others is a primary moral characteristic.[30] Responsiveness requires both a cognitive and an affective grasp of a situation. It does not require true empathy yet, nor does it require that children be aware of why they act as they do, only that they act to relieve another's suffering. In this view of moral development, what changes from childhood to adulthood is the amount and type of experience a person brings to a situation. For example, the adult might offer advice the young child might not yet know about, or the adult might have resources the child does not. Also, empathy develops over time from directly feeling the feelings of others, to being able to understand how another might feel because one has had similar experiences, to imagining the feelings of someone different from oneself in a situation one has not directly experienced.

This model of morality has some similarity to Carol Gilligan's model of care.[31] In Gilligan's model, it is the interrelationships among people that are important, and these are based on empathic responses between people. The basis of moral action lies in the response to another's pain or difficulty. This requires an empathic attitude toward others, a sensitivity to their needs, and a wish to act with these needs in mind. In this view, morality reflects sensitivity toward others, rather than a focus on reasoning about what is a principled or unprincipled act.

While Kohlberg's theory has been directly tested with gifted children, especially through use of the Defining Issues Test, there has been little direct application of Gilligan's theory to the gifted.[32] Like many researchers, Gilligan appears to use some data from gifted children, but does not distinguish between data obtained from gifted children and data from more average subjects.

To develop sensitivity to moral issues, children must understand rules and standards. Judy Dunn, an expert on child development, described young children's increasing understanding of social rules and explanations for consequences. For example, during the second year of life, young children began to understand how to tease others, and they showed an increased awareness of what is permitted and what is prohibited.[33] Jerome Kagan, one of the pioneers of developmental psychology, has described how children in the second year of life regularly explored, experimented with, and violated rules. These children eventually modified their behavior and incorporated standards within themselves because of the emotional responsiveness of the parent and the interaction between parent and child.[34] The early empathic response that most children feel when exposed to parental distress develops into responsiveness to parental approval and disapproval. In a later work, Kagan stressed the importance of emotions in the development of moral standards; in fact, emotions are the basis for acquiring morality.[35]

Thus, early mutual attunement of activity level, mood, and body movements between mother and child, as described by developmental psychologist Mary D. Salter Ainsworth and specialist in infant development Daniel Stern, is the basis for development of a personal identity, empathy for others, and a rules-based internal standard that evolves into moral reasoning about right and wrong.[36]

Rules about how to live and how to treat others come from this early sensitivity to others and from the standards that young children internalize. Many young gifted children develop early standards of conduct. They are idealists; they think of life in its purest measure. Thus, these children abide by absolute, rather than relative, standards. Because their concepts are so advanced, these exceptionally and profoundly gifted children may suffer from the asynchrony inherent in living out their ideals: they just can't live up to them.

A child who can reason at an exceptionally high level about moral issues may be no more able than age-peers to resolve social situations in an equitable and mutual manner. Having knowledge or the ability to reason is not the same as having the ability to make a good decision. Conversely, having the ability to take a moral stand (about what is fair or just) or to act with compassion does not necessarily mean a child can articulate why he or she behaved in this way.

A number of writers have noted the interplay between the asynchrony of gifted children's chronological age and their advanced sensitivity to moral concerns. In *Guiding the Gifted Child,* James Webb, Elizabeth Meckstroth, and Stephanie Tolan discussed the differences between gifted children and age-peers based on advanced moral development.[37] Young gifted children may not be ready to deal emotionally with the ideas they generate. Some try to assume adult responsibilities without the emotional maturity required to abide human fallibility, or to accept that a problem may have no good solution.

Linda Silverman, psychologist and director of the Gifted Development Center in Denver, suggested that the greater the moral sensitivity and asynchrony of gifted children, the more vulnerability they experience.[38] Thus, very young, highly compassionate gifted children are especially vulnerable when they express moral concerns about problems of the world. They risk being overwhelmed by the suffering they feel when viewing other's pain, because they have not developed effective ways to deal with strong emotional content. They may also have to deal with adult reactions that do not meet their expectations. For example, children who want to help the poor and homeless by giving away possessions may not comprehend parents' reluctance to have them do so.

Advanced concepts of moral justice and fairness are likely to get the gifted child into trouble. The child is likely to question, and even challenge, traditions and practices that their age-peers follow without question. No one likes to have someone criticize an accepted way of doing things— especially in childhood, when doing things a certain way becomes a ritual. A child who violates a group's expectations by questioning the fairness of rules may be ridiculed.

Miraca Gross discussed some of the ramifications of being advanced in moral development.[39] The exceptionally gifted children in her study showed more intense awareness in thinking and feeling, and this set them apart from their age-peers. For example, one boy's views of ethical and moral issues (such as justice, fairness, and personal responsibility) were above high school level when he was ten years old. Another child, who at age twelve scored as high as college students on the Defining Issues Test, was teased for his advanced interests in psychology and philosophy.[40]

From an early age, many exceptionally and profoundly gifted children question rules they feel are unfair or unjust, not only with adults but also with peers. For example, Nicholas, age eight, disliked how the boys at school treated each other while playing games. He complained about the unfairness they showed in choosing sides, in changing rules part way through, and in not letting certain children play. Nicholas, a good player, was usually welcome to play, but he chose not to do so after several smaller boys were excluded. He and these boys decided to form their own games and to allow anyone to play. Nicholas succeeded in this challenge to the norms of his peer group because he was popular. Other children joined him in his games. Similar behavior might not work for a less sports minded or less popular child.

While many gifted children are not especially advanced in moral development, those who are may be puzzled by their age-peers' usual responses in situations of moral choice. For gifted children who are advanced in moral reasoning, values and principles seem very clear. Their age-peers, with less well-developed thinking processes, may believe in eye-for-an-eye justice and may see situations as requiring either/or choices. A gifted child can perceive the many ramifications of moral decisions.

For example, most young children tease and see nothing wrong with doing so, especially if they are on the giving end. When they are on the receiving end, they want to make the teaser stop but still may not see that teasing involves a moral choice. The young gifted child, who does view teasing as a moral issue, is puzzled by why other children tease. For example, Bob, age eight, thought of teasing as a type of prejudice. He wondered why teasing about things a person can't help is considered acceptable, when it isn't all right to tease about race or religion. He reasoned that if teasing about race or religion is prejudice, then so is teasing about weight, hair color, or personality traits. Thus Bob decided that teasing was a form of injustice.[41]

Exceptionally and profoundly gifted children may also experience distress when they adhere to absolute standards. Andrew never lied, even to keep out of trouble or avoid punishment. Other gifted children in the literature also are known for their high standards of honesty.[42]

The issue of fairness causes many gifted children difficulty. To young gifted children, *fairness* often means adhering to an absolute standard.

Things are fair if they are exactly equal (equal turns, equal shares). An event is fair if it follows the exact rules. An action is fair if you really get a chance to do it—for example, to give a good throw to the dice. In a family that contains a young gifted child who is concerned with fairness, he or she often becomes the "justice person," the one who asks, "But is that really fair?"[43]

As the young gifted child gains experience and a more sophisticated point of view, he or she adds other ways of thinking about fairness. *Equality* begins to encompass more than equal shares or turns. *Fairness* means more than following the rules or getting a good chance. The original ideas remain important, but other ideas of justice come into play.

Suffering Fools Gladly

Leta Hollingworth described the difficulty that young exceptionally and profoundly gifted children have in understanding that most other people are different from themselves with regard to intentions, interests, and the ability to reason or make good choices.[44] Hollingworth pointed out that failure to learn how to tolerate the foolishness of others leads to bitterness, disillusionment, and misanthropy. Interactions with peers who miss the point are frustrating and alienating. Negative interactions with adults who are less intelligent, trustworthy, truthful, fair, or honest than the child thinks they should be are direct routes to disaster.

Difficulty with "suffering fools gladly" affects gifted children's interactions with adults, especially if the child will only work for those he or she considers most likable. The parent, teacher, or other adult whom the gifted child perceives as foolish or stupid will receive the child's contempt. Gifted children need a means of tolerating the less-than-ideal.

The adult's foolishness is not the true problem for these children, although arbitrary actions can be frustrating. More important is the child's lack of realization of what *ordinariness* means and of how arbitrary life itself is. Children who hold absolute standards in a world not organized around absolutes will act on the basis of an ideal fantasy, not reality. They need help in understanding the relativity within the absolute principle. Yes, lying is wrong because it breaks trust; but there are times we lie for good reasons, to maintain trust. Thus, the *words* of the lie are meaningless but the *intent* matters. Such an explanation broadens the idea of truth, and allows gifted children to build other conceptualizations onto the ideal. When they can see that there may be more than one point of view about how something should be, they find it easier to tolerate differences that appear foolish.

Embracing foolishness is a different matter. Just as gifted children need to think about the wide range of possibilities inherent in an ideal, they also need to know when something isn't true at all. Even adults have difficulty dealing with people whose foolishness results from stubborn adherence to wrong beliefs. Teaching gifted children how to respectfully disagree is an important part of teaching them how to suffer foolishness gladly. These children can also benefit from learning about people who have thwarted popular belief and have paid a price for doing so. An excellent example is Galileo, who was almost burned at the stake by the Inquisition for daring to refute foolish beliefs about the Earth's place in the universe.

Conclusion

Young exceptionally and profoundly gifted children are often natural philosophers in their observations, questions, hypotheses, and thought experiments about how the world works. The paradigms they produce form the foundations for later creative thought, as well as for the code and principles upon which they will base their beliefs and conduct.

Parents and teachers of these children need to allow them plenty of opportunity to explore the natural world without giving them predefined answers. In fact, predefined answers limit thinking because new directions the naive child might take are cut off prematurely as the child is shunted into preset paths. For this reason, even moderate exposure at an early age to media such as television, video games, and computers can damage this type of thinking. In most cases, the children mentioned in the vignettes in this paper, who explored the world so energetically, did so because their play encompassed free forms. That is, they did not use television and movie toys, but instead played with common household objects or old-fashioned toys, such as blocks. Reading extensively, or being read to from books with complex language, also promoted complexity of ideas.

One of the best ways to model thinking and hypothesizing about how things work involves simply talking with children about interesting ideas. Ongoing topics for discussion with gifted children include: moral dilemmas; the basis for making rules; types of assumptions made in discussing an opinion; the principles one chooses to live by; and how to make good choices. As the children grow in experience, their points of view should also develop more complexity.

All gifted children need opportunities to discuss their ideas about the paradigms they develop around moral, as well as intellectual, issues. Caring adults can help them discover their own internal resources, while providing the intellectual, emotional, and moral support the children need so they can integrate reasoning and compassion into wise moral choice.

Notes

1. Rogers and Silverman, "Recognizing Giftedness in Young Children," 3–28.
2. Lovecky, "Exceptionally Gifted Children: Different Minds," 116–120.
3. Hollingworth, *Children Above 180 IQ.*
4. Matthews, *Philosophy and the Young Child,* 8.
5. Gross, *Exceptionally Gifted Children.*
6. Lovecky, "Exceptionally Gifted Children: Different Minds."
7. Ibid.
8. Feldman and Goldsmith, *Nature's Gambit.*
9. Roberts, "Equilibrium and Intelligence," 201, 203–205.
10. Cohen and Kim, "Piaget's Equilibrium Theory and the Young Gifted Child."
11. Matthews, *The Philosophy of Childhood.*
12. Matthews, *The Philosophy of Childhood,* 13–14.
13. Hollingworth, *Children Above 180 IQ.*
14. Morelock, "The Child of Extraordinarily High IQ."
15. Ibid.
16. Columbus Group, transcript of meeting.
17. Galbraith, "The Eight Great Gripes of Gifted Kids," 110–116.
18. Terman, *Genetic Studies of Genius.*
19. Hollingworth, *Children Above 180 IQ,* 281.

20. Hollingworth, *Children Above 180 IQ,* 121.

21. Hollingworth, *Children Above 180 IQ.*

22. Gross, *Exceptionally Gifted Children.*

23. Silverman, "The Moral Sensitivity of Gifted Children."

24. Janos and Robinson, "Psychosocial Development."

25. Howard-Hamilton, "An Assessment of Moral Development," 57–59.

26. Gross, *Exceptionally Gifted Children.*

27. Kohlberg, *The Psychology of Moral Development*; Gilligan, *In a Different Voice.*

28. Piaget and Inhelder, *The Psychology of the Child.*

29. Kohlberg, *The Psychology of Moral Development.*

30. Blum, "Particularity and Responsiveness," 306–337; Matthews, *The Philosophy of Childhood.*

31. Gilligan, *In a Different Voice.*

32. Kohlberg, *The Psychology of Moral Development;* Rest, *Manual for the Defining Issues Test;* Gilligan, *In a Different Voice.*

33. Dunn, "The Beginnings of Moral Understanding," 91–112.

34. Kagan, *The Second Year: The Emergence of Self-Awareness.*

35. Kagan, *The Nature of the Child.*

36. Ainsworth, "Patterns of attachment behavior," 51–58; Stern, *The Interpersonal World of the Infant.*

37. Webb, Meckstroth, and Tolan, *Guiding the Gifted Child.*

38. Silverman, "The Moral Sensitivity of Gifted Children."

39. Gross, *Exceptionally Gifted Children.* The first child from Gross's study described in this paragraph is the one known as Ian; the second is Fred.

40. Rest, *Manual for the Defining Issues Test.*

41. Lovecky, "Identity Development in Gifted Children," 90–94.

42. Gross, *Exceptionally Gifted Children;* Hollingworth, *Children Above 180 IQ.*

43. Matthews, *The Philosophy of Childhood,* 66.

44. Hollingworth, *Children Above 180 IQ.*

References

Ainsworth, Mary D. Salter. "Patterns of Attachment Behavior Shown by the Infant in Interaction with His Mother." *Merrill Palmer Quarterly* 10 (1964): 51–58.

Blum, Lawrence. "Particularity and Responsiveness." *The Emergence of Morality in Young Children,* edited by Jerome Kagan and Sharon Lamb: 306–337. Chicago: University of Chicago Press, 1987.

Cohen, LeoNora M., and Younghee M. Kim. "Piaget's Equilibrium Theory and the Young Gifted Child: A Balancing Act." *Roeper Review* 21, no. 3 (1999): 201–206.

Columbus Group. Unpublished transcript of the meeting of the Columbus Group. Columbus, OH: July 1991.

Dunn, Judy. "The Beginnings of Moral Understanding: Development in the Second Year." *The Emergence of Morality in Young Children,* edited by Jerome Kagan and Sharon Lamb: 91–112. Chicago: University of Chicago Press, 1987.

Feldman, David Henry, and Lynn T. Goldsmith. *Nature's Gambit: Child Prodigies and the Development of Human Potential.* New York: Basic Books, 1986.

Galbraith, Judy. "The Eight Great Gripes of Gifted Kids: Responding to Special Needs." *Roeper Review* 8, no. 1 (1985): 15–18.

Gilligan, Carol. *In a Different Voice: Psychological Theory and Women's Development.* Cambridge, MA: Harvard University Press, 1982.

Gross, Miraca U. M. *Exceptionally Gifted Children.* New York: Routledge, 1993.

Hollingworth, Leta S. *Children Above 180 IQ: Stanford-Binet Origin and Development.* New York: World Book, 1942.

Howard-Hamilton, Mary F. "An Assessment of Moral Development in Gifted Adolescents." *Roeper Review* 17, no. 1 (1994): 57–59.

Janos, Paul M., and Nancy M. Robinson. "Psychosocial Development in Intellectually Gifted Children." *The Gifted and Talented: Developmental Perspectives,* edited by Frances D. Horowitz and Marion O'Brien: 149–195. Washington, DC: American Psychological Association, 1985.

Kagan, Jerome. *The Nature of the Child.* New York: Basic Books, 1984.

———. *The Second Year: The Emergence of Self-Awareness.* Cambridge, MA: Harvard University Press, 1981.

Kohlberg, Lawrence. *The Psychology of Moral Development.* New York: Harper and Row, 1984.

Lovecky, Deirdre V. "Exceptionally Gifted Children: Different Minds." *Roeper Review* 17, no. 2 (1994): 116–120.

———. "Identity Development in Gifted Children: Moral Sensitivity." *Roeper Review* 20, no. 2 (1997): 90–94.

Matthews, Gareth B. *Philosophy and the Young Child.* Cambridge, MA: Harvard University Press, 1980.

———. *The Philosophy of Childhood*. Cambridge, MA: Harvard University Press, 1994.

Morelock, Martha J. "The Child of Extraordinarily High IQ from a Vygotskian Perspective." Paper presented at the Esther Katz Rosen Symposium on Psychological Development of Gifted Children, University of Kansas, Lawrence, February 1992.

———. "Imagination, Logic and the Exceptionally Gifted." *Roeper Review* 19, no. 3 (1997): A1–A4. Also available online. Retrieved June 8, 2007, from www.gt-cybersource.org/Record.aspx?rid=11323.

Piaget, Jean, and Bärbel Inhelder. *The Psychology of the Child*. Translated from the French by Helen Weaver. New York: Basic Books, 1969.

Rest, James. *Manual for the Defining Issues Test*. Minneapolis: University of Minnesota, 1979.

Roberts, C. H. (1981). "Equilibrium and Intelligence: Individual Variation in Cognitive Development as a Function of CA, MA and IQ." Cited in LeoNora M. Cohen and Younghee M. Kim, "Piaget's Equilibrium Theory and the Young Gifted Child: A Balancing Act." *Roeper Review* 21, no. 3 (1999): 201–206.

Roeper, Annemarie. "Should Educators of the Gifted and Talented Be More Concerned with World Issues?" *Roeper Review* 11, no. 1 (1988): 12–13.

Rogers, Martin T., and Linda Kreger Silverman. "Recognizing Giftedness in Young Children." *Understanding Our Gifted* 1, no. 2 (1988): 5, 16, 17, 20.

Silverman, Linda Kreger. "A Developmental Model for Counseling the Gifted." *Counseling the Gifted and Talented*, edited by Linda Kreger Silverman: 51–78. Denver: Love Publishing, 1993.

———. "The Gifted Individual." *Counseling the Gifted and Talented*, edited by Linda Kreger Silverman: 3–28. Denver: Love Publishing, 1993.

———. "The Moral Sensitivity of Gifted Children and the Evolution of Society." *Roeper Review* 17, no. 2 (1994): 110–116.

Stern, Daniel N. *The Interpersonal World of the Infant*. New York: Basic Books, 1985.

Terman, Lewis M. *Genetic Studies of Genius*. Vol. 1, *Mental and Physical Traits of a Thousand Gifted Children*. Stanford, CA: Stanford University Press, 1925.

Webb, James T., Elizabeth A. Meckstroth, and Stephanie S. Tolan. *Guiding the Gifted Child*. Columbus, OH: Ohio Psychology Publishing Company, 1982.

---

*Parts of this paper have been excerpted from Deirdre Lovecky's book, *Different Minds: Gifted Children with AD/HD, Asperger Syndrome, and Other Learning Deficits* (London and Philadelphia: Jessica Kingsley Publishers, 2004).

4 Calculus, Pooh, and Tigger Too

BY COURTNEY JAMES

Courtney James and his wife, Anne, were born in Trinidad and Tobago. He is a software designer and homeschooling father. Over the years he has lived in Honolulu, Houston, Pittsburgh, Atlanta, and he now resides in Issaquah, Washington, with Anne and their two daughters.

Many parents, like Courtney and Anne James, have never heard of giftedness before their child teaches them the meaning of the word. Even though (or perhaps because) giftedness is a constant factor in their lives, they don't experience their daughter's giftedness as out-of-the-ordinary; it's simply one aspect of who she is. As parents, they have been guided from the beginning by their daughter's needs, first medical and now multifaceted. Only occasionally do they pause to reflect on what giftedness means to them as a family.

When Bambi was six years old, she told her mother, "Sometimes I feel like an adult and sometimes I feel like I'm two years old."

Anne responded by saying, "Well, you know that you're neither."

Then Bambi replied, "Mom, you don't understand—I'm both."

That, in a nutshell, is what living with a highly gifted child is like. Our eight-year-old, Bambi, will enjoy a video about differential equations and then delight in a Winnie the Pooh cartoon. She'll discuss with me the significance of the ongoing energy crisis, then fight with her baby sister over a toy. She is profound, sensitive, wise, unwavering in her convictions, and furious at the injustices of the world. She is frustrated by the limitations imposed by childhood and can't wait to grow up. She demands more freedom and likes to wrestle with boys. She is sweet, sassy, and so brave—willing to try anything. Yet her heart is so tender that I fear it will oft be broken. What's a father to do?

Before we had children of our own, Anne and I never paid close attention to what very young children were learning or the manner in which they learned. Because Bambi was our first child, we had no basis for comparison. All parents think their children are bright but, because of our background, we never thought of our daughter as gifted.

Understanding and appreciating giftedness has not come naturally to us. Anne and I were both born and raised in the West Indies and initially came to the United States to attend university. Before I came to this country, I had never met or even heard of anyone who had taken an IQ test. My experience in secondary school was that students who were exceptionally good at science, for example, were simply described as being "very good at science." As strange as this may seem, I had never heard of giftedness. There were no gifted programs, there was no mention of asynchronous development, and I had never heard of an IEP (individualized education program). Students at my school never received special testing of any kind. Those who performed very well academically were automatically skipped and no one thought it extraordinary. Everyone knew that some students were "brighter" than others, but truly outstanding academic or intellectual achievement was considered to be the result of hard work. Giftedness simply was not part of our cultural awareness.

Bambi was born with a complete, unilateral cleft of the lip and palate, so the first few years of her life were filled with visits to ophthalmologists, audiologists, orthodontists, geneticists, craniofacial and cosmetic surgeons, speech therapists, lactation consultants, and even social workers. Surgeons repaired her lip when she was four months old and her palate eight months later. She still has at least one more surgery, planned for the coming year. Our intense focus on her medical needs in the early years may have caused us to overlook the significance of her intellectual precocity.

As a baby less than four months old playing with her stuffed animals, she would spend most of the time looking intently at their labels. By six months, she sat in the children's sections of bookstores and carefully looked at books— one at a time, one page at a time. By this time, she had started speaking her first words.

Bambi was always extremely secretive about her abilities, never willing to reveal herself (even to us) until she had attained a level of mastery that satisfied her. The house in which we lived had a staircase with fourteen steps. When we took her up to bed at night, we would count them. Also, when I changed her diaper I would sing the alphabet song. Her only reaction was to smile. She never tried to count or sing along. It wasn't until she was almost eighteen months old and speaking in full sentences that she revealed to us that she could count to fourteen and recite the entire alphabet. She could also read and spell short words and had started to learn to use the computer.

When Bambi was eighteen months old, she was evaluated for speech therapy. The therapists were stunned that she could read a few words, write some letters of the alphabet, and spell many words—including *butterfly*, which was her favorite word at the time. We knew that these therapists usually worked with children with significant learning disabilities, so we did not put much stock in their amazement. They did recommend that we enroll her in preschool, so she could be around other children and further stimulate her speech development.

Bambi started preschool when she was almost two. After several months, the time came for our first parent-teacher conference to discuss her progress. We thought that the report would be fairly routine, but the teacher and her assistant seemed uncomfortable. Finally, the teacher said that she thought that Bambi was developmentally delayed. She was trying to say, in the kindest possible way, that Bambi was somewhat retarded. We asked the teachers how they came to this conclusion. They told us that Bambi did not seem able to follow along during circle time. Apparently, when all the other children were eagerly listening to stories, Bambi would turn away and not pay attention. As the teacher prepared to discuss remedial options with us, we asked if they realized that Bambi could count in three languages and also read a little. They looked at us and at each other for several seconds, and then said, "Oh . . . then maybe she's just bored."

Because we lived near the preschool, the drive there took only a few minutes. Early in the year, Bambi had asked me how far it was to the school. I told her I wasn't sure, but that we should count while driving and see what number we reached. We arrived at school when the count was a little past 100. She enjoyed the counting so much that we did it every day. After a week or two, I got tired of this so I suggested that I teach her how to count in Spanish. By the end of another week, she could count in Spanish. I then taught her to count in French. After about a month of driving to and from school, Bambi could count past 100 in English, French, and Spanish. I let her choose the language of the day. When we went shopping, she would look at price tags and tell me the prices in French and Spanish. She was two years old.

Since Bambi enjoyed playing with gadgets, we bought her a toy cassette player for her second birthday. We also gave her a collection of children's songs and a sing-along phonics cassette. We thought she would enjoy listening to the songs. Instead, without telling us, it seems that she used the phonics cassette to teach herself to read. By the time she was three years old, she was reading fluently at a second-grade level. She could also print all upper- and lowercase letters and she could type stories, using Microsoft Word, with correct spelling, punctuation, and grammar. She could operate the VCR and the CD player, and would regularly annoy me by changing my computer settings.

Bambi started reading Hardy Boys and Nancy Drew mysteries when she was four, but she still liked me to read to her at bedtime. One night, as I was reading a new Nancy Drew book, I came to a passage in which a character was described as having been orphaned when her parents were killed in a car accident. I decided to omit that sentence and smoothly moved on to the next. Bambi jumped up and said, "Daddy, wait, you missed something." She grabbed the book from me, found the passage I had been reading, and pointed to the sentence I had skipped. She had apparently read the book earlier and remembered it well enough to know that I had left out one sentence.

For kindergarten, we enrolled Bambi in a private Montessori school. The classes were multi-age and, though the work was not in the least bit challenging, she enjoyed herself immensely. She especially loved helping care for the younger children. She completed the entire academic curriculum about four months before the end of the school year. She only took that long because her teacher held her back and would only allow her to do a certain amount of work each day. Children who finished their work before the rest of the class were told to play with blocks and other toys until everyone else finished. We subsequently discovered that Bambi spent much of her school year playing with blocks and toys, because she always finished before anyone else. The school principal agreed to order the next level of curriculum for Bambi, but somehow she never received it. At our first parent-teacher conference, the teacher told us Bambi's work and behavior were excellent, but that during "practical life" training she sometimes got butter on her wrist while buttering a slice of bread. She told us that we needed to work with Bambi on her bread-buttering skills. At that moment, we sensed that we would need to change schools.

During the summer break before Bambi entered first grade, her school gave out reading lists. These came with the requests that all students read at least one book during the break, and that parents keep a record of the books read. Bambi read 213 books with reading levels ranging from first to eighth grade. These numbers, by themselves, do not give an accurate picture of how much she read. She read more than half of the books twice and some—her favorites by Roald Dahl and Louis Sachar—she read four times. Her reading voracity is complemented by her natural ability to speed-read. On an average day, she reads about five hundred pages. On bad-weather days, with nothing else to do, she'll read two thousand.

When we enrolled Bambi in first grade at her new school, we thought we had climbed Mount Olympus. This was a private International Baccalaureate school with a bilingual curriculum. The students followed an alternating schedule with one day in English, the next day in the language of their chosen track: French, Spanish, or German. Thus the students would cover the complete curriculum twice, once in each language. The foreign-language teachers were native speakers and the instruction and environment were superb. It was the perfect school and we thought that the level of challenge would be ideal.

We noticed right away, though, that the work was not as challenging as we had expected. Bambi was on the French track and we thought initially that the bilingual nature of the curriculum required a slow start with steady progress. We casually mentioned to the English teacher that Bambi could handle more difficult work. This teacher was wonderful, and a week later she gave me a second-grade reading workbook and asked me to let Bambi look at it over the weekend. She warned me that the workbook was a little challenging and I shouldn't let Bambi get discouraged if she had trouble with it. I believe the workbook was designed to last an entire semester. Bambi finished it in a couple of hours.

When we returned the workbook on Monday, the teacher just shook her head and said, "I don't have a clue, do I?"

Bambi's math homework usually consisted of ten addition and subtraction problems, which were hardly formidable since she would finish them in fifteen seconds or less. Hoping to challenge her a little, Anne and I decided to supplement her math with Saxon 54, which is a fourth-grade curriculum. She would do three to five lessons a day after school and complain when I told her to stop.

One day I couldn't work with her at the usual time, so I told her to read ahead in the lesson and let me know if there was anything she didn't understand. An hour later, I asked her how much she had read and found that she had gone through forty-five lessons. During the following three weeks, I went back and quizzed her on every new concept and gave her problems to solve. She had no difficulty whatsoever. This was probably the first time that I realized I didn't have a clue either.

Two months into the semester, the school's learning specialist tested Bambi to determine her academic ability. She administered the WRAT (Wide Range Achievement Test) and a subtest of the Woodcock-Johnson Tests of Achievement. As I understand the results, Bambi's performance was equivalent to that of a thirteen-year-old.

Anne and I had several meetings with teachers, counselors, and school administrators. A number of plans were proposed that, in theory, sounded good. However, there were unforeseen glitches in the execution. The main strategy was to give Bambi an individualized curriculum. However, her classmates noticed immediately that she was using different materials and, when they spoke about it, she felt uncomfortable and isolated. Soon she refused to use the new books in school any more. Then Bambi's best friend told her that she felt dumb compared to Bambi. We became concerned that Bambi would begin to underachieve in order to fit in with her classmates.

Bambi's teachers arranged for a high school student to tutor Bambi in mathematics. They also came up with another plan that involved pulling her out of class, on English days, and tutoring her one-on-one in German. Their feeling was that adding another foreign language would provide her with the challenge she needed. Bambi enjoyed German very much and handled the work with relative ease. There was, however, a reaction that we did not anticipate. Bambi's classmates were aware of the new arrangements and apparently some of them told their parents. Soon several parents approached us to ask if it were true that Bambi was being tutored in German and math. It was clear to us that they felt that Bambi was receiving "special" treatment and they were displeased that their own children were not. We told these parents that they should petition the headmaster themselves if they felt that their children needed similar accommodation.

I had casually toyed with the idea of homeschooling for a while, ever since I had realized how little effort Bambi exerted in order to excel at school. I realized that it would be nearly impossible for any schoolteacher to cater to her needs within the confines of a regular classroom. Ideally, Bambi needs one-on-one tutoring in almost every subject, because she learns so quickly.

We had a final meeting with school officials. The counselor suggested that Bambi skip middle school entirely. She felt that middle school students were extremely cliquish and that Bambi might be ostracized. However, she believed that the high school students were more mature and would probably accept her more easily. Our options were either to prepare Bambi for early high school or let her stay with her age mates. Since neither option seemed appropriate, we decided, with some sadness, to withdraw Bambi from school.

One immediate benefit of homeschooling is its flexibility. We can plan extracurricular activities to suit our schedule. Bambi takes art classes, as well as piano and ballet lessons. She is a junior Girl Scout. She wanted to learn Mandarin before she got "too old," so she attends Chinese school for two hours a week. We can do all this without feeling overwhelmed and pressed for time.

One of our initial concerns was whether we were capable of teaching Bambi all the required subjects. We anticipate that within a year or two we will need outside assistance, especially in the areas of math and science. Bambi's interest in math tends toward the esoteric. She reads scholarly books about zero, e (a constant approximately equal to 2.7182, which natural logarithms have as a base), imaginary numbers, Fermat's last theorem, the history of pi, and concepts related to multidimensional space. One day she hopes to have a math theory named after her. I support and encourage these interests even though I don't share them.

I spoke with someone at a local community college to explore the possibility of Bambi taking some math courses there. I was told that they would not even look at her application until she was ten and, even then, it was unlikely that they would accept her until she was at least twelve. We are fairly certain that, by then, she will have outgrown their offerings.

After one year of homeschooling, we're still trying to find the "right" curriculum. We need to be flexible and open-minded, so we mix and match everything. Bambi completed ten years of math in five months. She started calculus when she was seven years old, so now, if she wants to, she can take the AP Calculus exam next May. She's been begging to do some lab sciences, so we'll probably let her study physics, chemistry, and biology. Her love of reading makes the study of history and geography a pleasant pastime. This year, our main focus is on improving her writing skills. Next year is a universe away.

I intuitively feel that homeschooling is the best choice for us, though this past year has been extremely difficult. Not long after we began our homeschooling adventure, my mother died. She was only sixty-two years old and I was completely unprepared. She died suddenly and I never got to say good-bye. My mom adored her granddaughters, and now they'll grow up without really knowing her. She'll never see them turn sweet sixteen or tell them stories that only grandmothers can tell. My whole year has been tinged with sadness and disappointment. I feel like I was painting a rainbow and someone stole all my colors.

Life with Bambi is breathtaking and bittersweet. It is so exciting to watch her grow and imagine the possibilities that life may offer her. Yet it is sobering to realize that her intellect may take her places where we may not follow, and cause her to leave us long before we're ready to let her go.

For the most part, Anne and I experience Bambi's giftedness vicariously, through other people's reactions to her. We don't see her giftedness. We see a little girl who likes stuffed animals, video games, and junk food. We loved her from the moment we laid eyes on her, cleft and all. She is our baby and one of our treasures. For her sake and her sister's, I need to beg, borrow, or steal some new colors and paint myself another rainbow. Mom would be so proud.

Intellectual Assessment of Exceptionally and Profoundly Gifted Children

BY JOHN D. WASSERMAN

John D. Wasserman is associate professor of psychology at George Mason University and maintains a private practice in Fairfax, Virginia. A clinical neuropsychologist, he has directed development of psychological tests at leading test publishers for nearly a decade.

Being off the charts means the tests don't work for you. One of the hardest parts about figuring out which kids are profoundly gifted, and how to help them learn, is getting accurate test results. John Wasserman, an authority on testing instruments, looks at the options with an eye to their strengths and shortcomings.

Efforts to identify and follow the progress of children with exceptionally high levels of intelligence began with the work of Lewis M. Terman, the author of the first Stanford-Binet Intelligence Scale. In 1921, he described a child with an IQ of 188, and noted that she was functioning at a level more than six years above her chronological age of seven. At about the same time, Leta S. Hollingworth began identifying children above 180 IQ. She remarked upon their early reaching of developmental milestones (especially talking and reading), unusual levels of creativity, and superior capacity for learning. Terman and Hollingworth both followed

48

the progress of many of the gifted children they identified, noting the unique problems these children experienced in their education and social adjustment. They both advocated for early identification and educational acceleration of gifted children, with a differentiated curriculum and specially trained teachers. Ultimately, Terman viewed highly intelligent children as a national resource for the betterment of society. He encouraged teachers and parents to allow these children to develop in whatever directions their considerable abilities, talents, and interests would take them.

Unfortunately, our ability to effectively measure the highest-functioning of gifted children has declined, even as our understanding of their special needs has increased. To estimate IQ, Terman and Hollingworth used the intelligence quotient devised by William Stern in 1910: mental age (or test-age equivalent, in months) divided by chronological age (in months), all multiplied by 100 (expressed as MA/CA x 100). This method has been termed the *ratio IQ* and has been appropriately criticized, because it does not yield comparable scores at different ages. For example, an IQ of 200 can be obtained by a four-year-old child with the test-age equivalent of an eight-year-old, but it is not possible for the same child grown to age twenty to achieve the same level of IQ; intelligence does not continue to develop throughout life, so it is not possible to obtain a test-age equivalent of forty years. We note that newer, developmentally referenced, absolute scales of ability (rather than age) based on item-response theory may eventually offer a way to revisit the MA/CA x 100 formula.

For about fifty years, the preferred method of describing intelligence has been by computing a *deviation score* that compares an individual to his or her peer group. The deviation IQ, developed by Arthur Otis and popularized by David Wechsler, defines an individual according to rank order in a normal, bell-shaped distribution of scores. Assuming a normative mean of 100 and standard deviation of 15, the deviation method sets an IQ of 100 at the 50th percentile, an IQ of 130 at the 97.7th percentile (two standard deviations, or SD, above the mean), and an IQ of 160 at the 99.997th percentile (four SD above the mean). For most intelligence tests that sample between one hundred and two hundred individuals at every age band, it is unlikely that even one member of the normative sample will achieve a score greater than 160. Tests using the deviation method are simply not developed to make discriminations in ability far from the normative mean.

Having described this state of affairs, we now describe assessment approaches aimed at identifying children with intellectual ability four or more standard deviations above the normative mean (IQ above 160), or *exceptionally and profoundly gifted* children, who have been found to have qualitatively and quantitatively unique cognitive characteristics that differentiate them from intellectually gifted children performing at lower ranges of intellectually gifted ability (i.e., an IQ between 130 and 160). Of the estimated 3 million intellectually gifted students served in the United States,[1] there are probably no more than a few thousand who can be classified as exceptionally or profoundly gifted. The average educator will never personally encounter such a student, but the news media in every community will periodically cover an exceptionally or profoundly gifted child: a nine-month-old who names objects and uses words; an eighteen-month-old who knows the alphabet; a three-year-old who is able to read more than children's books; a six-year-old who designs and maintains his own Web site; or a ten-year-old who graduates from high school.

Although our focus is on intellectual assessment, we caution that the results of an intelligence test should never be the sole criterion for classification of exceptional children. Intelligence does not tell the whole story of the exceptionally gifted child, although it is the most traditional defining characteristic.

Current Intelligence Tests

In spite of their many limitations, measures of intelligence remain the most common and effective way by which children can be identified as intellectually gifted. Intelligence tests should always be used in conjunction with other evaluation methods, because they reveal little about the functional living skills, drive and motivation, and social-emotional characteristics that are also important in predicting life success. Testing is only one component of a full evaluation that will help parents and educators provide appropriate support for a gifted child's needs. Only a few intelligence tests, specifically the following, are commonly used to identify intellectually gifted children.

Stanford-Binet Intelligence Scales, Form L-M (SB L-M)

The Stanford-Binet L-M was published in 1972 as a normative update of intelligence-test items created in 1916 and 1937 by Lewis M. Terman (the latter edition with Maud Merrill), based in part upon assessment procedures pioneered by Alfred Binet and Théodore Simon. The SB L-M was organized by age level, with items tapping different kinds of abilities intermixed at each age. Although item content and the abilities tapped were not balanced across ages, the SB L-M remains unmatched in its breadth of procedures and is probably truer to the changing nature of cognitive-intellectual abilities over development than any test subsequently published. Its unique age-scaled format and liberal discontinue rules enabled testing to continue far beyond one's chronological age, thereby providing examinees with an opportunity to demonstrate considerably advanced competencies.

Spanning the ages of two through twenty-two years (and ability levels through three levels of superior adult), the SB L-M was normed on a nationally representative sample stratified by demographic variables as well as by verbal ability on a group-administered test, the Cognitive Abilities Test® (CogAT®). From ages two through thirteen years, the highest IQ scores yielded by the SB L-M using the standard IQ tables varied from 58 to 166 (equivalent to IQs of 154 to 161 when the SD is adjusted to 15), dropping lower for older ages. By using a mathematical formula based on the ratio IQ in appendix A of the manual, however, even higher scores can be obtained.[2]

The SB L-M uses a ratio IQ approach that was adjusted to provide accurate peer comparisons, based upon the patterns of typical development and normative distribution of scores at any given age. I consider this test appropriate only after an examinee has approached the ceiling of a more recently normed test (such as the WISC®-IV or SB5, or any of the following tests described), as a method of resolving just how far above the ceiling the examinee's true abilities may lie. When reported in an appropriately conservative manner (because of its limitations), the ratio IQ approach provides the only available means of estimating intelligence in exceptionally and profoundly gifted ranges that has any prior foundations in research (e.g., the work of Terman and Hollingworth).

Stanford-Binet Intelligence Scales, Fifth Edition (SB5)

The SB5, published in 2003, is the most recent revision of the oldest of intelligence tests.[3] It ranks as a distant second in popularity to the Wechsler intelligence scales. It spans the ages two through over eighty-five years and was designed to measure the theory of fluid and crystallized intelligence formulated by Cattell and Horn.[4] Fluid intelligence describes reasoning and problem-solving ability in novel situations (*fluid* because it takes different forms according to the demands of the problem), whereas crystallized intelligence refers to well-learned and well-practiced skills and knowledge sets. The SB5 continues the tradition of its predecessor editions by also measuring mathematical problem-solving and working memory. The SB5 yields a Full Scale IQ, as well as a Nonverbal IQ and a Verbal IQ, each with a normative mean of 100 and a standard deviation of 15. It also generates five factor-based standard scores: Fluid Reasoning, Knowledge, Quantitative Reasoning, Visual-Spatial Processing, and Working Memory. The SB5 has ten subtests, all with normative means of 10 and standard deviations of 3. Subtests are given in an age-scaled format, permitting the administration of adult-level items to high-performing children.

The SB5 offers several unique features that may be important to consider in the assessment of highly gifted children and adolescents. First, it decreases emphasis upon crystallized intelligence (contributing one-tenth to the overall IQ score) by restricting measurement of verbal acquired knowledge to a single vocabulary test. This decision may have the effect of enhancing its fairness for use in cross-cultural settings and with English-language learners, while simultaneously decreasing its capacity to recognize children with exceptional verbal knowledge bases. Second, the test is balanced between verbal and nonverbal content. The SB5 includes substantial testing content (about half) that involves minimal verbal instruction and requires minimal verbal response from the examinee. Third, the test emphasizes reasoning ability, as about forty percent of the content of the SB5 (the fluid reasoning and quantitative reasoning subtests) is intended to measure reasoning ability of some kind. Fourth, the SB5 has low emphasis on speed, with no bonus points for fast performance, thereby recognizing performance accuracy without penalizing for a contemplative or perfectionistic response style. Fifth, about twenty percent of the SB5 content is intended to recognize mathematical precocity, and the SB5 is the only major intelligence test to tap quantitative abilities as part of its overall composite scores.

The psychometric characteristics of the SB5 are fully adequate. It was normed on 4,800 examinees matched to 2001 U.S. census findings on the basis of age, sex, ethnicity, geographic region, and socioeconomic levels.

Its composite scales all have internal reliabilities meeting or exceeding the professional standard of 0.90, while those of the ten subtests average 0.84 or higher. The *Technical Manual* reports a variety of validity studies, including those that demonstrate somewhat lower-than-expected statistical sensitivity to students already identified as gifted in their respective school systems. It is possible that the increased nonverbal and less crystallized content of the SB5 may serve to identify gifted children with different cognitive characteristics than those currently being identified.

The SB5 Full Scale IQ (FSIQ) typically ranges from about 40 to 160, but guidelines for the use and interpretation of an Extended IQ (EXIQ) that produces scores up through a value of 225 appear in a separate *Interpretive Manual*. The EXIQ is recommended for use among children who obtain a scaled score of 19 (the highest possible score) on any of the SB5 subtests and a Full Scale IQ of at least 150. It may be computed with Table A.1 in the *Interpretive Manual* using the examinee's age and raw score total for all ten SB5 subtests. The EXIQ was derived through two steps: (a) conversion of SB5 raw scores into Rasch-based change-sensitive scores for the entire standardization sample, creating a single yardstick of cognitive development across the lifespan; and (b) transformation of smoothed change-sensitive age-group means and standard deviations into the familiar IQ metric ($M = 100$, $SD = 15$) for each separate age group. In analyses with the entire SB5 normative sample, the EXIQ is reported to yield a median correlation of 0.99 with the FSIQ, with a mean FSIQ-EXIQ difference of less than one point. At this time, the EXIQ is considered a promising experimental measure needing further research, but it appears to have a firm foundation in contemporary item response theory. Independent research will be necessary to establish its value with exceptionally and profoundly gifted children, but I recommend that the EXIQ be routinely included in SB5 psychological reports for children with very high FSIQs.

Wechsler Intelligence Scale for Children®, Fourth Edition (WISC®-IV)

The WISC® was most recently revised in 2003 and traces its origins to a model of intelligence first described by David Wechsler in 1939.[5] It is the most widely used intelligence test for gifted evaluations and will usually be the first individually administered test given to a candidate for gifted programs. It is intended for children between the ages of six and sixteen; preschool children are given the Wechsler Preschool and Primary Scale of Intelligence™, Third Edition (WPPSI™-III), and adults are given the Wechsler Adult Intelligence Scale®, Third Edition (WAIS®-III).

The WISC-IV balances verbal and nonverbal content while placing more emphasis on reasoning and less emphasis on speed than any prior editions of the Wechsler scales. The core battery of the WISC-IV consists of three verbal subtests, three performance subtests, two auditory working memory subtests, and two processing speed subtests. Five supplementary subtests are also available. The WISC-IV yields a Full Scale IQ and four factor indexes (Verbal Comprehension, Perceptual Reasoning, Working Memory, and Processing Speed), each with a normative mean of 100 and a standard deviation of 15. The Verbal IQ and Performance IQ scores are no longer available. WISC-IV subtests have a mean of 10 and standard deviation of 3, with scores extending up through 19.

The WISC-IV Verbal Comprehension Index (VCI) consists of measures of verbal abstraction (the Similarities subtest), word knowledge (Vocabulary), and social and practical knowledge (Comprehension). The decision by test developers to make the Information subtest (a measure of factual knowledge) supplemental means that acquired knowledge has been somewhat deemphasized on this index score, which is predictive of success in most academic settings, especially those that place a premium upon speaking, reading, and writing.

Substantial changes have been made on the WISC-IV performance scales, increasing the role of reasoning and decreasing speed and motor requirements. One new reasoning subtest (Picture Concepts) has been created, and two traditional performance subtests with time bonuses have been discarded (Picture Arrangement and Object Assembly). The Perceptual Reasoning Index (PRI) includes measures of visual-spatial pattern perception, analysis, and reproduction (Block Design), nonverbal conceptual and categorical reasoning (Picture Concepts), and analysis of nonverbal concepts and relationships (Matrix Reasoning). Two of the three core subtests have no motor requirements, other than pointing. For gifted students who are careful or thoughtful in their work, these changes to the WISC-IV nonverbal tests decrease the penalty for slow performance.

The Working Memory Index (WMI) provides an estimate of auditory working memory capacity, or the ability to temporarily store spoken information in mind while performing some active transformation or manipulation of it. The WMI estimates *how much* information a person can think about at any moment and is predictive of success in activities such as reading comprehension, applied math problems, or taking notes from a lecture, all of which require remembering information while organizing and interpreting it. The WMI includes measures of immediate number recall (Digit Span) and mental reorganization of numbers and letters (Letter-Number Sequencing). The sole WISC-IV measure of mathematical reasoning (Arithmetic) is now supplementary and does not contribute to any composite score.

Finally, the Processing Speed Index (PSI) provides an estimate of the rapidity with which a person can solve low difficulty problems over the span of a few minutes. It consists of timed measures of written associative learning (Coding) and visual discrimination and matching (Symbol Search), each of which estimates *how quickly* a person can accurately respond to tasks requiring sustained effort and attention.

The WISC-IV Full Scale IQ is now based primarily on knowledge, reasoning, and problem-solving and secondarily on cognitive efficiency. The VCI and PRI scores together constitute sixty percent of the Full Scale IQ, while the WMI and PSI together contribute only forty percent to the overall score. An alternative overall composite score called the General Ability Index (GAI), first introduced for the WISC-III in 1998, may provide a better estimate of intellectual giftedness for children who are slow, uncoordinated, distractible, or otherwise inefficient in their WISC-IV performance. Based upon the sum of scaled scores for the VCI and PRI only, the GAI tables are available in a separate volume and not in the WISC-IV manuals.[6]

The Wechsler scales are renowned for their rigorous standardizations, and the WISC-IV was no exception. The standardization sample consisted of 2,200 children stratified according to 2000 U.S. census data for age, sex, race, parent education level, and geographic region. The Full Scale IQ has an average internal reliability of 0.97, with three of the factor indices yielding fully adequate reliabilities ($r > 0.90$). The PSI yielded an average test-retest stability coefficient of 0.88. With the exception of the processing speed subtests, all WISC-IV subtests show adequate internal consistency. The structural validity of the WISC-IV has been strengthened with its new subtests, and its increased emphasis on reasoning ability is a positive development.

For exceptionally and profoundly gifted children, however, the low ceilings of the WISC-IV remain a significant limitation of the measure. From ages six through sixteen, the Full Scale IQ and GAI reach their highest possible score at 160.

Other Intelligence Tests

Four additional intelligence tests should be mentioned as showing promise in serving the gifted, although none has specific demonstrated utility with exceptionally and profoundly gifted children.

The Kaufman Assessment Battery for Children, Second Edition (KABC-II) is a cognitive-processing measure designed for use with children and adolescents between the ages of three to eighteen years.[7] It was developed to accommodate either of two theoretical approaches: an adaptation of a neuropsychological model formulated by A. R. Luria, and the psychometric model that synthesizes the work of Cattell, Horn, and Carroll. From a Lurian perspective, the KABC-II scales correspond to learning ability, sequential processing, simultaneous processing, and planning ability. From the perspective of the Cattell-Horn-Carroll model, the KABC-II captures long-term storage and retrieval, short-term memory, visual processing, fluid reasoning, and crystallized ability. Selection of subtests corresponding to the Luria processing model yields a Mental Processing Index (MPI), whereas a decision to include subtests of acquired knowledge/crystallized ability yields a Fluid-Crystallized Index (FCI) of overall performance. The KABC-II was standardized on 3,025 examinees stratified according to 2001 census figures. Reliability for composite scores is adequate, but results from a validity study with a gifted sample may be interpreted as indicating that gifted students are more likely to show superior functioning on measures of acquired knowledge than those tapping cognitive processing.

The Das-Naglieri Cognitive Assessment System (CAS™) is a cognitive-processing battery intended for use with children and adolescents from five through seventeen years of age.[8] Developed according to a Lurian model, the CAS taps four dimensions of processing: planning, attention, simultaneous processing, and successive processing. The CAS was standardized on 2,200 children and adolescents stratified on 1990 census figures. Sample stratification variables included race, ethnicity, geographic region, community setting, parent educational attainment, classroom placement, and educational classification. The internal consistency of the CAS is fully adequate. Exploratory and confirmatory factor analyses of the CAS provide support for either a three- or four-factor solution, although the integrity of the factor structure has been challenged. The CAS is the first cognitive-intelligence test to include measures of executive functions such as planning. It tends to show small racial and ethnic group mean differences compared to other intelligence tests, presumably because it emphasizes processing rather than acquired knowledge or crystallized intelligence. Consumers of the CAS should be aware that its planning and attention scales (fifty percent of the system) place a premium on speed, which is often an area of weakness among gifted students.

The Differential Ability Scales® (DAS®) is an ability profile test consisting of seventeen subtests, divided into two overlapping age levels and standardized for ages two-and-a-half through seventeen years.[9] It also includes several tests of school achievement. The DAS was developed to accommodate diverse theoretical perspectives and to permit interpretation at multiple levels of performance. The DAS is also characterized by exceptionally high attention to technical qualities. Unlike tests that include many measures of unique abilities, the DAS yields a composite General Conceptual Ability (GCA) score that emphasizes performance on subtests with strong associations to a factor of general intelligence, usually referred to as g.[10]

The Woodcock-Johnson III Tests of Cognitive Abilities (WJ III COG) represent the most recent revision of an assessment battery with prior editions from 1977 and 1989.[11] Normed for use from ages two through ninety-plus years, the WJ III COG is co-normed with a leading achievement test. The WJ III COG consists of twenty tests purporting to measure seven broad cognitive factors. The tests are organized into a standard battery (tests 1 through 7, with three supplemental tests) and an extended battery (tests 1 through 7 and tests 11 through 17, with six supplemental tests). The WJ III COG is designed to measure elements from the theory of Cattell, Horn, and Carroll.[12] The WJ III COG yields a composite General Intellectual Ability (GIA) score that is weighted to emphasize measures of general intelligence, but most of its subtests appear to measure unique abilities that are not good measures of g. The WJ III COG is reported to yield intelligence standard scores over 200, so it may be suitable for applications with exceptionally and profoundly gifted children. Its inclusion of measures of auditory processing and speeded performance, however, may act to depress very high scores.

Special Assessment Issues

|||||||||||||||||||||||||||||||||||||||||||||||||||||||||||||||||||||||||||||||||||||||||||||||||||||||||||||||||||||||||||||||||||||||||||||||||||||||||||||||||||||||||||||||||||

Not all intelligence tests are created equal, and selection of the appropriate intelligence test should consider what the test purports to measure, as well as what levels of giftedness it is capable of evaluating. Special assessment issues come into play when intelligence tests are used with exceptionally and profoundly gifted children.

Content of the Intelligence Test

Intelligence tests vary considerably in their content, and the results of an assessment depend in large part upon the abilities and cognitive processes being assessed. For example, a test emphasizing recall and application of verbal knowledge is likely to yield depressed scores (relative to a nonverbal test) in a gifted child with limited English proficiency. Accordingly, important questions concern (1) what the essential aspects of exceptionally and profoundly gifted behavior are, and (2) how these may be associated with formal psychological testing.

The essays in this volume contain numerous descriptions of exceptionally and profoundly gifted children. Characteristics of these children include an advanced ability to solve novel and unique problems; rapid learning of new material; an ability to integrate and synthesize seemingly diverse concepts; and an insatiable drive toward new experiences and new learning. Parents of gifted children report that advanced abstract thinking, expressive language, and unusual memory are among the reasons they think their children are gifted. Exceptionally and profoundly gifted children are usually described as verbally precocious, with large vocabularies and multiple forms of self-expression. These students also seem to process information across sensory modalities, encoding experiences in many different ways.

Beginning with the work of Charles E. Spearman a century ago, psychologists have sought to identify the essence of intelligence. Spearman discovered a mathematically derived general intelligence factor, usually referred to as the *g-factor* that may be computed from the shared variance that saturates batteries of cognitive-intelligence tests.[13] This general factor, rather than isolated specific or unique ability factors, is thought to explain the extraordinary abilities of exceptionally and profoundly gifted children. Spearman considered g to be a "general mental energy," but more recently researchers have presented evidence that g is synonymous with fluid reasoning ability. Others have argued that g is working memory capacity, an estimate of how much information an individual can hold and transform in mental operating space at any given time. Still others have posited that g is an index of neural efficiency or an index of mental complexity. Arthur Jensen has reviewed literature showing that correlates of g include scholastic performance, reaction time, success in training programs, job performance in a wide range of occupations, occupational status, earned income, socially significant creativity in the arts and sciences, and a variety of biologically anchored variables.[14]

Intelligence tests operationally define intelligence in many different ways, usually consisting of a mathematical average or composite score derived from performance on a wide range of tasks that tap diverse cognitive abilities. This is the approach utilized by the SB L-M, SB5, Wechsler scales, KABC-II, and CAS. Tests such as the DAS and WJ III COG derive composite scores based upon subtest g-loadings, with varying degrees of success. Exceptionally and profoundly gifted children, and most gifted children for that matter, tend to attain high scores on intelligence test batteries that emphasize general intelligence, either by including many high-g tests or by assigning more weight to high-g tests. Batteries with many subtests tapping low-g unique abilities may yield somewhat lower intelligence test scores in the gifted. For this reason, among others, different intelligence tests will yield varying estimates of intelligence.

John B. Carroll, whose 1993 work is frequently cited by researchers, conducted factor analyses of more than 460 archival sets of data and concluded that g was virtually identical to fluid reasoning ability. He specified descending g-loadings in tests that tapped the following factors: fluid reasoning, crystallized intelligence, general memory and learning, visual perception, auditory perception, retrieval ability, cognitive speediness, and decision speed. High-g subtests include matrix reasoning tasks, vocabulary, pattern analysis, and block design; low-g subtests include processing speed tasks and short-term memory tasks, such as digit span. Tests that emphasize reasoning and problem-solving tend to be high-g, whereas tests with high levels of dependency on speed tend to be low-g. The value of low-g tests tapping unique abilities may be to identify cognitive weaknesses that contribute to specific academic problems (e.g., reading disability) that are largely independent of general intelligence.

Levels of Giftedness

To effectively serve the needs of exceptionally gifted children, an intelligence test must have sufficient discrimination at the upper ranges of ability. It must differentiate levels of giftedness up to and including the exceptionally and profoundly gifted. The following table transcends the levels described in intelligence-test manuals, offering additional suggested descriptive terms and classifications for levels of intellectual giftedness. Using this framework, exceptionally gifted children perform more than four standard deviations above the normative mean, and profoundly gifted children perform more than five standard deviations above the normative mean.

Levels of Intellectual Giftedness

Descriptive Term	Composite Score Range	Normal Curve Scoring Range
Profoundly Gifted	175+	+ 5 SD and above
Exceptionally Gifted	160–174	+ 4–4.99 SD
Highly Gifted	145–159	+ 3–3.99 SD
Gifted	130–144	+ 2–2.99 SD
Advanced (or Superior)	120–129	+ 1.33–1.99 SD
High Average	110–119	+ 0.67–1.32 SD
Average	90–109	- 0.67–+ .66 SD

Note: SD means standard deviation(s). The descriptive terms and corresponding ranges vary among systems and tests. These are intended for a test with a normative mean of 100 and standard deviation of 15.

Only three major intelligence tests offer scoring methodologies that reach into the exceptionally and profoundly gifted ranges. Measures such as the WISC-IV and the KABC-II reach their upper limits at about 160. The SB L-M permits the calculation of an IQ beyond 160 (using an adjustment of the formula MA/CA x 100). As I have mentioned, this method may be criticized, but it formed the foundation for identification of the exceptionally gifted. The SB5 offers the experimental EXIQ that generates scores beyond 200. Also, WJ III COG offer General Intellectual Ability (GIA) scores that approach 200, based upon scoring extrapolation and Rasch scaling.[15] It has not yet been determined whether the WJ III COG GIA effectively identifies and discriminates between individuals within the exceptionally and profoundly gifted range, because no studies of intellectually gifted students have yet been reported with this 2001 test.

An alternative way to estimate intellectual ability in the exceptionally gifted is to administer an out-of-level test, one intended for much older children, such as the Scholastic Aptitude Test (SAT). The limitation of this approach is that SAT scores do not readily translate into peer-norm–referenced standard scores.

Subtypes of Exceptionally and Profoundly Gifted Children

Cognitive abilities develop at different rates. Those that are more strongly related to general intelligence tend to develop more uniformly, whereas more unique and low-*g* abilities often have distinctive developmental trajectories. Accordingly, it should be no surprise that both gifted and non-gifted children may show uneven patterns of performance on batteries of cognitive-intellectual tests. The term *asynchrony* has come to describe the uneven development and unusually wide scatter of abilities that is evident in exceptionally and profoundly gifted children, who appear very advanced in measures of general intelligence while appearing less advanced in measures of other abilities. Asynchrony is so prevalent among the higher levels of giftedness that within this population it can be considered "normal." Asynchrony also extends beyond cognitive functioning to include emotional development, functional living skills, physical maturation, and social competencies.

Asynchrony becomes more challenging to understand and evaluate in the twice-exceptional child, especially the gifted child with a learning disability. In the exceptionally gifted, the problem of twice-exceptionality is difficult to detect because it may be manifested in a slightly different form than with non-gifted children and because we do not know precisely what a learning disability means in an exceptionally gifted child. It may not represent an inability to read, but rather a reading ability that is not commensurate with expectations based upon general intelligence. For example, a girl with a measured IQ of 191 experienced difficulty reading and demonstrated a 70-point discrepancy between intelligence and achievement. In spite of this relative weakness in reading, her reading competency on a norm-referenced test was still above average! A discrepancy of this magnitude is possible when general intelligence is high but a unique, low-*g* ability contributing to reading proficiency, such as phonological processing, is substantially lower or less developed. Patterns of significant scatter or variability across abilities is common in exceptionally and profoundly gifted children and may result in extreme levels of frustration, given that these children strive to perform at consistently high levels in every area of endeavor.

Federal and state mandates usually do not clearly require assistance for twice-exceptional gifted/learning-disabled (LD) children, because their academic skills may not be sufficiently depressed to qualify for services. At the same time, their relative weaknesses in circumscribed abilities often meet criteria for LD diagnosis in terms of discrepancy approaches (in which ability is severely discrepant with academic skills) or process-based approaches (in which the unique cognitive processing abilities contributing to performance of academic skills are weak relative to general intelligence). Programs of special education are typically tailored to children who perform substantially below average in a given academic skill, whereas exceptionally and profoundly gifted children may still perform above the general population average while showing substantial weakness relative to their own level of general intellectual functioning.

Subtypes of twice-exceptional gifted children may include: (1) gifted/LD students with subtle or prominent relative weaknesses in specific academic skills including reading, written language, or mathematics, (2) gifted/ADHD (attention deficit hyperactivity disordered) students who have particular difficulty with attention, foresight, and impulse control, and (3) gifted/EBD (emotionally or behaviorally disordered) students whose problems with anxiety, depression, or oppositional behaviors significantly interfere with their ability to function effectively in school, social, and other situations. Gifted children with learning disabilities are thought to score at high levels on both intelligence and achievement tests, usually with intelligence higher than achievement, but over time the discrepancy between ability and achievement may widen as academic skills fail to keep pace with other aspects of cognitive development. The problem of coexisting ADHD and giftedness has also been reported in a number of anecdotal cases, but it is unclear to what extent behaviors that are characteristic of exceptional or profound giftedness are misinterpreted as evidence of ADHD. For example, many behaviors associated with giftedness may resemble those associated with ADHD (e.g., boredom and daydreaming, low tolerance for frustration, impersistence on tasks of low interest, impulsivity and poor judgment, and high energy). Kazimierz Dabrowski described gifted children as showing unusually intense reactions or *overexcitabilities*, which he defined as higher-than-average responsiveness to stimuli in psychomotor, sensory, affective, imaginational, or intellectual domains.[16] These overexcitabilities may closely resemble some symptoms of ADHD. Clearly, further research is needed to determine the relationship between symptoms of ADHD and giftedness, as well as EBD and giftedness.

Toward the Future

Assessment science and the publishers of intelligence tests still have a considerable distance to go before the special needs of exceptionally and profoundly gifted children can be identified and formally measured. The professional who wants to measure intellectual ability in these children finds a striking shortage of options; the SB L-M represents the only testing approach with a relevant research history. New promise may be offered by the Stanford-Binet EXIQ and the WJ III COG, but these tests are unproven in their ability to serve the exceptionally gifted.

Several research initiatives need to be undertaken. The first is a clear-cut and unequivocal validation with contemporary intelligence measures, preferably those that emphasize *g*, of the extraordinary intellectual gifts of exceptionally and profoundly gifted children. Few researchers since Terman and Hollingworth have had the assessment tools capable of identifying and serving these children. Second, there needs to be an examination of the ways in which intelligence tests with ceilings below 160 (e.g., the Wechsler intelligence scales) inadequately represent the abilities of children who are thought to be exceptionally and profoundly gifted. Given that intelligence tests measure a variety of constructs, it will be important to identify which of the contemporary tests provide the most meaningful information about a gifted child's learning abilities and special needs. A comparative study of intelligence tests with exceptionally and profoundly gifted children, along with objective measures of their capacity to predict successful functioning in everyday life, may be necessary in order to identify the best tests to use for assessment purposes. Finally, intelligence tests with adequate ceilings must be administered in conjunction with achievement tests and other measures of special abilities with adequate ceilings, in order to begin the process of arriving at clear and accurate identification of subtypes of gifted children with learning disabilities and other comorbid conditions. It is only with the right tools that we can measure the unique gifts and special needs of exceptionally and profoundly gifted children.

Notes

1. U.S. Department of Education, *Digest of Education Statistics 1996*.

2. Terman and Merrill, *Stanford-Binet Intelligence Scale: 1972 Norms Edition*.

3. Roid, *Stanford-Binet Intelligence Scales, Fifth Edition*. See also Roid, *Stanford-Binet Intelligence Scales, Fifth Edition, Interpretive Manual*.

4. The writings of Cattell and Horn are extensive, but the most complete accounts of their theories of intelligence appear in Cattell, *Intelligence: Its Structure, Growth and Action*, and Horn and Noll, "Human Cognitive Capabilities: Gf-Gc Theory."

5. Wechsler, *The Measurement of Adult Intelligence*.

6. Prifitera, Saklofske, Weiss, and Rolfhus, *WISC®-IV Clinical Use and Interpretation*.

7. Kaufman and Kaufman, *Kaufman Assessment Battery for Children, Second Edition*.

8. Naglieri and Das, *Cognitive Assessment System*.

9. Elliott, *Differential Ability Scales*.

10. This concept is explained in more detail later in the essay, and the ability of the DAS® to produce a General Conceptual Ability (GCA) score contrasts it with tests in which all subtests (high- and low-g-loading) contribute equally to the overall composite index of intelligence.

11. Woodcock, McGrew, Mather, *Woodcock-Johnson III Tests of Cognitive Abilities*.

12. Carroll, *Human Cognitive Abilities*.

13. Spearman, "General Intelligence."

14. Jensen, *The G Factor: The Science of Mental Ability*.

15. Rasch scaling and item response theory represent new approaches to measurement theory that may enhance assessment with children such as the exceptionally and profoundly gifted, who are functioning at the extreme high end of most existing tests. A good introduction to Rasch scaling is available in Embretson and Hershberger, *The New Rules of Measurement*.

16. Dabrowski, *Psychoneurosis Is Not an Illness*.

References

|||||||||||||||||||||||||||||||||||||||||||||||||||||||||||||||||||||||||||||||||||||||||||||||||||||||||||||||||||||||||||||||||||||||||||||||||||||||||||||

Carroll, J. B. *Human Cognitive Abilities: A Survey of Factor-Analytic Studies*. New York: Cambridge University Press, 1993.

Cattell, R. B., ed. *Intelligence: Its Structure, Growth and Action*. New York: Elsevier Science, 1987.

Dabrowski, K. *Psychoneurosis Is Not an Illness: Neuroses and Psychoneuroses from the Perspective of Positive Disintegration*. London: Gryf, 1972.

Elliott, C. D. *Differential Ability Scales*. San Antonio, TX: The Psychological Corporation, 1990.

Embretson, Susan, and Scott Hershberger, eds. *The New Rules of Measurement: What Every Psychologist and Educator Should Know*. Mahwah, NJ: Erlbaum, 1999.

Hollingworth, L. S. *Children Above 180 IQ Stanford-Binet: Origin and Development*. Yonkers, NY: World Book, 1942.

Horn, J. L., and J. Noll. "Human Cognitive Capabilities: Gf-Gc Theory." *Contemporary Intellectual Assessment: Theories, Tests, and Issues*, edited by D. P. Flanagan, J. L. Genshaft, and P. L. Harrison: 53–91. New York: Guilford, 1997.

Jensen, A. R. *The G Factor: The Science of Mental Ability*. Westport, CT: Praeger Publishers/ Greenwood, 1998.

Kaufman, A. S., and N. L. Kaufman. *Kaufman Assessment Battery for Children, Second Edition*. Circle Pines, MN: AGS Publishing, 2004.

Naglieri, J. A., and J. P. Das. *Cognitive Assessment System*. Itasca, IL: Riverside Publishing, 1997.

Prifitera, A., D. H. Saklofske, L. G. Weiss, and E. Rolfhus. *WISC®-IV Clinical Use and Interpretation: Scientist-Practitioner Perspectives*. San Diego: Academic Press, 2004.

Roid, G. H. *Stanford-Binet Intelligence Scales, Fifth Edition*. Itasca, IL: Riverside Publishing, 2003.

———. *Stanford-Binet Intelligence Scales, Fifth Edition, Interpretive Manual: Expanded Guide to the Interpretation of SB5 Test Results*. Itasca, IL: Riverside Publishing, 2003.

Spearman, C. E. "General Intelligence: Objectively Determined and Measured." *American Journal of Psychology*, 15 (1994): 201–293.

Terman, L. *Genetic Studies of Genius: Mental and Physical Traits of One Thousand Gifted Children*. Stanford, CA: Stanford University Press, 1925.

Terman, L. M., and M. A. Merrill. *Stanford-Binet Intelligence Scale: 1972 Norms Edition*. Boston: Houghton Mifflin, 1973.

U.S. Department of Education. National Center for Education Statistics. *Digest of Education Statistics 1996* (NCES 96–133). Washington, DC: U.S. Government Printing Office, 1996.

Wechsler, D. *The Measurement of Adult Intelligence*. Baltimore: Williams and Wilkins, 1939.

Woodcock, R. W., K. S. McGrew, and N. Mather. *Woodcock-Johnson III Tests of Cognitive Abilities*. Itasca, IL: Riverside Publishing, 2001.

Recommendations for Identifying and Serving Black Youth in Gifted Programs

BY TAREK C. GRANTHAM & LINDA A. LONG

Tarek C. Grantham is an associate professor in the Department of Educational Psychology and Instructional Technology at the University of Georgia. He teaches courses in and serves as coordinator for the Gifted and Creative Education Program.

Linda A. Long is the program coordinator for the bachelor's program in the School of Social Work at the University of Georgia. Her interests include socio-emotional, counseling, and family issues of academically gifted black children and adolescents.

It's always difficult to identify profoundly gifted children and to provide them access to appropriate educational opportunities. Children from backgrounds unlike that of the dominant culture they live in face extra sets of cultural barriers. Tarek Grantham and Linda Long look at the need for multicultural awareness in assessment of gifted children and make recommendations for finding abilities without regard to demographic categories.

School, personal, and family factors present challenges for gifted black students and schools. Gifted program personnel and parent advocacy groups who want to make sure that gifted black students receive appropriate educational opportunities must be proactive with recruitment and retention efforts. These efforts should focus on modifying identification procedures, recruiting black gifted-education teachers, promoting positive ethnic identity through multicultural gifted education, developing emotional resilience in students and teachers, and supporting black parents who advocate for their children's educational choices.

Modifications in Identification from a Multicultural Perspective

Gifted education identification procedures must be restructured to effectively include gifted students from diverse backgrounds. Ford, Grantham, and Wright have proposed a synthesis of goals and rationale that gets to the heart of restructuring.[1] These authors state that gifted education needs to identify and develop abilities without being confined by sociodemographic variables, such as ethnicity, culture, class (e.g., educational level, income, occupation), and gender.

Educators should consider one or more of the following options for more accurate assessment of ability and potential: (1) adapt instruments (e.g., modify the instruments relative to language); (2) re-norm the instruments to reflect local population and needs; (3) modify predetermined cut-off scores; and (4) use alternative instruments to measure a given construct (e.g., replace WISC® III as a measure of intelligence with Kaufman Assessment Battery for Children or Raven's Progressive Matrices). These options compensate for biases in identification that are caused by social injustices and educational problems. When minority students are not constrained by the boundaries of traditional identification procedures, they have a greater chance of being appropriately identified and served in gifted programs.

Recruitment of Black Teachers

The educational pipeline in gifted education at all levels—from kindergarten through graduate school—needs serious attention, particularly as it affects black and other minority teachers. Like other disciplines, the field of gifted education must aggressively recruit minority teachers.

Ford, Grantham, and Harris have recommended several measures that can promote diversity.[2] These include (1) educational loans that are forgiven following a certain amount of professional service to the field; (2) mentoring programs for high school and college students who are interested in teaching; (3) training in test-taking skills for those who would like teacher certification; and (4) increased peer and professional contact for minority teachers-in-training.

Cohort teams of minority individuals involved in the field of gifted education may include university faculty members, practicing teachers, school personnel, educators, gifted education teachers, and former student-participants in gifted programs. While these teams can help to create an educational pipeline that diversifies the teaching staff, they also promote awareness of the cultural needs of black and other special populations in gifted education. As the following discusses, a diverse teaching staff can help educators and parents from all backgrounds—mainstream and minority—promote culturally diverse teaching practices.

Development of Multicultural Competencies

Ford, Grantham, and Harris have also maintained that individuals must have the following characteristics in order to be competent with diverse groups of gifted children: self-awareness and self-understanding, cultural awareness and understanding, social responsiveness and responsibility, and culturally sensitive techniques and strategies.[3] In order to be competent in teaching gifted minority students, educators need early and ongoing exposure to and experiences with a variety of cultures.[4]

G. R. Howard's research suggests that caucasian educators can be more effective advocates for gifted blacks, and can work to reverse racial imbalances in gifted programs, if they develop an authentic and positive caucasian racial identity.[5] The suggested transformation involves attention to three modalities: (1) thinking (construction of truth; caucasianness; dominance); (2) feeling (level of self-awareness; emotional response to differences and to discussions of racism); (3) acting (approach to cross-cultural interactions; approach to teaching about differences; approach to leadership/management). This framework may help caucasian educators improve their multicultural competencies and increase their understanding of non-caucasian gifted students' experiences.

When educators and parents of the gifted develop multicultural competencies, they are better prepared to help gifted black students develop emotional resilience and positive ethnic identity. They can teach black students how to be resilient and how to persevere in the face of social injustices, instead of succumbing to negative peer pressures or to feelings that undermine self-esteem.[6] They can teach gifted black students that achieving one's potential is part of black heritage and is crucial to the development of a positive black identity. They can help parents of gifted black students transform their role as advocates for their children, teaching them to help their children successfully navigate through the triple quandary of majority, minority, and black cultural experiences.[7]

Multicultural awareness gives all educators and parents of the gifted the tools they need to effect social change for gifted black students. Black students continue to be under-represented and to underachieve in gifted education because we have not yet made a serious commitment to improvement and change. Competency in multicultural gifted education, which permits teachers to work with diverse populations, represents a serious and necessary transformation.

Notes

1. Ford, Grantham, and Wright, "Maximizing Potential of Minority Learners."

2. Ford, Grantham, and Harris, "The Recruitment and Retention of Minority Teachers."

3. Ford, Grantham, and Harris, "Multicultural Gifted Education."

4. Ford and Harris, *Multicultural Gifted Education.*

5. Howard, *We Can't Teach What We Don't Know.*

6. Gordon, "Self-Concept and Motivational Patterns."

7. Boykin, "The Triple Quandry."

References

Boykin, A. W. "The Triple Quandary and the Schooling of Afro-American Children." *The School Achievement of Minority Children,* edited by Ulric Neisser: 57–92. Hillsdale, NJ: Erlbaum, 1986.

Ford, D. Y. *Reversing Underachievement Among Gifted Black Students: Promising Practices and Programs.* New York: Teachers College Press, 1996.

Ford, D. Y., T. C. Grantham, and J. J. Harris III. "Multicultural Gifted Education: A Wake-Up Call to the Profession." *Roeper Review,* 19, no. 2 (1996): 72–78.

———. "The Recruitment and Retention of Minority Teachers in Gifted Education." *Roeper Review,* 19, no. 4 (1997): 213–220.

Ford, D. Y., T. C. Grantham, and L. B. Wright. "Maximizing Potential of Minority Learners with Gifts and Talents." *Advances in Special Education 12,* edited by Festus Obiakor, John O. Schwenn, and Anthony F. Rotatori: 91–104. Greenwich, CT: JAI, 1999.

Ford, D. Y., and J. J. Harris III. *Multicultural Gifted Education.* New York: Teachers College Press, 1999.

Gordon, K. A. "Self-Concept and Motivational Patterns of Resilient African-American High School Students." *Journal of Black Psychology* 21, no. 3 (1995): 239–255.

Howard, G. R. *We Can't Teach What We Don't Know: White Teachers, Multiracial Schools.* New York: Teachers College Press, 1999.

---

*The full text from which this article has been excerpted, "School, Personal, and Family Factors Impacting Under-Representation Among Black Adolescents in Gifted Programs," can be found in *Highly Gifted Children* 13, no. 2 (Winter/Spring 2000): 19–26.

Twice Exceptionality

Life in the Asynchronous Lane

BY LEE SINGER

Lee Singer is both the mother of a gifted child with special needs and an advocate for gifted/special needs children.

The word *asynchronous*, frequently applied to gifted children, refers to an essential fact of their lives: they are out of step, or not synchronized with, their age-mates. They surge ahead and they also lag behind, often simultaneously in different developmental areas, or, in school, in different subjects, like language and math. Lee Singer articulates the challenges of parenting a young man whose intellectual abilities span five grade levels, and tells of successfully creative solutions required to meet his learning needs.

I'm sitting here while my nine-year-old son takes a weekend of mini-courses for high school students at a prestigious local university. He is in heaven, running around with friends, constructing a computer, exploring the engineering library. His favorite reading material is "Garfield" and "Foxtrot" cartoons. He's happy to discuss black holes or why John Elway is the greatest quarterback ever. However, he kicks and screams at the thought of reading or writing about these things, even though they are his passions.

He's a joy to be with, but when his ADHD medication wears off he starts bouncing off the walls—literally. This is life with an exceptionally gifted child with special needs.

I sometimes feel like I'm spending my life on a tightrope. Always wondering when to push, when not to push. Trying to guess the fine line between presenting opportunities and pushing.

Being highly gifted and having special needs causes difficult dilemmas. My son has been diagnosed as being mildly dyslexic. He can read on age level, but finds it a chore. Certainly when there is information he wants in a user's manual or on a Web site, he reads it. And he's happy to read the latest issues of *Sports Illustrated for Kids, Cat Fancy,* or *Consumer Reports.* However, his "fun" reading is all cartoon books. This raises questions—is it worth trying to remediate? *Can* we remediate? Am I just being pushy because I want my son to love reading as much as I do? Or am I legitimately concerned about the world of information from which he is closing himself off because of his reading difficulties? There are no easy answers.

We gave up on school a year and a half ago—there was no way the system could meet the needs of a child whose abilities spanned more than five grade levels, and there was no way he could survive long days of mixed frustration and boredom followed by long evenings of fights over home-work. After a grade skip, he was still at way too low a level in math and science, but was unable to keep up in writing and foreign language; although social studies and English were at the correct reading level for him, the level of classroom discussion was far below him.

Now we homeschool, and things are much better. He has a writing tutor who understands the needs of a child with a written-language dis-ability, and who has made co-writing stories fun. He has attended special university programs geared to seventh- to twelfth-grade students. We listen to a lot of books on tape in the car, because his comprehension level is so much higher than his comfortable reading level. The child who hates to read anything harder than "Foxtrot" happily listens to *The Double Helix,* Helen Keller's autobiography, and essays by physicist Richard Feynman as we drive, leading me to quip that our main education method is "car schooling."

One big advantage to our shift in educational environments has been the lack of age-consciousness within the homeschooling community. Home-schoolers tend to reject the rigid age-stratification of the schools. This means that no one blinks an eye when my son participates in a homeschoolers' math class with children several years older than he is. The other kids in the class accept him without question; it's clear he belongs there and that's all that matters. Of course, it's an extra bonus when the laid-back teacher allows a fellow student to bring his pet python to class, so that math gets spiced with lessons in the care and physiology of snakes!

My son needs a great deal of physical activity and is athletically gifted. Homeschooling means that we can provide more opportunities for him to explore his talents without worrying about the homework getting done. When he was in school, we had to limit the number of sports he could participate in, and he wasn't able to do family gym night at the local community center because his homework load was too high. Now he has time to follow his athletic interests, which are as multifaceted as his academic ones. His ADHD actually gives him some advantages on the soccer field, as he can scan the whole field and be aware of everything going on around him. Unfortunately, his heightened sensitivities (whether due to those dratted Dabrowski's overexcitabilities or to sensory integration issues—it's hard to tell which) also mean that he is acutely aware of every bruise, slight muscle strain, or feeling "off," and he often needs to be coaxed to go to practice or a game—even though he forgets all about his concerns as soon as he gets immersed in play.

Part of my son's giftedness involves a level of sensitivity and insight into people and other creatures that never ceases to amaze me. He is very attuned to his friends' feelings about their special life circumstances; he will tell me of a relative's oscillating feelings about being adopted, or a friend's anger at having an older brother with a difficult neurological disorder. We have long discussions about what makes people tick. I've heard my son give explanations of other people's behaviors or why a cat acted a certain way that were striking for their levels of nuance. In fact, when he was in school, I found that the teachers often would not understand the depth of his answers to questions about interpersonal relationships. I revel in our discussions of philosophy, religion, politics, science, and the human condition.

Many parents of exceptionally gifted children talk about how they aren't pushing their children—instead, they are being pulled along and running as fast as they can to keep up. With an exceptionally gifted child who also has special needs, I find myself alternately pushing and being pulled—sometimes both at the same time! The degree to which asynchrony—that frustrating mixture of different levels of intellectual, emotional, and physical development—occurs in exceptionally gifted children with special challenges is so great that it challenges the ingenuity of even the most creative, knowledgeable parent to figure out how to properly meet these special children's needs.

I am very thankful that the Internet has made a wealth of information and resources available to help me figure out what my son needs. If it weren't for the support of Internet friends, I would never have had the courage to try homeschooling. If it weren't for the information I have gotten from a variety of email lists, I would never have known what to look for in testing, what our educational options are, and what resources are available to homeschoolers.

We still struggle, and I often worry about how we will handle the challenges that lie ahead. Then I take a deep breath and think about how much I love our deep discussions, our closeness when I read aloud to him (whether the topic is a fantasy story or astrophysics), his sheer joy in physical movement. And I muse that these are all facets of our life in the asynchronous lane.

An Anomaly

Parenting a Twice-Exceptional Girl

BY KIESA KAY

Kiesa Kay is the editor of this volume as well as of *Uniquely Gifted*, an anthology about gifted students who have other special needs, and a writer, playwright, and poet. She has been guest editor of the *Highly Gifted Children* magazine's special issues on adolescence and twice exceptionality and a featured speaker at regional and national conferences, including National Association for Gifted Children. Kiesa is also the mother of two profoundly gifted children, Benjamin and Ameli.

Kiesa Kay writes of her daughter, Ameli, who combines exceptional intellectual abilities with learning differences. In addition, Ameli is a girl with acknowledged gifts in mathematics. Kiesa points out the need to find appropriate education for profoundly gifted children whose learning styles differ from the norm, so that children like Ameli can reach their full potential. She also suggests that unusual perception—like that which accompanies conditions we call "disabilities"—may combine with extreme intelligence to produce rare and valuable mental capacities.

Definitions:

twice exceptionality: giftedness combined with other special needs, for example, learning disabilities, dysgraphia, or cerebral palsy *sensory integrative dysfunction:* the researcher who first described sensory integration dysfunction called it a "traffic jam" in the brain where bits of sensory information don't get to the parts of the brain where they need to be to do their jobs

asynchronous development: the condition of being advanced in some areas and lagging in others

My daughter's name is Ameli; we call her Filly. As a twice-exceptional person—very gifted and with a different learning style—she is also an anomaly.

Filly has a natural flair for mathematics. From a very early age, the opportunity to do math problems became a powerful motivational reward for her. Filly reads complicated texts and expounds upon them. Despite her voracious reading and obvious intellectual acumen, it takes her a long time to write a simple sentence. The letters leap and dance on the page, and only with the most painstaking effort can she write at all. She's been diagnosed as a profoundly gifted girl with sensory integrative dysfunction.

"Sensory integrative dysfunction would be much easier to diagnose and treat if the problem were the same in each child," writes Jean Ayres, who first described this condition. "Sensory integrative therapists have a somewhat bewildering diagnostic job since every child they see has his own set of symptoms."[1] The stereotype of the absent-minded professor resembles some of the traits of this kind of twice exceptionality, because despite all her disorganization, Filly's mind never stops discovering.

Asynchronous development is common to children with Filly's disability, just as it is common to children with her profound level of giftedness. Even as the sensory integration renders her unique, children with Filly's IQ of 191 are statistically one in a million.

In the classroom, her extraordinary ability and her disability seemed to cancel out each other, and she was identified early as a very bright child who balked at completing written work in class. She did not demonstrate any academic inadequacies at all, although she received criticism for losing materials and lacking organization. Her teachers were loving, kind women who reminded her daily to organize her work, and they struggled bravely in a public school system that offered little support. "In a national survey of teachers of grades three and four, the majority reported that they had no training in gifted education. Of the 2,300 respondents, 61 percent of the public school sample and 53 percent of the private school sample had no training in gifted education."[2] Even fewer teachers have training in assisting twice-exceptional or profoundly gifted students. What's more, as they strive to teach every school day in mixed-ability classes of twenty or more students, they often lack the time to obtain training when the need arises in the classroom setting.

When Filly was tested at the Gifted Development Center in Denver, Colorado, her lowest score was above-average and a seventy-point spread existed between her highest and lowest scores. Since even a ten-point spread indicates the presence of a learning disability, the test results pushed us toward further investigation. In a regular classroom, few resources existed for a child as unique as Filly. The classroom teachers had to teach twenty-five students, including students who were not performing at grade level. Since Filly performed above grade level even on those things that were extremely difficult for her, her needs often did not seem as pressing as the needs of other students. If she had not received testing, it's likely that her talents would have been subdued in a traditional classroom setting. Quite simply, no one would have known that she needed anything extra, because her brilliance covered up her learning problem, and her learning problem dimmed her brilliance just enough to make her appear somewhat gifted, instead of profoundly gifted. We had her tested because her brother had been identified for his intellectual gifts at an early age, and research showed that siblings tend to be within ten IQ points of one another. We feel glad to have discovered her abilities when she was seven years old.

"The necessity of finding gifted girls early in life is underscored by the fact that their advanced abilities, observable before they enter school, may be diminishing as a consequence of the educational process," writes Dr. Linda Kreger Silverman of the Gifted Development Center.[3] We found that risk factor affected Filly, despite the great efforts of her competent, caring teachers.

Due to her obvious advanced skills, Filly was assigned to do more difficult mathematics problems in the corner of a classroom while the other children learned in a large group. This attempt to differentiate instruction, without an ability-appropriate cluster group, meant that Filly spent learning-time alone, often wearing headphones to obscure the sounds of the lecture given to the other students. At the same time, acceleration was not an option, due to the constraints imposed by her lack of handwriting ability. Ideas crowded her mind, but she could not express them in writing. Since she made no trouble and excelled at learning, her disability and her giftedness both remained at risk for going underground and out of sight.

We began a desperate search for a more appropriate learning environment for our daughter. We finally chose a nearby school that promised to individualize the curriculum for students, the Rocky Mountain School for the Gifted and Creative in Boulder, Colorado.

The school's director, Barbara Mitchell-Hutton, writes that asynchronous development "is incorporated into our curriculum and the basis for our individualized education plans, individualized instruction, and grouping practices." She continues, "Every day I explain it to greatly relieved parents of gifted children."[4]

Unfortunately, the school was an hour's drive from our home in Estes Park, Colorado, down a winding mountain road. Filly has vestibular dysfunction, and her motion sickness occurred every time we went down that road to school, or up again to home.

Filly's unusual IQ places her in a very rare group, indeed, and allowing her the opportunity to develop her talent and strengths remains imperative. "The rarer the talent, the greater the responsibility of both the individual and society to develop that talent," writes University of Kansas psychologist Barbara A. Kerr, who specializes in optimal human development.[5]

"Since gifted girls excel at imitation and adaptation, they often blend into the group rather than demonstrating their unusual abilities," Dr. Silverman writes. "They need the safety of other gifted girls in order to value their talents." [6]

We took our parental responsibility seriously, and relocated on weekdays to Boulder, Colorado, so that our daughter would not have to be sick on the mountain roads every morning and every afternoon, and we also started occupational therapy for her. Once again, we have been lucky to have the resources that have allowed us to do this. It is my supreme hope that some day every profoundly gifted child with a disability will have easy access to individualized education.

According to Deirdre Lovecky, in 1942 pioneering psychologist Leta Hollingworth "noted that in the regular elementary classroom moderately gifted children wasted almost half their time and exceptionally gifted children almost all their time." Lovecky continues, "it is the exceptionally gifted whose needs are more difficult to meet by virtue of being so few in number and because of the differences of their cognitive skills."[7]

Now, more than fifty years after Leta Hollingworth's discovery, as we explore ways to meet the needs of profoundly gifted children, we must also identify and serve the children who have twice exceptionality. Early identification, coupled with individualization, could save more than a few minds. Much of the research in the area of twice exceptionality seems to focus on the needs of moderately gifted children with learning disabilities, perhaps because there is a larger pool of possible research subjects.

It may be that the presence of a learning disability enhances some aspects of perception, in combination with the workings of a highly brilliant mind. The unique perspective and experiences provided by the blending of these disparate intellectual factors already support creative problem-solving. Perhaps the most innovative thinkers include not only the ones with the greatest intellectual talents, but also the ones who blend that intellect with perceptive dysfunctions that allow them to function beyond the norm.

Notes

1. Ayres, *Sensory Integration and the Child*, 56.

2. Gubbins, "NRC/GT: Research Should Inform Practice," 2.

3. Silverman, "What Happens to the Gifted Girl?" 59.

4. Mitchell-Hutton, "Putting a Face on Asynchronous Development," 1.

5. Kerr, *Smart Girls Two*, 205.

6. Silverman, "Helping Gifted Girls," 122.

7. Lovecky, "Exceptionally Gifted Children," 120.

References

Ayres, A. Jean. *Sensory Integration and the Child*. Los Angeles: Western Psychological Services, 1979.

Baum, Susan, Steve V. Owen, and John Dixon. *To Be Gifted and Learning Disabled: From Identification to Practical Intervention Strategies*. Mansfield Center, CT: Creative Learning Press, 1991.

Gubbins, E. Jean. "NRC/GT: Research Should Inform Practice." *The National Research Center on the Gifted and Talented Newsletter* (Spring 1997): 1–2. Published by the National Research Center on the Gifted and Talented, Storrs, CT.

Kerr, Barbara A. *Smart Girls Two: A New Psychology of Girls, Women and Giftedness.* Dayton, OH: Ohio Psychology Press, 1994.

Lovecky, Deirdre. "Exceptionally Gifted Children: Different Minds." *Roeper Review* 17, no. 2 (December 1994): 116–120.

Mitchell-Hutton, Barbara. "Putting a Face on Asynchronous Development." *Highly Gifted Children* 11, no. 2 (Spring 1996): 1–2.

Silverman, Linda Kreger. "Helping Gifted Girls Reach Their Potential." *Roeper Review* 13, no. 3 (April 1991): 122–123.

———. "What Happens to the Gifted Girl?" *Critical Issues in Gifted Education: Vol. 1, Defensible Programs for the Gifted,* edited by C. June Maker and Shirley W. Schiever: 43–89. Austin, TX: Pro-Ed, 1986.

PART: 2

Take a Number

Despite a common focus on academic achievement, school systems aren't set up to teach high-IQ kids. Ingrained beliefs, misinformation, misunderstandings, even prejudice form a seemingly endless mass of obstacles that squat in the road, blocking the way to an appropriate education for these children.

If you're a parent, you've probably run into some of these obstacles: the school official who declares that gifted education is elitist and that all children must be taught in lockstep linearity. The gifted and talented director who defends the school's "one size fits any smart kid" approach to gifted programming. The teacher who thinks "average" means "normal" and "above average" means "abnormal." The special education expert who fails to recognize the impact of learning disabilities, asynchrony, and different levels of giftedness. The administrator who tells you that other children's "real" special needs are far more pressing than your child's, so take a number and wait your turn.

If you're an educator, you've hit obstacles, too. Not enough training in college and even less once you're in the field. Little or no access to innovative approaches to education, educational environments, and delivery methods developed for high-IQ kids and backed by research. All kinds of kids with all kinds of needs (special and otherwise) in overcrowded classrooms. Not enough mentors, not enough administrative support, too much paperwork, and never enough money.

As you'll see in this section, educating high-IQ kids is incredibly difficult—but it is not impossible. Parents become advocates, teachers become partners, researchers clear new roads.

And, when all this happens, high-IQ kids zoom along the educational paths that are right for them.

"So You're the Teacher of a Profoundly Gifted Child"

(And Then There Was Bill)

BY LAURA FREESE

Laura Freese holds a master's degree in Elementary Education with certification in Gifted Education from Indiana University. Laura has taught regular and gifted classes and provided professional development for classroom teachers. She presently teaches gifted children at an elementary school in Sarasota, Florida.

Teachers already have more tasks on their daily lists than can be accomplished in any twenty-four hours. Then a kid shows up who doesn't fit the curriculum, the desk space, or any part of teacher training—even for an instructor who's studied gifted education. Laura Freese writes a letter to her colleagues that embodies the discoveries she made after observing, "No one told me during my teacher-ed classes how I should deal with Einstein if he showed up in my class!" She demonstrates how determination and, maybe most importantly, humor provide the keys to actually teaching a profoundly gifted child in a regular classroom. Then she gives vital information for negotiating the territory between student, parents, and schools so that these kids have the opportunity to learn, which is what teaching is about, regardless of the students' abilities.

Dear Colleague,

You have just found yourself in a situation similar to one I was in several years ago when I first encountered Bill. Bill is one of those kids who comes into our classrooms without a set of directions that says, "You are a very lucky educator! You have been given an opportunity few teachers will experience in their lifetime! You will be working with the next possible Einstein!"

Oh, GREAT! So what am I supposed to do? No one told me during my teacher-ed classes how I should deal with Einstein if he showed up in my class.

If I casually mentioned in the lounge, "Guess what! I've got the next Einstein in my class," there would have been a few raised eyebrows. You see, the other teachers all knew Bill did not complete his assignments, had trouble getting along with other students, and seemed to space out when he should have been listening. Einstein, RIGHT! Not in the school's eyes!

In the world of gifted education, children like Bill are called *profoundly gifted* (PG) or, as I've heard, *severely gifted*. Nothing in my teacher training, including my endorsement in gifted education or my many years of teaching, prepared me to work with a student like Bill. Unfortunately, even when I realized I had a profoundly gifted student, I found few resources. Bill didn't fit the rules! No matter what we as educators believe or have been taught in our education classes, there are always exceptions to the rules.

Once we concede that we have found an exception, our next question is, "Now what do I do? Should I make the student fit the rules, or should I allow them to set out on uncharted territory?"

Let me save you time and trouble. Based on my personal experience, choose the uncharted territory! Think about it. Have you ever tried fitting a round peg in a square hole? Or is it "fit a square peg in a round hole"? Whichever, you get the picture. It just *won't* fit—any more than a profoundly gifted child can be made to fit a set of written and unwritten rules established for a majority of the students.

Not only don't profoundly gifted kids fit the educational mold of regular kids, I discovered they don't even fit the mold of most gifted kids. In the fall when Bill was six years old, his sixth-grade classmate Sam came back from taking the SATs. Sam asked me if I was going to have Bill take the SATs next year because Bill was a *true* genius! I refrained from responding, "So what does that make you?" Sam ended up with a score of 1180 as a sixth-grader, although he still hadn't learned to tie his shoes. (Bill at the time had no idea of how to talk on the telephone.) I did tell Sam that I thought we'd wait until Bill could reach the table without sitting on his knees. Looking back, however, I probably should have had Bill take the tests.

It was always interesting to watch Bill and Sam when they were intellectually challenged. They would get real quiet as they pondered, and then what I called "the thinking" would happen. They'd start with some rocking, some toe tapping, some pencil thumping, and maybe even some humming. I could tell when their thinking processes were in full gear, because they'd get up and start pacing. Back and forth, back and forth, until their new thoughts seem to flow together with all their incredible prior knowledge. When they hit the "AH HA!" stage, they were ready to share. All this physical activity drove me nuts until I realized they can't think and sit still because they think with their whole being. The more movement, the deeper their thinking seemed to be.

A friend who was at Princeton when Einstein was there told me Einstein used to do the same thing. He might be at a meeting, get up, pace the hallway, and then not even go back to the meeting.

You can be assured that all this physical movement does not endear these students to some of their teachers! I wonder what Einstein's teachers thought about him in school. I've read that he had trouble sitting still and doing simple math, too.

As for me, after Bill receives the Nobel Peace Prize and the news media come to interview me about what he was like as a student, I plan to point to that groove in the carpet. I'll say, "This is where the theory of [to be announced] was born."

When I reached this understanding, I realized the kids and their parents had broken through my educational paradigms and I was converted. I found myself out there trying to convert others. *Not* an easy task! It felt like I was beating my head against the wall when I tried to get others to understand why it was so important to do something really radical to help these radically gifted kids. These kids needed to have sacred educational walls come down. The response I got was the old "we've *never* done it that way before."

Using the term *gifted* got me nowhere. No one felt sorry for me or the kids. You know the usual phrases: "They have it all anyway," "They'll make it on their own," "They should slow down and wait for everyone else to catch up."

What? Wait for everyone to catch up? One of these kids has the cure for cancer up their sleeve! I'm from Kentucky and we never ask our race horses to slow down and wait for the rest of their age peers, so why not give our gifted kids the same opportunity we give race horses?

Then it hit me. EUREKA! My tactics were wrong. Maybe, just maybe, what I needed to do was to make people feel sorry for these exceptionally gifted kids! And then I came across a new concept: *asynchronous development*. Asynchronous development is where "advanced cognitive abilities and heightened intensity combine to create inner experiences and awareness that are qualitatively different from the norm. This asynchrony increases with higher intellectual capacity. The uniqueness of the gifted renders them particularly vulnerable and requires modifications in parenting, teaching, and counseling in order for them to develop optimally."[1]

That was it—these kids had a *severe* case of asynchronous development! Why, hadn't I seen six-year-old Bill memorize the periodic table with all the atomic numbers (and teach it to a sixth-grade girl) and then refuse to sing "I'm Getting Nothing for Christmas" in the school program because he thought the teachers were teaching the kids to lie since the teachers knew the kids were really going to get something? Sounds like a pretty severe case to me!

So . . . as you gather your wits and move ahead with your new assignment, let me share with you a few of the things I learned in the school of my hard knocks.

1. LISTEN to the parents. Thanks to parents who were willing to share and my willingness to learn, I learned more about these kids from parents than from anyone. Bill's parents provided many stories that helped me understand Bill's intensities and sensitivities. PG kids are so incredibly aware of the world around them: "We've got to help save the whales." "Who will feed the starving children if I don't?" "Why do kids call me [fill in taunting name]?" Important note here: when you're that intense and sensitive, name-calling doesn't roll off your back. The inner pain caused by teasing sticks like Superglue that has no solvent. Layers of verbal abuse build up over time. So *never* tolerate teasing by other students.

2. LISTEN to the parents! I started by giving Bill next year's work, because I knew he was ahead of his first-grade classmates. I assumed that skipping

him ahead one year would really challenge him. Boy, was that a bad assumption on my part! In talking to Bill's parents, I found out they had saved (and dated) a goldmine of stuff that I could use to figure out what Bill already knew. In looking over this treasure chest, I realized this kid was years ahead of the second-grade curriculum.

True learning only begins when I find out what my students already know and build my instruction on that foundation. If I didn't give Bill the opportunity to learn new material, I was going to be spinning his wheels and teaching him how to get by without working hard. You know, it's the old ten-minute-A trick! That's a poor work ethic and not one I should be teaching. No boss down the road will let my students get by with ten minutes of work for a full day's paycheck.

3. Watch and listen to the student. Bill's parents and I always had plans A, B, and C ready. We'd try plan A as long as it worked, but we'd also have plans B and C waiting. Bill learned new material at an incredible pace, and my preconceived schedule would have held him back. I never would have thought to give the periodic table to a six-year-old. Bill could spend hours researching a subject and then do something like design a program about his research on the computer.

Another educator described this kid as having a short attention span. Bill and I developed a different approach. Bill would let me know what he wanted to study. I provided lots of resources and time for him to explore, and reminded him when it was time for lunch. Can you imagine? These kids can become so engrossed that they forget to eat!

4. Let both the parents and the student know you believe in and will support them. Unfortunately, neither PG parents nor their kids find much support in the educational or the social community. Finding other parents with whom to discuss having a six-year-old who is ready to study algebra doesn't happen very often. Think about what it might feel like to be six years old and trying to find another six-year-old who wants to discuss the periodic table at recess. You can feel pretty alone in both instances. Students and their families need to know there is someone else who may not have all the answers, but who is willing to support and advocate for them. It's not easy being a lone duck.

5. Don't always believe what you see. I learned that temper tantrums (Bill's, not mine) were a sign of his total frustration because he was

being held back intellectually. I have seen this distress manifested in other ways, like stomachaches. When we met Bill's educational needs, these negative behaviors and symptoms disappeared. Think about it. What would your reaction be if you were six years old and had to sit there doing math papers that asked you to circle the correct number of birds in a nest (you do have a choice: is it 5 or 6?) when at home you got to make up your own problems, such as "If $5 \times 10 = 50$, should 5×20 be 100 and 5×180 be 900?" You'd be thinking, "How many more years of this do I have?" I don't know about you, but I don't like to sit hour after hour, day after day, listening to what I already know.

6. Face it, profoundly gifted kids are probably smarter than you. Admit you don't know something when you don't, and be willing to let them teach you. I learned all about computers by long-necking. I think these kids are born with computer language embedded in them. Since they are pros in areas of their passions, I let them keep me and the rest of the class up on the latest. I mean, who has time to keep up with it all. So become the guide on the side, not the sage on the stage.

   By the way, these students love to correct you and they love humor, so why not combine these strengths? I tell them, "I make three mistakes every day and your job is to find them and correct me." That sure gets them to pay attention—just for fun, make only two mistakes one day, and watch what happens!

7. Forget the sloppy handwriting. You'll never win. Get them on those computers! Ever look at your doctor's handwriting? Ask your doctor if he or she had to stay in at recess to practice handwriting. Did it help? These kids' minds work too fast to keep up with their hands. They'll probably use a computer anyway when you're not around, and they'll sure produce better work when they don't labor over that handwriting stress.

8. Discover the www.hoagiesgifted.org Web site sooner than I did. WOW— what a fantastic place to start learning about PG kids! Send everyone who doubts you and those who support you to this Mecca. Say, "It's not just me saying this. You can search the site yourself and find out what the 'experts' think." Use the site to help debunk the myths about PGers. Let others read for themselves about how radical acceleration doesn't produce warped children who have no friends. You've heard that one, haven't you?

My favorite story arguing against acceleration goes like this: "We can't let Mike accelerate, because we had a girl who accelerated ten years ago and she got pregnant." See why you have a challenge ahead of you?

9. Be nice to these kids! I wonder if the fifteen-year-old who just made a million selling his computer program had a teacher along the way who believed in him? And then, if my Bill had been Bill Gates and he remembered I got him out of the dungeon . . . hmm . . . I always say, "If I had the next Picasso in my class, I sure hope I would recognize the talent and would have the student sign and date that doodle. What a sweet retirement that would be!"

Thank goodness Bill had parents who advocated strongly for their child's needs, because no one else seemed to. I'm sure it's hard for you to believe, but some folks in my district thought Bill's parents were "pushy" because they didn't sit back and take "we've never done it that way before" for an answer.

If Bill's parents hadn't shared with me and hadn't believed things didn't have to remain status quo, and if I hadn't been willing to realize I had a few more things to learn myself, I might never have learned about Bill's unique abilities and had the opportunity to watch what can happen when you don't put a learning ceiling on a student.

Just imagine how embarrassing it would be for me to have Bill get up in front of a crowd some day and say, "I went to Such-and-such School and Ms. So-and-so was my teacher. Because I didn't complete my grade-level work, Ms. So-and-so didn't think I was gifted. My parents felt I wasn't being provided with academic challenges and the social/emotional support I needed, so they pulled me out of that school."

No, I don't have to worry about Bill saying that, because although Bill and I have both moved to other states and I haven't seen Bill in many years, I talked to his mother not long ago. I asked her if she thought Bill would remember me.

"Are you kidding?" she said, "You *never* forget the person who gets you out of the dungeon!"

Yes, you have been given a *very* special assignment this year. You have the opportunity to be a PG student's lifesaver. This may be a once-in-a-lifetime opportunity—the chance to bring forth incredible abilities.

Whether you choose to accept this mission or thwart it, it *is* your mission. You *can* do it! You *can* be just the lifesaver that child needs to become *all* that he or she can be. With the right environment, you can watch a student blossom!

Enjoy . . . and listen!

Notes

1. Columbus Group, transcript.

References

Columbus Group, unpublished transcript of the meeting of the Columbus Group. Columbus, OH: July 1991.

10 What Makes the Highly Gifted Child Qualitatively Different?

Implications for Schooling

BY KAREN B. ROGERS

Karen Rogers is a professor of Education and director of research for the Gifted Education Research, Resource and Information Centre at the University of New South Wales in Sydney, Australia. She has published a book for parents on how to develop an education plan for a gifted child, entitled, *Reforming Gifted Education: How Parents and Teachers Can Match the Program to the Child* (Great Potential Press, 2002). She has written fifteen book chapters and over ninety articles on gifted education.

Karen Rogers analyzed data on highly gifted and moderately gifted learners, and compared her results to statistics for average children. She learned that while highly gifted children have more differences from each other than they have common characteristics, their families, personalities, and behaviors also show certain patterns that can help educators plan appropriate and low-cost instructional approaches for them.

Scenario: *A young girl, age six, comments as she defines the first word on the Stanford-Binet L-M: "Well, it's a color and a juicy fruit and you can't find a word to rhyme with it . . . I've tried!"*

Needless to say, Sarah (as I will call her) is highly gifted. Her start on this test was auspicious, but not one-of-a-kind. She was able to look at the question from multiple perspectives and then "select" the best answer she would give. Since 1995, I have had the thrill of testing several children like Sarah. Each has shown unique yet marvelous ways of interpreting and reinterpreting the questions on the Binet, yet none has approached the test in quite the same way. So no matter how I go about answering the question that heads my chapter, I must begin with my opinion that these children are very idiosyncratic. Yet as a researcher I am driven to find patterns in their ways of processing.

In 1995, I spent several months with Dr. Linda Kreger Silverman at the Gifted Development Center searching for such patterns among the several hundred children with IQs over 160 whom she has tested over the years. We found many patterns, which I will share in this chapter. But it is important to remember that not a single child possessed all of these patterns—the uniqueness of processing and personality was perhaps the children's most common attribute.

What Are the Qualitative Differences of the Highly Gifted?

Since 1980, Dr. Silverman has tested the intelligence levels of more than 2,000 children. When I visited in 1995, she had located 241 children with IQs greater than 160 (their average was 170). Since that time, she has located another 60 or so children, but they have not been included in this description. The children I studied included 112 girls and 129 boys. Their ages when tested ranged from 2½ to 12½ years. The average IQs of the boys and girls were essentially the same, with the girls at 169.43 and the boys at 170.7.

There were some strong family patterns for this group of children. The mean age of the mothers at the birth of their highly gifted child (30.8 years) was considerably older than for the national population, as well as for mothers of moderately gifted children. A similar pattern was found for the fathers (31.7 years). Likewise, the educational backgrounds, work experiences, and personal interests showed a pattern for the parents of highly gifted children. Mothers tended to have an average of 18 years of schooling (master's degree) and the fathers averaged 19 years of school (master's plus). Forty-nine percent of the mothers worked outside of the home (according to the national average from 1998 U.S. statistics, 18 percent of mothers with children work full-time outside the home) and 90 percent of this working group held professional jobs, such as doctor, lawyer, professor, high-level business executive, etc. (the national average is 40 percent). Ninety-three percent of the fathers worked in the top professional categories (the national average is 29 percent).

The parents' interests included reading (55 percent of mothers, 35 percent of fathers), fine arts (34 percent of mothers, 25 percent of fathers), and sports (33 percent of mothers, 49 percent of fathers). How these interests differ from the general public could not be found, but comparisons with more moderately gifted research samples showed both reading and fine arts interests significantly higher for the highly gifted parents.[1]

Family "conditions" appeared to be comparatively more healthy among Silverman's highly gifted group. Two hundred five of the 241 children (85 percent) were living in two-parent homes, with a mean family size of 1.2 children. As of 1996, the national statistics suggested that in the general population, 68 percent of American families were two-parent families, and the mean family size was 2.5 children. This may suggest that there is significantly less divorce and family dissolution among families with highly gifted children, at least at the time of testing! Dr. Silverman has collected data on instances of abuse and trauma, and incidences of counseling, among her sample. She found that 0.5 percent of the children she evaluated had experienced physical or sexual abuse, and 5 percent had been traumatized through serious family problems (death, divorce, etc.); approximately 10 percent of the children had received counseling. Comparative national statistics have reported a 4.7 percent rate of physical abuse, 11 percent sexual abuse, and 3 percent psychological abuse, with 16 percent of children in the U.S. general population experiencing trauma.

Physically, the highly gifted group showed some interesting differences. Twenty-two percent of these fairly young children were reported to have "physical" problems such as colic, health issues, or difficulties with physical coordination. By comparison, among moderately gifted samples, approximately 3 to 4 percent reported problems with physical coordination or health. Allergies occurred more often among the highly gifted group. Forty-four percent of Silverman's sample suffered from some allergy, with 36 percent of that number having an allergy to milk and 8 percent to pollens, trees, etc. Among the general adolescent population, an average of 20 percent experience allergies or asthma. Among the more moderately gifted group, Wiley and Goldstein have found in Talent Search samples that allergy rates approximated 34 percent. Left-handedness was significantly less frequent for the highly gifted (11 percent) than for the regular population (15 percent).

Family conditions also can include relational dynamics. At the time testing was administered, 67 percent of the highly gifted sample were firstborn children (and of those 67 percent, 55 percent were "only" children). Among moderately gifted samples, 53 percent have been found to be firstborns with 22 percent being "only" children. Forty-four percent of the parents described their children as "easy" to handle, while another 37 percent described this as "it depends on the situation." Whereas 17 percent of the parents described their highly gifted child as "difficult," 3 percent of the moderately gifted parents did so. When siblings were present, relationships were described by the parents as "good" or "very good" for 49 percent of the children and "variable" for another 21 percent. Such statistics are difficult to compare with other, more moderately gifted samples as well as with the general population. Certainly the work of Nicholas Colangelo and Dewey Cornell suggests, however, that moderately gifted samples may contend with "dominance" issues, in which the gifted child becomes a focus of the family's efforts and energy, while other, less gifted family members may take a back seat.

It is difficult to compare the highly gifted with the general population on social issues, but comparisons were found with the moderately gifted. Whereas 86 percent of the highly gifted children in the Silverman sample preferred older children as playmates, 34 percent of the moderately gifted showed such a preference. At the same time, 82 percent of the parents sampled in Silverman's group felt their children "got along well" with same-age peers, while only 48 percent of the moderately gifted samples reported this. Among the highly gifted, approximately one child in five was described as "bossy," when parents were asked about their children's leadership skills.

No, girls were not significantly more likely to be considered bossy than boys! Among the more moderately gifted samples, no direct comparison could be made, but 8 percent were described as "aggressive" and 13 percent liked to "show off."

Parents of the highly gifted were also asked about the sizes of groups their children preferred when playing. Ninety percent felt their children did "very well" in one-on-one groupings, and the percentages declined progressively as the group sizes increased. Fifty percent of the highly gifted children in this sample reported a need for "one best friend," rather than a group of friends. These preferences were very similar to those reported for moderately gifted children. A huge difference was found in terms of interpersonal sensitivities, however. The highly gifted (90 percent) were described as having compassion and sensitivity to others: they could be easily hurt by others and would just as easily fly to the defense of other children who were being hurt. These behaviors were reported less frequently (63 percent) for the more moderately gifted samples.

Emotionally, the highly gifted children differed greatly from the more moderately gifted children. Eighty-eight percent of the highly gifted (versus 52 percent) were described as perfectionistic by their parents. Similar differences were found for questioning authority and self-confidence. Ninety percent of the highly gifted reported emotionally sensitive reactions to people, stories, and even ideas, whereas Joan Freeman has reported a rate of 29 percent for more moderately gifted samples. Fears and anxieties among the highly gifted group were in the 37 to 40 percent range, with the moderately gifted groups reporting rates around 6 percent.

The childhood milestones of the highly gifted were fairly similar to those of the moderately gifted in terms of when physical and verbal developments occurred. Both groups developed significantly more quickly than the average population in both physical and mental areas, with one noticeable difference. Parents of highly gifted children were significantly more likely to report long attention spans and extraordinary alertness in birth and early infancy (94 percent versus 71 percent). Eighty-three percent of the highly gifted group tend to want to concentrate on one activity at a time and to be allowed to pursue it in depth. Seventy-four percent "hate" to be interrupted, and 60 percent think about ideas before acting.

For the highly gifted sample I studied, the biggest school-related issues concerned having nothing to learn (53 percent), personality conflicts with a peer (36 percent), and a perceived lack of individual attention (36 percent). This may be a huge issue for these children, considered in light of the strong interests they reported. And the higher the IQ, the more intense these interests were. When I broke down the sample into the 160–180 group and a 180+ group, the 160–180 group showed the greatest attention spans and the strongest desire to be intensely involved in an in-depth study of personal interest. They showed greater creativity, a great need for privacy, and a desire to explore and satisfy their curiosity. They were more likely to love mazes and collections and less interested in numbers. Those children with IQs over 180 were the most all-around academically skilled, particularly in mathematics, reading, and computers. They possessed the most extensive vocabularies, were exceptionally quick learners, and showed extensive memory skills and keen abilities of observation. They were avid readers with a great interest in books and words. They were described as having the best sense of humor and were more likely to participate widely in extracurricular activities than were the 160–180 group. The greatest interests of the 180+ children tended to be in chess, computers, mathematics, number theory, and how things work.

What Are the Implications for Schooling?

I have developed a chart showing the possible schooling implications of this broad pattern of differences of degree and kind for the highly gifted child, based on the studies of Linda Silverman's sample of 241 children with IQs over 160. None of these implications truly requires the hiring of extra staff (if there is a gifted resource teacher on school grounds), presentation of additional courses, or an individualized education plan with district-level supervision. Many of the suggested provisions only require that the school show more flexibility in *when* the highly gifted child is "exposed" to challenge and *how frequently* that occurs.

I would also argue that I believe *most schools are willing to try to do these things, when specific requests are made of them.* Since most administrators and teachers have had little training in gifted education, let alone concerning highly gifted children, they are not likely to think of these provisions on their own. A principal in a small rural school district in Minnesota recently remarked, "When I am given a specific plan with an extensive description of what a child can do and what that child needs, I can get to work on it." In this case, the principal was dealing with a four-year-old boy with an IQ over 200 just placed in first grade who was already working at fifth- to sixth-grade level in mathematics and reading/language arts. The biggest "problem" she had found this year for him came from a physical education specialist concerned about the boy's "lack" of physical coordination in gym class. (He tended to want to count and measure the geometrical shapes in the gym, rather than practice dribbling a ball!) When the principal checked on the specialist's complaints, however, she discovered that "he was one of several in that first-grade class who didn't have their physical skills together," and she wouldn't consider placing him back with the kindergarten group for physical education.

Highly Gifted Pattern	Expectations Based on This Pattern	School Implications
Stable home environment, older parents, intact family	Parents can be counted on to work *with* the school, if/when the school works with them.	Long-term projects, assigned as an alternative to nightly mini-tasks, will be successfully completed.
Parents well educated and understand value of education	Parents may have critical questions about how school and teachers operate. School must be prepared to have a rationale for its practices.	Assignments for work outside of school must be relevant, challenging, and must focus on high-order applications, depth, and intensity rather than "drill-and-kill." Emphasis on or exposure to a "classical" education in literature and fine arts.
Health and allergy issues for child	School absences due to illness produce a corresponding need for "makeup" work outside of schooltime.	Regular communication about child's individual progress will be needed. Teacher can use opportunity provided by absences to compact regular curriculum and accelerate work through "makeup" assignments.

Highly Gifted Pattern	Expectations Based on This Pattern	School Implications
Difficulty in "handling" the child	Regular behavior modification strategies will not work. Child will almost always test the limits of any strategy that involves "consequences," rewards, or punishments.	Teachers must be capable of using techniques that "appeal to reason," instead of trying to manage the behavior or the child. One-on-one time for "conversations" between child and teacher at school.
Child gets along well in sibling relationships and prefers one-on-one play situations	Child may feel uncomfortable in larger group situations and may withdraw. Large-group mentality could lead to teasing or taunting about child's differences, which might happen less often in small groups. Parents will expect a positive climate and a toleration of differences to exist at school.	No need to focus on social-skills development for this child: just provide ample opportunities to develop friendships with one or two other gifted children who may function intellectually at a similar level. Frequent opportunities for paired learning with intellectual peer (or other gifted child). Frequent opportunities for independent study projects based on personal interests, with teacher supervision. Independent study skills must be "taught" to child.
Preference for older playmates	Child may gravitate toward dependence on the teacher for interactions of any kind.	Teacher will need to step out of "teacher role" and become an intellectual peer in learning. Acceleration options that allow grouping of child with older peers are needed, such as subject acceleration, grade skipping, concurrent enrollment, multi-age classes, mentorships, early entrance to school, and early admission to college.

(Continued)

Highly Gifted Pattern	Expectations Based on This Pattern	School Implications
Compassion, interpersonal sensitivity, issues of social and moral justice	Child will engage in "learned helplessness" or existential depression when she or he does not have skills or outlets for righting perceived wrongs.	Teacher must train child in social-action skills and encourage engagement in service and social-action projects, both at school and in the community. (Note: A good book for this is *The Kid's Guide to Social Action.*)
Strong achievement drive with tendency toward perfectionism when work is not recognizably challenging	Child will become nonproductive in school if not challenged often enough.	Student and teacher jointly plan what student will learn in each area, starting from what child already has accomplished. Teacher keeps pacing fast, realizing that child is more likely to retain information when it is paced many times faster than for regular students. Practice will be minimal. Specific, corrective feedback must be given on all tasks done.
Strong ability to concentrate, stay focused, and resist interruptions	Child will become nonproductive in school when learning periods are short and time-based, rather than task-completion-based.	Frequent opportunities for independent study projects, done alone or in pairs, with systematic supervision. Flexible project requirements and deadlines, when possible.
Child truly "loves" reading, numbers, and computers	Child will be perceived as different by age peers and may not have much in common with them.	Group child with intellectual peers for: reading discussion, accelerated math study, instruction in computer programming and languages.

Highly Gifted Pattern	Expectations Based on This Pattern	School Implications
Different pattern of interests outside of school, including computers, games of strategy, and planning	Child will be perceived as different by age peers and may not have much in common with them.	Group child with intellectual peers (older students) who have similar interests in competitive situations, such as Knowledge Masters (computers), Word Masters, Knowledge Bowl, Academic Decathlon.
Powerful capacity to reason, conceptualize, and think critically	Child will apply these processes to everything she or he encounters, at times inappropriately. Can become cynical about ways of the world if left unguided.	Need for instruction in advanced thinking skills, Philosophy for Children program, curriculum that integrates higher order reasoning applications. Opportunity to discuss critical concepts with others of like ability and inclination.

Last Words

It must be repeated that highly gifted children are more likely to be different from each other than similar to each other. Even so, there are strong developmental, family, interest, emotional, social, and physical patterns that can guide parents in how they approach schools and ask for the services their child needs. These patterns can also "free" schools to intentionally create programs that will meet the needs of highly gifted children, whether these children come one at a time to the school or happen to occur as a cluster.

The keys to schooling these children are to link them whenever possible with the others closest to them in intellectual functioning; to provide consistent, daily challenge with appropriate pacing and little practice; and to accelerate their exposure to content and skills they will need to be successful in college and in their adult lives. Their teachers must move away from the teacher-versus-student mode of operation and focus on a facilitator/learner relationship, in which the teacher and student work together in joint learning and in planning the child's foundational learning outcomes.

Parents of a highly gifted child must vigilantly search out teachers who can work in this way, and must ensure that the child is able to connect with such mentors.

Notes

1.   Rogers and Silverman, "Differences of Profoundly Gifted Children."

References

Rogers, K. B., and L. K. Silverman. "The Physical, Social, Emotional, and Environmental Differences of Profoundly Gifted Children: A Comparative Study." *Talent Development IV: Proceedings from the 1998 Henry B. and Jocelyn Wallace National Research Symposium on Talent Development,* edited by N. Colangelo and S. G. Assouline: 419–423. Scottsdale, AZ: Great Potential Press, 2001.

Lewis, B. *A Kid's Guide to Social Action.* Minneapolis: Free Spirit Publishing, 1996.

Too Smart for School?

A Lesson About Teaching and Learning

BY MARILYN WALKER

Marilyn Walker is a former research ecologist for the U.S. Forest Service and the author of many articles on arctic ecology. She now owns a toy store in Boulder, Colorado, and lives with her son Daniel and their parakeet Einstein in Louisville, Colorado.

Gifted infants and toddlers can be charming, although their behaviors and ideas can cause raised eyebrows in parents (and others). In the right educational setting, the amusing trends continue. But in the wrong school—even one called "excellent" by normal standards—everyone's quality of life can deteriorate rapidly. Gifted-ness and the gifted child become problems. The parent must become a full-time advocate, regardless of other responsibilities. Marilyn Walker, who learned these things while her son was young, argues that even our *smartest* children need to be loved and accepted . . . and appropriately educated in public schools.

My name is Marilyn, and I am the mother of an exceptionally gifted child. There—I am out of the closet with the dirty secret I have not dared to whisper even to my closest friends. My son is a *very* cute, usually sweet, little boy who could be your neighbor, grandson, child, or nephew. This same bouncy boy just happens to have an IQ that is among the rarest of the rare. His intellectual abilities are, indeed, a gift,

101

but being among the millionaires of the intellectual world is not a way to gain broad favor. As we have painfully discovered, this "gift" can be a good way to make others hope you will fail.

Unfortunately, unlike financial millionaires or their heirs, these children cannot simply buy out of our educational system. The system that should sustain them fails them miserably. Surely, we all surmise, a person who has been given such a mind can do almost anything, deal with almost any situation.

I only wish it were true.

This is a story about a boy and three schools. It is a story about the ordinary magic that an appropriate education can bring into the life of a child, and a story about the pain a school can cause, even when intentions are good. I hope that in telling our story I may help some other child, and that our family's healing may progress.

Enjoying My Baby

The story begins with a tiny baby—one who seemed, from his earliest days, quite determined to get his needs met! I have a vivid memory of the day on which my son, Daniel, turned six months old. He had been scooting and squirming around the floor, using various bodily contortions. On that day he suddenly, with almost no warning, pulled himself up onto his knees and crawled across the floor. The huge toothless grin on his face absolutely shouted with pride and joy and seemed to say, "Today, the living room—tomorrow, the world!"

I soon found out that this was not far from true. Within the hour, he pulled himself to a standing position. In a bittersweet moment, I realized that the joy of having a helpless baby had lasted far too short a time, and that my life for the next few years would consist of keeping a toddler safe from harm.

I also thought, "How unusual that he both crawled and pulled to a stand on the same day! I suppose each child develops in his own way and pace."

Daniel's early standing blossomed into independent walking at 10½ months, followed shortly thereafter by running. This was a bellwether of what became a common statement for me: "Hmm, I don't think that is common for a child of age X." His precocity was both physical and otherwise, and it was clear early on that he was "quite bright." When a speech therapist casually estimated that his two-year-old vocabulary and enunciation were that of a child twice his age or more, I was surprised but still assumed the variation fell within the range of normal. Daniel was a toddler, and I assumed all these developmental differences would even out with time. Wouldn't they?

Some moments were hard to deny—moments when he stood out as different. There was the day, at twenty-two months, when he walked around a shop singing "Kum Bah Yah" in perfect key. I was used to him and thought little of this, but a woman told me—with her eyebrows raised in astonishment—that he sounded like a little angel. I shrugged and gave a weak smile, thinking he was sweet, but surely this wasn't *that* rare.

Daniel started making jokes at about the same time, but I never recognized that a sense of humor could be a sign of precocity. I was a typical mother whose main child-rearing philosophy was to "enjoy my baby" while I had him. The jokes just made that job more fun.

Respect, Freedom, and Magic: Early School Experiences

Daniel started his formal schooling at the age of 2½. School #1 turned out to be, by all reasonable measures, the ideal environment for him. A Montessori school, it had thirty-six students ranging from age 2½ through kindergarten. The school's philosophy was to: (1) hold deep and true respect for every person in and associated with the school, and (2) meet the students where they were, rather than according to any presupposition of where they should be. In this special "children's house," children were lovingly and consistently disciplined. The message was always, "You can do this," rather than, "You are not measuring up." The message, "You are only a child," was replaced by, "You are capable."

Daniel was neither treated nor labeled as a "gifted" child at this school, although the staff recognized quite early that he was gifted by all standard measures. His precocity did not stand out in an environment where all children appeared remarkable. He was a member of a community that respected all but did not expect them to be intellectual equals. Provisions were made where they were clearly called for. For example, a teacher would create a substitute lesson or activity when a student had already mastered the group activity. The teachers engaged my husband and me in helping find appropriate materials to keep Daniel interested. We brought in books as he moved beyond their available offerings. This was all done without conferences or written plans, but with frequent, informal communication.

But there were also times when they "met me at the door," as I came to call it. Frequently Daniel did something that stood out so strongly that several teachers would make sure that I heard about it. Some of these incidents were funny, others were astounding, and all of them pointed toward an unusual little boy. These included outstanding feats of memory—for example, when he recognized the name of a painting that he had been shown only once several weeks earlier. That might not be so astounding if he had not been only four years old and the painting had not been Diego Rivera's "Vendedora de flores" and its name spoken to him only in Spanish. Then there was his ability to grasp concepts and languages with essentially no repetition. The Spanish teacher, a Mexican native, told me that Daniel learned words as soon as he heard them, and that his pronunciation was the best in the school. He was barely three at the time. Then one day, about one month past his fourth birthday, he suddenly "got" reading, in a blast of understanding. This surprised the teachers more than me, whom it merely pleased. After all, I was the woman who had watched him crawl and then cruise within a two-hour period.

The only thing I knew for sure about this child was that once he did get something, he would go for it with all his power.

The Extent of the Gift Comes to Light

I had Daniel evaluated by the Gifted Development Center (GDC) in Denver in March of his kindergarten year. I agonized over the testing decision for a long time, spending hours poring over the GDC literature. Why was I thinking of spending hundreds of dollars on testing, and what would I do with the results? It seemed likely that Daniel was "gifted," but what good would confirmation do? If his intelligence became a problem, then the school district would evaluate and act, right?

Yet my intuition knocked at my conscience, loud and clear, saying, "Get more data. You'll be glad you did."

The GDC assessed Daniel with the Wechsler Intelligence Scale for Children®, version III (WISC® III). It revealed an IQ within the range called *moderately gifted*, encompassing 95 to 99 percent of the gifted population. So, yes, he was gifted, and that implied a certain level of special needs. But he was not different from most gifted children.

I assumed this meant that we would have an easy time in school with this polite, bright, eager-to-learn child. I imagined that he would easily find himself at the top of his class in most subjects.

The GDC tester and counselor pointed out something else about the scores, however. The WISC III gives a composite score based on ten subtests, each of which is individually scored. Each subtest has an absolute maximum value, beyond which the score never increases, no matter how far the child might have gone. Because the test is normed to a certain age, once a child has scored at the high end for his or her age, the test is not continued (or if it is continued, then the additional questions are not counted).

For Daniel, four of those ten scores were at the maximum and one was just below it. This meant that his composite IQ was probably artificially depressed by the test's construction. The GDC professionals explained that his real IQ more likely lay at the high end of the moderately gifted range, just below the cutoff for highly gifted. I was also told that we could do additional testing to get a more accurate number.

My immediate thought was that we did not need more testing. I could see little value in knowing if the IQ value I had was off by ten or fifteen points. But something still nagged at me. The words of Dr. Linda Silverman, the GDC director, kept haunting me: "Parents are the best indicators of their children's gifts." My intuition and experience did not match the test numbers.

I cannot describe precisely what was behind my intuition. Daniel was not severely precocious in academic areas, but he was *different*. His mind, even when very young, seemed to probe corners of the universe where few people could or would go. I saw the differences in his fantasy play, in his sense of humor, and in his questions. I saw a difference when, at the age of four, he would describe complex "Rube Goldberg" devices that would do silly things, like put paste on a toothbrush. These were uniformly funny and complex, and usually described in rapid-fire speech while he barely drew a breath.

I eventually decided to proceed with further testing. My investigations had convinced me that the needs of highly and profoundly gifted children were sufficiently unique that I needed to know if this applied to Daniel. Having done this research, I was emotionally unprepared for the second set of test results, which indicated that my child was neither moderately nor highly gifted, but well into the range known as *profoundly* or *exceptionally gifted*.

Realizing that my kindergarten son was mentally close to eleven years old was a great shock, and also a moment of sadness. In his weakest areas, as measured by the test, he was mentally about two years ahead of his chronological age. In other words, he was moderately gifted as his baseline. In some areas he did as well as the average fourteen-year-old. Yet he still had his baby teeth.

Now that I knew our truth, I searched in vain for success stories of profoundly gifted (PG) students who had successfully navigated public school, where their mental ages were anywhere from one and a half to two times ahead of their chronological peers. And what I found was a bleak landscape indeed.

Those who survived intact appeared to be either homeschooled or radically accelerated by two or more years. Depression, dropping out, behavior problems, belligerence, withdrawal—these were the stories I found for children who had been forced to fit a mold many, many sizes too small.

Kindergarten graduation was one of the proudest and saddest days I have had. I hope I never forget the absolute sparkle in Daniel's deep-blue eyes as he accepted his diploma and a hug from his teacher, who said, "These children have learned their letters, their colors, and their numbers. They are ready for first grade. But much more importantly, they have learned how to be a friend. And I know that they will take all the love that they got from being here out into their next school and the world."

Here were children and teachers who had formed a true community, where everyone was loved and respected, and where everyone thrived. The love and magic in that graduation room was so thick you could slice through it.

But our time there had ended. This school went no higher, and it was time to leave. The next day our family made a 3,200-mile move and continued our hopeful journey into our future.

We Learn About Mainstream Schools

By the time I realized that Daniel's "gifts" (the term seems so ironic now) would almost surely be a liability in a normal classroom, we had sold our home in an area with multiple educational options and committed to move to a small, isolated town. I worried about the schools there, but everyone I asked assured me that they were *excellent*. That was the single descriptor—*excellent*.

There were no private elementary schools, but there was a public charter Montessori school. I placed Daniel's name on the waiting list, with the grim realization that there were about a hundred students on that list for ten spots.

Despite the glowing reports about the local schools, I felt only cautiously optimistic, thinking of all the PG children who had been failed by other *excellent* schools. The words of Leta Hollingworth sprang up at me with a dreadful foreshadowing:

> In the ordinary elementary school situation, children of 140 IQ waste half their time. Those of 170 IQ waste practically all of their time.
>
> —Leta Hollingworth, *Children Above 180 IQ*

Could this be avoided? Could we find a school in which he would not "waste practically all" of his time? I chatted with the school district and with everyone I knew who had school-age children. I spoke with principals. I learned that one neighborhood school was considered to be the "best of the best." It offered multi-age classrooms spanning grades first through third and fourth through sixth, was close to the university where we would be working, and served children whose parents were often professors and other professionals.

We bought a home that would make this our neighborhood school. I spoke with the "gifted and talented" resource teacher there, who assured me that Daniel would be eligible for participation in their gifted and talented (GT) program. I asked if they had experience with PG children, and was told that since fully 10 percent of the school's population was "gifted," they had lots of experience with very, very gifted children.

Things seemed as good as they could get for a public school. I started the year confident that our transition would be a smooth one, that we were in the best of possible situations—among caring, skilled educators who would know what to do.

From Teacher-Pleaser to Classroom Problem

The long story of what happened in that school is not worth repeating in full. The very short version is that Daniel began school there described as a "teacher-pleaser" and a "sweetie." That did not surprise me, as I knew how sincerely he wanted to learn. But things went downhill quickly from there.

Daniel's behaviors became increasingly problematic and frequently annoying, and he suffered teasing and exclusion by other children. He began to appear extremely distressed. When I sought help with the behavior of others toward him, I was told that these things happened because he annoyed the other children. Since his behavior was problematic, he was apparently responsible for whatever happened to him. He was afraid of the playground and hated recess, when three hundred children ages five to twelve were under the supervision of two adults.

The GT program gave Daniel access to a special teacher and resources for ninety minutes each week. He always looked forward to that time. Although an individualized education program (IEP) was prepared, there was little "individual" about the plan. It said nothing about his educational levels, goals, or anything else that could not be accomplished during the once-a-week GT pull-out program. It appeared that Daniel was allowed to be gifted ninety minutes per week. That one period of letting him go beyond the norms was expected to be enough. The classroom teacher was given complete freedom, and no guidelines, to direct the rest of his education.

Daniel survived School #2 by "becoming invisible." He was convinced that he could blend into the walls. While doing this, he would listen to the other children talking—about him. I observed this once. Daniel could not find some of his class work, and another child began haranguing him about it. His reaction was to sink back into a wall and to stand facing the wall. His face told me that he was putting every ounce of energy he could muster into the act of not crying. It took nearly an hour for that look to disappear, at which time he was engaged in an activity and was beginning to seek ways in which to make it more interesting (translation: he began to do things that annoyed those around him).

The Roots of the Problem: The Simple Is Complex, and Teaching Versus Learning

Any spare energy that I had, and then some, went into advocacy. I tried to help the school reach and help Daniel. But the teachers and administrators seemed to move in a different dimension from me. *The information necessary to help Daniel was there—it was available to the staff—but it was never acted upon, primarily because it was not believed.*

Although the staff felt that their past experience with gifted populations would help them, instead this history became a barrier to seeing beyond what had happened before. I often felt that if they would just step back and view Daniel as a PG child, and pay attention to a few key research studies on such children, then they would understand him perfectly. He was a "textbook case."

Yet he was outside their experience and they never admitted this. Instead, they compared him to other gifted children, assuming that because other gifted children thrived in their school, then any child's failure to succeed must be his fault and not theirs. Some of the key phrases I recall that were red flags included "many children much smarter than him," "most gifted-friendly classroom in the school," "not giftedness but a problem with personality," and "10 percent of our children are gifted and no one else has these problems."

Although his IQ *per se*, and the characteristics that went along with it, were a large part of the problem, I soon learned that these educators thought mainly in terms of academic achievement. I tried to focus on that, instead of the IQ score. But this helped no more than talking about IQ, because it was again beyond their experiences.

When I told the teachers that Daniel had mastered all the first- and second-grade material described in their curriculum guide, and essentially *all* the elementary-school social studies and science curricula, their faces and words told me they did not believe me: "What do you mean by 'mastered'?"

When I told his teacher that he had mastered all the listed math topics for first and second grades, she replied, "But can he write his own word problems? For example, 'If you have three elephants and two tigers, how many animals do you have altogether?'"

All I could think was that Daniel, when posed this problem, would see no reason to make up a silly question merely because someone asked him to do so. The answer was obviously five, but what was the purpose of the question? Why would one write a question for the sake of writing a question?

But could he write word problems? Yes! He "wrote" word problems all the time. Why, I was practically bombarded with them on a daily basis! Questions about "How many?" and "How long?" and "How far?" filled our days. These came out as, "How many seconds have I been alive?" or "How far apart are the stars?" or "How long would it take me to walk to school (four miles away)?" I then worked with him on solving the problems. His questions went far beyond adding elephants and tigers. He might, however, wish to know how gravity worked, and when he learned that a satisfactory answer was not available, he would decide quite seriously that he wanted to work on it.

The word-problem example illustrates the heart of Daniel's difficulties. He knew that he wanted to learn, and he knew that he wanted to learn *new things*. He absolutely loves *learning* new things.

The school, on the other hand, wanted to *teach*, and it wanted *him* to show *them* what he could do. They sincerely believed that unless Daniel progressed through a linear sequence of materials, doing all the necessary practice for each step, he might "miss something" and they would have failed him.

It was evident to me that Daniel often *could not succeed* at the tasks set before him because *he could not simplify them to the degree required*. For example, if told to write a story, a bright six-year-old will write a short, simple story about something like attending a birthday party, walking to school, or another detail of life. When Daniel was told to write a story, he would simply stare at the page. A story? *Write* a story? But stories are hundreds of pages long! How could he be expected to write one down?

All the teachers could see was that he either could not or would not do the work. When Daniel saw that often others could do the required work and he could not, he quickly developed a self-image of someone with little competence. At least two well-described characteristics of profoundly gifted children were operating to make this situation such a failure.

The first is that *the simple is complex and the complex is simple.*[1] Daniel's ability to conceptualize ideas far exceeded that of other children his age and of many adults. But he simply could not think like an average six-year-old, which made his schoolwork appear difficult to him. Because he could *not* think like a six-year-old, and since he was given few or no opportunities to think at a higher level (beyond about third grade), he did not look smart. He stopped saying much of anything.

The other important principle, one that has been demonstrated repeatedly, is that placing PG children in a classroom in which they have no true peers causes them great social angst. I believe that Daniel seriously wanted to fit into the classroom, and that he tried hard to act like the other children. But the internal pain that this caused could not be hidden, and after five months he was beginning to behave in ways that would be associated with a moderate to severely emotionally disturbed child.

A New School and New Hope

After five months, we decided to withdraw Daniel from school, although we had no idea how we were going to do this. We simply could not continue to make him experience the pain. On the very day that we decided we could take it no more, I walked into my office, despondent and prepared to place an ad for full-time child care. Serious questions ran through my head. Was my career at risk? How could I do what I needed to do for my child, to take full responsibility for his education?

As I sat down to make the call, a message was waiting, and I learned that a position was available for him at the Montessori charter school. He began there the next morning, and although we are still in a transition phase, the future looks bright.

The classroom is quiet and orderly, and Daniel goes in each morning and gets right to work. When asked how school is going, he answers positively. He spent the first two days in the classroom reading a children's encyclopedia, and he announced to me at the end of day one, "My brain isn't starving now!" He has slowly begun to explore the rest of the classroom, and has successfully communicated to the teacher, without my help, that the science materials available are not challenging enough for him. The teacher immediately supplemented with new materials, and Daniel was encouraged to express his own desires to work on projects and to explore topics. He has written a full-page poem, "Insects," by his own hand, more writing than he accomplished in the previous five-month period.

I gave School #3 the GDC report, but I avoided using any terminology that I thought might be unfamiliar to them. My observations of the school suggested that it might not be necessary to treat Daniel as a special case, because the staff was committed to meeting students wherever they were. This seems to have worked well.

After the first week, we were "called in" for a conference and the teacher explained how her first days with Daniel had gone. She had learned, all on her own, that he simply would not respond to "power trips," and she could tell that he had experienced many. The school had graduated another similar student, and she talked about how challenged they had been to keep up with that child academically. Finally, instead of telling me that my child did not "fit" the school, they had recognized that he had intellectual gifts that would constantly challenge them.

But they seemed determined to meet those challenges and to *enjoy the child*. He is easy to enjoy when his world makes sense, and life can become difficult for those around him when it does not.

Some of Daniel's dark shadows have followed him to this new place, but I feel confident that they will soon fall away. He was initially afraid of the playground, but once he learned that no one would force him out there, he became interested again. Within a few days, he was busy building complex snow structures and enjoying outdoor recess. He shies away from most group activities, preferring instead to spend time exploring on his own. This may never change. He has always needed plenty of time every day to be with himself. But with such strong acceptance, and if he is never forced, he will soon join the group for part of each day. He will do this when he is ready. He loves other children and people in general, and is still young enough that his reality cannot accept anything less than full acceptance of him by others. His world is falling back into order now, and he can again fly.

Did I Learn Anything? Can I Teach Anything?

I am sure that our experience contains many lessons, but I am not certain they can be neatly packaged. I had a better experience at one school where I engaged in mild and subtle advocacy than I did at another school where I did serious, sustained advocacy. But I do not conclude that the advocacy was the problem.

My advocacy efforts got Daniel into the GT pull-out program very early on, which was a positive experience for him, albeit a limited one. My advocacy did eventually get him more difficult work—when we left School #2, he was in a reading group with gifted third-graders, reading at a middle school level. Without advocacy, I think the time at that school would have been much worse.

I think that three things pained Daniel most deeply about School #2. The first was being told what to do, even if there was a degree of freedom in when to do it. The second was feeling unsafe around other children and being allowed to behave in ways that he knew were inappropriate. The third was being expected to "perform" and to work in areas that he had mastered years before.

Techniques that may have worked with moderately or highly gifted children were simply not enough. I have often wondered if *anything* could have been done within that school environment. Would radical acceleration from the very beginning have worked? I suspect not. The cognitive differences would still have been there.

The state law defining giftedness contains a large clue to meeting the needs of all gifted children, but one that has not been embraced by the school system. Gifted children are, by definition, sufficiently different that they require different techniques of instruction. That is the specific language—*different techniques of instruction.* Unless that concept is fully embraced, the system cannot be effective. The words of the principal of School #2 ring through my mind as a sign of why it might never work: "But this is only a public school."

If there is a single lesson to be learned from our experience, it is that PG children indeed *exist,* and they are different from other children, *including other gifted children*, in fundamental ways. Although it has been said that PG children are a heterogeneous group, I was struck by the similarity of our experience to the stories of other families. Child psychologist Deirdre Lovecky summarized how the cognitive processes of PG children differ from those of moderately gifted children, listing seven specific differences (the simple is complex, need for precision, complex is simple, early abstract reasoning, early grasp of essential elements, high capacity for empathy, and inclination toward immersion).[2] Recognition of these qualities and how they affect classroom behavior and success is absolutely essential to the healthy social and emotional development of these children. Recognition of *who they are* is the key to *meeting their needs*.

All children, *even our very "smartest" children*, deserve our love and acceptance. Whether or not they deserve a chance to learn *while in public school* remains one of the most pressing questions of our age.

Postscript: At press time, Daniel is in third grade at the Montessori charter school. He is feeling very limited by the materials available there, and that solution may soon have reached its limit. He has become a prolific author and is now on book #14 of his "Sherman the Shortfin Mako" series, which his mother hopes to help him publish some day.

Notes

1. Lovecky, "Exceptionally Gifted Children."

2. Ibid.

References

Hollingworth, Leta. *Children Above 180 IQ*. Yonkers-on-Hudson, New York: World Book Company, 1942.

Lovecky, D. "Exceptionally Gifted Children: Different Minds." *Roeper Review* 17 (2): (December, 1994): 116–120.

Becoming an Educational Advocate

Dolphin's Story

BY CAROLYN KOTTMEYER

Carolyn Kottmeyer is the winner of the 2005 National Association of Gifted Children (NAGC) Community Service Award for her work as author and webmistress of Hoagies' Gifted Education Page (www.hoagiesgifted.org) and Hoagies' Kids and Teens Page (www.hoagieskids.org). She writes for the *Gifted Communicator* and speaks nationally for a variety of gifted conferences. She served on the Board of Directors for SENG (Supporting Emotional Needs of the Gifted) and helps with several other gifted organization Web sites and the Hollingworth Center for Highly Gifted Children. Carolyn shares the parenting of two wonderful and profoundly gifted girls with her husband, Mark.

"Parents are notoriously slow learners—so I've heard, from many gifted children," Carolyn Kottmeyer says, as she tells how her very young daughter turned her into a reluctant, then an avid, advocate for the needs of profoundly gifted children. She shows how parents need to mediate between educators—who often think they know what a child needs—and the child as an individual, who often *does* know what is needed, but doesn't know how to self-advocate yet. The parents have to learn quickly to understand the child's needs and convey them effectively to the educators.

There are two ways to do everything: the easy way and the hard way. One way to become an educational advocate is to go to school and get your bachelor's, master's, and perhaps a doctorate in education. Then, as an expert in education, take a job with a school system and advocate for educational programs there. That's the easy way.

Anyone who knows me knows I *never* do anything the easy way.

So I went to college and got my bachelor's degree in software engineering. And everyone wants to know: how did *I* end up an educational advocate?

The hard way. I married another software engineer; together we got our master's degrees in software engineering; and together, we had kids ("No mom, not kids, *children*. We're not baby goats!").

And our life rolled merrily along. Dolphin (her chosen nickname) walked at nine months, ran at ten months, and never stopped. She rode her bike without training wheels by the age of four. We noticed that most of the kids in our neighborhood were a bit slower to develop, but . . . you hate to make judgments about kids. They'll all catch up eventually, we thought. We really didn't notice anything else. Our daughter was a wonderful infant, a terrific toddler—a bit active, but lots of fun. She quizzed us on addition and subtraction from her car seat, and insisted that we *not* give her the right answer the first time, so she could correct us. We didn't know that most three-year-olds didn't do that.

She questioned us on everything, from "How does the sun rise and set?" to "How did the baby get inside of you, Mommy?" She laughed at the stork story, and insisted, "Seriously, Mom!" So we told her more, but still she insisted, "Mommy, if the egg came from you, and the sperm came from Daddy, how did they get together inside you?" She was almost four at the time, and being pregnant, I didn't suspect that other four-year-olds of expectant mothers didn't ask the same questions. I quickly found a cartoon-style book that helped me answer her questions.

There was another hint, just before her new sister was born. Dolphin chose to switch rooms, and she picked her own wallpaper (with a little subtle guidance from us). It was decided: a fish print, pastel (not my choice). It was pretty and suited her. As we left the wallpaper store, she turned to us and stated, "You know, my new wallpaper won't go with the carpet in that room." I went home and checked—she was right. So we went to the carpet store, she walked in and picked up a sample: pale purple (definitely not my choice). We got out the wallpaper sample, explained about the long and arduous process of selecting coordinating carpet, and she played under the racks for two hours while we looked at nearly every sample in the store. Of course, she was right. The best choice was the carpet she picked the moment she entered the store. She wasn't yet four.

Parents, however, are notoriously slow learners—so I've heard, from many gifted children.

The next fall, Dolphin entered pre-kindergarten right on time. It only took three weeks before she, her teachers, and the director (in that order) decided that perhaps she should move into the kindergarten room, for social reasons—she got along much better with the kids in kindergarten. They played her games and talked her talk. And the director added, as an afterthought, "Academics won't be an issue." That turned out to be the understatement of Dolphin's life!

Kindergarten went well. Dolphin completed the kindergarten curriculum, the first-grade curriculum in math and reading, and a second-grade math CD from the math-curriculum company that the teacher didn't know what to do with. Dolphin figured it out. She absorbed every tidbit of science the teacher offered, and then some, so the teacher gave the class, mostly Dolphin, more and more detailed science. It was a great school—a daycare with an accredited kindergarten. But no first grade.

We registered Dolphin for first grade in our public school. That's when I became an educational advocate. At registration, the staff tested Dolphin and she answered every question right, yet they still recommended that she repeat kindergarten. Why? Because she was young, and her feet weren't big enough for first grade. Yup, that's what they told us. I think they were trying to say "because of her size," but since she was taller than all the incoming kindergartners, most of the first-graders, and some of the second-graders, they went for shoe size. Dolphin, on the other hand, was expecting to move directly into second grade. When she heard us talking about putting her in first grade, she thought we meant *right then*, in the spring of her kindergarten year, with a move to second grade in the fall. We still don't know where she got that idea. So we compromised, and against the school's better judgment, she started first grade.

Things went well for . . . about a week. Then Dolphin realized that the class was going to go through the alphabet, one letter at a time, just like they had started in pre-kindergarten, and then perhaps get to words. The class was also going through the numbers, one digit at a time, and by the end of the year they were going to learn how to add and subtract single digits. When she came home each day after school, her behavior told us that we had better do something about this young lady's educational experience. So we started to advocate.

Being a computer programmer, I searched the Internet and the public library. I read every book I could find about gifted children. I found every site in the world on gifted children, and bookmarked them all. My bookmark file was a mass of educational sites, so crowded that I couldn't find a single reference when I wanted it.

Back in school, Dolphin was having a terrible time in first grade. The school placed her in a second-grade class for math, which helped, but the first-grade teacher was very unhappy with her from day one. On that day, the teacher had handed out a very old science book and told the students to "look at the book" while she did some required paperwork. After a while, Dolphin raised her hand. It seems the old science book started by talking about the earth, and how it was made of solid rock. Dolphin didn't agree. She explained to the teacher that the earth wasn't made of solid rock, but of liquid rock and fire. Okay, not exactly right, but closer than the book description. The teacher chastised her for *reading* the book when she was told to *look* at it.

Things didn't improve over the next few months. The teacher thought Dolphin answered questions in too much detail, and asked her to keep her answers simple. So Dolphin stared out the window at the playground. By the first parent-teacher conference, the teacher was convinced that Dolphin did not belong in the first-grade classroom. She even told us that Dolphin had gotten something wrong on an assignment once. When we asked to see it, she admitted it might have been another child.

In the second-grade math class, Dolphin was doing quite well. The reading made things a little complicated. Although she wasn't a particularly proficient reader, she read as well as the average student in the class, and she had no difficulty with the math. She was also making friends in the class.

A month before the winter holiday, we sat down with school officials to discuss what to do. From her behavior and comments at home, it was clear to us that Dolphin needed to move full-time to the class where the teacher appreciated her, away from the class where she had nothing to do but stare out the window. Thus her second grade-skip took place only eighteen months after the first one.

To be honest, I was worried. The school officials were worried. I think the only people who weren't worried were Dolphin and her dad. But they prevailed . . . and she did very well in second grade. Her scout troop included both grades, so that didn't change. Her swimming and soccer programs were organized by age and/or level, so nothing changed there. The only glitch was school gym: Dolphin's slight nearsightedness (not enough to correct) made her less than perfect at some activities. As soon as the gym teacher learned about her vision (and her skiing, swimming, soccer, and biking outside of school), that "problem" went away.

At the end of the school year, we did something we hadn't intended to do for several years. We moved to another district. We wanted to live where our children would be appreciated, and where we wouldn't have to fight the schools for their education. We didn't want to spend our time advocating. We wanted to spend our time with our family.

But moving didn't provide the solution we had hoped for. The next three years in the new school district . . . well, we were back in the advocacy business.

About then, I was asked to create a class at work for my fellow programmers on writing Web pages for the Internet. *Voilà!* Hoagies' Gifted Education Page was born, at www.hoagiesgifted.org. Later, I was asked for a class on Web-page design, and Hoagies' Page got a facelift. Nothing motivates me more than teaching the subject!

At first, Hoagies' Page wasn't much: a single page with all my bookmarks, organized and annotated, so that I could find what I needed. It is still all of that—except it is not a single page. Three and a half years after it first launched, Hoagies' Gifted Education Page involved more than 150 Web pages of information, and had more than 300,000 visitors. It has continued to grow and evolve. It contains success stories from parents with different methods of success, original articles by some of the biggest names in gifted education, and even some gifted-child humor for the moments when you need to sit back and laugh at it all. And it still includes an organized, annotated collection of every useful gifted-education Web site, book, and journal that I've found.

So in addition to using all the information to advocate for my children's education, I share what I've learned with the rest of the world via the Internet. Any parent or educator of a gifted child can use this information to help advocate successfully for a gifted child's education.

And that is the *hard* way to become an educational advocate.

You'd think our being well versed in gifted education would help, but . . . it didn't. Before we moved, we did all our homework: interviewed lots of districts; talked to parents, teachers, and administrators; and eventually decided on a district. We registered Dolphin for school in early August. A few weeks later, we got an idea of the magnitude of our mistake. The principal called and scheduled a meeting. We weren't worried—Dolphin was coming from another district in the same state, with a valid IEP already negotiated for her third-grade year, with no special accommodations. Everything should be fine.

The principal spent more than two hours trying to hold Dolphin back. First, she wanted Dolphin back in kindergarten. After second grade?

"She won't even be the oldest," the principal added.

After an hour of listening politely, we declined. A three-grade demotion, for no academic, social, or emotional reason, didn't sound good for Dolphin.

Next the principal tried to persuade us to place Dolphin back in first grade. When we again declined, she suggested second grade. Finally she admitted that, with a valid IEP, she couldn't change Dolphin's placement without our approval. Dolphin was placed in third grade. But as you can imagine, this wasn't the end of it.

As an advocate, I assumed the best motives: the principal had probably never encountered another child like Dolphin, and would like to learn more about profoundly gifted (PG) children. We'd had various testing done since kindergarten, and we now knew what we were dealing with: a profoundly gifted child with an intense desire to learn, and with social and emotional levels well above her chronological age. But this was probably new to this school. At the next meeting, I brought a few articles by professionals on educating the PG child. The principal told us if she wanted to learn more, she knew where to look, and she did not need any help from us. The articles were tossed in the trashcan as we left the meeting.

So much for advocacy.

The next three years were full of ups and downs. In third grade, we pulled Dolphin from the high math class midyear, after a situation with the teacher. Dolphin spent the rest of the year proving she already knew fourth-grade math, documenting her accomplishments with the teacher of the gifted. But when fourth grade rolled around, all the records had been lost and she was again assigned to fourth-grade math. This was a better year, with a wonderful teacher, but there was only so much the teacher could do. Dolphin had long since mastered all of the year's math, and most of the other material to be taught. But Dolphin enjoyed the social aspects of school, and she didn't want to be homeschooled. We worked with the teacher, and persevered.

During Dolphin's fourth-grade year, we were advised by friends in gifted education to apply on her behalf to a new program for PG children, the Davidson Young Scholars program. Our application was accepted, and the Young Scholars program has turned out to be one of the best things that ever happened for Dolphin (and, a year later, for our second daughter, Cheetah). She has made many friends—peers—all over the country. We attend gatherings where these children and their families are accepted for being themselves, no matter what age or grade—whether they are nine and in elementary school, or eight and in college, or ten and home-schooled with tons of advanced materials. And the Davidson program offers a wonderful support system for us, the parents. It connects us with educational experts and with other parents, struggling to raise and educate PG children, so we can share information and ideas.

Thanks to our Davidson support with our IEP meetings for fifth grade, Dolphin was finally permitted to take math outside the classroom, where she zipped through both Education Program for Gifted Youth (EPGY) sixth-grade math and Academic Systems pre-algebra with amazing speed and accuracy. Taking her first comprehensive final exams didn't faze her (though it scared me). She took the Johns Hopkins Talent Search PLUS test, an eighth-grade achievement test. On the quantitative section of the test, only 37 fifth-grade girls in the country scored higher than she did, although she had not begun her pre-algebra course. She did nearly as well on the verbal section. We were again surprised.

During this time, she also took sixth-grade science and did very well, presenting each of her units to the gifted classes in school. She seemed happy. She made a best friend. We thought things were good.

The following summer, our IEP team had two options. One was cross-grade placement, where Dolphin would take some classes with sixth- and some with seventh-graders, a very difficult schedule in a middle school that emphasizes team teaching. The other option was full-time seventh grade, with the same self-paced math she had taken in fifth grade (now for high school credit), high language arts, high concert band, and French I (also for high school credit). This was Dolphin's choice and the team quickly agreed (with one dissenter), because the choice facilitated scheduling and made everyone happy.

The oddest thing happened at this meeting: when the dissenter made his speech and insisted that an appropriate placement would not be sixth *or* seventh grade, but instead holding Dolphin back in the elementary school to repeat fifth grade, we didn't argue. We didn't have a chance. An administrator, one we never thought was on our side before, spoke up immediately. She agreed that three years ago, she held the same belief, but she had since seen Dolphin's performance and social fit and she could no longer hold onto those beliefs for this child. She supported Dolphin's move to seventh grade.

The best was yet to come. School started on a Monday. I'd had the privilege of seeing Dolphin come home from the first day of school five times before, but this was different. I have *never* seen such a happy child in my life. She literally bounced into the house, and joyously gave me the details of her day, and went off to do her homework . . . all new material! And though school has only been in session a few weeks, she is still thrilled with her teachers and classes, her new friends whom she lunches with daily, and everything about her new grade.

It's a year later now. Seventh grade was a success, but . . . it wasn't as good as we hoped. Science was slow, and very repetitive—the new material was few and far between. The rest of the classes weren't much better—some worse. We were floored. Dolphin had straight A's the first marking period, but the brightest kids in the seventh grade, whom she had quickly become friends with, teased her for doing so well. She made sure to get a B every other marking period. We weren't sure what to do for eighth grade, but . . . they had a plan!

The principals of the middle and high school came up with a great idea: Honors tenth grade classes at the high school in the mornings, and afternoons at the middle school. They even provide transportation! Dolphin was thrilled—she picked Latin I (she'd wanted Latin all along, but it wasn't offered in middle school), Chemistry I, and Geometry. And she still takes band and TV studio with her eighth-grade friends. And with the Honors high school classes, she's actually learning new things! She's thrilled!

Now we have her sister Cheetah, just starting second grade: a totally different child, as different as night and day; brunette and blond; tall and petite; extrovert and introvert. First grade was great—she had a terrific teacher—but . . . we learned today that this year will not be the same. I've read that PG children are as different from each other as they are different from other children. These two certainly are! But their needs are equally strong. Looks like we're back in the advocacy business!

The Underachievement of Gifted Students

Multiple Frustrations and Few Solutions

BY SALLY M. REIS

Sally M. Reis is department head and a professor of Educational Psychology at the University of Connecticut, where she also serves as principal investigator of the National Research Center on the Gifted and Talented. She was a teacher for fifteen years, eleven of which were spent working with gifted students in elementary, junior high, and senior high levels. Sally has presented workshops and professional development on enrichment programs and gender equity programs throughout the United States. She is the author or coauthor of many articles, book chapters, monographs, and technical reports, including *Work Left Undone: Choices and Compromises of Talented Females*. Sally serves on the editorial board of the *Gifted Child Quarterly* and is past-president of the National Association for Gifted Children.

Underachievement is a significant problem in gifted children, and solutions are often elusive. Sally Reis discusses causes, frustrations, research findings, and possible answers.

Student performance that falls noticeably short of potential, especially for young people with exceptionally high ability, is bewildering and perhaps the most frustrating of all challenges faced by both teachers and parents. Why do so many talented students fail to realize their potential? Some underachieving students lack self-regulation skills; others suffer from obvious or hidden disabilities. Still others may underachieve in response to inappropriate educational conditions. These comments suggest possible causes, but we need to look further to find ways of defining and reducing the too-frequent occurrence of academic underachievement among our most capable learners.

The literature describing the problem dates back to Agnes Maria Conklin (1940) and her research about high-IQ students who were failing.[1] Decades later, underachievement among high-ability students is still a major problem. As early as 1955, John Gowan described the gifted underachiever as "one of the greatest social wastes of our culture."[2] In 1990, a survey conducted by the National Research Center on the Gifted and Talented showed that most educators of gifted students identified underachievement as their number-one concern.[3]

Some students underachieve or fail in school for obvious reasons that affect all young people: excessive absences from school, poor performance, disruptive behavior, low self-esteem, family problems, and poverty. Yet additional factors place gifted or high-potential students at risk of failure. These involve the inappropriate curriculum and content that they endure on a daily basis. High-ability students spend hundreds of hours each month in classrooms where they rarely encounter new or challenging curriculum. They are bored by the assignment of routine tasks they mastered long ago, by low levels of discussion, and by a constant mismatch between content and their ability. These events lead to frustration for many of our brightest students. In fact, dropping out of school is the only way that some students believe they can address these issues effectively. How do I know this? For the past decade, I have been involved in research about underachievement and I have also experienced this problem firsthand.

A Personal Story

My husband was my friend and colleague for a long time before we married. When we did, my new stepsons, Mark and Scott, were teenagers and the transition to having a new stepmother was not easy for them. Scott loved school and was an excellent student, but Mark's work in school had frustrated his family for years. When Mark lived with his father and me, I became more involved in his life, both in school and at home.

Mark was always a child of remarkably high potential. Yet his grades fluctuated in elementary, junior high, and senior high school. Mark took advanced math classes and achieved a near-perfect score on the math section of the SAT during his junior year of high school. However, he was labeled an "underachiever" because of his variable attitudes toward school.

Figuring out the situation was not difficult. If Mark liked his teacher, he would do well in class, regardless of the content. If Mark liked the content of the class but not the teacher, he would do enough to get by, usually with Cs. But if Mark did not like either the teacher or the content, or the content was well below his achievement level, Mark usually failed the class or pulled through with a D. He did well on exams, even when he had done none of the assigned classwork. He simply lost credit for every bit of homework and classwork that he did not do.

The problem wasn't that Mark was idle. In fact, we usually had to plead with him to go to bed at an appropriate time because he was reading books about artificial intelligence or pursuing his own interests, which happened to be designing software and building computers. In his senior year, Mark got recruitment letters from the best colleges in the country because of his near-perfect SAT scores. Unfortunately, he did not graduate from high school because he failed both English and history. He did not like his teachers, and the work was too easy in the lower-track classes to which he had been assigned because of his lack of effort in earlier years.

Not graduating from high school was for Mark the lesser of two fates. The worse fate, in his opinion, was pretending to be interested in boring, uninspiring classes taught by teachers who he believed did not care about him. Was he wrong? Or in some way did he respond honestly to a bad situation? When I remember these difficult months in his life, I am troubled by the dilemmas his father and I faced when we tried to give him advice. Should we have told him to pretend to be interested and to play the game?

We encouraged Mark to try to negotiate with his English teacher about substituting more challenging and enjoyable assignments. He even tried to show his teachers some of the work he was doing at home, but few of them cared. He did not fit the model of the student who "goes to school well" and was, in their words, an enigma. We were asked repeatedly how someone so bright could fail to do such relatively easy work, and we were blamed and felt helpless, despite our experience and background in education.

Almost fifteen years have passed since Mark flunked his senior year of high school and happier events have unfolded. After a few years of switching jobs and searching for the right school and the right program, Mark started college part time, despite his lack of a high school diploma. Eight years after leaving high school, he had completed both bachelor's and master's degrees in systems engineering. He currently works on cutting-edge software design. The reversal of his underachievement occurred when he made up his own mind that he wanted to succeed academically, and also when he found the right academic program for him. He didn't get high grades in every class, but he learned to put out enough effort to pass required classes, which in turn enabled him to continue taking the classes he loved.

Background

The problem of academic underachievement among high-ability youth has long been believed to be widespread.[4] Some people estimate that between 2 and 10 percent of high school students are underachievers. For high-ability students, the proportions are thought to be far greater. Pirozzo suggests that up to one-half of high-ability students underachieve.[5] In *A Nation at Risk: The Imperative for Educational Reform*, the National Commission on Excellence in Education pushed the bar higher: "Over half the population of gifted students do not match their tested ability with comparable achievement in school."[6] Underachievement in school is clearly an issue of great importance for young people, their parents, and society, despite difficulties in defining and assessing what is meant by underachievement.[7]

Defining Underachievement

The process of producing both conceptual and operational definitions of underachievement has been complicated and problematic. Most people agree on a general definition of underachievement as it applies to education: "the underachiever is a young person who performs more poorly in school than one would expect on the basis of his mental abilities."[8] This conceptual definition identifies a discrepancy between actual and expected performance, and it applies to students at all ability levels.

Categorizing different types of underachievers, and the consequent development of operational definitions, continues to be problematic. Some types of underachievement affect all students, including the gifted. While some additional types of underachievement are unique to gifted students, we have no agreed-upon definitions of gifted and talented learners or of gifted underachievement. While defining gifted underachievement should be a fairly straightforward task, it has not been.

Following the Soviet launching of Sputnik in 1957, both public and educational critics expressed concern over technological ability in the United States and alleged that our country was not doing enough to educate its most capable students, many of whom were performing at mediocre levels in school. Social, political, and educational attention focused on these students,[9] and in 1960, Shaw and McCuen provided educators with an early definition of the gifted underachiever: "the underachiever with superior ability is one whose performance as judged either by grades or achievement test scores, is significantly below his high measured or demonstrated aptitudes or potential for academic achievement."[10] This approach to definition implies that it is important to recognize a learner's level of potential. It also provides a rationale for the idea that appropriate academic performance constitutes the fulfillment of potential. Most research on high-ability underachievers involves learners with high scores on some standard measure of ability whose academic performance is not correspondingly high.

The most common component of the various definitions of gifted under-achievement involves a discrepancy between ability and achievement, neither of which can be measured with any degree of precision.[11] Potential is especially difficult to assess, in large part because students identified as gifted and talented learners are not a homogeneous group. Their talents and strengths vary widely, just as talents and strengths vary within any diverse sample of students. Yet even more difficult than assessing a learner's potential is the task of evaluating the level of academic performance that indicates underachievement.

Initially, the most commonly applied standard appeared to be simply performing below average for the current grade level.[12] Instead of basing classification on performance during a single year, some researchers regard gifted underachievers as students who evidence a longstanding pattern of academic underachievement.[13]

This brings us to the need to differentiate between *chronic* and *situational* underachievement, a distinction initially made in the 1950s and 1960s.[14] The academic performance of a *temporary* or *situational* underachiever temporarily declines, often in response to personal or situational stress, such as a divorce, a particular teacher, or a family move. In contrast, a *chronic* underachiever displays the underachievement pattern consistently over a long period.[15] Both types can affect students at all levels of potential. Sylvia Rimm cautions that while underachievement may be a result of a particularly negative school year or a highly competitive environment, and therefore a situational problem,[16] the pattern of underachievement may continue because of reinforcement from home or school. Unfortunately, no specific length of time has been found to distinguish chronic from temporary or situational underachievement.[17]

When Does Underachievement Begin?

It is commonly reported that underachievement begins during the late elementary grades, certainly by junior high school, and that it begins earlier for males than for females.[18] The research findings that underachievement begins in elementary school may be meaningful to educators and may assist them in preventing later, more serious problems. For example, the amount of assigned homework usually increases in upper elementary and junior high school. At this point, students who refuse to complete homework or who do the work with little care or effort can be easily identified.

Some gifted students may achieve easily and without effort through the early years in school, but falter when they encounter challenges that require effort. The identification of smart students who underachieve raises an important question regarding the stability of underachievement and the resulting problem in defining underachievement. McCall, Evahn, and Kratzer explain:

> The very fact that underachievers do not learn as much in school as would be expected will mean that their mental ability may decline to match their grades, at which point they will no longer be underachieving. Prolonged underachievement, then, may be unusual, not because of lack of stability

in the psychological characteristics of such students, but because their mental ability has not been nurtured by effort in school.[19]

Causes of and Contributors to Underachievement

Determining why some high-ability students demonstrate low levels of achievement is difficult because underachievement occurs for many reasons. However, practitioners must explore causes if they plan to help these children. Research indicates that, in the vast majority of cases, bright students underachieve for one of three basic reasons:

1. Underachievement masks more serious physical, cognitive, or emotional issues.

2. Underachievement indicates a mismatch between the student and the school environment.[20]

3. Underachievement results from a personal characteristic, such as low self-motivation, low self-regulation, or low self-efficacy.[21]

What would cause a capable learner to engage in behaviors that mask ability? No definitive answers exist to this perplexing question, but several theories and some speculation provide a background for studies. Research concerning underachievement among gifted students has examined many possible causes that fall into the three categories listed above, including biology, environment, self-pressure, school pressure, peer pressure, parental pressure, boredom with school, and inappropriate teaching methods.[22]

Many researchers point to school as the place where bright students lose their interest and drive. Some teachers may be satisfied with minimal work and their low expectations may have a negative impact on bright youngsters. Some teachers may feel threatened by high-ability students and may fail to provide them with appropriate, creative activities.[23] Banks suggested that the formal school structure may not encourage imagination or creativity, creating an environment in which bright youngsters are unwilling to achieve.[24] In an educational setting where conformity is valued, classroom standards may promote rote learning rather than critical thinking and problem solving. Thus bright students are left without challenge.

In addition to the rigidity of the school system, an inappropriate curriculum was also found to contribute to underachievement in high-ability high school students in a study we conducted at the National Research Center on the Gifted and Talented.[25] Thirty-five students participated in this three-year study in a large urban high school. We compared high-ability students who were identified as high achievers with students of similar ability who underachieved in school. Using qualitative methods, we examined the perceptions of students, teachers, staff, and administrators about why some academically talented students fail to achieve in school. Interestingly, my colleagues and I found many similarities between high-ability students who achieved and students of similar ability who underachieved in school.[26] This study indicates that achievement and underachievement were not disparate concepts. In many cases, students who underachieved had been high-achieving in the previous year or semester.

The students who underachieved recalled "breezing" through elementary school and indicated that previous schoolwork required no major effort. They simply never learned how to work hard at learning, or they became so accustomed to learning without effort because the work was so easy that when they had to exert effort they thought they were no longer smart.

Although data from this study cannot be generalized to other groups of students, the identified underachievers were more often male and from lower socioeconomic levels and from larger families than the achievers.[27] Although divorce is commonly reported to be more frequent in families of underachievers, we found no relationship between parental divorce and underachievement; between poverty and underachievement; or between family size and underachievement.

Some high-achieving students had experienced periods of under-achievement and were supported in their achievement by a network of high-achieving peers who refused to let their friends falter. To these students, achievement was like walking up a crowded staircase. If one student started to underachieve and tried to turn and walk down the staircase, many other students pushed the student back up. However, once the cycle of underachievement began and the student went down that crowded staircase, it was extremely difficult to turn around and climb back up.

Behavioral Characteristics of Underachievers

A variety of personal and psychological characteristics have been attributed to underachievers and their parents, often based on clinical impressions and on the subjective reports of professionals, teachers, and parents, rather than on systematic, objective measurements and observations.[28] *Self-concept*, or an individual's cognitive view of self, is closely tied to the more important measure of *self-esteem*, the feelings of worth that one's self-image produces. Most literature on self-esteem among bright underachievers agrees that these children perceive themselves as inadequate,[29] especially with regard to their academic abilities. They are described as self-critical, fearing both failure and success, and could be anxious or nervous, especially about their performance.

Poor self-perception is one of the most commonly cited characteristics of this population.[30] Numerous researchers have discovered underachieving gifted students with overall low self-esteem,[31] although they differ in whether they see low self-esteem as a cause or a byproduct of underachievement. Sylvia Rimm reported negative comments made by underachieving youngsters about themselves,[32] which she perceived as a defense mechanism stemming from a low sense of self-efficacy. She concluded that these youngsters would achieve if they could see a direct relationship between their efforts and positive classroom outcomes.

Other studies report that underachievers have poor peer relationships, and that they lack friends and may be socially withdrawn.[33] Fine and Pitts found that bright underachievers usually had a strong interest in something outside of school, and that this interest frequently kept them isolated from their peers.[34]

Parental Issues with Underachievement

Most research about parents of students who underachieve indicates a series of negatives. Some anecdotal reports cite inconsistent, overly strict, or overly indulgent familial discipline as contributors to underachievement. Other researchers suggest that conflicting attitudes between two parents toward the child will also lead to underachieving behaviors.[35]

The most commonly described characteristics of parents of underachievers include indifference, lack of interest, distant relationships with little affection, and neutral to negative attitudes toward education.[36] These characteristics may occur singly or in combination with several other themes. One is an authoritarian, restrictive, and rejecting parental style, especially by the father.[37] Another involves permissiveness and freedom, bordering on parental neglect. With a gifted underachiever, the latter configuration may occur because the youngster leads the parent, who treats the child as a miniature adult.[38] Overindulgent, overprotective parents may also contribute to underachievement, producing youngsters who believe that they can't do anything independently and fail to develop self-sufficiency, a sense of responsibility, or feelings of self-fulfillment.[39]

Parental inconsistency may worsen the situation for underachievers in several types of families.[40] In one type, the father restricts and controls the child in an authoritarian fashion while the mother capitulates to the youngster, trying to compensate. In a second type, the opposite dynamic occurs. In a third type of inconsistency, the father is uneducated or simply withdraws from childrearing in the face of the mother's dominance. In each case, one parent is strong and one is weak, and the child receives conflicting messages that enable the youngster to play one parent against the other and do not promote achievement.

Often the conflict within the family is directly related to the high ability of the child. Parents push the youngster to excel and often the goals set by the parents—separately or as a unit—are unrealistic or do not coincide with the goals of the child. All of these instances produce emotional conflict for the young person and may contribute to underachievement.

Students who underachieve are reported to have problems relating to authority figures, such as parents, teachers, and other adults. These students may be overly aggressive and hostile to authority figures, may exhibit discipline problems and high rates of delinquency, may lack self-control, and may be irresponsible. They may have serious problems establishing independence from their parents and may be regarded as rebellious. Others may perceive these children as frequently attempting to manipulate situations or people.[41] Bricklin and Bricklin suggest that some underachievers "hit" their parents where it hurts the most—that is, through underachievement—while McIntyre perceives the dawdling, stubborn, procrastinating, and daydreaming underachiever as rebelling through inaction.[42]

Interventions

The causes and correlates of gifted underachievement have received considerable attention through case studies and qualitative research.[43] However, few researchers have attempted true quasi-experimental studies of how effective various interventions may be. Most interventions reported in the literature were designed to effect immediate results with a group of acutely underachieving gifted students.[44] Results of interventions designed to reverse underachievement in gifted students have been inconsistent and inconclusive.[45] Furthermore, most interventions have shown limited long-term success.[46]

Interventions aimed at reversing gifted underachievement fall into two general categories: counseling and instructional interventions.[47]

Counseling interventions concentrate on changing the personal and/or family dynamics that contribute to underachievement. They may involve individual, group, and/or family counseling. In most situations, the counselor's goal is not to force the underachiever to become a more successful student but to help the student decide whether success is a desirable goal, and, if so, to help reverse counterproductive habits and cognitions.

The most well-known educational interventions for gifted underachievers are instructional. They involve the establishment of part-time or full-time special classrooms in which educators strive to create an environment favorable to achievement by altering the traditional organization.[48] There is usually a smaller student/teacher ratio; teachers create less conventional types of learning activities; students have more choice about and exercise more control over the atmosphere; and students are encouraged to utilize different learning strategies. Two programs of this type were designed and implemented for gifted underachievers in elementary school. Whitmore put together a full-time program and Supplee instituted a part-time one.[49] Both stressed the importance of affective education, as well as the necessity of student-centered classroom environments. Because neither study used a control or comparison group, the results of these studies may not be generalizable to the entire population of underachievers. Ethically, it may be difficult to have a true comparison group in such studies, because the researcher must withhold valuable treatment from one group.

Emerick investigated the reasons that some students are able to reverse academic underachievement without the assistance of formal interventions.[50] Her qualitative research study examined the patterns of underachievement and subsequent achievement of ten young adults. All of Emerick's participants believed that a specific teacher had the greatest impact in reversing their underachievement. In addition, participants were most likely to develop achievement-oriented behaviors when they were stimulated in class and were able to pursue topics of interest. Participants perceived that several additional factors appeared to play a part in their reversal of underachievement: out-of-school interests and activities, their parents, the development of goals associated with grades, encounters with particular teachers, and changes in their "selves." Other research suggests that student involvement in extracurricular activities reduces the likelihood of underachievement.[51]

Emerick observed that her findings suggest that "reversing the underachievement pattern may mean taking a long, hard look at the underachiever's curriculum and classroom situation. The responses and actions of the students in this study suggest that when appropriate educational opportunities are present, gifted underachievers can respond positively."[52]

Emerick's study indicates that one type of effective intervention may be based on students' strengths and interests, and Renzulli Type III enrichment offers one approach that works with this idea.[53] In a recent study that specifically targets student strengths and interests in order to help reverse academic underachievement,[54] researchers systematically used self-selected Renzulli Type III independent projects with underachieving gifted students. For these projects, the student investigates a topic that he or she is interested in, resulting in a product or service. The projects often address problems in the school or community and result in creative works, for example, books, articles, plays, scientific projects, and historical investigations.

In a qualitative study of this technique, five major features of the Type III enrichment process contributed to the intervention's success: (1) the relationship with the teacher, (2) the use of self-regulation strategies, (3) the opportunity to investigate topics related to their underachievement, (4) the opportunity to work on an area of interest in a preferred learning style, and (5) the time to interact with an appropriate peer group. Almost all of the students who completed Type III investigations showed positive gains in either behavior or achievement during the school year. Of the seventeen participants, eleven showed improved achievement, thirteen appeared to exert more effort within their classes, and four showed marked improvement in classroom behavior. These results suggest that flexible, student-centered enrichment may be an effective intervention.

Summary

Most researchers conclude that we need more specific definitions related to gifted or high-ability underachievement. Most agree that the sooner concerned adults are able to identify underachievers, the more opportunities we have to reverse underachievement patterns.

High-ability students who underachieved in high school acknowledged that their underachievement began in elementary school, when they were not provided with appropriate levels of challenge.[55] Students who achieved acknowledged the importance of being grouped together in honors and advanced classes. Successful students received support and encouragement from each other and from adults, including teachers, guidance counselors, coaches, and mentors. Students who achieved took part in multiple extracurricular activities, both after school and during the summer.

Students who underachieved did not exhibit a high belief in self; often came from families that experienced some problems; and were not resilient enough to overcome environmental factors, such as gangs and drugs.

What, then, does the current research tell us about underachievement?

First, it appears that underachievement often begins in elementary school, perhaps due to an unchallenging curriculum. There appears to be a relationship between inappropriate or too-easy content in elementary school and underachievement in middle or high school.

Second, underachievement appears to be periodic and episodic, occurring in some years and not others, and in some classes but not others. However, increasing episodes of underachievement may produce a more chronic pattern.

Third, parental issues interact with the behaviors of some underachievers, yet no clear pattern exists about the types of parental behaviors that may influence underachievement.

Fourth, peers can play a major role in keeping underachievement from occurring in their closest friends, making peer groups an important part of preventing and reversing underachievement.

Fifth, adolescents who are involved in clubs, extracurricular activities, sports, and religious activities tend to be effective learners in school.

Sixth, helping gifted students develop regular patterns of work and practice seems to be very beneficial. Music, dance, and art lessons, combined with regular time for homework and reading, can be helpful for developing positive self-regulation strategies.

Seventh, a caring adult in school can help reverse the process of underachievement. This adult may be a counselor, a coach, or an academic teacher.

Eighth, some students may underachieve as a direct result of an inappropriate and unmotivating curriculum. Before we try to "fix" these students or punish them for their behavior, perhaps we need to try drastic curriculum changes. If the curriculum can't be changed, we may want to reconsider our attitudes toward students who make conscious decisions *not* to put their best efforts into schoolwork that fails to motivate, engage, or challenge them.

Finally, too few interventions have been tried to reverse underachievement, and some interventions do not match the reasons for underachievement.

The heart of the matter is this: our school personnel should consider implementing interventions for gifted students who are underachieving. These young people are too precious a resource to squander.

Notes

1. Conklin, *Failures of Highly Intelligent Pupils.*
2. Gowan, "The Underachieving Child."
3. Renzulli, Reid, and Gubbins, *Setting an Agenda.*
4. Gowan, "Dynamics of the Underachievement of Gifted Students."
5. Pirozzo, "Gifted Underachievers."
6. United States, National Commission on Excellence in Education, *A Nation at Risk*, 8.
7. McCall, Evahn, and Kratzer, *High School Underachievers.*
8. Ibid., 2.

9. Ibid., 2.

10. Shaw and McCuen, "Onset of Academic Underachievement."

11. Baum, Renzulli, and Hébert, "Reversing Underachievement"; Dowdall and Colangelo, "Underachieving Gifted Students"; Emerick, "Academic Underachievement Among the Gifted"; Redding, "Learning Preferences and Skill Patterns"; Rimm, "An Underachievement Epidemic"; Supplee, *Reaching the Gifted Underachiever*; and Whitmore, *Giftedness, Conflict, and Underachievement.* For a more thorough review of issues surrounding the definition and identification of underachievement in gifted students, see Reis and McCoach, "The Underachievement of Gifted Students."

12. Morrow and Wilson, "Family Relations of Bright School Boys."

13. Lukasic, Gorski, Lea, and Culross, *Underachievement Among Gifted/Talented Students.*

14. Fine, *Underachievers: How They Can Be Helped?*; Fliegler, "Understanding the Underachieving Gifted Child"; and Shaw and McCuen, "Onset of Academic Underachievement."

15. Whitmore, *Giftedness, Conflict, and Underachievement.*

16. Rimm, "Underachievement."

17. McCall, Evahn, and Kratzer, *High School Underachievers.*

18. McCall, Evahn, and Kratzer, *High School Underachievers*; and Shaw and McCuen, "Onset of Academic Underachievement."

19. McCall, Evahn, and Kratzer, *High School Underachievers*, 18.

20. Siegle, "Parenting Achievement-Oriented Children."

21. Reis and McCoach, "The Underachievement of Gifted Students"; Siegle, "Parenting Achievement-Oriented Children."

22. Lukasic, Gorski, Lea, and Culross, *Underachievement Among Gifted/Talented Students.*

23. Observations in the previous two sentences are based on Pirozzo, "Gifted Underachievers."

24. Banks, "How Would You Like It if You Were Gifted?"

25. Reis, Hébert, Diaz, Maxfield, and Ratley, *Case Studies of Talented Students.*

26. Ibid.

27. Reis and McCoach, "The Underachievement of Gifted Students."

28. McCall, Evahn, and Kratzer, *High School Underachievers.*

29. Lukasic, Gorski, Lea, and Culross, *Underachievement Among Gifted/Talented Students.*

30. McCall, Evahn, and Kratzer, *High School Underachievers.*

31. Thiel and Thiel, "A Structural Analysis of Family Interaction Patterns"; Whitmore, "The Etiology of Underachievement"; and Whitmore, *Giftedness, Conflict, and Underachievement.*

32. As reported by parents and teachers; Rimm, "Underachievement."

33. Dowdall and Colangelo, "Underachieving Gifted Students."

34. Fine and Pitts, "Intervention with Underachieving Gifted Children."

35. Fine and Pitts, "Intervention with Underachieving Gifted Children"; Thiel and Thiel, "A Structural Analysis of Family Interaction Patterns."

36. Fliegler, "Understanding the Underachieving Gifted Child"; Gowan, "Dynamics of the Underachievement of Gifted Students"; Gurman, "The Role of the Family in Underachievement"; Pirozzo, "Gifted Underachievers."

37. Fliegler, "Understanding the Underachieving Gifted Child"; McIntyre, "Dynamics and Treatment of the Passive-Aggressive Underachiever"; Pirozzo, "Gifted Underachievers."

38. Gurman, "The Role of the Family"; McIntyre, "Dynamics and Treatment of the Passive-Aggressive Underachiever"; Rimm, "Underachievement."

39. Bricklin and Bricklin, *Bright Child, Poor Grades*; Gurman, "The Role of the Family"; McIntyre, "Dynamics and Treatment of the Passive-Aggressive Underachiever."

40. Rimm, "Underachievement"; McIntyre, "Dynamics and Treatment of the Passive-Aggressive Underachiever."

41. McCall, Evahn, and Kratzer, *High School Underachievers*.

42. Bricklin and Bricklin, *Bright Child, Poor Grades;* McIntyre, "Dynamics and Treatment of the Passive-Aggressive Underachiever."

43. Dowdall and Colangelo, "Underachieving Gifted Students"; Whitmore, *Giftedness, Conflict, and Underachievement.*

44. For example, those reported in Supplee, *Reaching the Gifted Underachiever,* and Whitmore, *Giftedness, Conflict, and Underachievement.*

45. Emerick, "Academic Underachievement."

46. Dowdall and Colangelo, "Underachieving Gifted Students"; Emerick, "Academic Underachievement."

47. Dowdall and Colangelo, "Underachieving Gifted Students."

48. Supplee, *Reaching the Gifted Underachiever;* Whitmore, *Giftedness, Conflict, and Underachievement.*

49. Whitmore, *Giftedness, Conflict, and Underachievement;* Supplee, *Reaching the Gifted Underachiever.*

50. Emerick, "Academic Underachievement."

51. Colangelo, Kerr, Christensen, and Maxey, "A Comparison of Gifted Underachievers"; Reis, Hébert, Diaz, Maxfield, and Ratley, *Case Studies of Talented Students.*

52. Emerick, "Academic Underachievement," 145; Renzulli, *The Enrichment Triad Model.*

53. Renzulli, *The Enrichment Triad Model*; Renzulli and Reis, *The Schoolwide Enrichment Model*; Renzulli and Reis, *The Schoolwide Enrichment Model,* 2nd ed.

54. Baum, Renzulli, and Hébert, "Reversing Underachievement."

55. Information in this paragraph drawn from Reis, Hébert, Diaz, Maxfield, and Ratley, *Case Studies of Talented Students.*

References

Banks, R. "How Would You Like It if You Were Gifted?" *Special Education in Canada* 53, no. 2 (1979): 12–14.

Baum, Susan M., Joseph S. Renzulli, and Thomas P. Hébert. "Reversing Underachievement: Creative Productivity as a Systematic Intervention." *Gifted Child Quarterly* 39, no. 4 (1995): 224–235.

Bricklin, Barry, and Patricia M. Bricklin. *Bright Child, Poor Grades: The Psychology of Underachievement.* New York: Delacorte, 1967.

Colangelo, Nicholas, B. Kerr, P. Christensen, and J. Maxey. "A Comparison of Gifted Underachievers and Gifted High Achievers." *Gifted Child Quarterly* 37 (1993): 155–160.

Conklin, Agnes Maria. *Failures of Highly Intelligent Pupils: A Study of Their Behavior by Means of the Control Group.* New York: Teachers College, Columbia University, 1940.

Dowdall, C. B., and Nicholas Colangelo. "Underachieving Gifted Students: Review and Implications." *Gifted Child Quarterly* 26 (1982): 179–184.

Emerick, L. J. "Academic Underachievement Among the Gifted: Students' Perceptions of Factors That Reverse the Pattern." *Gifted Child Quarterly* 36 (1992): 140–146.

Fine, Benjamin. *Underachievers: How They Can Be Helped?* New York: E. P. Dutton, 1967.

Fine, M. J., and R. Pitts. "Intervention with Underachieving Gifted Children: Rationale and Strategies." *Gifted Child Quarterly* 24, no. 2 (1980): 51–55.

Fliegler, L. A. "Understanding the Underachieving Gifted Child." *Psychological Reports* 3 (1957): 533–536.

Gowan, J. C. "Dynamics of the Underachievement of Gifted Students." *Exceptional Children* 24 (1957): 98–122.

———. "The Underachieving Child: A Problem for Everyone." *Exceptional Children* 21 (1955): 247–249, 270–271.

Gurman, A. S. "The Role of the Family in Underachievement." *Journal of School Psychology* 8 (1970): 48–53.

Lukasic, Mary, Vicki Gorski, Melinda Lea, and Rita Culross. *Underachievement Among Gifted/Talented Students: What We Really Know.* Houston, TX: University of Houston—Clear Lake, 1992.

McCall, Robert B., Cynthia Evahn, and Lynn Kratzer. *High School Underachievers: What Do They Achieve as Adults?* Newbury Park, CA: Sage Publications, 1992.

McIntyre, P. M. "Dynamics and Treatment of the Passive-Aggressive Underachiever." *American Journal of Psychotherapy* 19 (1964): 95–108.

Morrow, W. B., and R. C. Wilson. "Family Relations of Bright High-Achieving and Under-Achieving High School Boys." *Child Development* 32 (1961): 501–510.

Pirozzo, R. "Gifted Underachievers." *Roeper Review* 4, no. 4 (1982): 18–21.

Redding, R. E. "Learning Preferences and Skill Patterns Among Underachieving Gifted Adolescents." *Gifted Child Quarterly* 34 (1990): 72–75.

Reis, Sally M., Thomas P. Hébert, E. I. Diaz, L. R. Maxfield, and M. E. Ratley. *Case Studies of Talented Students Who Achieve and Underachieve in an Urban High School.* Research Monograph 95114. Storrs, CT: The National Research Center on the Gifted and Talented, University of Connecticut, 1995.

Reis, Sally M., and D. B. McCoach. "The Underachievement of Gifted Students: What Do We Know and Where Do We Go?" *Gifted Child Quarterly* 44, no. 3 (2000): 152–170.

Renzulli, Joseph S. *The Enrichment Triad Model: A Guide for Developing Defensible Programs for the Gifted and Talented.* Mansfield Center, CT: Creative Learning Press, 1977.

Renzulli, Joseph S., B. D. Reid, and E. J. Gubbins. *Setting an Agenda: Research Priorities for the Gifted and Talented through the Year 2000.* Storrs, CT: The National Research Center on the Gifted and Talented, University of Connecticut, 1990.

Renzulli, Joseph S., and Sally M. Reis. *The Schoolwide Enrichment Model: A Comprehensive Plan for Educational Excellence.* Mansfield Center, CT: Creative Learning Press, 1985.

———. *The Schoolwide Enrichment Model: A How-To Guide for Educational Excellence.* 2nd ed. Mansfield Center, CT: Creative Learning Press, 1997.

Rimm, Sylvia B. "An Underachievement Epidemic." *Educational Leadership* 54, no. 7 (April 1997): 18–22.

———. "Underachievement . . . Or If God Had Meant Gifted Children to Run Our Homes, She Would Have Created Them Bigger." *Gifted Child Today* 31 (1984): 26–29.

Shaw, M. C., and J. T. McCuen. "The Onset of Academic Underachievement in Bright Children." *Journal of Educational Psychology* 51, no. 3 (1960): 103–108.

Siegle, Del. "Parenting Achievement-Oriented Children." *Parenting for High Potential,* December 2000: 6–7, 29–30.

Supplee, Patricia L. *Reaching the Gifted Underachiever: Program Strategy and Design.* New York: Teachers College Press, 1990.

Thiel, R., and A. F. Thiel. "A Structural Analysis of Family Interaction Patterns, and the Underachieving Gifted Child." *Gifted Child Quarterly* 21, no. 2 (1977): 267–276.

United States, National Commission on Excellence in Education. *A Nation at Risk: The Imperative for Educational Reform: A Report to the Nation and the Secretary of Education, United States Department of Education.* Washington, DC: National Commission on Excellence in Education, 1983.

Whitmore, Joanne Rand. "The Etiology of Underachievement in Highly Gifted Young Children." *Journal of the Education of the Gifted* 3, no. 1 (1979): 38–51.

———. *Giftedness, Conflict, and Underachievement.* Boston: Allyn and Bacon, 1980.

14 Surviving in Spite of It All

BY SHAUN HATELY

Shaun Hately has worked in the Australian software industry. In addition, he spent over ten years as a voluntary mentor to gifted children trying to help them avoid some of the problems he encountered, and because of that experience, he is now studying to become an educational professional.

Shaun Hately talks bluntly about what it can *cost* the individual members of a family—emotionally, physically, and financially—to raise and educate a profoundly gifted child. He is a strong survivor. Yet he also copes with clinical depression, an all-too-common "side effect" of giftedness today. In particular, he discusses the ways in which bullying and a rigid school system resulted in suicidal tendencies that fortunately he did not act on. Others among the gifted population are not as well-supported, personally strong, and/or lucky.

I am writing here as someone who had to grow up as a gifted child. That is my perspective. It is a personal one, naturally enough, and cannot be considered representative of the experiences of all gifted children. Regrettably, however, it seems that negative experiences as a result of giftedness, while not universal, are all too common.

I write here as a survivor—I've been lucky enough to have made it. At the age of twenty-five (as I write this), I am well on the path to building a decent career in a field where my gifts are valued and useful. I made it this far because of one overriding reason. My parents went above and beyond all reasonable expectations to do everything in their power to help me. I was lucky to have parents who were both willing and able to do whatever they could to help me.

Their sacrifices were not minor. My mother put her plans for her own future on hold for me. My father died while still a relatively young man from causes that I feel must be attributed, in part, to the stress of having to constantly deal with the problems I placed upon my family. I mention this so that people may understand that my survival and the future I am now (hopefully) beginning to enjoy did not come easily for anyone involved. I am concerned that some people could look at me and feel that I am proof that my experiences weren't that bad, and that my survival by itself means there are no real problems with the experiences some gifted children have to endure. I want it understood that my survival only came at the expense of great sacrifices by others—sacrifices they should not have been expected to make—and that even with those sacrifices, a great deal of luck was involved.

Although I have survived and now look forward to my future, I did not emerge from my schooling unscathed. I bear physical and emotional scars.

Most notably, I am a clinical depressive and the current prognosis is that this condition may have to be controlled by medication for the rest of my life. I spent a great deal of my adolescence suicidal. Although I never actually attempted to take my own life, I seriously considered the idea and came very close on several occasions. Perhaps worse, I contemplated doing harm to others on many occasions. I was a victim of severe bullying, largely because I was different from others, and at times I planned the murder of those who tormented me. Even I am not sure how serious I was about those plans—whether they were simply a release valve for the pain I was feeling, or whether there was more to it. But the feelings were real.

Although my overall school experiences were quite bad, they were not universally so. At times I was lucky enough to have excellent teachers who had a positive effect on my life. And I believe that most of my teachers, even those whose actions hurt me, were honest, committed, and decent people. Some of them were simply unequipped to deal with a child like me.

Because my experiences are now part of history, it is only fair to point out that what happened to me should not be viewed as indicative of how the schools I attended function today. They may have changed dramatically since I left them.

While I firmly believe that no child should ever be placed in a situation where such experiences are likely, I also could have handled things far better. I did not make full use of help, support, and opportunities that were available to me and that would have made things considerably better. I was a child, and like all children I made mistakes. However, the price I paid for those mistakes was far higher than it should have been—and, in most cases, I don't believe I should have had to make those choices.

I will focus here on my experiences and what didn't work to help me. I realize it is much easier to criticize than to find solutions to these problems, but there are people who are far more qualified to find solutions than I am. What I have is my experience in the not-too-distant past, in a modern education system that was not equipped to deal with gifted children. I can highlight some things that didn't work for me, and perhaps give insight as to why they didn't work. But I do not claim to have the answers as to what should be done.

My worst experiences relating to my giftedness involved bullying. Without the bullying, I don't believe I would have experienced anywhere near the same level of problems. Giftedness is not the only cause of a child being bullied, of course. But in my case, I believe it was the most important cause for a number of reasons. And I believe that being bullied because you are gifted carries with it certain aspects that set it apart from more general bullying.

The first aspect relates to self-esteem. Being gifted—being smart— should be a positive element in a person's life. It should be a good thing. When I was bullied because of my intelligence, I had two available choices. I could alter my behavior to hide my intelligence—I could deliberately underperform so nobody would realize I was intelligent. This wasn't good for my academic performance or for my self-esteem. Or I could continue to reveal my intelligence—which meant the bullying continued and I was constantly under pressure from the attitudes expressed by the other kids around me. In this case, I gradually came to wonder if they were right, if something was wrong with me. Again, not good for my self-esteem.

The second aspect to being bullied because I was gifted involved the attitudes of my teachers and the seriousness with which they took the bullying. This affected their attempts to prevent it.

Too often, schools do not take bullying of any sort seriously. Some people regard it as a normal part of childhood. Some even regard it as a positive thing that helps a child to develop a thick skin.

Things weren't quite that bad during my education. Bullying wasn't ignored, but I don't believe it was handled particularly well. Some help and protection was usually available for victims, but far less protection was available for those who were bullied for being more intelligent than others.

When a child was bullied because of a physical infirmity, or for being "slow," or because of race, height, or weight, action was likely taken to try to stop the bullies—and rightly so, because no child should be bullied for any reason. However, when I was bullied or teased, either directly because of my intelligence or indirectly for some other excuse, help and protection were far less likely to be forthcoming.

I was viewed as the problem, not the victim. I was accused of antagonizing the bullies by doing better in class, or by showing off by reading books. Sometimes I was punished for allowing myself to be bullied, while the bullies got off scot-free. The double standard in operation suggested that bullying was not wrong when the victim had an "acceptable" reason for being a target.

I experienced bullying in many forms: verbal taunts, by individuals and by groups of thirty or more; physical assaults, including quite serious attacks; the routine theft and destruction of my homework by other students; deliberate attempts to humiliate me. These were not occasional and isolated instances that could have been missed by my schools. This treatment was systematic and deliberate.

It was also largely ignored, because, in the opinion of at least one school, I was unwilling to hide what I was. A child being teased because of race would not have been told to "act white." Yet I was told, implicitly and explicitly, to "act dumb." The teachers who told me this also told me that I should always do my best, for the sake of my marks.

Bullying and teasing always need to be taken seriously. My experiences lead me to believe that special vigilance is needed when the bullying occurs because a child is gifted. This is not because that child has a greater right to or need for protection, but because that child has the same right and the same need as other children.

The third aspect for my negative experiences as a gifted child at school relates to the rigidity of the education system and its attitudes toward gifted children. Most of my schooling took place in a state where the educational system believed in "equality of outcomes" and that "differences among learners are quantitative, not qualitative in nature." Special educational accommodations for gifted children were seen as elitist or unnecessary.

This is neither unusual nor usual, but, I think, points to one reason why my educational experiences were far less successful than they should have been. Educational practice was based on political theory, or on educational theories that came from politically acceptable sources.

My experiences have led me to believe that decisions about the education of gifted children should be based on evidence about and studies on gifted children. An education system that has already eliminated these children from consideration has little hope of making decisions that will meet their needs. Drawing on my personal history, I can think of several instances when decisions that directly affected my education were made with little consideration of my needs, as compared to the needs of the hypothetical average child.

One example is group work—the idea of children working in groups rather than individually. I am not opposed to this idea. I think it can work well. Yet it was often used in a counterproductive way during my education.

The simple fact was, in most cases, my abilities exceeded those of my classmates. The groups were not balanced and did not benefit me. If group assignments had been made so the assigned tasks required a variety of skills to complete, then group work might have helped me learn. But, for the most part, group tasks were simply larger versions of normal assignments that required only a few specific skills that I already knew.

I was often faced with the reality that if I allowed other people in the group to do any of the work, our group would get a lower mark. So I either had to do all the work (which defeated the point) or accept that my marks would be lowered by the rest of the group. In an academic sense, other members benefitted from my presence in the group, but I suffered because of theirs. I was expected to make my rights subservient to theirs.

Because of the educational philosophies in place, "equality of outcomes" meant placing the most academically able students with the least proficient to even out the marks. This was considered a good idea. If the grouping had been by ability, or even random, this might have been less of a problem for me. As it was, all I could see was that I was expected to put up with an education that didn't meet my needs for the sake of others. And I was in private schools, isolated from the full effects of the political decisions that affected education in my state—so my experiences easily could have been worse.

Different grouping methods were used. I was grouped with the slowest students, on the principle that I would help them achieve better marks, without consideration for my own academic needs. I was grouped with the kids who bullied me, on the principle that this would help us get along better, without consideration that it gave them the opportunity to intimidate me into doing their work. We were allowed to group ourselves with our friends, with no consideration of what this meant for students like me who often had no friends and were put in the position of being forced into a group where we were not wanted. Not once was a group formed with any consideration of my needs. The needs of the gifted child were not considered important in comparison to everyone else's.

As a result, the work offered was only rarely challenging. It was aimed at the supposed average standard in the class. I often had been capable of the material years earlier. Even when a new concept was introduced, it rapidly became boring again as we were required to perform more or less identical problems over and over again. It didn't matter if you answered the first ten questions perfectly—if there were twenty questions, you had to answer twenty. If you happened to finish the twenty before everyone else, then you could do another twenty. Other kids got extra problems as a punishment for talking in class; I got them for working too fast and too well. I rapidly came to view this as a major disincentive to working to my potential.

Other problems resulted from the work being too easy, of course. I found it hard to develop a decent work ethic or study skills, because I did not need these skills. How is somebody supposed to learn how to study when it only takes ten minutes' work to know everything that is expected? The problem is, this doesn't last. At some stage (in my case, around the age of thirteen), work and studying do become necessary. Unlike other people in my classes, I didn't learn this gradually. Most of them progressed from fifteen minutes of homework to thirty minutes, then to an hour or two hours. I went almost instantly from having to do no more than a few minutes to needing an hour. Objectively, the work was still easier for me than for other people. But my learning curve was much steeper and harder to deal with.

As I understand it, children go to school to learn. If so, shouldn't they be taught at a standard that consistently requires them to learn something? Aiming classes at the average student neglects everyone but the average student. Somehow—through genuine individualized instruction, special accommodation in a regular classroom, ability grouping, acceleration, or some other method—it seems critical to make an effort to ensure all children have an education targeted to their needs.

I didn't receive that, and although I made it through, I believe a person should succeed in life *because* of their education, not *in spite of* it. Education should not be a handicap race.

Some opportunities available to me, in many cases, I didn't take full advantage of. Some problems I experienced were partly self-inflicted. Even acknowledging that, it seems like access to those opportunities was based on fundamentally flawed ideas about education.

If I had been willing to work harder in my regular classes, I might have been offered more advanced work—work I really needed. But there is something illogical in requiring success in an inappropriate environment before you may have access to an appropriate one.

A gifted child in a regular heterogeneous classroom with no special support is in an environment not designed to meet that child's needs. Requiring the child to perform in that environment as a condition of access to a more appropriate environment makes about as much sense as throwing an eagle chick into the ocean and requiring it to learn to swim before you let it try to fly.

The education of gifted children should be based on what works for gifted children. Surely that makes sense. Yet in too many cases, it seems like decisions in education are based on how the decision-makers would like the world to be, and not on how it is. Theories have to change to fit the facts, not facts to fit the theories.

It's not an easy life, being one of the facts that needs to be changed.

15 Curriculum Issues for the Profoundly Gifted

BY JOYCE VANTASSEL-BASKA

Joyce VanTassel-Baska is The Jody and Layton Smith Professor of Education at the College of William and Mary, Virginia, where she has developed a graduate program and research and development center in gifted education. She initiated and directed the Center for Talent Development at Northwestern University, and served as a state director of gifted programs, a regional director of a gifted service center, coordinator of gifted programs, and a teacher of gifted high school students. She is widely published and has worked extensively as a consultant on gifted education. She is currently president of the Board of Directors of the National Association of Gifted Children. Her major research interests are the talent development process and effective curricular interventions with the gifted.

As the personal stories have demonstrated, profoundly gifted students need to be educated differently than their age-mates—whether those age-mates are "regular kids" or "gifted." Most parents and school systems feel their way to solutions that work, more or less, but that have high emotional or personal costs, and that certainly evolve more slowly than the kids wish they would.

Joyce VanTassel-Baska provides a clear road map—or more accurately, it's the atlas that so many parents and teachers have been wishing existed—for developing appropriate educational programs for profoundly gifted young people.

Curriculum for gifted students in general requires a careful selection of appropriate materials, learning experiences, and assessment practices that are adapted to the students' advanced learning rates and need for complex opportunities. Yet within the gifted population there exist vast differences with respect to educational, and therefore curricular, need. The profoundly gifted student has a great need for multiple levels of curriculum opportunities at each stage of his or her development.

As a general rule of thumb, this level of student should be provided with work at least two or three grade levels beyond the norm in basic content strands, and instructors should also carefully diagnose levels of functioning in order to document the need for more advanced work. Moreover, in comparison with other students, the profoundly gifted need both more intense and more extended learning opportunities, based on their aptitude areas and interests.

Two guiding principles for judging the appropriateness of curriculum for the highly gifted are that (1) the *rate of learning* must be flexible and sped-up and (2) the *learning experiences* must be complex enough to be challenging. Both parents and teachers need to ensure that highly gifted students are adequately served in these two dimensions through the curriculum experiences that they have.[1]

The most important step in prescribing curriculum for this population is to ensure that the level of challenge is slightly above their tested instructional level in all areas. In order to facilitate this, it may be necessary to engage in multiple forms of acceleration at different stages of development. A grade-skip into first grade and bypassing kindergarten may offer one propitious opportunity, as would early entrance into middle or high school. Early entrance to college by one or two years may also be considered.

Such acceleration alone will be insufficient, however, because it only slightly reduces the disparity between age and intellectual functioning. Moreover, many highly gifted learners have uneven profiles and require tailored curricula that address their "peaks and valleys." Otherwise, disaffection for school-based learning is likely to set in early. Students with highly uneven profiles can also experience increased angst in social-emotional aspects of their development.[2]

Because of the complexity of devising appropriately individualized curricula for these students, this article contains a planning form that parents and educators may use to help them structure appropriate curriculum options.

Peer-Group Issues

Not only do these students require advanced curriculum, they usually also require a small group of students around them who share their interests, passions, and abilities. The nature, scope, and extent of advanced curriculum offerings need to be carefully planned at each developmental stage, necessitating early contact with university-based programs for gifted learners and summer residential experiences, like those run by the Talent Search universities, so the students may acquire an appropriate intellectual peer group.

The profoundly gifted also need access to the encouragement, skills, and conversation of gifted adults, to whom they may relate better than they do to most same-age children. These gifted adults can serve as mentors and role models for these children, providing an informal but readily available support structure. Much of the value of these relationships lies in the social-emotional bonds, built over time, that allow the profoundly gifted to feel comfortable with themselves.

Teachers can be important supports for highly gifted children, too, if they can effectively individualize and personalize learning experiences for them. An enthusiastic and encouraging teacher can spur these students to new heights, if an ethos of care underlies the teacher's effort.[3]

Intervention Areas

Appropriate, high-level challenge in all subject areas is critical to the development of profoundly gifted students as learners. It is particularly important for students who have already distinguished themselves as exceptional learners to receive a curriculum commensurate with their nascent abilities. These students should be challenged by curriculum experiences that extend their knowledge base and deepen their fundamental understanding of key ideas.

In general, curriculum experiences for profoundly gifted learners should provide the following types of components, singly or in combination:

- Challenging, advanced work in traditional subject areas.

- Opportunities to engage in independent and group investigation of problems of interest within and across study areas.

- Opportunities to learn about the world of ideas, as portrayed in various products of civilization over time.

Specific recommendations follow, arranged by area of learning, to illustrate how these three types of curriculum experiences may be integrated.

Recommendations for the Language Arts

Of the academic subjects critical to the healthy development of the profoundly gifted, individualized reading programs may be at the top of the list. These children need books that are suitably advanced and also complex in language and situation. In addition, they benefit from early and ongoing opportunities for reading biography and poetry.

Books may also play a role as bibliotherapy. Reading about characters faced with the same types of problems these students may be having (in such vulnerable areas as developing relationships, perfectionism, and coping with giftedness) may provide a healthy outlet for understanding and expressing feelings.

Literature. In literature, students should have many opportunities to read quality texts, and to respond to them in a variety of ways. Students should read broadly across subject areas, and should be exposed to the genres of poetry, plays, essays, biography, and autobiography. Students should develop a familiarity with favorite authors and their lives. Study should emphasize critical reading and the development of skills in analysis and interpretation.

Writing. The writing program should emphasize the kind of writing that these students will be expected to do in high school and college. It should help them develop skills in expository and persuasive writing, and should teach them the processes of draft development, revision, and editing, as well as techniques for developing ideas and arguments on current issues.

Language study. The formal study of English and word power should be a major component of language study. They should learn to comprehend the syntactic structure of English (grammar) and its concomitant uses (usage), develop vocabulary, understand word relationships (analogies) and origins (etymology), and develop an appreciation for semantics, linguistics, and the history of language.

Oral communication. Profoundly gifted students can profit from a balanced exposure to oral communication, through both listening and speaking. They need to develop evaluative listening skills, debate skills (especially for use in formal argument), and discussion skills (question-asking, probing, and building on ideas stated).

Foreign language. By the time they graduate from high school, profoundly gifted students should learn two foreign languages. Ideally, the primary language would be one for which geography offers abundant follow-up opportunities for use. Good choices for second- and third-language study include Spanish, French, German, Japanese, and Latin.[4]

Recommendations for Science

Science needs to be taught as active inquiry, where the students are real investigators making meaning out of their world. In order for science to be real inquiry, it must have a strong emphasis on concepts, on real problems, and on its integration with other disciplines. Profoundly gifted learners exhibit an unusual readiness to engage in inquiry and exhibit intense curiosity about the world; they are eager to participate in doing real science. Independent investigations involving science can most easily be initiated at the elementary and middle-grade levels, and at that time scientific processes can also be explored in an interdisciplinary framework.

Five key emphases are necessary in science curriculum for these learners:[5]

- Developing an understanding of scientific concepts, especially the concepts of scale, models, change, systems, reductionism, and evolution.

- Developing scientific process skills in collaborative settings.

- Developing a high-level knowledge base in physical, biological, and geological science.

- Engaging in investigations of real problems.

• Developing the scientific habits of mind of curiosity, skepticism, and objectivity.

Recommendations for Mathematics

Work with students who are profoundly gifted in mathematics should employ two approaches. One is to allow these students to go as far as they can in the elementary math sequence and to begin algebra as soon as they indicate readiness. Thus some students may begin algebra at age ten while others may wait until they are twelve or thirteen. In addition, these students need to explore mathematical topics in depth and learn to use mathematics as a tool for learning in other areas. Topics such as probability, statistics, spatial reasoning, problem-solving, and logic may be especially useful to develop across the elementary years, so that these higher-level skills can be effectively applied when they engage in independent work and special interdisciplinary projects.

Interdisciplinary Work

Profoundly gifted students can also profit from well-structured inter-disciplinary programs. *Philosophy for Children* and *Man: A Course of Study* are packaged programs for use at the intermediate and middle school levels that promote an interdisciplinary approach to the humanities. *Challenge of the Unknown* and *Voyage of the Mimi* are mathematics- and science-based programs with excellent interdisciplinary features.[6] Each of these programs uses Socratic questions to stimulate intellectual discussion among students on an issue or theme. They encourage the creation of analogies across a field of inquiry, and they place a high value on interdisciplinary thinking.

Early and ongoing assessment of these children keeps their teachers and parents attuned to the development profiles that emerge over time, as interests and aptitudes come together in new ways. Areas of strength need to be assiduously addressed with commensurate opportunities. Co-curricular options like art, music, chess, or individual sports also form a critical component of their education, because these students will need to have a creative outlet throughout life. These options can be cultivated as mental-health safeguards that will help them stay balanced.

Parental Guidance Concerns

Parents need to know what curriculum is appropriate for their child at the various stages of development. The Center for Gifted Education at the College of William and Mary has published a number of articles and guides to help in identifying these features.[7] Checklists of criteria may be used to ascertain appropriateness of curricula for high-ability children in core subject areas. Parents who have a sense of what would be challenging for the child in each subject domain and strand of the curriculum can better keep track of the child's educational progress in the context of school.

As a follow-up, parents need to monitor curriculum progress. All students have the right to learn something new every day in school. This includes profoundly gifted children. Parents must be in a position to ascertain the extent to which that is a reality. This is difficult for them to do unless they understand how a curriculum is, or is not, appropriate.

For these reasons, parents need to know about curriculum levels and needs. In addition, teachers should use pre-assessment as a diagnostic tool to determine whether students really need a segment of the curriculum. Parents must also be vigilant about making sure this is done. As an important first step, parents can query the principal about the regularity with which pre-assessment is used in a given school. Then they can initiate conversations with the teachers on the same topic. Pre-assessment should be a regular staple in the learning approach, especially at elementary levels. Parents should especially insist on its use at the beginning of the school year in all core subjects.[8]

Ability Grouping

Some form of ability grouping should also be part of the profoundly gifted child's educational trajectory each year. Different and flexible patterns of grouping are fine, as long as the student has intellectual peers for core areas of the curriculum.

This is frequently accomplished by having students move up to the necessary level by changing classrooms for particular subjects, by joining other students in the resource room, or by having a similarly advanced study-mate within the regular classroom. When grouping patterns are flexibly implemented and coordinated, the profoundly gifted child may blossom.

Even better, however, are the comprehensive and integrated settings provided by full-time gifted classes or special schools. Here, with more students likely to be similar in ability and interest, they may flourish.

Nurturing the Profoundly Gifted at Home: Curricular Advice

Many parents think that school will provide these children with their optimum challenges, but often home and out-of-school experiences carry these students through childhood and adolescence. Thus it is incumbent on parents to assume responsibility for providing a high level of challenge and stimulation at home. Ways of doing this include travel, regular trips to museums and libraries, and reading and viewing together as a family. Parents can also share their own passions with their children. A mother's love of archaeology can be taught to the child, and then the pleasures can be shared. A father who loves nature can help a child begin to collect leaves and flowers, and both can experience the wonder of their diversity. These home-based activities are also crucial in the profoundly gifted child's development. They give the parents a chance to get to know the child well and they model a natural give-and-take of educational activities. Even in homes with limited fiscal resources, a rich library of games, puzzles, and books can be built up through the careful selection of presents that meet intellectual needs and interests.

Parent and child can also learn together—taking watercolor lessons, or engaging in a book discussion group. A family can learn a foreign language and then travel to a country where it is spoken, creating a wonderful community connectedness in their learning.

Because building relationships can sometimes be difficult for profoundly gifted children, parents need to help by finding families with parallel interests. A crucial part of effective parenting involves arranging special gatherings where these children can interact at many levels and in many different kinds of activities. A profoundly gifted child may only relate well to a few other children; maximizing exposure to these children will enhance satisfying social relationships.

Parents also need to provide rich supplies of books, magazines, and newspapers, encouraging their profoundly gifted children to read and also to discuss current events or a great book or an interesting idea at the dinner table. For daily stimulation of high-level thinking, the family can consider together these three questions each evening:

- What did you learn today?

- How can you apply that learning to your life?

- How can you use the learning to help others?

Parents who instill a clear respect for knowledge and its power to make a better world begin to create their children's value systems and pave the way for future contributions to the larger society.

Older profoundly gifted students need opportunities to try out their abilities and skills in "real world" settings and to discover how interests and predispositions affect career planning. One high school girl, who had just completed a one-semester internship/mentorship working with a female pediatrician, opened her project report with this insight: "I was so pleased to have had this internship as I learned that I never want to be a doctor." This unexpected conclusion constituted a real growth experience for her. Providing service to others in the community can also spark deeper appreciation for hidden gifts and talents.

Conclusion

Planning effective curriculum for profoundly gifted children remains a unique challenge for parents and schools. The effort must balance an appreciation of these students' abilities with a profound respect for their interests; their cognitive developmental needs with their social and emotional levels; and their strengths with their relative weaknesses. The ongoing task requires great skill and patience from caring adults. Hopefully, concern and a good plan of action for each stage of development can guide these exceptional learners on a positive trajectory for talent development.

Notes

||||||||||||||||||||||||||||||||||||||||||||||||||||||||||||||||||||||||||||||||||||||||||||||||||||||||||||||||||||||||||||

1. VanTassel-Baska, *Excellence in Educating Gifted and Talented Learners.*

2. VanTassel-Baska and Little, *Content-Based Curriculum for High-Ability Learners.*

3. VanTassel-Baska, "The Development of Talent Through Curriculum."

4. VanTassel-Baska, Johnson, and Boyce, *Developing Verbal Talent.*

5. VanTassel-Baska, *Excellence in Educating Gifted and Talented Learners.*

6. See the special list of resources for interdisciplinary work, following the references at the end of this chapter.

7. Johnson, Boyce, and VanTassel-Baska, "Science Curriculum Review."

8. VanTassel-Baska, *Curriculum Planning and Design for High-Ability Learners.*

References

||||||||||||||||||||||||||||||||||||||||||||||||||||||||||||||||||||||||||||||||||||||||||||||||||||||||||||||||||||||||||||

Bruner, Jerome S. *Man: A Course of Study.* Cambridge, MA: Educational Services, 1965.

————. *Toward a Theory of Instruction.* Cambridge, MA: Belknap Press of Harvard University, 1966.

Johnson, Dana T., Linda Neal Boyce, and Joyce VanTassel-Baska. "Science Curriculum Review: Evaluating Materials for High-Ability Learners." *Gifted Child Quarterly* 39, no. 1 (Winter 1995): 36–43.

Rogers, Karen B. "Using Current Research to Make 'Good' Decisions About Grouping." *NASSP Bulletin* 82, no. 595 (February 1998): 38–46. Bulletin published by National Association of Secondary School Principals.

VanTassel-Baska, Joyce. *Comprehensive Curriculum for Gifted Learners.* Boston: Allyn and Bacon, 1994.

————. *Curriculum Planning and Instructional Design for Gifted Learners.* Denver, CO: Love, 2003.

————. "The Development of Talent through Curriculum." *Roeper Review* 18, no. 2 (December 1995): 98–102.

————. *Excellence in Educating Gifted and Talented Learners.* Denver, CO: Love, 1998.

VanTassel-Baska, Joyce, Dana T. Johnson, and Linda Neal Boyce, eds. *Developing Verbal Talent: Ideas and Strategies for Teachers of Elementary and Middle School Students.* Boston: Allyn and Bacon, 1996.

VanTassel-Baska, Joyce, and C. Little, eds. *Content-Based Curriculum for High-Ability Learners.* Austin, TX: Prufrock Press, 1991.

Resources for Interdisciplinary Work

||||||||||||||||||||||||||||||||||||||||||||||||||||||||||||||||||||||||||||||||||||||||||||||||||||||||||||||||||||||||||||||||||||||||||||||||||||||||

Challenge of the Unknown. A series of seven films on math and problem solving. New York: W.W. Norton, 1984. A description of the program is located at www.wbra.org/html/edserv/teach/ITVProgPDF/challenge_unknown.PDF (accessed May 2, 2007). Public television stations sometimes schedule airings of the series.

Man: A Course of Study (MACOS). Developed by Jerome Bruner for middle school and upper elementary grades. A good description of the course can be found at www.coe.ufl.edu/CT/Projects/MACOS.html. Some films used in the curriculum, developed by the National Film Board of Canada and the Education Development Center, Inc., in Newton, Massachusetts, can be located at secure.edc.org/publications/list.asp?97. (Sites accessed May 2, 2007.) See also Bruner listings under references for this chapter.

Philosophy for Children. Developed by the Institute for the Advancement of Philosophy for Children (IAPC), Montclair State College, 14 Normal Avenue, Montclair, NJ 07043, 973-655-4278; cehs.montclair.edu/academic/iapc/ (accessed May 2, 2007).

The Voyage of the Mimi and *The Second Voyage of the Mimi.* Developed by The Bank Street College of Education. Multimedia, interactive, and interdisciplinary programs, including thirteen video episodes for the first voyage and twelve for the second, plus software and print materials. Information is available at www.bankstreetcorner.com/voyages_of_mimi.shtml (accessed May 2, 2007).

16

Of Importance, Meaning, and Success

Application for Highly and Profoundly Gifted Students

BY CHRISTINE S. NEVILLE

Christine S. (Tee) Neville has served in education as a teacher (kindergarten through graduate school), elementary administrator, teacher center director, supervisor of gifted and talented, teacher trainer, high school principal, and college gifted program founder and director (Mary Baldwin College Program for Exceptionally Gifted). She is currently founder and head of school of The Academy for Gifted Children of Greater Cincinnati, Inc. (www.giftedacademygc.org).

When she was a student herself, Christine "Tee" Neville began to consider the process of learning and the ability of schools to support students' growth. Over the following decades, she continued her analysis and ultimately defined the critical components of effective learning in the form of three simple concepts: *importance, meaning,* and *success.* Her path to this understanding blends personal discovery with the educator's natural desire to make learning rewarding for others.

My concern for the least-supported population of students in the nation, the highly and profoundly gifted, began as far back as high school. Considering the needs of this special population has been part of every job I have held in education, and at times it has been my primary focus. After thirty-five years as a professional educator, I have distilled most of my concerns and questions about the critical components for effective learning into three simple concepts: *importance, meaning,* and *success.*

Personal Perspective

I began to look at schools and the process of learning during my junior year of high school, when I was told to think about college and what I might do with my future. The search for a college became complicated, because I had no particular focus and had been largely untouched by the academics of high school. At the time, I was captivated by animals and was considering veterinary science—until I saw a documentary film and watched a vet's arm disappear inside a convulsing cow. Nor did the bedpan aspect of nursing appeal to me. I did know that I enjoyed tutoring younger students, thanks to successful sessions helping ninth-graders make meaning out of the mysterious (to them) subject of social studies. So I began to think about a career in teaching and learning.

I was acutely aware that little that had been offered to me as a student up to that point had made much of an impact. I remember some excitement from the elementary level, but nothing academically intriguing about junior high school. Although I attended an excellent, college-preparatory high school in a well-funded school district, I had long since stopped working for high As because I could not force myself to do the required minutiae. I poured my abundant energy into drama, the school political process, musicals, being social, and learning to ski. I remember having fun with several groups of friends, but I can't recall much about the academic side of high school. The only math class that made sense was geometry. Biology and public speaking seemed practical, and I enjoyed the challenge of one English teacher. But the only classes I really remember were AP International Relations and French V, both from my senior year.

Learning in college was a whole new experience for me. I began to enjoy the small, interactive, seminar classes, and I found my voice. My ideas became important to professors and classmates, so I shared them. I studied for the first time *because I wanted to know,* not because the work was assigned. I attended a women's college, so I had many strong women as role models and all of the student-body leadership positions were held by young women. I was learning every day about human interaction and the science of getting things done. In addition, there were few male/female distractions during the week.

I joined an experimental program in elementary education that emphasized the needs of the individual student, diversity of activities, and discovery-and-mastery learning. I learned to teach by being observed every day by my college professors, with daily constructive feedback. We had no methods courses, because we were required to discover ourselves as learners and then to create our teaching profile as it applied to the needs of our students. We had to be clear about how to match our teaching strengths to the needs of each student. The experience was a minute-by-minute, day-by-day discovery of learning. For once, I was on fire with a wonderful passion. As a byproduct, I found myself on the dean's list.

My passion for the art and science of teaching and learning never abated. Since 1966, I have served as a teacher from kindergarten through upper elementary school, middle school, high school, college, and graduate school. In public schools, I have supervised instruction as an elementary school principal, teacher-center director, supervisor of gifted and talented education, high school assistant principal for instruction, and high school principal. I designed and founded the Program for Exceptionally Gifted (PEG) at Mary Baldwin College, now in its seventeenth successful year. I am currently head of school for The Academy of Greater Cincinnati, Inc. It is one of two schools in Ohio specifically designed for gifted children.

After all of these rich experiences, I have concluded that the public education system is too big and entrenched to provide for the needs of students who do not fit. Until recently, I held onto my faith that a dedicated, passionate, informed individual teacher could make the changes required to accommodate the needs of special students. But I have finally had to admit that it is next to impossible to meet the learning needs of highly and profoundly gifted children in public schools, as those schools are currently structured. Most schools cannot, or will not, institute the flexibility that values highly or profoundly gifted youngsters, the learning activities that ensure a meaningful experience for such students, and teachers skilled enough to construct rigorous learning sequences that lead these students to a profound sense of success.

Simply put, it takes the application of *importance, meaning,* and *success* to ensure learning for our most capable children. These three critical elements must be present for any learning to take place. Unfortunately, the schools that recognize and design programs for our most able learners are few and far between. Effective learning occurs when the student feels valued or *important* in the learning process, when that which is to be learned holds *meaning* for the learner, and when the learner is supported through the entire learning progression until *success* is achieved.

Of Importance

What is required to give highly and profoundly gifted students a sense of their own value in the learning process? First, they must be recognized for who they are. Their teachers must be able to see, enjoy, and *value* highly and profoundly (H/P) gifted students. And the students' asynchronous development is a given, and must be understood.

The idea of asynchronous development was first articulated in 1991 at a meeting of theorists, practitioners, and parents in Columbus, Ohio. The group devised this definition:

> Giftedness is *asynchronous development* in which advanced cognitive abilities and heightened intensity combine to create inner experiences and awareness that are qualitatively different from the norm. This asynchrony increases with higher intellectual capacity. The uniqueness of the gifted renders them particularly vulnerable and requires modifications in parenting, teaching, and counseling in order for them to develop optimally.[1]

As a result of the qualitatively different way in which H/P gifted children interpret their life experiences, they have a deep understanding of how the world works that can't be denied. They cannot hide it, and other people have difficulty grasping what they are thinking.

One kindergarten child said to her mother, "Mommy, I like school well enough, I just miss learning so much!" Nothing new had been introduced to this youngster in the first four months of kindergarten. Under the circumstances, it would be difficult for this child to feel that her learning needs were important.

In a similar instance, a first grader stood at the morning bus stop with her neighbors. Everyone was talking and laughing. The first grader remarked,

"This is so much fun, we could have a sleepover." As all the children cheered in excitement, the first grader continued, " . . . and we could all play chess!" The idea was met with dead silence. A child who enjoys the complicated strategies of chess will feel very lonely in a group of children whose development doesn't include even a vague interest in such a game.

Classmates and teachers who do not understand that these children are *normal for who they are* could consider these two children strange.

In another example, a math teacher was working with a class of six-year-old gifted children on combinatorics, or ways to combine numbers to get a particular number as an answer. Examples might be $2 + 5 = 7$, $21 / 3 = 7$, $-12 + 19 = 7$, $56 - 49 = 7$, and so on. After the class had been working for about ten minutes, one six-year-old raised his hand and asked the following question: "If we kept going, there wouldn't be an end, would there? I mean, we could just keep combining forever. . . ." He had discovered the concept of infinity. The teacher was blown away, and no other child in the class had a clue what he meant. If the teacher of a child like this cannot help him learn conceptually appropriate math and find other children of similar ability to interact with, the child will not feel important.

In order to feel valued or important, H/P gifted children need H/P gifted adults who are master teachers and they need an intellectual peer group with whom to learn. A solitary H/P gifted child in a class with students of differing abilities leads a lonely existence. High anxiety penetrates the child who cannot be understood because his thoughts are too far out, or whose intense reactions to situations are perceived to be way out of line.

If a highly capable child remains in such an educational wasteland, excitement over learning will dwindle away before long. The child may either withdraw or express anger and hostility toward those who don't get it. Both aggressiveness and withdrawal lead to social isolation, feeling badly about oneself, and an overwhelming sense of frustration at not learning anything. Children in this kind of a situation quickly learn that they are not important enough to have their needs met.

As a critical component of their learning experiences, H/P gifted children need intellectual peers with whom to share their learning activities. In order to feel normal in their own skin, they need to be with other people who can appreciate the ways they think, understand their humor, and share in their unalterable drive to learn. Learners who have similar abilities and interests need to be together in the thrill of discovery, to be mutually respected for the depth of their knowledge, and to have the opportunity to enjoy the company of other complex thinkers. They need to see themselves reflected back in the actions and words of other people who care deeply about the issues of life, who feel a deep emotional reaction to art or music, who feel revved all the time and may have little need for sleep. They need to experience others who love the structural logic of an explanation or enjoy similar flights of fancy and imagination.

Polish psychologist and psychiatrist Kasimirez Dabrowski identified five overexcitabilities (OEs), or areas of intensity, that explain ways in which H/P gifted children express heightened response to stimuli.[2] The five areas of intensity as explained by Dabrowski are: *psychomotor, intellectual, sensual, imaginational,* and *emotional.* The recognition of seemingly greatly exaggerated responses to events and specific stimuli are a bonding force among highly and profoundly gifted individuals. Gifted young people experience great relief when they see and feel the heightened intensities of the people—young and old—around them. When they can associate with people who respond as they do, H/P gifted children begin to accept themselves and their intensities as normal. They can then begin to let go of their instinctive tendency to hide their intense reactions for fear of being misunderstood.

To help a group of H/P gifted third-grade children understand one another and learn a level of tolerance, I taught them the Dabrowski OEs. Once the students had studied the psychomotor intensity, the group began to understand very differently an annoying overabundance of energy that three students exhibited. They saw that the energy was inherent, a part of the person that was quite difficult to curb. The class became much more accepting of classmates who were wildly creative or exceptionally emotional. Students could recognize the intensities in each other, and they learned to enjoy the vigorous intellectual give-and-take of argument, discussion, and debate.

Another group of upper-elementary H/P gifted children seemed to be bouncing off the walls. They were unable to focus and constantly aggravated one another. A presentation of the OEs helped them see themselves accurately and helped the teacher understand them as a group. When they charted their OEs as a group, everyone in the class had imaginational OE as their greatest intensity, followed closely by psychomotor OE. The class was naturally revved with energy. Throwing a new idea out to the group was like throwing gasoline on a fire! They simply had to have time to emote, babble, express, and allow their excitement to run its course before they could move on. The increased understanding changed the direction of classroom management from *controlling* to *channeling* the high energy. When the students knew who they were and knew that their teacher understood their intensities, the class became more relaxed and could develop a sense of community. Very different kinds of learning became possible. Students who feel valued are much more open to the behaviors of others.

In magnet schools, special schools for gifted children, summer programs, conferences, and institutes designed for H/P gifted children and adults, you can see and feel the positive excitement and self-acceptance that occur when H/P gifted folks recognize their own qualities in other people. You can also see these results in H/P gifted students who return from a summer experience. They walk down the school corridor with new self-confidence and belief in themselves, thanks to the summer's challenges and safe environment. You can feel these students emoting, *"I am OK. I am not alone. I know, because I spent the summer where there were lots of kids just like me."*

"You may wonder why we continually enter contests and work together to create things. It is because our math classes and some others do so little for us." This was the opening statement made by two high school seniors for the presentation of their completed project for the Discovery Program at a well-respected high school in Maine. They had spent all year creating a working model of a remote-controlled submersible with video capabilities, which they had tested successfully in the harbor down the street from the school. This project carried no grade and none of the limitations of a class assignment. Both boys designed and constructed their submersible for the pure joy of the challenge. The thrill of success showed all over them as they described their process of invention to the Community Committee. They needed the excitement of figuring out all of the project details and they clearly came away from the experience with a deeper sense of their own worth than they had received from typical high school classes.

The Program for Exceptionally Gifted (PEG) at the Mary Baldwin College provides a college program in which high school girls complete high school and college in four to five years. Students live together in an environment they help design and govern. They take their academic courses in the college community, and many go off to graduate school at age 18. The program has been successful because the girls feel valued in that learning environment. Their emotional and social needs are met in an appropriate teenage residential setting, while their high intellects flourish with the rich array of college courses under the guidance of highly capable professors.

Meaning

Learning activities must be connected to meaning for the learner. Whatever is to be learned will become part of a student's repertoire more effectively if it is connected to a student interest or extends from an existing foundation. Highly and profoundly gifted children experience the world from their own qualitatively different point of view. What they see and interpret, based on their accumulated life experience, is very different from that of their average age-peers. At a very early age, they may have a sophisticated under-standing of our symbol systems for language and math, an understanding that opens them to a deeper interpretation of the world and an asynchronous way of receiving and processing information. As toddlers, they observe and wonder about things. They ask, "Why?" They see the gap between what is and what ought to be in the world, a gap that may cause unusually strong reactions and the development of a remarkable sense of universal rights and wrongs. What holds meaning for an H/P gifted student will be very different from what holds meaning for average children and for children at lower levels of giftedness. A teacher must be highly skilled in the art and science of teaching to build learning in a context that holds meaning for H/P gifted students.

An illustration from my past has haunted me over the years. I was placed in an advanced Algebra I class, where I was one of two girls grouped with twenty-two boys. I knew everyone from the year before, so I wasn't concerned about being in the class. Our youngish male teacher was passionate about mathematics. He posed ideas and possibilities that I had never considered before, and I soon became aware of how happy and excited all the boys seemed to be as they played with the mathematical concepts. Much of the "playing and messing around" with math was done verbally, and I couldn't always follow the thinking. I had no frame of reference to use as a foundation, and at the time I didn't know that I was a visual learner. Intimidated, I began to dread the class. I felt so limited, and scared of what I thought I didn't understand. A few written examples on the board tied to my previous learning might have been all that I needed, but without that assistance I became less confident and more terrified each day.

I never asked questions for clarification and never requested help. I thought I had lost my ability to do math, so my mother had me changed to regular Algebra I. Result: algebra and its derivatives—Algebra I, Algebra II, and Trigonometry—were lost to me forever, because arithmetic never held any meaning for me. I slogged through the classes with good grades but no understanding. I aced geometry because it all made sense, but avoided any other contact with math. Not until the math analysis part of my doctoral program did I see that math was just another symbol system for representing information and actions. Then, the system held clear meaning because I could use it to carry out and explain my research. I enjoyed the course and was the top student.

I have seen situations similar to mine over and over again. Highly gifted students who learn from a conceptual framework die on the vine in a classroom where learning is not anchored in meaning, specifically meaning *at their level*. I suffer with students who are held back from conceptual math because they cannot master addition or multiplication facts in a void. I wince when highly gifted learners are given massive long-division practice sheets, or are told they cannot do algebra until they produce perfect scores on timed tests of basic facts. I have watched students wither under those conditions.

Because the human need to make meaning is so intense, many H/P gifted students might be considered *connective learners*, a concept coined by writer and researcher Stephanie Tolan and clinical child psychologist Deirdre Lovecky to explain what happens to H/P gifted students in school situations that do not require the engagement of the brain. During an unmotivating lecture or while trying to complete repetitive worksheets, they may leapfrog from idea to idea and disappear entirely from the task at hand. A term that was often directed at me in similar situations was *daydreaming*, but today I call students who disappear into their own learning modes my *Ozone Walkers*. Their minds go off on wonderful tangents as their ideas connect on and on—off into the "ozone." It is beautiful to watch this happen when two H/P gifted students come together on a classroom task, which may not tantalize them. One idea leads to another, and they take off together into a world that may have nothing to do with the assignment. Alert teachers who see and properly interpret these wonderful flights have at their disposal valuable information they can use to build tasks based on students' interests and meaning frameworks.

I'm not sure we can blame students for gliding away on the excitement of intricate ideas when their assigned activities are not grounded in personal meaning. Too often, the Ozone Walking is seen as wasting time and is punished. One of my students was struggling mightily with Algebra II. During lecture or class work, his mind would take flight and he would be off to the "ozone." While he was "gone," his hand would move, creating a doodle on his paper. He could often explain where his head had been by looking at the doodle. His teacher once threatened to throw him out of class if he doodled again. We both knew he was doomed, so I found a retired college professor to tutor him. Together they gave meaning to Algebra II and worked on it with respect, humor, and intensity. The student learned avidly because his new teacher accepted and valued him as a good thinker. I watched his confidence and mathematical understanding grow every time he and his tutor met.

Integrated learning works well with H/P gifted children at all ages. A kindergarten teacher who provides experiences in all subject areas dealing with, for example, oil, could offer children cooking activities using math; science projects involving oil properties; discovery activities about an oil spill, including cleanup methods and environmental implications; all the different uses of oil and how oil affects our lives; and on and on. Students could write, speak, experiment, read, discover, and do social studies for days using oil as a focus. Similarly, older students studying inventions in science could incorporate all of the core-curriculum subject areas into the topic and then move into a unit on frontiers of many realms other than science, still including all of the disciplines. The obvious high school humanities classes that include history and English could also incorporate the fine arts, to add depth and richness.

Science at the high school level has been artificially separated into distinct disciplines for over a hundred years. It makes no scientific sense to study biology, chemistry, and physics separately. It also makes little sense to keep math separate from science. Science uses mathematics, and courses that can naturally be combined ought to be.

In the early years of PEG, the students came to the program with no high school science, and the biology professor taught a chemical biology that incorporated both disciplines. He believed that the PEG students could learn the content and the processes needed for both chemistry and biology in one intense course built around laboratory experimenting. He was correct. Some PEG students majored in the sciences, and when they reached a personal knowledge gap or a weak spot in later, higher-level courses, they simply received extra help at the time. H/P gifted students are quick studies when challenged and engaged. They were able to keep up and do exceptionally well academically because everything worked together to build meaningful understandings. Many PEG students have gone on to earn doctorates in the sciences.

All high school science courses need to integrate physics, chemistry, and biology. The math that students need can be a prerequisite, and the math course they take along with the science could use the science topic of the week for the applications. Another way of integrating disciplines for H/P gifted children is working in a similar way for a group of H/P gifted second graders. They opened the school year with *relationships* as the theme. They looked at *relationship* in all the disciplines and developed a community of caring in their classroom. They researched the relationship between early cultures and modern times; studied where words come from; and used *The Phantom Tollbooth* to understand parts of speech, explore humor, and see what happens when words are put together in different ways. Students also worked hands-on using the inquiry method to determine relationships in the field of science.

At this writing, this same group of H/P gifted second graders has embarked on a library project, approved by the faculty in a gifted school that has no librarian. Using computers and an interdisciplinary approach, the students will organize the school library. They will categorize books, implement an electronic check-out system, determine where the school collection has gaps, and run an entire e-commerce system over the Internet to get books donated to the school and shipped to the library by United Parcel Service. They will sort the books according to use. Then they will negotiate with a nearby used-book dealer to sell him the books the school doesn't need, using the resulting credit to buy books the school does need. The students have already used math to figure expenses, possible revenues, and percentages. They have written the project proposal, advertisements, and newsletter articles, and are creating the e-commerce Web site. They have studied supply and demand, cost-benefit theory, and the Library of Congress cataloging system. They are keeping an ongoing list of library materials that the school needs. Everyone in the class is involved with the project, which they designed to meet a real need. They are learning so much that they are about to burst with excitement.

An amazing difference can be made in the lives of H/P gifted children by guaranteeing that every learning activity builds on an established foundation and extends understanding into new realms. In order to accomplish this with H/P gifted children, a teacher or co-learner needs to know what students already know and what interests them, and then needs to devise a wide variety of ways to reach intended outcomes. We all know that H/P gifted children can be avid learners. The personal connection is the key. It provides them with the opportunity to figure things out for themselves in an environment that safely provides continuous feedback toward improvement.

Success

What does *success* mean? How does one measure it? When does a learner feel most successful? *Success* in this context would mean meeting preset goals or expectations. Success could be measured by demonstrating knowledge or skills actively performed; on a test using paper and pencil or computer; by making an oral presentation; or by participating in group discussion, debate, simulation, case study, and/or problem-solving. Highly and profoundly gifted children feel most successful when they have had to work to meet an expectation. They need challenges, as well as the time, resources, and support to meet those challenges. Learning takes effort when the learner is stretching to make new meaning, figuring out how something works, or solving an unknown problem. The presentation of an idea, research results, or a plan of action requires effort when a learner meets high standards. For H/P gifted students, the feeling of being successful comes after the insatiable drive to find out about something is complete. A strong set of emotions is unleashed when an important set of criteria is met. It just feels good to accomplish something that has taken effort and intellectual prowess. It is the completion of the task that is the reward, not necessarily the assessment that is attached. The amazing light that glows on a student's face is the best reward both for teaching and for learning.

Highly and profoundly gifted learners are filled with questions, ideas, and an amazing drive to find out about things. They have dreams and big ideas that may or may not be realized, because they may not have the tools for learning how to learn. They may be excited about an idea but not know how to begin—how to brainstorm and organize all of their questions. They may see an amazing model or prototype but lack the resources to put it together if they had a plan, or the simple perseverance it takes to complete a complex assignment. People who succeed have a plan. They work the plan to meet expectations. They do not quit when they find an obstacle. They figure out a way around the obstacle and they ask for help when they need it. They put in the necessary effort, accept support from interested people, and pay attention to the criteria spelled out in the expectations, or create and meet criteria they set themselves.

Highly and profoundly gifted students need certain skills if they are to successfully follow their dreams, and many books provide long lists of these skills. For example, the compendium of communication skills includes listening, active listening, giving appropriate response, note-taking, informal writing, formal writing, written presentation, effective discussion, debate, public speaking with and without visuals, reading for information, reading to respond, and using computers. The *Schoolwide Enrichment Model*, edited by Joseph Renzulli and Sally Reis, includes comprehensive lists of learning-how-to-learn skills. Joyce VanTassel-Baska presents many skills in the *Comprehensive Curriculum for Gifted Learners* that must be included in curriculum developed for gifted students. Lists of necessary skills are presented for learning across the various disciplines, for creative and critical thinking, problem solving, inquiry learning, research, locating resources, and the use of computers as tools to support learning. Highly and profoundly gifted students can be effective in teams of students with similar abilities, but because these youngsters have experienced isolation in general-education programs, they often have not had much opportunity to work cooperatively. For some students of extreme ability, becoming an effective team member takes time, constructive feedback, and consistent practice. They are much more successful at mastering teamwork with intellectual peers.

Highly and profoundly gifted students do not always demonstrate perseverance. Our most capable students may not stick with tasks to completion. It is disturbing to watch them come up against an obstacle, perceive that they cannot succeed easily, and quit. I find myself wondering whatever happened to, "If at first you don't succeed, try, try again," or "It will take lots of elbow grease to accomplish this." I remember my family reading the story of *The Little Engine that Could* to me as a child, and that story made an impression. The little engine took on a heavy burden, faced a large hill, and got to the top by repeating to itself, "I think I can! I think I can!" Another often-repeated slogan in my youth was, "Anything worth doing takes effort." Highly and profoundly gifted children who have slithered through in general education without much effort do not know how to work at something that does not come easily to them.

According to Larry Lezotte of the Effective Schools Movement, the research on effective schools shows that effort is the most vital ingredient in the formula for success.[3] If effort is critical to success, then H/P gifted students need human support to help them put forth effort often enough to understand the difference it makes. An understanding but determined mentor can make all the difference in the world to a student who does not know the meaning of trial and error, especially when solid family backing is missing. Young people with big ideas get discouraged when they run into roadblocks, discover that their idea won't work the way they envisioned it, don't know how to access the resources they need, or are too proud to admit that they need help. We—their families, teachers, friends, and mentors—need to help them deal with defeat, learn perseverance, and open themselves to the principle of multiple approaches to challenges. We may need to force them to finish so they will develop the habit; we may need to stand back so they can figure things out on their own; and at other times we may need to be right there, close by, every step of the way, cheering them on and coaching them to successful completion.

Success has a delicious taste. On the other hand, students who put forth effort but do not reach success may not try as hard the next time, and may eventually give up altogether. Students who work hard and meet success will often try again because they know what success feels like. In the 1970s, William Glasser, the American psychiatrist who developed Reality Therapy and Choice Theory, told a story to make this point. A young man on his way to catch a bus sees the bus pull up to his bus stop. People begin to board. He starts to run, because he really wants to make the bus. But as he draws near, the bus pulls out into traffic and moves away. The young man puts more power into his run and shouts for the bus to wait. If that extra energy pays off and he makes the bus, he will likely try to make the bus again or will plan his timing better. If he cannot catch the bus in spite of his extra effort, he will be less likely to run after it the next time. If he learns over and over that extra effort does not end in success, he will eventually decide that the goal of making that bus is not worth the effort.

In the context of H/P gifted children, we could focus on the student who can hardly wait to go to kindergarten. She has watched for four years as the neighbor children have left on the bus for school and come home on the bus at the end of the school day. She loves learning more than anything, so with great anticipation she goes off to kindergarten to learn all those dreamed-for things. If she could read at age two or three and at three-and-a-half was donating her piggy bank full of pennies to help world hunger, she may have her own asynchronous sense of how the world should be. She may think naively that all the other children are just like her. If she understands that a tree gets water from the dirt into its roots, that the water goes up into the tree and out through the leaves where it goes to the sky and then comes down to the earth again in the form of rain, and she thinks about fairness in terms of universal justice, what may happen to her passion for learning when no one else in the class is comfortable with her thinking? What happens when her teacher and classmates are appalled by her intense reactions to pain or beauty? What will happen to her excitement if she is reminded to be quiet so that the others can answer some of the questions, or when she finishes the number puzzles and there are no more? What happens to the light in her eyes if she goes day after day with nothing new to learn? What happens to her high energy when she is rarely, if ever, given an opportunity to stretch her thinking? What happens to her will to succeed when everything she is asked to do is something she already knows how to do? What happens to her ability to interact with her classmates when they don't understand why she wants to design the Alaska pipeline with her blocks, or why she refuses to play in a game if they don't follow the rules? If she finds no understanding or support for her unusual needs, she may decide that she doesn't want to ride that bus after all.

Being highly or profoundly gifted makes a child stand out in a crowd of average learners. A child who is "twice-gifted," and has a learning difficulty as well as exceptional ability, inhabits an almost unbearable situation. A student who is highly gifted, with several additional complications, recently said to her mother, "I know I am unique but it is so hard to be this different!"

Students with unusual educational needs beyond their giftedness need to have the giftedness addressed first, and then their other learning needs. They must study and learn with intellectual peers so their minds are continually engaged at challenging levels. Learning disabilities in spelling, handwriting, reading, and other forms of processing must be supported within the context of giftedness. The anthology *Uniquely Gifted: Identifying and Meeting the Needs of Twice-Exceptional Students,* edited by Kiesa Kay, provides detailed information on helping twice-gifted children achieve success. Highly and profoundly gifted students with sensory integration difficulties, hyperactivity, illnesses such as asthma or diabetes, or an array of specific learning disabilities need to be with their intellectual peers. Fortunately, their difficulties are more likely to be understood and accepted by H/P gifted students, who have themselves experienced the pain of being isolated. Parents and learning-disability specialists must be enlisted to help teachers of twice-gifted children adapt assignments, shorten writing requirements, and change testing situations as needed. Twice-gifted children may need parent volunteers or mentors to provide support for the many complex thinking activities expected of H/P gifted children.

Highly and profoundly gifted children tend to be rapid thinkers. A single story idea may flow rapidly into an amazing complexity of scenarios. I have worked closely with extreme giftedness in the elementary grades, and have witnessed brilliant students who turn in disappointing writing consisting of bare-bones thoughts presented in simple sentences. It is discouraging to read such spare writing from these students, when their oral communication can be so eloquent and rich. I have come to name this situation the "train effect." Using this metaphor, the thoughts of H/P gifted children can be seen as moving through the brain like a rushing train. It is exceedingly difficult to write down the words as they speed by. If fine-motor control is not well developed and a child lacks rapid keyboarding skills, what too often ends up on paper are a few key words put together as simple sentences. The complex wording that occurs in the brain rushes by like the string of lighted windows on a train. It is next to impossible for rapid thinkers to write down each window as it rushes by. This becomes extremely frustrating for the H/P gifted child. Writing is seen as a pain-fully inadequate process to be avoided at all costs. So you have amazingly bright children who cannot or will not express themselves in written form. This is a major problem in any school setting where writing is expected. The extreme frustration could be relieved somewhat by providing an adult or older student to take dictation from students, so the richness of their thinking is not lost. If the teacher wants to assess the thinking, he or she can ask the parents to listen to their children and write down answers that demonstrate the quality of that thinking. Students with writing difficulty due to the "train effect" will benefit greatly from voice-to-print computer programs when they become more user-friendly and effective. In order for "train effect" children to achieve success, they need special consideration and support when a written presentation is necessary.

Highly and profoundly gifted children find increased success as members of a group of intellectual peers. Because their special learning needs are understood and honored by those around them, they feel important. A child who feels valued in a given learning environment will be much more likely to participate. With learning opportunities designed to draw on personal student repertoires, H/P gifted children will engage further because they love to use what they know to create new understandings or to tease out meaning from something as yet untackled. If they know that the students in their group will help them learn and that a teacher or co-learner is standing by to support that learning, they are likely to jump into exciting activities with no holds barred. We have all experienced the thrill of such learning, and thus each of us carries the responsibility to find or create rich learning possibilities for highly and profoundly gifted learners. All it takes is clear expectations of *importance, meaning,* and *success*.

Notes

1. Columbus Group, transcript, 1.
2. Silverman, *Counseling the Gifted and Talented*.
3. Lezotte, "Effective Schools."

References

Columbus Group. Unpublished transcript of the meeting of the Columbus Group. Columbus, OH, July 1991.

Gross, Miraca U. M. *Exceptionally Gifted Children.* London: Routledge, 1993.

Kay, Kiesa, ed. *Uniquely Gifted: Identifying and Meeting the Needs of the Twice-Exceptional Student.* Gilsum, NH: Avocus Publishing, 1999.

Lezotte, Larry. "Effective Schools." Keynote address, Effective Schools Conference, 1992. Clarke County High School, Berryville, Virginia.

Renzulli, J. S., and S. M. Reis, eds. *The Schoolwide Enrichment Model: A How-To Guide for Educational Excellence.* Mansfield Center, CT: Creative Learning Press, 1997.

Silverman, Linda Kreger, ed. *Counseling the Gifted and Talented.* Denver, CO: Love, 1993.

Tolan, Stephanie S., and Deirdre Lovecky. Personal correspondence between the author and Stephanie Tolan, 1993.

VanTassel-Baska, Joyce, ed., and John Feldhusen, Ken Seeley, Grayson Wheatley, Linda Silverman, and William Foster. *Comprehensive Curriculum for Gifted Learners.* Needham Heights, MA: Allyn and Bacon, 1988.

Homeschooling with Profoundly Gifted Children

BY KATHRYN FINN

Kathryn Finn is mom to five and (at the time of this writing) grandmom to one. She has been homeschooling for over eighteen years and was a member of John Holt's staff. She is the director of Tagfam.org, an Internet-based support community dedicated to building and strengthening relationships between individuals, families, and organizations for the benefit of intellectually gifted children and adults.

At the very least, parents of profoundly gifted children will need to enrich the educational experiences their children receive from standard schools. At the most, they assume responsibility for the whole learning process. Whether they use an unstructured (unschooling) or structured (curriculum-based) approach, Kathryn Finn shows how home-based education can grow, expand, and accelerate to meet the needs of these nonstandard learners.

A great many parents of profoundly gifted children end up homeschooling their children for part of their education. These children are so different from the typical child, and so different from each other, that it's a rare school that has the perfect program all set up. And even if the school offers good options, they are rarely sufficient. These children often eat curriculum in great gulps and come back raging for more. So common is this phenomenon that there's a word for homeschooling children who also go to school. It's called *afterschooling.*

Like all parents, we work out solutions for our children as we go along. It often takes us a very long time to use the term *gifted*, never mind *profoundly gifted.* I didn't use these words for over a decade of mothering. I didn't use them when my first child turned over when she was less than twelve hours old. I didn't use them when she was smiling at me within a week, or when she failed to be distracted when I took things out of her range of vision at the same age. And I sure didn't use them when she wanted to stay up most of the night looking me in the eyes and cooing at me. Nor did I use them when she demanded to be taught to read when she was four years old. Or when her little sister suddenly learned to read over one weekend the same year.

Discovering my children deep in conversation about whether the universe had edges or not didn't clue me in. Nor did having a three-year-old look up from counting blocks and announce that math is real. I didn't take seriously another three-year-old announcement, when my daughter said that she wanted to go to school, MIT by preference. Nor did her wondering joy when she looked up at the stacks of the Boston Public Library help me. She announced that she was going to read all the books, and I told her that we'd start with the children's room.

It didn't strike me as odd when my one-year-old learned to choose a computer-game cartridge, insert it properly, start the computer, and happily play games rated for four- to six-year-olds. It didn't even surprise me that she always picked the right cartridge.

Not that I was displeased with most of these things. I could have used more sleep, and I knew my children possessed a phenomenal ability to disorganize a house, but mostly I thought they were cute. All children are cute, aren't they? And all children are full of energy, and they all make a mess. I knew my neighbors had neater houses, but I blamed myself rather than my children.

I learned to mother the children I had. I did notice that the developmental timetables in the baby books were off, but I thought that was probably to keep people from worrying. I learned that you *can* read even when you have a baby who wants constant interaction. You simply read out loud, for hours and hours and hours. You also go for walks and name everything you come across.

We joined the Children's Museum and the Science Museum and went to each roughly twice a week. In the grocery store, we discussed menus and read labels together. We visited the library daily, and quickly developed a rule that no one could borrow more books than she could personally carry. We went to concerts of all sorts, and investigated all the inexpensive and free activities that a large city offered. And along the way we made the most wonderful friends.

Eventually school came into our lives for my older child, and passed out again quite quickly. It didn't work. My daughter didn't fit in. The teacher didn't like her, and made that clear all around. My child wasn't supposed to ask *why* about every little thing. She wasn't supposed to point out every inconsistency or say, "Teacher, you made a 'stake." She wasn't supposed to bring in books in other languages and ask to have them read to the class. And above all she wasn't supposed to derail every lesson plan with her questions. Even then, I didn't conclude that my child was different. I thought the school was dreadful.

We brought her home to learn. My mother donated a small chalkboard to the cause, which led to the discovery that chalk dust causes my second child to break out in dramatic welts. The doctor suggested we avoid any school with chalkboards. We didn't even consider school for years after that.

Another mother had to name for me what I was dealing with. (Thanks, Bev.) The revelation came as a shock. I had to consider for a long while before I agreed and then proceeded to deal with the information. You may have had your own challenge named for you by a teacher, a doctor, a professional in gifted education, or another parent. The naming will give you a new view of your child, but remember that you still have the same child you had before. You've been learning to deal with this child all along. You will be all right.

The word *gifted* gave me two things. It made some of what we had been living with more understandable. And it gave me permission to do things that I wouldn't have otherwise considered.

The first thing is to forget the picture of a little classroom in your house. You may find it convenient to set up a study room for yourself and your child. You may prefer to do different tasks in different places in the house. But you are not embarking on school in miniature. This is an individual tutoring situation.

Lessons can happen anywhere that works. You can have set hours for schoolwork or use the Montessori concept of the prepared environment.

You also don't have to teach everything yourself. Consider yourself the administration, not the staff. Feel free to make use of all of your community's resources, including the schools, if you like. It isn't unusual these days for schools to work out part-time arrangements, in which a child studies some subjects in school and others at home. But your community will contain many other resources as well. Colleges offer weekend and summer classes for kids. So do museums and nature preserves. Consider incorporating Scouts or Camp Fire into your program. Think in terms of volunteer work, as well as classes. Volunteer time at a museum site, or regular visits to a nursing home, can teach a great deal of history. Programs designed for adults are also an option. Depending upon your child's age, you may need to attend, too. But children as young as ten regularly take college courses successfully, and younger ages are not unknown.

Friendship is important to any child. For the profoundly gifted child, I have found that homeschooling offers a great advantage. Basing the child's education throughout the community allows the child access to a wide range of possible friends. It also circumvents the false impression so many children receive that friends ought to be exactly one's own age. Instead, the child develops friendships based upon activities and interests.

Finding a soul mate who can share all of a child's interests is a matter of luck. Sometimes it happens, and sometimes it doesn't. But even if the magical best friend doesn't come along, there are soccer buddies and swimming buddies, friends from Scouts and friends from church. There is the book group from the library, the elderly gentleman who plays chess in the park, the neighbor with the toddlers, and on and on. Find your child opportunities to share his or her interests, to run around and be silly, to be the leader and the follower, the older guide and the younger one as well. And try to have friends you share with your child. It would be sad if there were no one who could delight you both.

Homeschoolers range between two poles. The *unschoolers* rely on life to motivate their children to learn all that is needed. They impose nothing, following the lead of the child's interests at every step. At the other end of the continuum are the *curriculum-based*. They buy textbooks in grade-level packages and run small schools in their refurbished garages.

People on both ends of the continuum do excellent jobs of educating their children. I have always been most comfortable somewhere in the middle. In part this is a matter of my own personality, and in part it is a reaction to my children and my community.

I live in a state where the law requires regular achievement testing of homeschoolers. The existence of a minimum standard is therefore at the back of my mind. Not that any of my children ever scored near the minimum. They usually miss few questions, or none. But I admit that the testing has influenced my choices. You will want to find out what your state requires. This is information easily come by. In some other countries, education laws are made on a national basis. The United States sets these regulations state by state. There are few places in the world where home-schooling is not a legal option for parents who choose it.

Additionally, I live in a college town and so we have always had access to excellent library facilities. This has led us to make our studies more book-oriented than they might otherwise have been. It also has meant we have not bought as many books as we might have needed to. (This will come as a surprise to my husband, who will not believe that anyone buys more books than we do.)

Find out the strengths of your community and your family, and use those resources to the maximum. Grandparents and other relatives are often delighted to share their knowledge and skills with children. The children are often as delighted to learn.

I have never felt any hesitation in requiring my children to learn material they feel disinclined to master. This is, to my mind, what parents do. If I can reasonably insist on toothbrushing and baths, I can equally insist that my children learn to make change or to write a letter of thanks.

My youngest recently informed me that she "doesn't do bathrooms." Unfortunately for her, adults "do bathrooms" as a general rule. I can't let her leave home without the skill. Equally, she needs to be able to change a tire, cook a meal, figure out a budget, and acquire a long list of other practical skills. Under normal circumstances, the natural desires of children to be independent and mature will drive them to acquire such skills. If they don't, that's what parents are for.

But I feel free to require other things, as well. I feel an obligation to pass on my religion to my child. I also feel an obligation to pass on my culture. My child is therefore, willing or not, going to discover such things as classical music and Shakespeare's plays and sonnets, and will become familiar with such people as Archimedes and Einstein.

As a general rule, however, the child's interests can be allowed to drive. It's so much less work that way. Topics of lesser interest can be connected to the passions as necessary. Showing real interest in something yourself will almost always convince your child to take a closer look.

One question you will encounter regularly is what grade your child is in. This can be difficult to answer, because these children are often all over the place. At first, the question is really one of age. Since that's all the inquirer wants to know, just tell them that.

You will, of course, keep track in your own mind the level at which your child is working in any given subject. For the most part, you needn't have this nailed down to a specific grade. If you are using a textbook, it will be marked with a grade or a grade range. If not, you will know a little more roughly how to label your child's learning level. But you will know. A gifted child rarely works across all subjects at the same level. Don't expect this.

I have dealt with this unevenness by adjusting myself to it. The level of *input* that the child can handle is often very high. I read material out loud for most of the early years. My child's reading level was adequate for amusement reading. But for information input, we used books written for adult readers almost from the beginning. The material written for children rarely contained enough information and often had a patronizing tone that made my children wild. Their *output* was also oral for most of the elementary grades. They used writing for letters and stories. I checked their comprehension of the content areas by asking them to tell me what they understood, or to tell Daddy what they'd learned that day.

This led to a rediscovery of something we'd known when they were very small. My children were completely capable of absorbing information without understanding it at all. Later, when understanding arrived, out would pop the information. I repeatedly found myself staring in amazement at children who were reciting material I could swear no one ever taught them. When asked, sometimes they'd explain that the information was taught to an older sibling within their hearing, often when they were only toddlers. Occasionally I've been told that the child has always known it, but only just understood.

This information-sponge nature comes with a flip side: an aversion to repetition. When asked to repeat what they already know, you can watch the brain switch into the off position. If you find your child forgetting material that was known in the past, the problem is probably too much repetition. Repetition kills learning for gifted kids. Don't do it any more than you can help. Life itself will contain more than enough practice in handling repetition.

Textbooks repeat to a shocking extent. So if you choose to use textbook material, you will have to select. Textbooks repeat within each volume and they repeat from grade to grade. Don't ever expect to use all of any textbook. Your child will use up the benefits long before you've gone through every page. If possible, borrow textbooks instead of buying them.

The stage of happy exploration can last throughout the childhood years. Adolescence is different. Adolescents want to adventure into the wide world. They arrange this in individual ways. Some go from part-time jobs into their own businesses. Some choose to go to high school. Some begin with college.

At this point, the yardsticks of the educational system come into play. The records you have kept become very important. You will want to be able to document what you have done. In addition, this is the stage at which my family has found distance-learning programs very useful. They allow the child to try out a more directed style of learning and evaluation while still remaining in the familiar environment and controlling the pace. Distance-learning makes a good transition device. And while a transcript can be made up by parents, in my experience transcripts from these programs are easier for schools and colleges to accept. A gradual transition has worked best for my family. I would suggest beginning to find serious mentorships no later than age nine or ten, and to think about college courses starting by age fourteen, if possible.

One day you will discover that the homeschooling years have passed for at least one child. Enjoy them while they last.

18 Unfettered Innovation

The Promise of Charter Schools

BY AMANDA P. AVALLONE

Amanda P. Avallone has worked as a teacher, administrator, and curriculum writer since 1985 in public, independent, and charter schools, as well as in corporate settings. At present, she teaches English and literacy, serves as assistant principal for curriculum and instruction, and directs the in-house teacher training at Summit Middle School. She serves on the National Assessment Governing Board (NAGB), an independent, non-partison board appointed by the U.S. Secretary of Education to set policy for the National Assessment of Educational Progress (NAEP), and currently chairs NAGB's Assessment Development Committee. Amanda is also a freelance writer, consultant, teacher trainer, workshop facilitator, and a frequent speaker at conferences.

Educational standards and organizational structures can make it difficult for teachers to meet the varying needs of their students. In some places, like Colorado, the formation of charter schools offers an alternative. Under the aegis of the public system, they develop clear missions and obtain some freedom from the constraints of standardized education. Amanda Avallone describes some ways in which Colorado's charter-school option offers choices, and hope, for unusually able learners.

I recently asked a young teacher I am mentoring to accompany me to a district middle-level curriculum-council meeting. As a relatively new teacher at our charter middle school, he had never attended one of these meetings. The debate surrounding one agenda item in particular, a remedial reading class, seemed to distress him, as it might any advocate for the needs of the talented and gifted.

Our local district, like all districts in the state of Colorado, is trying to find ways to meet the needs of students who do not yet read at grade level or do not qualify as "proficient" in reading on our state tests. One solution under consideration in some public schools is to require all middle school students to take a reading class in addition to language arts. The discussion went something like this:

"What if we teach reading as a separate class?"

"Well, that could work, but what about the students who are excellent readers already?"

"Couldn't we offer an accelerated version, something like reading for pleasure?"

"Wait a second—we're not allowed to ability-group—all of these classes would have to be heterogeneous."

With frustration: "But how will that solve the problem? If the class is remedial enough to reach the students it's designed to help, won't it bore the strong readers to tears? And where will we find time in the schedule?"

With a sigh: "I guess they'd have to give up an elective, like art or music."

At this point, my young colleague grew increasingly agitated. Finally, he scrawled a note and passed it to me: "Do we have to abide by what they decide? Forcing bright students to give up their elective courses to take a class they don't need is totally against our mission, isn't it?"

Relief flooded his face as he read my answer: "Relax—we are a charter school. We'll find another way."

I chose to begin with this anecdote because it highlights two important truths about charter schools: (1) charter schools do enjoy a greater degree of freedom and flexibility than regular public schools, and (2) many people, including those of us who work with charter schools, are still defining what a charter school is and can be. A relatively recent phenomenon, these schools are a work-in-progress, an ongoing inquiry into ways of meeting the needs of diverse learners.

Based on my observations of my own school and others throughout Colorado, I see much promise in the area of gifted and talented education. Still, it will take time to explore fully the possibilities in the charter-school model.

It is not my intent to suggest that quality education for the gifted is impossible in a regular public school, nor am I claiming that charters are better suited to gifted students. Still, by definition, charter schools are freed from some of the constraints that may hamper innovation in public schools. Charter schools, with their autonomous boards, can create an institution that not only permits teachers to meet the needs of the gifted, but also establishes a culture where such teaching is encouraged, rewarded, and supported.

In this article I will identify key differences between charter schools and regular public schools, focusing on those aspects that are most promising for meeting the needs of gifted and talented students. Along the way, I will share some of the ways my particular school, Summit Middle School, has tried to realize the potential underlying the charter school model.

What Are Charter Schools?

A charter school is a public school of choice that is sponsored either by the local district or the state. It operates under a renewable contract, typically granted for three to five years. This contract, or charter, specifies the school's mission, curriculum, goals, and indicators of success. To renew its contract, a charter school must demonstrate both academic results and sound fiscal practices. To thrive, it must remain highly accountable to its sponsoring institution, to the public that provides funding, and to the parents who choose to send their children to the school.

In exchange for this higher level of accountability and uncertainty, charter schools are liberated from regulations that might hinder them from fulfilling their stated mission. Therefore, they operate with greater autonomy concerning curriculum, the hiring and training of teachers, scheduling, and allocation of resources, all of which have implications for serving the needs of talented and gifted students.

Consensus of Mission

||||||||||||||||||||||||||||||||||||||||||||||||||||||||||||||||||||||||||||||||||||||||||||||||||||||||||||||||||||||||||||||||||||||

When working with charter-school leaders on any project—from writing standards to teacher training to communicating with parents—the first question I ask is, "What's your mission?" Developing a mission is the first step in building a charter school, and the mission must likewise be the foundation for all decisions about how the school should function.

One distinguishing feature of a charter school is that it usually has a precise mission statement that, at least in part, identifies how the school differs from the other schools in its area. In order to start a charter school, the founders must identify a new approach, an unfulfilled need, or an underserved population and must state how their school will address the perceived lack.

Summit's founding parents were critical of the local district's philosophy regarding middle school education and expressed a concern that highly motivated and gifted students were not sufficiently challenged. Envisioning a school where the needs of those students would be met, they wrote a mission that reads, in part, "To provide a rigorous, academic curriculum that promotes high levels of student effort and academic achievement. To foster high self-esteem through stimulating intellectual challenge and meaningful academic accomplishment."

From that mission statement stem all school decisions: the curriculum and materials, school calendar, number of minutes in each class period, student placement, types of classroom activities and assessments, whether or not a field trip is worthwhile, even how much homework to assign.

Every school I've worked for has had a mission statement, but many are too broad and idealistic to serve as practical guides for school decisions. Public schools today are indeed expected to do all things for all people, a daunting task. Charter schools, in contrast, do not claim to be right for everyone; rather, each charter school offers an alternative approach that may be right for certain learners.

Because the charter school's mission identifies clear priorities, it can marshal its resources in accordance with those priorities. Field trips, for instance, do not consume a significant part of Summit's yearly budget. Instead, Summit spends far more than a typical public school on curriculum development and teacher training to fulfill its mission—to challenge and stimulate learners. As our coaches and physical education teachers might observe, Summit's gymnasium is not state-of-the-art, but its faculty consists of content specialists, most with advanced degrees and several with doctorates. Thus, if a charter school decides to adopt a mission to serve the needs of gifted and talented students, it has the guiding principles and the power to make the decisions that will accomplish that mission.

Finally, the consensus of mission that guides the school's decisions extends to the parent and student communities as well. Because charter schools are an alternative to the regular public schools, parents must go out of their way to choose one.

In Summit's case, this school is not the "default-value" school for even a single child. For its very existence, Summit must articulate its mission to the community and invite like-minded parents to enroll their children. Without clarity about who we are and credibility that we are true to that identity, we would cease to attract students. Our teachers would show up next August to lead empty desks to greater understanding of Mesopotamia, protozoa, and Shakespeare. To justify our right to exist, we must remain accountable to our mission. Each enrollment cycle is a new test of our credibility in the eyes of our parents.

Imagine the potential for student growth at a school where parents, teachers, and students all share similar philosophies of what education is for and how it should unfold in children's lives. This vision, although lofty, at least becomes possible when there is unity of mission.

Curriculum and Instructional Program

As long as charter schools in Colorado meet the state standards, they are given considerable latitude in the areas of curriculum, course offerings, assessment, and student placement. Although Summit students participate in both the state-mandated and district-level proficiency tests, Summit's own standards and benchmarks are unique.

Using the school's mission as a guide and the state's content standards as a foundation, Summit set out to create a one-of-a-kind curriculum that articulates precisely Summit's goals for student achievement. Working intensively and year-round during the school's first few years of existence, Summit staff and administration, guided by the parent governing board, reviewed existing curricula from the United States, Canada, Europe, and Asia. They met with each other, with consultants, and with content experts to develop a challenging curriculum, one that was specific enough to be clear to parents and teachers, but open-ended enough to allow for a great deal of flexibility in both instruction and assessment of students.

Although many schools and teachers have autonomy over classroom units and activities, one aspect of the curriculum that affects gifted and talented students is the lineup of particular courses in a program of studies and student placement within them. A charter school's power over its instructional program—which courses to offer, what textbooks to purchase, and how to place and group students—is a key feature that distinguishes it from a regular public school and endows it with greater potential to meet the needs of gifted students. Unlike the other public schools in our district, Summit features mixed-age classes based on ability and interest. Even though students spend only three years at Summit, we offer four English classes, four science classes, and seven math classes in an effort to give each student optimal challenge. Moreover, all of our electives are mixed-age, based on student interest and not on grade level.

However, Summit's program is not tracked in the traditional sense, because students are free to mix-and-match advanced or accelerated classes in one subject area with less accelerated classes in other subject areas. In this way, Summit's curriculum responds to the many gifted students who have domain-specific talents. For example, an incoming sixth-grade student gifted in math but average in reading and writing can enroll in accelerated algebra with many seventh graders, English I with primarily sixth graders, and philosophy with a majority of eighth graders.

Summit's program also takes into consideration the peaks and valleys so characteristic of gifted students. In math and English especially, the flexible sequence of classes permits acceleration throughout the middle school years. If, for example, a student enters sixth grade in English I but suddenly blossoms as a reader and writer, he or she can move to English II at mid-year or possibly skip English II entirely, taking English III as a seventh grader and English IV, the most advanced and accelerated class, in grade eight. Similarly, incoming sixth-grade students can choose between pre-algebra (a grade-level course), pre-algebra honors (an accelerated grade-level course), algebra I (an above-grade-level course), or accelerated algebra (an accelerated above-grade-level course). Needless to say, offering so many courses makes scheduling a challenge, but it is possible in this way to accommodate the skill level, aptitude, and interests of a diverse student body.

Hiring and Professional Development of Teachers

To parents and students, the teachers *are* the school. How many of us owe our choice of "favorite subject," college major, or even our adult vocation to the inspiration of an exceptional teacher? A vision of a "gifted-friendly" school is meaningless without teachers who share that mission and have the training to implement it.

Like many charters, Summit is not required to hire teachers licensed by the state of Colorado. Instead, it has sought out teachers from across the United States, educators from universities and private institutions, and potential teachers from other professions who share the belief that middle school students are capable of high academic achievement. In its five-year history, Summit has employed research scientists, linguists and translators, writers, university professors, an astronomer, an artist, an orchestra conductor, and a software engineer, as well as experienced teachers and administrators.

For Summit's founding parents, subject-area expertise was of paramount importance to a school serving a high percentage of gifted students. As a charter school, Summit could hire teachers who were skilled in and passionate about their subject areas, even if they did not hold Colorado teaching licenses. Recognizing, of course, that effective teachers possess both subject knowledge and strong pedagogical skills, the Summit board and administration developed in-house training in teaching methodology.

In 1996, for example, Summit became a designated agency for Alternative Teacher Licensing through the Colorado Department of Education. This allows Summit, in conjunction with an advisory board of mentors and representatives from higher education, to train its own teachers while they are teaching. Not only does this attract potential teachers who cannot afford to quit their jobs in order to pursue a license at a university, but it also allows Summit to tailor its teacher-training program to meet the needs of its mission and its student population. For example, the program requirements include training in promoting critical thinking; understanding learning styles; and meeting the needs of bright, gifted, and twice-exceptional students.

Summit's ongoing professional development for experienced teachers is also independent of the school district. As a charter school, we can control the content and format of workshops and presentations so that they match the needs of our teachers and students. While district teachers are attending in-service training about motivating and providing remediation for reluctant readers, Summit might concentrate on curriculum compacting or on differentiating instruction for the gifted.

The freedom to hire noncertified teachers also allows Summit to offer an expansive array of electives based on student interests. Gifted students work best in situations where they are given a range of options, and Summit's elective program is varied, ever-changing, and responsive to that need to make individual choices. One of our PE teachers spent a year teaching English in Japan, and his conversations about that country and its language inspired a group of students to learn more. The teacher proposed a new elective, "Japanese Culture," that was offered the very next semester. Though knowledgeable about his subject and popular with the students, this young teacher does not hold a teaching license. His students certainly don't mind; his lack of a teaching license does not curb their enthusiasm for learning Japanese one bit.

If given the chance, many professionals would enjoy working with a group of eager and talented young people for a semester—or even for an hour every other morning—if they did not have to obtain a teaching license in order to do it. Interactions with scientists, writers, and other "real world" practitioners provide students with potential role models and a more authentic context for learning. Instead of seeing themselves as passive recipients of knowledge, students view themselves as partners in an inductive process, working side-by-side with fellow scholars and mentors. A charter school's more flexible approach to hiring teachers can increase the probability of such interactions.

The School Calendar and the Daily Schedule

Because charter schools do not need to adhere to the public-school calendar or traditional daily schedules, they can become laboratories for innovations in the use of time. Both Summit's school day and its school year are longer than those elsewhere in the district, and we are free to schedule parent-teacher conferences and teacher professional days as needed. This past fall, for instance, an additional day was scheduled for conferences, to accommodate parents who had been unable to see all of their children's teachers. Next month, Summit teachers will have a workshop day to write curriculum and receive software training.

Until this year Summit shared a site and a bell schedule with a standard public school, so our experimentation with scheduling is just beginning. Still, Summit teachers are full of ideas for the future: extended blocks for scientific inquiry; immersion mini-courses; and assemblies for student performances, exhibitions, and enrichment activities. The key for teachers is knowing that they are free to innovate. If they can conceive of a schedule configuration that will better serve Summit's mission, they have confidence that Summit can adopt it.

Responsiveness and Speed of Implementation

The final, and perhaps most significant, advantage for charter schools is the ability to respond quickly to staff and student needs. Skilled, dedicated teachers in all public schools can make their classrooms fertile grounds for learning, but the slow rate of change in large public-school districts can frustrate innovative teachers, as well as parents. Relatively minor changes—such as adopting a new textbook or retooling the curriculum of one course—can take months or years. More significant, systemic changes—like those needed to maximize the potential of all students—seem to inch along at a glacial pace.

In contrast, layers of bureaucracy, interminable studies, and focus groups do not hamper charter schools. Instead, charter schools are governed by their own boards (usually a combination of parents, teachers, and community members), in conjunction with the school's principal. Parents and teachers can bring concerns and proposals to the board, knowing that the board is empowered to act immediately. Last year, the social studies teachers conducted research to find a new geography textbook. They presented their findings at a board meeting, and a new text was approved in less than an hour. A few weeks later, the books were in students' hands. Such expeditious handling of business is the rule, not the exception.

More sweeping changes can also be implemented quickly. One of the best examples from Summit's history concerns cross-curricular skills.

In 1998, parents and teachers noticed that many students, even the most talented ones, were not prepared to accomplish some of the tasks assigned in their challenging courses. Specifically, students had not been trained in research skills, formal public speaking, and reading nonfiction for information. Upon arriving at Summit, students were suddenly asked to research a Greek god, prepare notes, and make a formal presentation—with visuals—to the class and adult guests. Not surprisingly, the students became anxious, the parents became concerned, and the curriculum stalled as teachers hurriedly tried to backfill the missing prerequisite skills.

Alerted to the problem, the Summit board immediately approved two teacher workdays, one right away and the other at the end of the year as a follow-up, to solve the problem. The entire faculty met for eight hours in a classroom, filling out grids and preparing assignments, scrawling notes on whiteboards, proposing, bargaining, compromising, and planning.

The result was a calendar for teaching cross-curricular skills. It spanned all subject areas and all three years a student would spend at Summit. Every major project and its respective skills was identified and sequenced so that students would receive the necessary instruction prior to being asked to tackle a major project like Science Fair or History Day. As part of the plan, each subject department took responsibility for one of the key cross-curricular skills: English teaches formal presentation, science teaches research skills, social studies teaches how to gather information from nonfiction sources, and so on. The skills calendar proved to be a godsend; students are challenged but not frustrated, and all subject areas work together to help students build the skills they need to develop their talents.

What is remarkable here is the speed with which Summit was able to address a perceived weakness. Concerns were first expressed late in the fall semester, and even though the changes affected all subjects, teachers, and grade levels, students and parents were able to perceive improvement by the fourth quarter of that same school year.

Potential, Not Panacea

There is no such thing as a perfect school, and the charter-school movement is not a cure for every weakness, real or perceived, in the public-school system. Nevertheless, I hope this discussion and the illustrations from my own school hint at the potential within the charter-school movement to meet the needs of talented and gifted students.

Within the current climate of back-to-basics, minimum proficiencies, tight budgets, and standardized assessments, parents and teachers of exceptional learners can feel, understandably, that they are at the bottom of every school's "to do" list. A charter school can be the answer for some communities.

Finding one with a mission you share may be difficult, and starting your own is a gargantuan undertaking (ask our founders), but a school that makes reaching a child like yours its first priority, its raison d'etre, is at least worth a closer look.

An Early Entrance Program

A Well-Rounded College Experience for Young Students

BY TRINDEL MAINE
& RICHARD S. MADDOX

Trindel Maine enjoys living in the Southern California desert with her family. She and her husband, Rich, have three children, two of them still living at home. She is a retired aerospace engineer.

Richard S. Maddox now directs the Cal State L.A. Early Entrance Program (EEP). In doing this, he draws on his own early experiences as a gifted student in the 1960s and 1970s—where, he says, "I struggled through a public school system not designed for or competent in educating students whose talents, needs, and abilities exceed those of traditional students." He studied psychology and taught at the secondary and college levels before discovering the Early Entrance Program, where he has helped young people nourish their minds in an environment that also allows them to be children. He is now completing his doctorate in educational psychology at the University of Southern California (USC), Rossier School of Education, while he continues his nationally recognized work for the EEP as an expert in gifted adolescent accelerated education at the university level.

Early entrance programs, where young people take on a full college-level program before completing high school, provide a comprehensive university education for some groups of accelerated kids. In looking at the options for providing this, we always need to remember that these kids aren't simply miniature adults.

(Continued)

A number of programs serve young people who are ready for college in tenth, eleventh, or twelfth grade. They usually serve local populations, require a manageable academic and social leap on the student's part, and keep the child within the established family support system. A good starting point for researching these programs is located at www.hoagiesgifted.org/early_college.htm.

But what about the profoundly gifted child who needs similar intellectual challenges before the age of fifteen? Perhaps before eleven? Or eight? That's harder! A small handful of programs in the United States have been set up to accommodate the social and emotional, as well as intellectual, challenges some of these children encounter. Some programs are residential and some require the family to live in, or move to, the program's locale. Well-established alternatives include the Program for the Exceptionally Gifted (PEG) at Mary Baldwin College, in Staunton, Virginia (ninth grade and up; young women only; residential); the Early Entrance Program of the Halbert and Nancy Robinson Center for Young Scholars at the University of Washington in Seattle (entrance before age fifteen; area residents); the Early Entrance Program at California State University, Los Angeles (eleven and up; area residents); and Simon's Rock College of Bard, in Great Barrington, Massachusetts (completion of tenth grade, possibly as young as fourteen; residential). An additional program is in development through the Davidson Academy and University of Nevada, Reno (sixth grade and up; Nevada residents).

Many of these options require a level of emotional maturity that not all profoundly gifted kids can muster. All early entrance college situations that intend to help very young students successfully ramp up to an appropriate academic level must provide a depth and breadth of support for the whole child that is not required for older students.

This insiders' look at the California State University, Los Angeles program, co-written by a parent and an educator, describes in detail one program that is designed to nurture very young college students. It offers guidance for evaluating—or establishing—early entrance opportunities to serve profoundly gifted young people. Trindel Maine is the parent of a 1996 graduate of this Early Entrance Program (EEP) and Richard Maddox is the program's director.

Introduction

The Early Entrance Program (EEP) for extraordinarily gifted students at California State University, Los Angeles (Cal State L.A.) provides the opportunity for highly gifted young students to begin their college studies early with the extra support, guidance, and counseling necessary to prepare them for success at the university level. The EEP was introduced and formally approved by the university in 1983. Initiated by Dr. Estelle Gregory, a former professor in the psychology department, the program was originally sponsored by the Psychology Department and the Office of Undergraduate Studies. Since 2001, the program has fallen under the auspices of the Division of Student Affairs.

Program Description

The EEP at Cal State L.A. is one of a small handful of early entrance programs in the United States, all of which follow somewhat different models. The Cal State L.A. EEP started with five to ten students but now supports about one hundred full-time, degree-seeking students between the ages of eleven and eighteen.

All EEP students are admitted before their sixteenth birthdays. The average entering age is currently thirteen and a half years. Most students bypass high school, and a few also skip part of junior high. Students carry between twelve and eighteen quarter-units of normal university classes. A private lounge area provides these young students with a safe place to congregate and socialize between classes. This is not a residential program and all students live at home.

Approximately 150 full-time EEP students are pursuing their baccalaureate degrees in any given school year. All EEP students participate in Cal State L.A.'s General Education Honors Program and, at present, hold the majority of positions on the G.E. Honors Board of Directors. EEP students frequently participate in the university's research symposium. Sought after by faculty members who need student research assistants, many EEP students have also become coauthors of research papers. EEP students have received numerous awards, scholarships, and grants.

EEP students have historically been very active in campus events, social programs, and organizations. They are well represented in Cal State L.A.'s chapter of the community-service organization, Circle K, as well as in student government, academic clubs and organizations, intramural sports, orchestra, jazz ensembles, the university newspaper, and the university's tutoring service.

These young scholars bring to Cal State L.A. a "spirit of community" by involving their families in campus events. After graduation, they form valuable links to some of our country's most prestigious universities.

The EEP reaches prospective students in the Los Angeles area by conducting a biannual talent search, typically testing between two hundred and nine hundred highly gifted middle school students each year. This Search for Exceptional Academic Achievement (SEAA) utilizes the Washington Pre-College Test (WPCT), which provides estimated SAT scores as part of its report. These scores are used to qualify students for three programs supported by Cal State L.A.: the full-time EEP and two part-time options, the Pre-Accelerated College Enrollment (PACE) program and the Accelerated College Enrollment (ACE) program.

To qualify for a provisional summer quarter of EEP study, students must achieve a total estimated SAT score of at least 1,100, with neither math nor English sub-score below 450. Approximately 10 to 20 percent of the students who take the test meet this threshold and are invited to apply. The provisional summer quarter allows the EEP staff, the individual student, and the family a chance to determine whether the EEP is a good choice without disrupting the normal flow of a student's education. The average qualifying score for EEP students is over 1200, which is substantially higher than the average SAT score achieved by college-bound high school seniors throughout the United States.

Students and parents complete an interview process and remain in close contact with EEP staff throughout the provisional quarter. During the quarter, prospective EEP students choose two entry-level college classes and must earn at least Bs. They are expected to display the motivation, maturity, and academic skills required for success in the college environment. In addition, an attempt is made to ascertain the student's need for this type of radical acceleration.

After conferring with all the provisional students and their families, and upon receiving final grades, the EEP staff submits recommendations to the Faculty Admission Committee for their approval. Typically, the EEP admits no more than thirty students per year.

The Admission Process: Deciding If EEP Is a Good Choice

The decision to start college much earlier than normal is a big one—from the perspectives of the student, the family, and the university. The student must be socially, emotionally, and academically ready for the largely adult university environment. The university justifiably does not want to juvenilize an environment primarily designed to meet adult educational needs. Parents don't want to put their adolescent children in an environment that isn't safe and sensitive to their needs.

The basic outline of the admission process has already been laid out. This section will attempt to address the more subjective decision-making process faced by the student, family, and EEP staff. As authors of this essay, we come at this from opposite perspectives. Richard S. Maddox is the current EEP director and Trindel Maine is the parent of a 1996 graduate of the EEP. We will attempt to blend these two viewpoints, but it may be evident that they don't always correspond.

The WPCT scores provide evidence of competency in both quantitative and verbal areas, which is necessary but not sufficient to predict success for a potential early entrant. The EEP uses the provisional quarter to attempt to sort through the intangible and difficult-to-measure issues. Like any subjective process, evaluation is not perfect and techniques are constantly being revised.

A student's desire to achieve in a more challenging atmosphere often predicts success far better than do test scores and previous academic record. Critical factors include the student's ability to adapt to the university environment, overall maturity, deportment, communication skills (both oral and written), and passion to learn.

A single summer session is a very short time in which to evaluate all of the forty to fifty students who try out the program each summer. Doing an acceptable job of assessment requires active involvement of the EEP staff, EEP student mentors, university faculty, the provisional students, and the families. It takes a consensus decision of all of these parties to make the EEP a successful choice.

The EEP staff begins assessment with their very first contact, when interested, WPCT-qualified students and their parents are invited to a preliminary meeting in the EEP lounge and a visit to campus. While this meeting and the students' interactions may be influenced by anxiety and a level of culture shock, a lot can be learned from observing a student's initial reaction. The EEP lounge, a critical component in the program's success, is a vibrant, active, and fascinating environment. Most applicants have never experienced a single location with so many other like-minded peers, so this first visit to the lounge can elicit a wide range of emotions. Students who have strong positive reactions tend to be excellent program candidates. Some other reactions—ranging from apparent lack of awareness of the EEP and the purpose of the meeting to discomfort, displayed through body language and terse verbal responses—often provide an early indicator that the EEP isn't the right choice. Like most first impressions, it would be a mistake to rely heavily on this first encounter as a means of identifying a student's potential for EEP, but it is a starting point.

Parents should also be alert for clues as to whether EEP is a good choice for their child. Trindel notes, for example, her son's early responses: "We were beset by very determined lobbying for EEP all the way home from the WPCT test. Our son had met instant soul mates among the EEP students working as test proctors during the midway test break!"

During all interviews, the staff attempts to evaluate the student's overall interest in radical acceleration. Staff questions typically focus on a student's awareness of the EEP and the meeting's purpose, current school situation, and feelings about possible accelerated placement through the EEP.

Ironically, a poor fit with a student's current or former school is often a strong indication that EEP will work well. Students who need college are probably not happy in junior high or high school, and thus may be more motivated to meet the challenges inherent in the college environment. Conversely, students who enjoy their regular placement have little reason to pursue a radical change in environment.

Parents and students need to actively air any concerns they have. Parents commonly wonder about the effects of missing important high school prerequisites, notably laboratory science and foreign language. (The EEP experience has been that the highly gifted students who join the program effectively fill these gaps within roughly the first year, by taking an appropriate selection of the university's lower division general education classes.) Students and parents also have an opportunity to ask about the university's support for particular interests.

It's important to consider how radical acceleration will mesh with existing hobbies, social activities, family dynamics, and friendships. For instance, if school-based competitive sports are important to the student, early college entry is probably a bad idea. The student will lose the opportunity to compete at the high school level, but is probably not physically ready for college-level competition.

The almost cliché question for any early college entrant is, "Won't they miss the senior prom?" Most early entrants view this as a joke, but it is a serious question when generalized to include the whole set of high school social events. Like the sports issue, the importance of this aspect of high school varies widely from one individual to another. In general, students with high extracurricular involvement may not want or be able to handle a more challenging academic load on top of their existing activities. Allowing time for outside activities is important.

The important word *maturity* conjures up different images in different people's minds. What does it mean to be socially and emotionally mature enough to handle a jump from junior high to college? Interestingly, there is a significant split in the answer to this question. Task-related maturity requirements are high. Yet program students are not subject to certain types of peer pressure and find that it is socially acceptable to continue enjoying their childhood interests.

In terms of personal responsibility, an early college entrant has to be way ahead of what we normally expect of a young teenager. The student must get to class on time with little prompting and must keep up with class requirements and long-term assignments without the reminders and checkpoints that abound in junior high. Conduct standards are high, with little tolerance for childish behavior or adolescent thoughtlessness. Fundamentally, the student must take responsibility for his or her education and behavior.

On the other hand, students find themselves free to talk about beloved childhood toys and activities. There is substantially less pressure to be up on all the latest pop culture fads or to experiment with sex, alcohol, tobacco, and other drugs. Those forces are not absent in the college environment. However, kids with those types of inclinations tend not to enter the EEP, and members of the regular student body who indulge in those pursuits feel no need to encourage a thirteen-year-old to join them.

After the initial interview, interested applicants are given the necessary paperwork and invited to an orientation meeting for all interested students and their families. At this meeting, information on the program, the university, and personal experiences is presented by students, alumni, parents, and staff. This is a wonderful opportunity for candidates and their parents to meet prospective, current, and former students and their families. These contacts can be reassuring and informative.

At this point, prospective students are given a list of recommended courses for the required, provisional summer quarter. Students are expected to choose two four-unit classes that interest them. All applicants participate in a three-week series of orientation meetings, which involve campus tours, study, and lectures on library skills given by university faculty, as well as presentations by each of the university's school advisement centers. Students complete a series of interview questionnaires and a writing-skill exam scored by members of the EEP faculty advisory board. Students also take two university assessment exams in mathematics and English. These tests enable students to qualify for entry level coursework in these disciplines should they be accepted as full-time students. Also, in smaller groups of between five and seven students, led by an EEP student mentor of their choice, candidates form social bonds that help the new students adjust to the university environment.

During the summer, the student's academic and social abilities are observed by the staff, with the assistance of an ensemble of EEP student mentors and university faculty. The goal is to get a solid feel for the student's motivation, maturity, communication skills, academic skills, and over-all attitude toward scholarship. At the same time, the student examines whether he or she wants to make a long-term commitment to the program. Most parents anxiously watch to see how their son or daughter handles this greatly increased level of academic and personal responsibility and form their own judgment of the option. Because spaces in EEP are generally limited, it is easy to fall into a semi-competitive mind-frame of wanting a slot just for the honor of getting in, and to neglect the family-level introspection needed to determine if this really is the right choice. Ideally, the end of the summer brings consensus on whether to continue the program full-time or to resume a more traditional path through school, at least for the time being. All students are invited to participate in an end-of-summer EEP ritual, a weekend camping trip. This serves as a fun ending for those who will not continue, and as a bonding experience for the new admits to the program and the established EEP students, many of whom have been off for the summer.

Succeeding as an Early Entrant

Early college entry is an exciting opportunity, but navigating the university bureaucracy and making wise course selections can be daunting to a student coming from junior high! Certain aspects of the EEP structure have evolved to facilitate this transition. Other issues must be addressed by early entrants and their families. It does take work on the part of all involved to make this transition work well. Typically, one or two of the thirty students admitted each year either withdraw or are removed from EEP participation during their first year.

From a parental perspective, the first concern is always safety. Despite recent events, we have the perception that public schools are relatively controlled environments. Sending our youngsters to a big-city university where they are only minimally supervised is scary. The university is probably farther from home than the "regular" school, and the youngster may need to rely on public transit to get there. It takes a bit of work to come up with a commuting plan that feels comfortable. Practice the route and work out contingency plans for what to do if things don't go as expected. Students should know what to do if they accidentally get off at the wrong stop, and how to get help if they need it. It is worthwhile to proactively invest some time into making students relatively street-safe.

A junior high student seldom needs money at school. A college student needs access to money for books, school supplies, train passes, meals, and as an emergency resource. The amount required tends to exceed the acceptable level of pocket change for a twelve-year-old. Parents will likely need to negotiate with their bank to get a young college student some combination of a checking account and a debit or credit card, with the parents as co-signers. This can be challenging to arrange and may require persistence, especially for the younger EEP students. The university's federal credit union can assist students in obtaining such cards with a parent's permission. In California, the Department of Motor Vehicles (DMV) will issue a non-driver identification card that serves as a good substitute of a driver's license for identification purposes. The DMV ID card, combined with the university student ID, tends to be adequate to get checks and credit cards accepted.

The EEP staff facilitates a regular schedule of required group meetings and individual counseling sessions to make sure that EEP students get the information they need in a timely manner. The content of these meetings varies. Sometimes staff reminds the kids to clean up their messes; or makes sure they know when, where, and how to sign up for upcoming classes; or tells them how to get extra help when they need it.

There is an EEP-specific general education program, devised by the EEP staff in conjunction with the university faculty and the general education honors program. It consists of an augmented combination of the university's general education requirements and the honors program requirements. This program is designed to meet normal university expectations, to fill common background holes of students moving from junior high to college, and to ensure that these students have a reasonable breadth of learning. The freshman curriculum also serves to ease the transition to university life by providing students with a natural group of same-age peers with whom they attend classes.

This set of courses constitutes a large percentage of the EEP student's first year or two. Many of these classes are offered through the university's General Education Honors Program (GEHP), which maintains small classes with professors who have expressed an interest in teaching advanced material to top-performing students. EEP students currently account for roughly a quarter of the GEHP enrollment, so they are well represented in these classes and have an opportunity to form friendships and study groups.

During the first couple of years, parents need to be actively involved in course selection and scheduling. Students are generally expected to be on campus at least four days per week. To avoid aimless drifting through college, students are expected to explore possible major fields during the first year or two, to have a rough idea of possible majors by the end of the second year, and to make a firm commitment to a major or majors during the third year.

It is worth noting that the parents of very young college students may have a strong tendency to steer kids into majors that lead to well-paid or prestigious careers. As parents, we need to be very careful to offer practical advice but not to push our children into fields that they don't like. The typical adult college student is more socially and emotionally able to tell parents, "But I don't want to be a doctor" than the most brilliant twelve-year-old.

Many incoming EEP students, especially those who haven't previously skipped grades, have unfortunately developed poor work habits. They have been able to get good grades for half-hearted, rushed efforts. There's a huge jump in expectations between junior high and college—any college. Midterms and finals replace chapter tests, and they cover a much greater quantity of material. Term papers should represent the work of many weeks, not thoughts the student threw together a day or two before they were due. College offers few opportunities to make up for a blown test or a poorly done assignment. It's all too easy to skip classes, and professors don't constantly remind students of their responsibilities.

In junior high, students often received high grades for knowing more than their classmates. In college, they are more likely to run into fixed standards that demand mastery of the material. The whole college system is designed around the assumption that students are responsible adults. New EEP students sometimes need to grow up quickly in terms of organizational skills, time management, and general responsibility for their own education. While these students typically hate the "spoon feeding" of junior high, to some extent they also tend to rely on it. Success in adapting to the new expectations usually depends on a combination of parental and EEP staff guidance. Beginning EEP students usually need their parents' help while they learn to keep up with their classes and to spread out the workload over the quarter.

Once the student has made a commitment to a major, it is reasonable for parents and EEP staff to back off a little and expect more of the academic advising to come from the major department. Yet it is worth noting here that Cal State L.A. is a less competitive institution than many of the graduate and professional schools these kids are likely to move on to. It is worthwhile to get course catalogs from one or more of those institutions to see whether their undergraduate majors have more demanding course requirements. Where possible, students will want to see if they can meet the more stringent course requirements.

Another opportunity open to EEP students at this point is the establishment of a real mentor relationship with one or more of the faculty members in their major department. Mostly this involves hanging around the department and regularly offering to assist the professors with whatever they can use help on. Cal State L.A. has fewer graduate students than other, larger, universities, so graduate research assistants are not widely available. EEP students have features that make them very attractive research assistants. They are inherently very bright, and they don't tend to have external adult responsibilities so they can afford to donate significant amounts of time for free. In exchange, they can get real exposure to their professor's research and a chance to go well beyond the standard course work. Assistantships and coauthorship of publications also look good on graduate school applications, and these relationships can generate really useful letters of recommendation.

Course content in most junior and senior high schools is pretty tightly regulated, and school boards tend to have conservative ideas of what is appropriate. Trindel remembers a high school English teacher who profusely apologized for the juvenile level of the reading for a literature course called "Aspects of War," saying, "It's hard to find literature with a serious war theme that doesn't have any four-letter words in it." The situation is very different at the college level. College professors have a great deal of latitude in selecting course materials and they assume that their students are adults.

Some classes will require material that you doubt your twelve-year-old is ready to handle. Trindel experienced qualms on discovering that her eleven-year-old was scheduled to read *A Clockwork Orange,* by Burgess, during his first quarter at Cal State L.A. She hastily reread the book and made a point of discussing it with him when the time came. She was impressed with his level of understanding and analysis of the topics addressed in the book, and relaxed some.

If you are highly concerned about this issue, early college may be a bad idea. In general, EEP staff and parents have found that most of these concerns can be handled just by being on top of the situation and having frank discussions. Realistically, this exposure to adult material is almost guaranteed to be healthier than what goes on in high school locker rooms.

Different families will have different comfort levels and will make different judgment calls. Parents of students who start the program between the ages of eleven and thirteen will be more concerned than those whose children are in their mid-teens. Matters of this type are usually more likely to occur in humanities and social sciences than in math and science classes. Classes with known sensitive content might be postponed, and different professors do make different selections of materials. The EEP staff and other EEP students can help a student choose classes that minimize the problem. Each EEP student must submit class choices for approval prior to the registration period, which allows staff to address course materials and or faculty that may be inappropriate.

One of the biggest attractions of EEP is there are a lot of similarly radically accelerated students and they make a wonderful peer group. These kids are good for each other! College schedules inherently have big holes in the day that are great for socializing. The level of interaction among these students is exciting, and they bring with them a wonderfully diverse array of backgrounds.

The private EEP lounge provides a great place for the students to hang out. Given time, this environment has worked wonders at drawing shy, withdrawn, or socially awkward kids out of their shells. Unfortunately, some students let the socializing get out of hand and they lose track of the academics. Parents and staff need to watch out for this.

Because these students are drawn from a large geographical area and are young, parents will need to provide taxi service and similar supports for out-of-school social opportunities. Maintaining close friendships can be hard when your best friend lives fifty to a hundred miles away.

Campus special-interest clubs, GEHP, and student government all provide good opportunities for EEP students to get involved with regular college social activities. Most majors have an affiliated special-interest club. Planning field trips, fund-raising, and lining up speakers for club events are all valuable life skills that these clubs foster. The special-interest focus minimizes social difficulties related to age differences, and helps EEP students fully participate in the college community. Being involved in these types of activities is crucial to getting the most out of a college education.

What Does It Take to Create (and Maintain) an Early Entrance Program?

We would like to see programs like the EEP available throughout the world. A well-run EEP can meet a critical need in the surrounding community and can attract very high-caliber students from that community to the local university, students who might otherwise leave the area after high school graduation.

While this may seem to be a strange comment, in many ways the EEP lounge is what makes the program. Adequate and appropriate space is needed before a program can successfully work with adolescents on a large university campus. EEP students need a place where they can work and socialize between classes, and that space needs to be adjacent to the EEP staff offices. The EEP space needs to provide a safe haven from the adult campus community. It must be large enough to house the EEP population and should include multiple rooms to serve a variety of needs. Ideally, it will have kitchen facilities, social areas, and quiet study rooms. Because EEP students use the space for group meetings, individual and group study, and socializing, it will be thought of as a home-away-from-home and should be comfortable.

EEP staff must be nearby, so they can monitor, counsel, supervise, and advise. The staff also needs adequate office space. On numerous occasions, privacy and confidentiality will be required. Meetings with students, faculty, parents, prospective parents, media representatives, and the interested public can take place only in an office protected from student noise. A great deal of program business must be conducted in a relatively quiet, adult environment close to, but separated from, the students themselves. If the program conducts its own talent search, as the Cal State L.A. program does, it will need adequate facilities for extensive record-keeping and outreach support.

If possible, there needs to be a buffer zone between the EEP space and other university activities. EEP students, like all adolescents, can be loud, boisterous, and full of youthful exuberance that can annoy nonparticipants. At the same time, the EEP should be close to general university support services and classes.

Early entrants have very different backgrounds than the high school graduates who make up most of the college population. The admission process needs to take this into account and be customized for this population. Clearly, specific high school course requirements need to be waived, because these kids haven't been to high school. They don't have a high school record that can be used to guide admission decisions. The provisional summer session helps compensate for this lack, but those admitted to the full program must then be very rapidly processed for enrollment in the immediately following fall quarter. Planning also needs to recognize that a twelve-year-old middle school student who achieves a

WPCT combined score of 1,100 possesses a *far, far higher level of academic potential* than an eighteen-year-old who receives the same score after a full high school program!

The staff needed to run a successful EEP will vary with the size of the program. Most programs will start small and gradually build to a stable size, driven by the community's need for this kind of program and limited by the university's resources and willingness to support the program. At a minimum, the program needs an overall director who works well with highly gifted adolescents, their parents, and the regular university administration and faculty. This director also needs access to adequate administrative support. An EEP also needs a counselor, someone with a background in clinical psychology or other related field, to monitor and assist the students with any emotional problems. As the program starts to grow, the staff will need to expand to provide additional support, encompassing such functions as counseling students, coordinating any talent-search outreach programs, and coordinating social events.

Those interested in exploring this option for their college or university in more depth are encouraged to contact the Cal State L.A. EEP program director and coauthor of this essay, Richard S. Maddox, for more detailed information and discussion.

A Longitudinal Study of Radical Acceleration with Exceptionally and Profoundly Gifted Children

BY MIRACA U. M. GROSS

Miraca U. M. Gross is professor of gifted education and director of the Gifted Education Research Resource and Information Centre (GERRIC) at the University of New South Wales in Sydney, Australia, and author of *Exceptionally Gifted Children*.

Australian researcher Miraca Gross has studied how radical acceleration affects profoundly gifted individuals in the long run. She carefully and comprehensively examines the academic, social, and emotional costs and benefits of meeting the intellectual needs of this special population and concludes that radical acceleration is a practical and effective response to the intellectual and psychosocial needs of the extremely gifted.

Substantial portions of this chapter originate from an article that discussed the early educational experiences of five of the six radical accelerands described in this chapter by the author.

Someone has said that genius is of necessity solitary, since the population is so sparse at the higher levels of mental ability. However, adult genius is mobile and can seek out its own kind. It is in the case of the child with extraordinarily high IQ that the social problem is most acute. If the IQ is 180, the intellectual level at six is almost on a par with the average eleven-year-old, and at ten or eleven is not far from that of the average high school graduate. . . . The inevitable result is that the child of IQ 180 has one of the most difficult problems of social adjustment that any human being is ever called upon to meet.

—B. S. Burks, D. W. Jensen, and Lewis M. Terman, 1930[1]

While the research of cognitive psychologist Lewis Terman and his colleagues is rightly credited with refuting the myth that intellectual giftedness is closely linked to nervous instability and emotional maladjustment,[2] we cannot afford to ignore the associated warning that extraordinarily gifted young people are nonetheless at serious risk of social isolation and rejection by age-peers.

Terman's "early warning" has been validated by several subsequent studies. While four comprehensive overviews of international research on the socio-affective development of intellectually gifted children and adolescents—conducted by Austin and Draper (1981), Janos and Robinson (1985), Schneider (1987), and Robinson and Noble (1992)—report generally positive findings, the authors of all four research syntheses caution that the considerable majority of the findings they reported originate from studies of moderately gifted children, and that the picture may be very different for children of very superior intelligence.[3] B. H. Schneider, for example, reports that his own study of peer acceptance of gifted students found significant negative correlations between IQ and peer nomination.[4] He cautions: "There is considerable reason to believe that the social status of the very highly gifted is not as consistently elevated as that of the moderately gifted."[5] P. M. Janos and N. M. Robinson warn:

> The most highly talented are the most vulnerable, probably because they are exceedingly "out of sync" with school, friends and even family. . . . They may become superficially adjusted but sacrifice possibilities for outstanding fulfillment and significant, socially valued, contributions. These are, in our opinion, problems of clinical proportions, but research devoted to exploring them pales in comparison with that devoted to virtually any other maladaptive set of behaviors.[6]

The relatively few studies which have investigated the social and emotional development of the extremely gifted suggest that exceptionally gifted (160–179 IQ) and profoundly gifted (above 180 IQ) children do indeed tend to have greater problems of social acceptance.[7]

Leta Hollingworth was the first psychologist to undertake a systematic study of peer relationships of children scoring at different levels of intellectual giftedness.[8] She defined the IQ range 125–155 as "socially optimal intelligence."[9] She found that children who scored within this range were well-balanced, self-confident, outgoing, and able to win the confidence and friendship of age-peers. She claimed, however, that above the level of 160 IQ the difference between the exceptionally gifted child and his or her age-mates is so great that it leads to special problems of development that are correlated with social isolation, and that these difficulties appear particularly acute between the ages of four and nine.[10]

Hollingworth was convinced that the difficulties in peer relationships experienced by highly gifted children arose not from social maladjustment but through the unlikelihood of their easily finding others who share their abilities and interests.

> This difficulty of the gifted child in forming friendships is largely a result of the infrequency of persons who are like-minded. The more intelligent a person is, regardless of age, the less often can he find a truly congenial companion. The average child finds playmates in plenty who can think and act on a level congenial to him, because there are so many average children.
>
> —Leta S. Hollingworth, 1936[11]

Research both in the United States and in Australia has noted the decrease in motivation among extremely gifted children confined to a regular classroom.[12] After many years of studying the extremely gifted, Hollingworth became convinced that enrichment alone was not a sufficient response to their academic and social needs. She became a persuasive advocate of full-time, self-contained classes for exceptionally gifted children.[13] Terman strongly endorsed Hollingworth's findings[14] and argued forcefully that for extremely gifted children the more conservative accelerative procedures, such as skipping a single grade, are not sufficient. He and his colleagues advised radical acceleration through several grade-skips, spaced appropriately throughout the student's school career.[15]

The subsequent research of P. M. Sheldon, P. M. Janos, and Linda Kreger Silverman strongly supported these recommendations. It also endorsed Hollingworth's contention that the social isolation experienced by exceptionally gifted children is not the clinical isolation of emotional disturbance, but rather a condition imposed on the child by the absence of a peer group with whom to relate.[16] When extremely gifted children who have been socially rejected by age-peers are removed from the inappropriate grade placement and placed with children of similar mental age, the social difficulties disappear.[17]

The Present Study

Since the early 1980s, this author has conducted a longitudinal study of the intellectual, academic, social, and emotional development of fifty-nine young people who have scored 160 IQ or above on the Stanford-Binet Intelligence Scales, Form L-M. The subjects of this study live in seven of the eight states of Australia and are presently between the ages of five and twenty-five. All entered the study before the age of ten, and their development has been followed over several years. Aspects of the children's academic and psychosocial development have been reported in numerous publications.[18] The first decade of the study was reported in depth in *Exceptionally Gifted Children* (1993).

Until the mid-1980s, the Stanford-Binet L-M was generally regarded as the best single measure of general intellectual ability[19] and the most reliable measure of determining very high levels of intellectual giftedness.[20] Unfortunately, the newer version, Revision IV, is much less suitable for use with highly, exceptionally, or profoundly gifted children, and researchers report that it generates significantly lower scores for even moderately gifted children than its predecessor did.[21] Indeed, the Revision IV manual itself reports that the mean composite score for a group of eighty-two gifted children (average age: seven years and four months) was 135 on the L-M, but only 121 on the Revision IV. This is a score depression of almost a whole standard deviation for these moderately gifted children. Even greater discrepancies are noted for highly and exceptionally gifted children. The newer test generates a punitive depression of scores for students in the entire gifted range, much greater than can be accounted for simply by the mean shift downward on the new test to accommodate the higher performance standards of the 1980s. Silverman points out that for average-ability children the same raw score yields an IQ approximately 8 points lower in 1991 than in 1960, whereas for gifted children the average downward shift is 31 points—a loss of one point per year![22]

An additional problem in the construction of Revision IV is that it has eliminated the mental age, which could be used in its predecessor to calculate a ratio IQ score for exceptionally and profoundly gifted children. The many problems with Revision IV have led psychologists with a special interest in the highly gifted to recommend that the Stanford-Binet L-M should be retained for use with children suspected of being very highly able.[23] Silverman and Kearney further recommend that a child who obtains three subtest scores at or near the ceiling of any current instrument should be tested on the Stanford-Binet L-M, and that ratio IQs should be computed for any child who scores beyond the test norms.[24] Riverside Press, the publisher of the Stanford-Binet L-M and Revision 4, endorsed the continued use of the L-M to assess intellectually gifted children, pending the development of a newer test (the Stanford-Binet Revision 5) and its return to the developmental age-scale format of the L-M.[25]

The present study uses the Stanford-Binet L-M to assess the cognitive abilities of its extremely gifted subjects, and will continue to do so until the publication of Revision 5.

The study employs a wide range of qualitative and quantitative observation techniques, triangulated to increase the study's validity and reliability.[26] The children take standardized achievement tests in several academic areas, and their tested achievement levels are compared to the levels of work they are permitted to undertake in class. This enables the researcher to judge the degree of "fit" between the children's demonstrated achievement and the programs provided for them by their schools. In addition, because Australian schools generally communicate with parents through written reports on a child's academic progress, the children's school reports from different grade levels are examined to determine their teachers' perceptions of their levels of ability and achievement.

Many educators and psychologists studying the gifted and talented have emphasized the significance of a healthy self-concept in the realization of intellectual potential.[27] Self-esteem, an affective aspect of self-concept, largely derives from the positive or negative feedback individuals receive from significant others about the value or effectiveness of their actions.[28] Particularly in a society where a highly egalitarian social ethos is based, in large part, on "cutting down the tall poppies" (such as Australia), there is the danger that extremely gifted students will receive deliberately misleading feedback about their abilities and potential from teachers as well as classmates.[29] This study uses the Coopersmith Self-Esteem Inventory (SEI) to measure the children's self-esteem in social relationships, relationships with family, and academic work. Many commonly used self-esteem inventories have a ceiling effect when used with intellectually gifted children. The Coopersmith SEI does not.[30]

Surveys of the reading interests of extremely gifted children reveal that they often read, with full comprehension and enjoyment, literature written for young people between five and seven years older.[31] At regular intervals, surveys are made of the hours each child spends daily in voluntary reading over a twenty-one-day period; the title, author, and subject classification of all materials read; books the children currently class as favorites; and their reasons for preferring these particular books. Regular surveys are also made, over several weeks, of the nature and extent of television viewing, computer usage, hobbies and play interests, and interest or participation in sports.

Developmental and demographic data have been acquired from many sources including questionnaires, medical records, parent diaries, and family documents. Semi-structured interviews are held, at regular intervals, with the parents of each child and with the children themselves. These interviews follow up, clarify, and expand on the material gathered through the questionnaires, the achievement and personality testing, the school reports, and all other sources of information. The interviews also elicit the parents' opinions on more sensitive issues such as the children's educational programs, their relationships with teachers and classmates, and their social and emotional development. Similarly, the student interviews elicit the children's views on their progress at school, their feelings about school experiences, their social relationships, and their perceptions of themselves and their abilities.

Of the fifty-nine young people in this study, a minority have been recognized, by their schools, as being young people of truly remarkable intellectual potential. However, most of the children's teachers have remained unaware of their extraordinary intellectual potential or, where psychometric evidence has been made available, the school has refused, on ideological grounds, to develop any form of differentiated curriculum for the gifted child.[32] The majority of the extremely gifted children in this study have spent, or are spending, their elementary-school years working through a lock-step curriculum in a heterogeneous classroom without access to other gifted—even moderately gifted—students.

However, sixteen of the fifty-nine children have been radically accelerated and are undertaking part or all of their schooling with students several years older. This chapter reports on the school histories of six of these children and discusses the factors that have contributed to the success of the individualized programs. The children and their families are identified in publications arising from this study by pseudonyms chosen by the children themselves.

It should be noted that the Australian school system is based on the British system. Accordingly, Australian children enter preschool or kindergarten at age four and formal schooling at age five, one year earlier than their American counterparts.

Christopher Otway

Christopher is a profoundly gifted young man. As stated earlier, psychologists with a special interest in the extremely gifted advocate that a ratio IQ should be computed when a child scores significantly beyond the ceiling of even the Stanford-Binet.[33] Tested on the Stanford-Binet L-M at the age of ten years and eleven months, Chris achieved a mental age of twenty-two years, and thus a ratio IQ of approximately 200. At the age of eleven years and four months, he achieved the remarkable score of 710 on the math section of the SAT (SAT-M).

From his earliest years, Chris displayed prodigious talent in math and language. He taught himself to read when he was two, and by the age of four he was reading children's encyclopedias and had acquired a level of general knowledge that would be unmatched by the majority of fifth- or sixth-grade students. His math ability developed almost as precociously. Shortly after his third birthday, he spontaneously began to devise simple addition and subtraction sums. By the time he entered kindergarten at the usual age of four, he was capable of working at the fourth-grade level in math. A psychometric assessment established that shortly after his fourth birthday, Chris had a mental age of at least seven.

The principal and teachers of Chris's primary school recognized his remarkable abilities within a few days of his enrollment and were willing to ensure that he received an appropriate education. Chris's parents had studied the literature on giftedness, and were aware of the educational and psychosocial benefits of acceleration. They suggested to the building principal that Chris might be a suitable candidate for subject-matter acceleration or grade-skipping. After some thought, the principal agreed to the experiment. By a fortunate chance, while on study leave, he had visited professors Julian Stanley and Camilla Benbow of the Study of Mathematically Precocious Youth (SMPY) at Johns Hopkins University and was aware of the advantages of acceleration.

At first, Chris was withdrawn from his first-grade class for a few hours each day to join the second grade for English and the fifth grade for math. Even this intervention did not address the full extent of Chris's advancement. The following year, as a second-grade student, he attended seventh-grade math each day. At the end of this year, Chris was permitted to skip directly into fourth grade. His subject-matter acceleration continued, with eighth-grade math and, in addition, the start of flute lessons with his eighth-grade classmates in recognition of his obvious aptitude for music. Several of the highly gifted young mathematicians in this Australian study also display high levels of musical precocity.[34]

Chris's program of grade-skipping and subject acceleration has been extremely successful. At the age of twelve, he was based in ninth grade (with students two and three years older), but took physics, chemistry, English, math, and economics with eleventh-grade students (who were seventeen).

On his own initiative, Chris then took the rather unusual course of "repeating" eleventh grade with a further five subjects—English, legal studies, Australian history, accounting, and biology. This proved highly successful, and he repeated the process in twelfth grade, doing twice the number of subjects spread over two years. He consequently graduated with ten university-entrance subjects, instead of five. In both his twelfth-grade years, he was one of the top-scoring students in his state.

This broadening of curriculum choice over eleventh and twelfth grades was not an attempt to "reverse" his acceleration. Rather, Chris used time he had saved with his early accelerations to "purchase" the opportunity to pursue a much broader and more enriched path to university entrance than was possible for his age-peers. He also felt that he personally would not be mature enough to enter university at thirteen or fourteen.

Chris entered the most prestigious university of his state two months after his sixteenth birthday, two years earlier than is customary for

Australian students. He participated enthusiastically in both the academic and the social life of the university. Only a few weeks after enrollment, he joined the university's Science Fiction Association and was promptly elected to the committee. One benefit he has experienced from university clubs is that they give him access to students at all different levels of the university. Although he formed several good friendships with other first-year students (two or three years his senior), he also enjoyed the company of second- and third-year students. Like many exceptionally gifted students, even in later adolescence Chris preferred the company of people several years older than himself.

Chris graduated with first-class honors in his B.Sc. in computer science and mathematics at the age of twenty. He won a highly prestigious scholarship to a major British university. At age twenty-four, he is currently in his final year of Ph.D. study. He maintains a wide range of intellectual and social interests. He plays competitive tennis; was, until recently, the captain of a mixed-sex netball team; plays piano and flute; enjoys contract bridge; takes a keen interest in the Stock Market; and, as he has always done, reads voraciously.

Roshni Singh

Roshni Singh, age sixteen, has a Stanford-Binet IQ of 162. Sarah, Roshni's mother, is Australian. Juspreet, her father, is of the Sikh religion and was born in Singapore.

Like many children in this study, Roshni's speech developed unusually early; she spoke her first word at six months.[35] Most of her early speech was in Punjabi, the first language of her father. By the time she was ten months old, she could identify and name several household objects in both Punjabi and English; at fourteen months, she could name most parts of her body, and a range of colors, in both languages.

Roshni was reading by the age of three, and by four was writing letters to her relatives in Singapore on the family's personal computer. At five years and five months, she scored at the 84th percentile for eight-year-olds on the Leicester Number Test, a standardized test of math achievement commonly used in Britain and Australia.

Roshni's exceptional abilities were recognized in early childhood. She was permitted early entrance to kindergarten at the age of three and a half, and to primary school at the age of four and a half, on the basis of her accelerated reading capacities. Yet neither the kindergarten nor the school was at first prepared to modify its curriculum in response to the very talents which had prompted them to offer her early entrance. Although she could read as well as the average second grader, the kindergarten presented Roshni with large cut-out letters as an introduction to the alphabet. Although picture books were freely available, they provided no books with printed text. Not surprisingly, Roshni stopped reading. The kindergarten was giving her the unequivocal message that three- and four-year-olds were not supposed to read, and that to do so was somehow "wrong." To conform to her teacher's wishes and her classmates' expectations, Roshni did her best to pretend to be a "normal" three-year-old. With tact, loving encouragement, and a great deal of patience, Sarah and Juspreet were able to reassure Roshni that she should not be ashamed of her reading capacity, and after a few weeks she began to read again. When Roshni entered formal schooling the following year, however, the pattern was repeated. She entered an environment in which all knowledge and learning was assumed to flow to the children through the teacher. The teacher believed that reading should be taught at age five, not four, and was disturbed by Roshni's self-acceleration. Obediently, Roshni stopped reading again.

This time, the setback was more serious and Roshni's deliberate underachievement became more difficult to reverse. She had no one in her class of five-year-olds who shared her ability or interests, and she became very bored, lonely, and depressed. After some months of unsuccessful negotiation with Roshni's teacher, Sarah and Juspreet expressed their concern to the principal. They asked whether the school might be willing to consider some form of acceleration, since they seemed unwilling to extend her academically within the regular classroom. Fortunately, both the psychologist attached to the school and one of the primary-school teachers knew something of gifted education. The school somewhat reluctantly agreed. Eight weeks before the end of the school year, Roshni was permitted to move from the reception class into first grade. Because this intervention was highly successful, she moved to second grade with her new classmates at the start of the following year. She entered second grade at the age of five years and four months, fully two years younger than is customary.

By the time she turned seven, Roshni was enrolled in fourth grade (with children two and three years her senior). The class was grouped by ability, and Roshni was in the top group in every subject. Although she was aware that the math she was exposed to was still considerably below her ability, she enjoyed most other subjects and reveled in the social aspects of school. She was liked by her teachers and extremely popular with her classmates. As noted earlier, most Australian schools send home regular written reports on the children's progress. On Roshni's fourth-grade report, the principal wrote: "Roshni has applied herself diligently to all tasks and maintained her high position. She is very settled in her peer relationships despite the age difference, and this allows her to use the opportunities presented to develop and extend her own knowledge. I do enjoy Roshni's lively personality with her mischievous sense of humour!"

A further grade advancement halfway through elementary school placed Roshni with students three years her senior. Like many other highly gifted children, particularly girls, she reached puberty earlier than her age-peers. By the time she was thirteen, and in tenth grade, she was taller and more physically mature than many of her classmates. At this stage of her school career, she experienced some unpleasant sexist teasing from boys in her class who resented being very visibly outperformed by a much younger girl; this was relatively short-lived, due to the support of the other girls, with whom she had become firm friends, and due also to Roshni's own faith in her abilities. The self-confidence she had gained over the years of appropriate education, and developmentally appropriate grade placement, allowed her to resist the temptation to underachieve that had plagued her early school years.

Roshni's early talent for language had been translated, in elementary school, to a flair for learning foreign languages. She excelled in her studies in Japanese and German, winning regional prizes for oral and written presentations. In eleventh and twelfth grades, she gained extremely high marks in all subjects and graduated from high school with excellent grades in a range of math, humanities, and language subjects.

Roshni entered university when she was fifteen and is currently, at sixteen, in her second year of a combined arts/law degree program.

Ian Baker

Ian Baker taught himself to read, write, and count before he was two. At four, he assisted his kindergarten teacher by reading stories to other children.

By the time he entered school, at five, he was reading, with great enjoyment, E. B. White's *Charlotte's Web*. He took an equal delight in mathematical problem-solving, having taught himself to add, subtract, multiply, and divide.

The teacher's response to Ian's remarkable abilities was to place him, along with the other five-year-olds, in a reading-readiness program and a math program which involved recognizing the numbers one through ten.

Six months into Ian's first school year, his parents were called for an emergency conference with the school vice-principal, who informed them that the school wished to have Ian psychometrically tested as a preliminary to referring him to a special school for behaviorally disturbed children. According to the vice-principal, Ian had become uncontrollable in class and was displaying frightening bouts of physical violence toward other children.

The school psychologist assessed Ian on the Stanford-Binet L-M as having an IQ of 170+. On a standardized test of reading achievement (the Neale Analysis of Reading), he had reading accuracy and comprehension ages of twelve. He was just over five and a half years old.

The psychologist was appalled at the school's mismanagement of Ian's education. He informed the principal that the child's behavioral difficulties arose not from emotional disturbance but from severe intellectual and social frustration. He advised the school that Ian desperately required an educational program adapted to his needs, along with regular access to other intellectually gifted students.

For a short time, the school adapted the curriculum for Ian. He was permitted to do seventh-grade math (but without leaving his first-grade classroom) and they established a small pull-out program. Ian's intellectual frustration abated somewhat and his behavior improved. However, the appointment of a new principal, whose extremely egalitarian ideological views precluded any special provisions, ended the pull-out program and put Ian back into a lock-step curriculum based on his chronological age, rather than his mental age and levels of achievement. This led to astonishing mismatches between the curriculum and Ian's levels of tested achievement. When he was nine and in fourth grade, Ian took the math section of the SAT (SAT-M) as part of the data collection for this study. He made a scaled score of 560, 0.6 of a standard deviation above the mean, on a test that is standardized on seventeen- and eighteen-year-old American students planning to enter college. Meanwhile, in his fourth-grade classroom, Ian was required to work lockstep with his nine-year-old classmates on fourth-grade math. The antisocial behaviors returned, together with psychosomatic disturbances such as migraines, bouts of nausea, and abdominal cramps. The mornings became a battle to get Ian "well enough" and subdued enough to go to school.

At the age of nine years and three months, Ian was again assessed on the Stanford-Binet L-M. On this occasion, he achieved a mental age of eighteen years and six months. A ratio computation places Ian's IQ at approximately 200.

At the end of Ian's fourth-grade year, his parents withdrew him from this state (government) elementary school and enrolled him in an independent (private) school whose principal had a special interest in the gifted and talented. Ian was at last permitted to flourish. To address his needs, the school developed an individualized program that incorporated radical subject-matter acceleration, grade-skipping, "relevant academic enrichment,"[36] and mentorship. In sixth grade, he was permitted to study tenth-grade math. Through the success of this initiative, the school agreed to let him skip to seventh grade. At age eleven, he was based in eighth grade with thirteen-year-olds, but took math and computer science with eleventh grade, and science, history, and geography with tenth grade. While in ninth grade, he successfully undertook the twelfth-grade university-entrance math examination. In eleventh grade, he took first-year university math, involving two lectures and one tutorial at university each week after school. He was popular with his teachers and accepted by the other students. He finally began to accept that, although he differs in many ways from his age-peers, this need not prove a barrier to supportive social relationships, as it did when he was isolated from intellectual peers in the regular classroom.

Like Chris Otway, Ian used his subject acceleration to buy time to take a wide range of university-entrance subjects. Over two years, he accumulated eight twelfth-grade subjects, rather than the usual five.

Ian entered university at sixteen and graduated at twenty, with first-class honors in a Bachelor of Engineering degree. Currently twenty-one, he is enjoying his first year of Ph.D. study in computer systems engineering.

Ian is grateful to have had the opportunity to accelerate through the last few years of school, but he honestly acknowledges that school life was never easy, and for the majority of time it was extremely unpleasant. He and his parents believe that ideally his school program should have included some form of ability grouping from a much earlier age, so that he would not have had to wait so long to experience the intellectual stimulation and social acceptance that arise from working and socializing with young people of like abilities and interests.

Fred Campbell

Fred Campbell is a wiry, continuously alert young man with an eager, inquiring mind. He is an exceptionally able and multi-talented student with a Stanford-Binet L-M IQ of 163. At the age of twelve years and one month, he scored 640 on the SAT-M and 500 on the SAT-V (verbal section). He taught himself to read before his third birthday and his remarkable math skills developed soon afterward. He is, furthermore, a highly gifted artist.

Fred was bitterly unhappy in elementary school. Like many exceptionally gifted children, he had an overwhelming thirst for knowledge. He read deeply in many fields, burying himself in a subject until he had exhausted the available resources, then moving to another topic, which he absorbed with equal enthusiasm. At nine, he developed a keen interest in psychology and devoured adult texts that he borrowed from libraries in the large city in which he lives. In his school, however, he was a social outcast, derided and rejected for being different. Fred's classmates could not understand his interests in psychology, philosophy, and music. They were unable to understand his passion for mathematics. His actions, reactions, and opinions, when he tried to express them, were utterly alien to their system of values. They taunted, derided, and attacked him mercilessly and made his life a misery.

The school refused to offer Fred any form of differentiated curriculum. Their attitude was that he would be more readily accepted if he would stop "trying to be different," take a "healthy interest" in sports, and work at the level of the class. This disturbingly echoes the findings of A. J. Tannenbaum (in the United States) and N. Carrington (in Australia) that academically brilliant students are tolerated in the child community only when their academic talent is accompanied by a keen interest in sports or athletics.[37] Ironically, Fred had won his school's swimming championship and placed third in his age group in a prestigious regional swimming competition, but he had little interest in sports as such, and even less interest in the other boys' Monday morning post-mortems of weekend sporting events. Fred's undervaluing of a talent so highly esteemed by his classmates must have made him seem even stranger in their eyes.

Finally, during Fred's fifth-grade year, his parents in desperation approached the local high school (most Australian high schools comprise seventh through twelfth grades) and asked the principal whether they would consider admitting Fred a year early. After meeting Fred, and noting his academic achievements and emotional maturity, the principal agreed enthusiastically. Consequently, at ten Fred entered seventh grade, an immediate grade-skip of one year. The following year, he was based in eighth grade but took math and chemistry with the eleventh grade. This combination of grade-skipping and subject acceleration was so successful that he was next permitted to skip ninth grade while continuing his subject acceleration in math, science, and computing. He enrolled formally in eleventh grade two weeks after his fourteenth birthday and graduated from high school a few weeks before his fifteenth birthday.

Both academically and socially, his radical acceleration program has been, in Fred's own words, "the best thing that ever happened to me." His eleventh-grade year opened up a world of social relationships that he had never experienced. For the first time, he had access to students who understood, valued, and accepted him.

At fifteen, Fred enrolled in undergraduate studies at his local university, taking a B.Sc. degree specializing in math, physics, and chemistry. He graduated at nineteen with first-class honors.

Fred had no problems adjusting to university life. He felt he was where he had always belonged—with older students who shared his passion for learning—and he felt very much at home. Life was very different from the enforced segregation by chronological age that he experienced for his first five years of school.

Currently twenty-three, Fred is in his final year of Ph.D. study.

Sally Huang

From her earliest years, Sally Huang displayed a phenomenal gift for mathematics, and her English abilities were similarly astonishing. By the age of two, Sally could read the daily newspaper. At seven, she was reading medical textbooks brought home by her father, a doctor.

She is a well-rounded young woman who has won numerous prizes for music, debating, and academic excellence. She speaks fluent Chinese and Japanese, is an accomplished pianist, and holds a first dan black belt in Tae Kwon Do.

Sally's elementary and high schools, in a large country town, allowed her radical acceleration through a series of carefully planned and monitored grade-skips coupled with subject acceleration. She entered second grade at age six, fourth grade at age seven, and seventh grade at age nine. Then she progressed swiftly through high school, completing twelfth grade at age thirteen. She entered university, on scholarship, at thirteen and a half, as one of her state's top-scoring twelfth-grade students. Her studies focused on the physical and mathematical sciences, but she has also continued with her language studies and music. She was allowed to skip first-year university math and to enroll in second-year pure and applied math classes.

Over the years, Sally had a few gentle confrontations with teachers who were reluctant to let her progress at her own rate. But she is a determined and confident young lady who expresses her feelings politely but with quiet conviction, and in general her teachers have acceded to her wishes. Sally herself requested that she skip from fifth grade to seventh grade, because she was finding fifth-grade work unrewarding.

Sally experienced no particular nervousness about her entry to university. She spent some time on campus while in eleventh grade, as part of a high school work experience program, and enjoyed the academic and social atmosphere. As she pointed out, calmly, being with people older than herself was hardly a new experience, as her program of progressive acceleration through school allowed her to work and socialize with older students for virtually her whole school career. She prefers to be with people older than herself and is valued and accepted by them.

Her undergraduate study required her to move to the city. For these four years she stayed near the university during the week, in the home of friends of her parents. She traveled home each weekend. This gave her ongoing access both to the social life of the university and to her parents and older sister, with whom she has a close and warmly supportive relationship.

She graduated with first-class honors in her Bachelor of Science degree a few months before her seventeenth birthday. Like Chris Otway, Sally won a full postgraduate scholarship to a major British university. Currently nineteen, she is enjoying the second year of her Ph.D. study in theoretical physics. She participates fully in the academic and social life of the university and has many warm and supportive friendships.

As in the case of Chris Otway, Sally's path through school was assisted by educators—in this case, her math teacher and the elementary school principal—who had a strong interest in the educational needs of gifted and talented children. The principal has since taken a postgraduate degree in gifted education. A wealth of research demonstrates the strong, positive effects of teacher training and in-service in gifted education on educators' attitudes toward gifted students and on their interest in developing appropriate educational programs for these students.[38]

Hadley Bond

Hadley Bond has a Stanford-Binet L-M ratio IQ of 178. His phenomenal mathematical ability was evident very early. At eighteen months, he was already fascinated by the math drill programs his two older brothers used on the family's computer. He delighted in simple addition problems. He would work out the answer to a question using plastic beads and then type it into the computer, laughing with pleasure when the response was verified. He was reading small books before the age of two, and at three and a half he had the reading skills of a child of eight.

Like Roshni, Hadley was permitted early entrance to school because of his remarkable abilities in math and language, which had been identified and assessed in preschool. Unfortunately, Hadley's school was similarly unwilling to adapt the curriculum to his needs. Three years after teaching himself to add and subtract, Hadley, along with the other five-year-olds, was being invited to place in order the numbers one through ten! Hadley was bored and resentful, and announced frankly to his parents that school was a waste of time. Concerned that continued negative experience might leave the child with a lasting dislike for school, his parents removed him. A few months later, at the "proper" age, they enrolled him in a different school a few miles away. The principal of this school recognized Hadley's remarkable abilities and placed him in first grade, rather than in the reception class, an immediate skip of one year.

Extremely gifted children often realize very early that their abilities and interests differ radically from those of other children, and they may come to blame themselves for being out of step.[39] At his second school, Hadley took care to disguise, as much as possible, the fact that he was "different" from other five-year-olds. He carefully modeled his behavior on that of his classmates, even mimicking them by selecting picture books or books that contained only a few words of text. Despite the psychologist's assessment, which placed his full-scale IQ at 150 on the Wechsler Preschool and Primary Scale of Intelligence™ (WPPSI™), the classroom teacher took Hadley's reading performance at face value, and some months passed before the school recognized and responded to his exceptional reading abilities. Fortunately, subject-matter acceleration formed part of this response, and Hadley was permitted to go to second grade for math and third grade for computer instruction.

Hadley responded much more positively to acceleration than he had to the school's initial attempts at individualized instruction and in-class enrichment. He was much happier with the third-grade students, with whom he worked in computer class, than with his own classmates who were only twelve months older than he. Accordingly, at the end of first grade, Hadley was advanced into third grade, to be with children two years his senior.

Hadley's mother described his response to third grade as being in "a social wonderland"—for the first time, he was truly accepted by the other children in his grade and he made many warm friendships, despite scoring at the top of the class in every subject. His social self-esteem soared and his new-found happiness led to a surge in his motivation to achieve. At the end of his fourth-grade year, the principal, Hadley, and his parents decided that he should skip directly to sixth grade. Like the previous two grade-skips, this one proved extremely successful. At the start of 1991, nine-year-old Hadley moved with his twelve-year-old classmates into seventh grade. To his surprise and delight, he topped his year of 125 students in the math placement test.

He needed no further acceleration. Hadley's six years of high school were extremely successful, both socially and academically. He scored at or near the top of his class in all subjects and participated enthusiastically in many extracurricular activities, serving as captain of the under-seventeen soccer (football) team and playing on his school's First XI cricket team, which toured England in his twelfth-grade year and competed against a range of English schools. He played clarinet in the school orchestra and, also in twelfth grade, served as chair of the organizing committee that managed the orchestra's interstate tour. It is a measure of his social acceptance, and the respect and affection in which he was held, that Hadley's classmates elected him to the soccer captaincy and to the orchestra committee chair, even though he was younger than they by a margin of three years!

Hadley entered university a few months before his sixteenth birthday, and is now, at eighteen, in his final year of undergraduate studies, specializing in economics and enjoying his program of advanced math, accounting, and actuarial studies. He has an excellent grade-point average and is one of the most successful and popular students in his year. He plays competitive squash and is recognized as one of Australia's most outstanding young players. He will enter Ph.D. study in 2001.

During Hadley's final year of school, his mother reflected on his academic and social development in a letter to me: "He really has become very socially competent—he has many good friends and spends lots of time with them and on the telephone. The 'social wonderland' of his early acceleration pales into insignificance compared to now. I am convinced that this aspect of his development will be far more significant to his future than any other during the last few years."

Examples of Inappropriate Educational Provision

The young people described previously are six of the sixteen exceptionally and profoundly gifted students in this study who have been fortunate enough to experience programs of radical acceleration. Of the fifty-nine students in the study, the remaining forty-three have been retained in regular classrooms or have been offered token grade-skips of one year. The school programs of several of these children are textbook cases of educational mismanagement.

At four, Richard (160 IQ) amazed a math professor at a major Australian university by doing arithmetic mentally in binary, octal, and hexadecimal. At twelve years and six months, he scored a remarkable 780 on the SAT-M. He is a gifted musician and composer, and won two state-wide elementary-school chess championships. Throughout his school career, Richard was retained with age-peers in all school subjects, including math. He gained entrance to a first-class university, but dropped out in his second year, saying that he had lost his will to learn. Actually, he had lost it several years earlier.[40]

Anastasia has a Stanford-Binet ratio IQ of 173. At six, her favorite out-of-school reading was *National Geographic*. At seven, she was reading Richard

Adams' *Watership Down*. At eight, she read an English translation of *Les Misérables*; having seen the show, she wanted to read the book. Anastasia was grade-skipped by one year. It is doubtful whether placing an eight-year-old who reads adult novels with nine-year-olds could provide anything more than a temporary alleviation of her boredom and social isolation.

Adam (162 IQ) was a competent and enthusiastic reader by the age of three. He spent his earliest years of schooling in a small country school, where the first three grades were contained in the same classroom. His teacher, who stated that he was the brightest child she had encountered in her teaching career, permitted him to complete the work of the three grades in eighteen months. At six years and ten months, he was reading Charles Kingsley's classic *The Water Babies* and his reading accuracy and comprehension were assessed at seventh-grade level.

The building principal, however, shared the concern of many school administrators that acceleration would lead to social or emotional damage.[41] Adam's accelerated progress was halted, and his third-grade teacher insisted that he read and study the same materials as the other students. He repeated much of the work he had already covered. Adam's consequent boredom, depression, and intellectual frustration manifested themselves both at school and at home. His teachers reported him as arrogant, disruptive, and unmannerly. At home, he was aggressive and short-tempered. However, as the year progressed he lost even the will to rebel. He began to conform to the requirements of his teachers and the academic standards of his classmates. His teachers were delighted with the "improvement" in Adam's behavior and expressed their approval to his parents. Halfway through the school year, Adam's father expressed his fears in a letter to the author:

> What I find it hard to tell them, because I can't define it, is that he has lost, or rather is no longer able to display, the "spark" that he always had. This was the sharpness; the quick, often humorous, comment; the sudden bubbling over of enthusiasm when he starts following through a series of ideas. It is rather like a stone with many sharp edges; they have knocked these edges off and as a result he is rolling more smoothly in class and they are happy about that. I feel that they have caused him to bury an important part of himself. It is still there; it bursts out at home now and again, but he has learned to keep it hidden. I hope you know what I mean, because I have tried to explain it to the teachers and I fail every time. They believe they have had great success, but I know they are depressing some vital spark.[42]

Richard, Anastasia, Adam, and the other forty exceptionally and profoundly gifted students who spent, or are spending, their school careers in the inclusion classroom, or with students one year older, could have benefited from well-designed individualized programs of radical acceleration as well as did Fred, Sally, Hadley, and the other students previously described.

Factors in the Success of the Acceleration Programs

Program Design and Planning

As discussed earlier, sixteen of the fifty-nine young people in this study have been radically accelerated. In each case, the grade-skips and subject-matter acceleration have been carefully planned and monitored, addressing the children's social and emotional maturity as well as their academic achievement. With the exception of Sally Huang, who underwent an unusually fast-paced but extremely well-monitored and evaluated program, no child has skipped more than one grade at a time. As recommended by Terman and Oden, the skips have been spaced appropriately as the child progressed through school, with at least one year of consolidation between skips.[43] As advised by J. F. Feldhusen, T. B. Proctor, and K. N. Black in their guidelines for grade-advancement of precocious children, each student was psychometrically assessed to establish his or her intellectual capacity, and to ensure that the child would be able to perform at a level considerably beyond the average for the receiving grade.[44] In each case, it was understood that acceleration would be undertaken on a trial basis, and the children knew that they had the option, at any time, to return to their earlier placement. In every case, however, the acceleration proved overwhelmingly successful.

In each instance, the children's parents and the children themselves were involved in planning and monitoring the acceleration program. Indeed, in most cases the initial grade-skip was proposed not by the teachers but by the parents, who had familiarized themselves with the research on appropriate education for the gifted. In several cases, the school was extremely reluctant to permit any acceleration and concurred only when it became obvious that retaining the child with age-peers, with token in-class enrichment or pull-out, was quite inadequate to the child's academic and social needs.[45]

The relative merits of acceleration and enrichment have been much debated. Many researchers conclude that the most effective intervention for highly gifted students combines both procedures and enhances them with other provisions, such as individual study and mentorships.[46] With the exception of Roshni, the children's acceleration has been supplemented with enrichment and ability-grouping, in the form of pull-out programs, mentorships, or streaming in specific academic subjects. Further extension has been provided for Chris and Ian by permitting them to enter state and national math competitions at ages much younger than usual. Even with radical acceleration, the mental ages of these children were considerably higher than those of the average students in the classes they entered, and additional educational adaptations were necessary to ensure that they were, indeed, provided with academic challenge and intellectual peers.

Provision of an Intellectual Peer Group

It is now generally understood and accepted that a child's level of social and emotional development is more highly correlated with his mental age than with his chronological age.[47] The significance of this is immense when dealing with the extremely gifted, because the higher the IQ, the greater the discrepancy between chronological and mental ages, and thus the wider the gap between the psychosocial development of the gifted child and that of his age-peers. Children tend to make friendship choices on the basis of mental, rather than chronological, age.[48] Researchers over the last sixty years have noted that, as a rule, intellectually gifted children prefer companions somewhat older than themselves.[49] Christopher, Ian, Fred, and the other radical accelerands in this study have been given access to a group of children who are at similar stages of intellectual and emotional development.

Extremely gifted children may be hampered in socialization because their reading interests and preferred leisure activities tend to lie completely outside the average child's realm of capability or interest.[50] This can lead to severe problems of salience and social rejection if the extremely gifted child tries to share his reading interests with age-peers. Few eight-year-olds choose, like Anastasia, to read *Les Misérables*. Fred, at the age of nine and in fourth grade, had no access to friends who would understand his passionate interests in psychology and the history of art. By contrast, Hadley, also nine but in seventh grade, had teenage classmates who share his enjoyment of science fantasy; the novels he preferred would have been completely above the heads of his age-peers. When Christopher, at twelve, was enthralled by Dickens and the Brontës, he could share his enthusiasm with his eleventh-grade classmates.

The Reversal of Underachievement

The common perception of the extremely gifted as eager, academically successful young people who display high levels of task commitment has been refuted by research demonstrating that many highly gifted children underachieve seriously in the regular classroom, and that, by the end of elementary school, many have almost completely lost the motivation to excel.[51]

The majority of the extremely gifted young people in this study state frankly that for substantial periods in their school careers they have deliberately concealed their abilities or significantly moderated their scholastic achievement in an attempt to reduce their classmates' and teachers' resentment. Generally, the radical accelerands have acknowledged that even the considerably advanced curriculum provided by their acceleration has not challenged their intellectual abilities to the fullest; however, they state uniformly that the emotional security they have experienced through being placed with intellectual peers alleviated or completely removed the pressure to underachieve for social acceptance.

However, there may be a temporal limit to the reversibility of underachievement. Attempts to reverse academic underachievement in gifted high school students who have been working significantly below their potential for several years meet with variable success.[52] Ian Baker's father recognizes how close Ian came to losing—perhaps irretrievably—his motivation to learn. "He has had to start all over again and learn to work in school," he wrote, when Ian was first permitted radical subject-acceleration in math. "It's years since he had to think about anything that was presented to him in class, and it has come as quite a shock to him to have to apply himself. At first, he even resented it. However, his attitude towards school has definitely improved. A few times in the last few weeks he has come home with the gleam in his eye that we remember from when he was little. Only now have we realized how much he had turned off. I think we've arrested the slide, but I also think we went very close to him switching off altogether."

The exceptionally gifted children who have not been permitted radical acceleration are not so fortunate. In many cases, the parents of children retained in the regular classroom with age-peers or grade-skipped by only one year report, like the parents of Adam, that the drive to achieve, the delight in intellectual exploration, and the joyful seeking after new knowledge—which had characterized their children in the early years—have seriously diminished or disappeared completely. Unfortunately, the schools attended by these children have in many cases viewed the student's decreased motivation, and attendant drop in academic attainment, as indicators that the child has "leveled out" and is no longer gifted.

Summary

The work reported here is the only longitudinal study of exceptionally or profoundly gifted children conducted outside the United States. The findings support the conclusions of American researchers (such as J. C. Stanley and C. P. Benbow, L. D. Pollins, and P. M. Janos and N. M. Robinson) that radical acceleration is a practical and effective response to the intellectual and psychosocial needs of the extremely gifted.[53]

In every case, the students who have been radically accelerated, and their teachers and parents, believe strongly that they are now much more appropriately placed, both academically and socially. These students display high levels of motivation, they report that pressure to underachieve for peer acceptance has significantly diminished or disappeared completely, and, although the curriculum that they are offered does not completely address their academic needs, it provides a challenging and stimulating intellectual environment when enhanced with ability grouping, enrichment, or mentoring. The radical accelerands have positive attitudes toward school and believe that they are warmly regarded by their teachers. They have a greater number of friends and enjoy closer and more productive social relationships than they did prior to their acceleration. They have significantly higher levels of social and general self-esteem than do children of equal intellectual ability who have been retained with age-peers or grade-skipped by a single year, and their academic self-esteem is healthy, rather than unrealistically inflated (as is the academic self-esteem of many of their ability peers who have been retained in the regular classroom without access to work that requires them to strive for success).

Prior to acceleration, many of the accelerands displayed the negative attitudes and behaviors that still characterize extremely gifted students who have not been radically accelerated. These unaccelerated children display disturbingly low levels of motivation and social self-esteem; are more likely to report social rejection by their classmates; and state that they frequently underachieve in an attempt to gain acceptance by age-peers and teachers. Several of these children are required in class to work at levels seven or more years below their tested achievement.

In Australia, as in the United States, many teachers argue that acceleration may jeopardize a child's social and emotional development. This study finds no evidence to suggest that social or emotional problems arise through well-planned and carefully monitored programs of radical acceleration, and suggests that we should instead concern ourselves with the maladjustment that can arise as a result of prolonged educational misplacement. Accelerating exceptionally or profoundly gifted children by a single year is no more effective than retaining them in the regular classroom with age-peers.

Let us end with comments from three of the six young people whose programs of radical acceleration have been reported here. Not one of the sixteen radical accelerands regrets having taken an accelerated pathway through school.

Sally Huang is certain that acceleration has brought her nothing but benefits.

> If I had not been accelerated, I feel sure that I would have become quite frustrated, as indeed I often did at various stages and still do when I attend things like mixed-ability language classes. . . . But the frustration in that case would have been prolonged and severe, having a detrimental effect not only on my love for learning but also on me as a person. Given the existing educational framework, acceleration was the best option for my particular situation and I certainly don't feel that I've suffered any ill effects as a result; indeed, all the effects have been beneficial. But this is only because of the support and watchful eyes that were kept trained on my progress academically and as a person all throughout.

Sally is a forceful and articulate advocate of teacher training and in-service in gifted education.

I really can't emphasize enough how important a role has been played by the nurturing, supportive home environment I've had right from Day One. This has made my progression relatively smooth, given that at first there wasn't much support from school—it was all initiated by my mother. Nothing like this had ever happened before in these schools and most of the teachers had absolutely no idea of what to do with me. Some even felt threatened. So it was important that my parents were well-informed and that there were a few key figures in school who were receptive to new ideas. This is where I think it is crucial that the educators are educated about the gifted, so that they are able to give more support to the child if it isn't forthcoming from the home.

Roshni Singh comments, "In a way I'm sorry it was necessary to do something that was so unusual at that time, and I didn't like the teasing that emerged when I was about thirteen, although I realized even then that it arose through jealousy or at least a certain resentment on the boys' part, but I certainly don't regret doing it. The alternative—staying with age-peers—would have been intolerable."

In 1991, when he was ten and before the start of his acceleration program, Ian Baker accepted the author's invitation to speak about his life at school to a postgraduate class in gifted education at the University of Melbourne, where she then taught. He bleakly encapsulated his life in the heterogeneous classroom in a single word: "Hell."

With appropriate teacher training, it need not have been.

Notes

1. Burks, Jensen, and Terman, *Genetic Studies of Genius*.

2. Tannenbaum, *Gifted Children*; Grinder, "The Gifted in Our Midst," 5–35.

3. Austin and Draper, "Peer Relationships of the Academically Gifted," 129–134; Janos and Robinson, "Psychosocial Development in Intellectually Gifted Children"; Schneider, *The Gifted Child in Peer Group Perspective*; Robinson and Noble, "Social-Emotional Development and Adjustment of Gifted Children," 4: 56–76.

4. Schneider, et al., "The Social Consequences of Giftedness."

5. Schneider, *The Gifted Child in Peer Group Perspective*, 33.

6. Janos and Robinson, "Psychosocial Development in Intellectually Gifted Children," 182.

7. Burks, Jensen, and Terman, *Genetic Studies of Genius*; Hollingworth, *Children Above 180 IQ*; Gallagher, "Peer Acceptance of Highly Gifted Children"; DeHaan and Havighurst, *Educating Gifted Children*; Barbe, *One in a Thousand*; Janos, "The Psychological Vulnerabilities of Children"; Silverman and Kearney, "Parents of the Extraordinarily Gifted," 1–10; Morelock, "The Profoundly Gifted Child in Family Context."

8. Hollingworth, *Gifted Children*; Hollingworth, *Children Above 180 IQ.*

9. Ibid.

10. Hollingworth, "The Child of Very Superior Intelligence."

11. Hollingworth, "The Development of Personality."

12. Janos, "The Psychological Vulnerabilities of Children"; Silverman, "The Highly Gifted"; Gross, *Exceptionally Gifted Children.*

13. Hollingworth, *Gifted Children*; Hollingworth, "The Development of Personality"; Hollingworth, *Children Above 180 IQ*; Hollingworth and Cobb, "The Special Opportunity Class"; Hollingworth and Cobb, "Children Clustering."

14. Burks, Jensen, and Terman, *Genetic Studies of Genius.*

15. Terman and Oden, *Genetic Studies of Genius.*

16. Sheldon, "Isolation as a Characteristic"; Janos, "The Psychological Vulnerabilities of Children"; Silverman, "The Highly Gifted"; Hollingworth, "The Development of Personality."

17. Hollingworth, *Children Above 180 IQ*; Silverman, *Counseling the Gifted and Talented*; Gross, *Exceptionally Gifted Children.*

18. See, for example, the following: Gross, "Children of Exceptional Intellectual Potential"; Gross, "The Use of Radical Acceleration"; Gross, "The Early Development of Three Profoundly Gifted Children"; Gross, "Radical Acceleration"; Gross, "'Fishing' for the Facts"; Gross, "Small Poppies"; Gross and Feldhusen, "The Exceptionally Gifted Child"; Gross and Start, "'Not Waving but Drowning.'"

19. Stanley, "Identifying and Nurturing the Intellectually Gifted."

20. Hagen, *Identification of the Gifted.*

21. Kitano and DeLeon, "Use of the Stanford-Binet Fourth Edition"; Silverman and Kearney, "Parents of the Extraordinarily Gifted"; Silverman and Kearney, "Don't Throw Away the Old Binet"; Tyler-Wood and Carrie, "The Identification of Gifted Children"; Robinson and Robinson, "The Use of Standardized Tests."

22. Silverman, *What We Have Learned About Gifted Children.*

23. Vernon, "The Demise of the Stanford-Binet Scale"; Silverman and Kearney, "Parents of the Extraordinarily Gifted"; Silverman and Kearney, "Don't Throw Away the Old Binet."

24. Silverman and Kearney, "Don't Throw Away the Old Binet."

25. Wasserman, personal letter.

26. Kidder and Fine, "Qualitative and Quantitative Methods."

27. Hollingworth, *Gifted Children*; Silverman, *Counseling the Gifted and Talented.*

28. Foster, "Self-Concept, Intimacy and the Attainment of Excellence."

29. Ward, *The Australian Legend*; Goldberg, *Issues in the Education of Gifted and Talented Children*; Start, *Submission to the Australian Senate.*

30. Gross, "How Ability Grouping Turns."

31. Burks, Jensen and Terman, *The Promise of Youth*; Hollingworth, *Children Above 180 IQ*; Gross, *Exceptionally Gifted Children*.

32. Gross, *Exceptionally Gifted Children*.

33. Silverman and Kearney, "Don't Throw Away the Old Binet."

34. Gross, "Relationships Between Musical Precocity."

35. Gross, *Exceptionally Gifted Children*.

36. Stanley, "Identifying and Nurturing the Intellectually Gifted."

37. Tannenbaum, *Adolescent Attitudes Toward Academic Brilliance*; Carrington, "Australian Adolescents' Attitudes Towards Academic Brilliance."

38. For an overview of these studies, see Gross, "Changing Teacher Attitudes."

39. Hollingworth, *Gifted Children*; Gross, "The Pursuit of Excellence."

40. Richard's school history is described in detail in Gross, *Exceptionally Gifted Children*.

41. Southern, Jones, and Fiscus, "Practitioner Objections to the Academic Acceleration."

42. Gross, *Exceptionally Gifted Children*, 222.

43. Terman and Oden, *The Gifted Child Grows Up*.

44. Feldhusen, Proctor, and Black, "Guidelines for Grade Advancement."

45. Gross, *Exceptionally Gifted Children*.

46. Hollingworth, *Children Above 180 IQ*; Sisk, "Acceleration Versus Enrichment"; Feldhusen, "Eclecticism: A Comprehensive Approach."

47. Hallahan and Kauffman, *Exceptional Children*; Tannenbaum, *Gifted Children*; Janos and Robinson, *Gifted and Talented*.

48. O'Shea, "Friendship and the Intellectually Gifted Child"; Gross, *From "Play Partner" to "Sure Shelter."*

49. Davis, "Personal and Social Characteristics of Gifted Children"; Terman, *Mental and Physical Traits of a Thousand Gifted Children*; Hollingworth, "The Child of Very Superior Intelligence"; Janos and Robinson, *Gifted and Talented*; Silverman, *Counseling the Gifted and Talented*.

50. Zorbaugh and Boardman, "Salvaging Our Gifted Children"; Hollingworth, *Children Above 180 IQ*; Gross, "Radical Acceleration."

51. Pringle, *Able Misfits*; Painter, *Gifted Children: A Research Study*; Whitmore, *Giftedness, Conflict and Underachievement*; Gross, *Exceptionally Gifted Children*.

52. Tannenbaum, *Gifted Children*.

53. Stanley and Benbow, "Extremely Young College Graduates"; Pollins, "The Effects of Acceleration"; Janos and Robinson, "Psychological Development in Intellectually Gifted."

References

Austin, A. B., and D. C. Draper. "Peer Relationships of the Academically Gifted: A Review." *Gifted Child Quarterly* 2, no. 3 (1981): 129–134.

Barbe, W. B. *One in a Thousand: A Comparative Study of Highly and Moderately Gifted Elementary School Children.* Columbus, OH: F. J. Heer, 1964.

Burks, B. S., D. W. Jensen, and Lewis M. Terman. *Genetic Studies of Genius.* Vol. 3, *The Promise of Youth.* Stanford, CA: Stanford University Press, 1930.

Carrington, N. "Australian Adolescents' Attitudes Towards Academic Brilliance." *Australasian Journal of Gifted Education* 2, no. 2 (1993): 10–15.

Davis, H. "Personal and Social Characteristics of Gifted Children." *Report of the Society's Committee on the Education of Gifted Children,* edited by G. M. Whipple: 123–144. The Twenty-Third Yearbook of the National Society for the Study of Education. Bloomington, IL: Public School Publishing Company, 1924.

DeHaan, R. F., and R. J. Havighurst. *Educating Gifted Children.* Rev. ed. Chicago: University of Chicago Press, 1961.

Feldhusen, J. F. "Eclecticism: A Comprehensive Approach to Education of the Gifted." *Academic Precocity: Aspects of Its Development,* edited by C. P. Benbow and J. C. Stanley: 192–204. Baltimore: Johns Hopkins University Press, 1983.

Feldhusen, J. F., T. B. Proctor, and K. N. Black. "Guidelines for Grade Advancement of Precocious Children." *Roeper Review* 9, no. 1 (1986): 25–27.

Foster, W. "Self-Concept, Intimacy and the Attainment of Excellence." *Journal for the Education of the Gifted* 6, no. 1 (1983): 20–27.

Gallagher, J. J. "Peer Acceptance of Highly Gifted Children in the Elementary School." *Elementary School Journal* 58 (1958): 465–470.

Goldberg, M. L. *Issues in the Education of Gifted and Talented Children in Australia and the United States.* Canberra, Australia: Commonwealth Schools Commission, 1981.

Grinder, R. E. "The Gifted in Our Midst: By Their Divine Deeds, Neuroses and Mental Test Scores We Have Known Them." *The Gifted and Talented: Developmental Perspectives,* edited by F. D. Horowitz and M. O'Brien: 5–35. Washington, DC: American Psychological Association, 1985.

Gross, Miraca U. M. "Changing Teacher Attitudes to Gifted Students Through In-Service Training." *Gifted International* 9, no. 1 (1994): 15–21.

———. "Children of Exceptional Intellectual Potential: Their Origin and Development." Ph.D. diss., Purdue University, 1989.

———. "The Early Development of Three Profoundly Gifted Children of IQ 200." *To Be Young and Gifted,* edited by P. N. Klein and A. J. Tannenbaum: 94–140. New Jersey: Ablex, 1992.

———. *Exceptionally Gifted Children.* London: Routledge, 1993.

——. "'Fishing' for the Facts: A Response to Marsh and Craven." *Australasian Journal of Gifted Education* 7, no. 1 (1998): 16–28.

——. *From "Play Partner" to "Sure Shelter": How Conceptions of Friendship Differ Between Average Ability, Moderately Gifted and Highly Gifted Children.* Keynote presentation at 5th Wallace National Symposium on Talent Development, University of Iowa, May 19, 2000; in press.

——. "How Ability Grouping Turns Big Fish into Little Fish—or Does It? Of Optical Illusions and Optimal Environments." *Australasian Journal of Gifted Education* 6, no. 2 (1997): 18–30.

——. "The Pursuit of Excellence or the Search for Intimacy? The Forced-Choice Dilemma of Gifted Youth." *Roeper Review* 11, no. 4 (1989): 189–194.

——. "Radical Acceleration: Responding to the Academic and Social Needs of Extremely Gifted Adolescents." *Journal of Secondary Gifted Education* 5, no. 4 (1994): 27–34.

——. "Relationships Between Musical Precocity and High Intellectual Potential." *Australian String Teacher* (June 1990): 7–11.

——. "Small Poppies: Highly Gifted Children in the Early Years." *Roeper Review* 21, no. 3 (1999): 207–217.

——. "The Use of Radical Acceleration in Cases of Extreme Intellectual Precocity." *Gifted Child Quarterly* 36, no. 2 (1992): 90–98.

Gross, Miraca U. M., and J. F. F. Feldhusen. "The Exceptionally Gifted Child." *Understanding Our Gifted* 2, no. 5 (1990): 1, 7–10.

Gross, Miraca U. M., and K. B. Start. "'Not Waving but Drowning': The Exceptionally Gifted Child in Australia." *The Challenge of Excellence: a Vision Splendid,* edited by S. Bailey, et al.: 25–36. Proceedings of the 9th World Conference on Gifted and Talented Children. Wagga Wagga, Australia: The Australian Association for the Education of the Gifted, 1991.

Hagen, E. *Identification of the Gifted.* New York: Teachers College Press, 1980.

Hallahan, D. P., and J. Kauffman. *Exceptional Children.* Englewood Cliffs, NJ: Prentice Hall, 1982.

Hollingworth, Leta S. "The Child of Very Superior Intelligence as a Special Problem in Social Adjustment." *Mental Hygiene* 15, no. 1 (1931): 3–16.

——. *Children Above 180 IQ: Stanford-Binet Origin and Development.* New York: World Book, 1942.

——. "The Development of Personality in Highly Intelligent Children." *National Elementary Principal* 15 (1936): 272–281.

——. *Gifted Children: Their Nature and Nurture.* New York: Macmillan, 1926.

Hollingworth, Leta S., and M. V. Cobb. "Children Clustering at 165 IQ and Children Clustering at 145 IQ Compared for Three Years in Achievement." *Nature and Nurture: Their Influence Upon Achievement,* edited by G. M. Whipple: 3–33. The Twenty-Seventh Yearbook of the National Society for the Study of Education, Part 2. Bloomington, IL: Public School Publishing Company, 1928.

———. "The Special Opportunity Class for Gifted Children, Public School 165, Manhattan." *Ungraded* 8 (1923): 121–128.

Janos, P. M. "The Psychological Vulnerabilities of Children of Very Superior Intellectual Ability." Ph.D. diss., New York University, 1983.

Janos, P. M., and N. M. Robinson. "The Performance of Students in a Program of Radical Acceleration at the University Level." *Gifted Child Quarterly* 29, no. 4 (1985): 175–179.

———. "Psychosocial Development in Intellectually Gifted Children." *The Gifted and Talented: Developmental Perspectives,* edited by F. D. Horowitz and M. O'Brien: 149–195. Washington, DC: American Psychological Association, 1985.

Kidder, L. H., and M. Fine. "Qualitative and Quantitative Methods: When Stories Converge." *Multiple Methods in Program Evaluation,* edited by M. M. Mark and R. L. Shotland: 105–139. New Directions for Program Evaluation, no. 35. San Francisco: Jossey Bass, 1987.

Kitano, M. K., and J. DeLeon. "Use of the Stanford-Binet Fourth Edition in Identifying Young Gifted Children." *Roeper Review* 10, no. 3 (1988): 156–169.

Morelock, M. J. "The Profoundly Gifted Child in Family Context." Ph.D. diss., Tufts University, 1995.

O'Shea, H. "Friendship and the Intellectually Gifted Child." *Exceptional Children* 26, no. 6 (1960): 327–335.

Painter, F. *Gifted Children: A Research Study.* Knebworth, England: Pullen Publications, 1976.

Pollins, L. D. "The Effects of Acceleration on the Social and Emotional Development of Gifted Students." *Academic Precocity: Aspects of Its Development,* edited by C. P. Benbow and J. C. Stanley: 160–178. Baltimore: Johns Hopkins University Press, 1983.

Pringle, M. L. K. *Able Misfits.* London: Longman, 1970.

Robinson, N. M., and K. D. Noble. "Social-Emotional Development and Adjustment of Gifted Children." *Handbook of Special Education,* edited by M. Wang, M. Reynolds, and H. Walberg, vol. 4: 56–76. Oxford: Pergamon Press, 1992.

Robinson, N. M., and H. B. Robinson. "The Use of Standardized Tests with Young Gifted Children." *To Be Young and Gifted,* edited by A. J. Tannenbaum and P. N. Klein: 141–170. New York: Ablex, 1992.

Schneider, B. H. *The Gifted Child in Peer Group Perspective.* New York: Springer-Verlag, 1987.

Schneider, B. H., M. R. Clegg, B. M. Byrne, J. E. Ledingham, and G. Crombie. "The Social Consequences of Giftedness in Ontario Schools." Research report, Social Sciences and Humanities, Research Council of Canada and Ontario Ministry of Education, 1986.

Sheldon, P. M. "Isolation as a Characteristic of Highly Gifted Children." *The Journal of Educational Sociology* 32, no. 1 (January 1959): 215–221.

Silverman, Linda Kreger. *Counseling the Gifted and Talented.* Denver: Love, 1993.

———. "The Highly Gifted." *Excellence in Educating the Gifted,* edited by J. F. Feldhusen, J. VanTassel Baska, and K. Seeley: 71–83. Denver: Love, 1989.

———. *What We Have Learned About Gifted Children, 1979–1995.* Denver: Gifted Development Center, 1995.

Silverman, Linda Kreger, and K. Kearney. "Don't Throw Away the Old Binet." *Understanding Our Gifted* 4, no. 4 (1992): 1, 8–10.

———. "Parents of the Extraordinarily Gifted." *Advanced Development* 1 (1989): 1–10.

Sisk, D. A. "Acceleration Versus Enrichment: A Position Paper." *Educating the Gifted: Acceleration and Enrichment,* edited by W. C. George, S. J. Cohn, and J. C. Stanley: 236–238. Baltimore: Johns Hopkins University Press, 1979.

Southern, W. T., E. D. Jones, and E. D. Fiscus. "Practitioner Objections to the Academic Acceleration of Gifted Children." *Gifted Child Quarterly* 33, no. 1 (1989): 29–35.

Stanley, J. C. "Identifying and Nurturing the Intellectually Gifted." *Educating the Gifted: Acceleration and Enrichment,* edited by W. C. George, S. J. Cohn, and J. C. Stanley: 172–180. Baltimore: Johns Hopkins University Press, 1979.

———. "The Predictive Value of the SAT for Brilliant Seventh- and Eighth-Graders." *The College Board Review* 106 (1997): 31–37.

Stanley, J. C., and C. P. Benbow. "Extremely Young College Graduates: Evidence of Their Success." *College and University* 58 (1983): 219–228.

Start, K. B. *Submission to the Australian Senate Standing Committee on the Education of Gifted and Talented Children.* Canberra, Australia: Australian Commonwealth Government, 1986.

Tannenbaum, A. J. *Adolescent Attitudes Toward Academic Brilliance.* Talented Youth Project Monograph. New York: New York Bureau of Publications, Teachers College, Columbia University, 1962.

———. *Gifted Children: Psychological and Educational Perspectives.* New York: Macmillan, 1983.

Terman, Lewis M. *Genetic Studies of Genius.* Vol. 1, *Mental and Physical Traits of a Thousand Gifted Children.* Stanford, CA: Stanford University Press, 1925.

Terman, Lewis M., and M. H. Oden. *Genetic Studies of Genius.* Vol. 4, *The Gifted Child Grows Up.* Stanford, CA: Stanford University Press, 1947.

Tyler-Wood, T., and L. Carrie. "The Identification of Gifted Children: The Effectiveness of Various Measures of Cognitive Ability." *Roeper Review* 14, no. 2 (1991): 63–64.

Vernon, P. E. "The Demise of the Stanford-Binet Scale." *Canadian Psychologist* 28, no. 3 (1987): 251–258.

Ward, R. *The Australian Legend.* Melbourne: Oxford University Press, 1958.

Wasserman, D. Letter to Dr. Linda Kreger Silverman, December 23, 1997.

Whitmore, J. R. *Giftedness, Conflict and Underachievement.* Boston: Allyn and Bacon, 1980.

Zorbaugh, H. W., and R. K. Boardman. "Salvaging Our Gifted Children." *Journal of Educational Sociology* 10 (1936): 100–108.

---

*The article was published in *Gifted Child Quarterly* 36, no. 2 (1992). The author acknowledges, with thanks, the permission of *Gifted Child Quarterly* to reproduce portions of the article.

PART: 3

More Than a Number

Numbers and categories are useful tools, but they no more define "high-IQ" than a yardstick defines the space-time continuum. High-IQ kids are so much more than test scores and intellectual potential.

High-IQ kids don't experience the world the way most people do. Their intense awareness, ability to understand and explore complex thoughts and situations deeply, and exceptional sensitivity affect their social and emotional, as well as their intellectual, experiences. Not only do high-IQ kids think differently, they feel and react differently.

This difference doesn't mean they're wrong or "broken," but it does mean they are vulnerable in ways that may be surprising.

High-IQ kids are more susceptible to social and emotional difficulties than their average-IQ peers. They recognize their differentness and often feel that being smart gets in the way of having more (or any) friends. Their capacity for understanding can lead to a sense of urgency as well as impatience and frustration. Behaviors that are a direct result of their high IQ, from acting out and challenging authority to daydreaming and perfectionism, get labeled as problems or emotional disturbances.

But along with the pain, high-IQ kids are often filled with a sense of wonder and awe. They're compassionate and concerned with fairness and justice. They delight in good relationships and passionate interests.

This section holds the heartbeat of high-IQ kids: stories of pain, perseverance, and triumph. Observations on volatility and vulnerability. Thoughts about being different and fitting in. Guidelines for nurturing heart and spirit.

Welcome to the *whole* world of high-IQ kids!

21 Red Zone

BY DEBORAH ROBSON

Deborah Robson is copublisher of Nomad Press, a small press that specializes in traditional and ethnic knitting books and in young-adult fiction. She also works as a freelance editor to support her passions for writing and visual art, especially traditional fiber work and oil painting, which she has recently rediscovered. She has learned, and still learns, more than she could imagine possible from her daughter, Bekah, who (thank heavens) no longer has to deal with compulsory "educational" systems.

When profoundly gifted children enter school, their differences become pronounced. The experience of attempting to fit in can cause serious psychological damage. Yet adults who don't ever give up—even when everyone's run out of obvious answers, even when the only advocate is a single parent who works full-time—can give a child whose teachers have labeled her a "social zero" the opportunity to become a well-adjusted success. Deborah Robson and her daughter know this better than most. Heartache, fear, and sorrow dogged them for many years, but neither surrendered to despair. Both rejected the pronouncements of a school system that refused to acknowledge her daughter's unique gifts. They carry scars from those years, but the scars pale in comparison to the triumph they ultimately found.

Second Crisis, Fall 1993

Fact: My daughter, age twelve, sits next to me in the front passenger seat of the van. We are in front of the public junior high school by the red-painted curb. Parking here is illegal. I've just come to drop off my daughter. But the emotional weight in the car prevents her from opening the car door and entering the school and keeps me from attempting to force her to do the same. We have driven across town to this school, because it offers the best possibility for her education. This is the second week of classes. Success eludes us. I take my hands off the wheel and practice yoga breaths.

There's nothing visibly wrong with this tall, lovely-to-me child, except that fear constricts her. Public school quit working two years ago. We dodged her into a private school for a year and a half. There are no private junior highs.

Bekah has dressed carefully this morning, wearing a blue dress made by my cousin. She looks neat, and far more mature than the other kids. Part of her wants to belong to the world of her age-mates. A bigger part knows she doesn't. Neither of us knows why. Soon we will both break free from the effort to be normal because we will clearly acknowledge our two options: the adolescent psych unit or a path of our own invention.

My daughter is brave and very strong. She is not physically disabled. Within a few months, we will have learned that she is extraordinarily intelligent and that learning disabilities have seriously impeded her. We don't know that yet. Nor do we know that some types of diversity are still simply pushed away, regardless of the laws.

Many vehicles have pulled up to the red-painted curb and dropped off young people, who run into the building carrying backpacks and sports equipment. I have turned off the engine, so we don't generate pollution as well as frustration. The first bell rings, then the second. Bekah holds her body rigid. Something scares her enormously. We both know her fear is illogical.

Bekah isn't even certain whether I am friend or foe. She's twelve. I'm forty-four. I'm the one who's supposed to know how to handle the world. Right now, I don't.

I look past her toward the closed doors of the school. Inside, other kids and adults go through routines that make sense, or are at least acceptable. We can't see through the glass that reflects the outside world back at us.

I envision the building's doors as a membrane through which I need to teach my daughter to pass, in and out, fluidly, repeatedly, and comfortably, before she can be fully enfranchised as a member of contemporary society.

If I get out of the car, open the door from her side, and attempt to move her physically, she will fight me with all her terrified strength. I'm wiry and agile, but she has been fiercely powerful since she was a toddler. At twelve, she weighs half again as much as I do. Even if I won the physical battle today, the hysterical child I would wrestle kicking and screaming into the building would not be ready to learn.

As long as we sit side by side, facing the situation together, we both have a chance of success. If we turn against each other—and yes, I am tempted to yell at her; to strike my fist against the steering wheel or the car seat; to try to force her into the school; to let someone else deal with her—if we turn against each other, we will both lose something irreplaceable.

Opinion 1: The public school system believes that my daughter is severely emotionally disabled.
Opinion 2: I don't.

Intervention: Someone within the school has seen us, recognized who we might be, and placed a call for the school psychologist. He also handles a high school and an elementary school, for a total of about 2,500 students. We've reached the top of his list again.

His car pulls up behind our van. He appears at the window on my side, talking across me to Bekah. He tells her she's being obstinate and making life difficult for everyone else. This is the wrong approach, although he has been one of the most helpful people we have found in the district. He's running out of patience. Now Bekah is crying, and tries to hide her tears. She has wrapped her arms more tightly around her chest, lowered her head farther, coiled her spring of resistance to its limit.

I say, flatly, "We're not getting anywhere. I'm taking her home." In this instant, I have also decided to spend the money and time driving to Denver, an hour away, for as much testing as we need.

The psychologist shrugs, then mutters to me, "If you don't get this under control, her weight's going to balloon. She'll end up weighing three hundred pounds."

He may be right. But I'm more afraid that she'll numb her pain through suicide.

As we drive away from the red zone, I strike a bargain with Bekah. She doesn't have to go to school, but she does have to be my full partner in a search for alternatives.

As her mother and the adult, I impose a few requirements. She has to stay connected with the world beyond our house, and she has to get an education. By that I mean she has to be actively engaged in learning. I don't care how she achieves those goals. I do care about the results, and I care that we make steady progress in the right direction. Slow is okay. Backward or stalled is not.

An Odyssey of Schools, 1982 to Fall 1993: From Daycare to Seventh (Eighth? Ninth?) Grade

Many years later, Bekah and I know a great deal about the learning environments that work for her. We gained that knowledge through trial and error, over many years. The testing that began in fall 1993—psychological profiles, educational evaluations, and experimentation with different learning environments—provided clues, not answers. It helped us ask the right questions and be more savvy about which one of many steps to take next.

In retrospect, the signs that Bekah was not a typical student first appeared in preschool, although they looked like positive attributes, not the foreshadowing of problems.

Schools #1, #2, and #3 (all private, all successful), ages 1½ to 4½: Within a few weeks after Bekah's birth, fatigue altered my state of consciousness. I felt semi-transparent. This child did not sleep more than ninety minutes at a stretch. Even when her father woke in response to her fussing, he didn't have the patience to walk the floor with her. We tried everyone's suggestions to help Bekah sleep, without success.

When Bekah was seventeen months old, I started taking her to home daycare in the morning at nine. Then I went home to bed. I awoke in time to pick her up at three. Here are memories I have from the time Bekah spent at Nina's house. In corduroy overalls, with diaper-plump butt, Bekah climbs onto a short chair to reach the kitchen table. She grins as she picks up one egg at a time and cracks it into a big bowl to help make lunch. Six eggs in all. The family's cat lets Bekah and the other toddlers haul him around. The kids make lots of things, including many messes. We are blessed.

Nina only operated the daycare for a year, as part of her Ph.D. program, but we were also blessed the next year, with Jane. I think back on Jane's collection of live-wire charges and wonder at her perpetual calm. When Jane moved out of the state, we parents and children used fabric crayons to make quilt squares and I assembled a blanket to keep her warm and to remind her of us all.

At three and a half, Bekah was not old enough for kindergarten, but she was ready for more structured learning. She was accepted for one of a handful of preschool slots at a private elementary school. If we could have kept her there through sixth grade, we might never have noticed any school "problems" at all.

Bekah's preschool reports discussed her preference for adults and older students, as well as her kindness toward younger kids. Over time, she evolved an individual schedule. She spent mornings happily in the preschool area. For science, the children created huge bubbles and mixed color solutions. For writing, they typed and explored printing techniques. Students who needed solitude or, like Bekah, one-on-one time with friends could retreat into several "quiet spaces." Multiple activity stations kept the classroom orderly, while the students chose their own pursuits from the options. In the afternoon, Bekah moved easily into an adjacent classroom of older kids and studied volcanoes by helping build a model the size of a sheet of plywood. Her teacher wrote, "During this year, Bekah has established herself in the group as a friend, a model worker, and a resource. This has been a gratifying experience for all of us."

Bekah's dad came down with pneumonia. His income as an independent musician stopped for a year, and I began taking the bus to work in town as a shop clerk. Then I obtained a better-paying job with a 120-mile round-trip commute. My income covered the mortgage, heat, and groceries, but not much else.

Schools #4, #5, and #6 (all public, mixed results, including the first crisis), ages 4½ to 10: In the fall, unable to pay the modest private-school tuition, we enrolled Bekah in full-day public kindergarten. Bekah objected to having to line up outside in the New England cold until the bell rang. All the children's construction-paper artwork looked similar. However, the teachers and students assembled a rainbow of colors and cultures, and each morning the class gathered in a circle for greetings in five spoken languages plus sign. Bekah especially loved the signing.

Our finances continued to plummet. Bekah's dad and I agreed that I would accept a job offer in Colorado. We visited schools before we moved, and chose as well as we could. Bekah's second semester of kindergarten consisted of a half-day program (the district had no full-day kindergarten). She sat in a room I remember as colorless working on photocopied worksheets under the supervision of a very sweet woman. Bekah began to experience boredom, although her teacher reported that "Bekah is a very capable, talented student." We were told that enrichment would be available in first grade.

The next year, Bekah began to resist going to school. "Enrichment" finally consisted of six sessions of parent-provided instruction in French, each one hour long. I visited the city's non-parochial private elementary school and decided that in Bekah's case that school would be different, not better. I heard about a clinic in Denver that tested gifted children, and if we'd had the money (or had been as desperate as we later became), I would have had Bekah tested then. Bekah's first-grade teacher said that she was "very creative and fun to have in class."

In second grade, Bekah's teacher observed that she was not reading fluently on her own. She suggested that I read to Bekah less. I compromised. I kept reading aloud, but I also sought out books for Bekah to read on her own. I looked for material written at an appropriate level concerning topics that interested her. Some English-as-a-second-language books worked well; others were far too adult. I found enough. Bekah became a reading addict. She apparently had not been motivated by the contemporary equivalent of Dick, Jane, and Spot. Her teacher said, "I am certain she is capable of doing better if she would concentrate more. . . . She has a happy attitude in school. . . ."

Divorce and family reconfiguration temporarily distracted us from school concerns. Yet Bekah began to arrive at school late, despite consistent on-time departures from home, and she started to see the school counselor. Adjusting to the family changes, or something else?

At the beginning of fourth grade, this school became so overcrowded, because of its excellent reputation, that the principal asked for volunteers to attend another school. Bekah and I listed pros and cons. She had no particular friends at this school, although she played occasionally with the girls on our block. Bekah thoughtfully decided to make the shift. She hoped the new school would be better. Maybe it would offer smaller classes and more personal attention.

Bekah was the only student out of six hundred who volunteered to change schools. The principal and the school counselor personally thanked her and acknowledged her maturity and sense of adventure.

She lucked out that year. From a class of more than thirty, she moved to a group of twenty-three, taught by an imaginative teacher who used creative problem-solving methods. Bekah packaged eggs so they could be dropped off the top of the school and land on the asphalt without breaking (hers was the only set where both eggs remained intact). She played with a couple of other girls during recess, and even stayed in touch with them through the next few years of changes.

Yet signs of academic difficulties appeared on her report cards. She was a "pleasure to have in class . . . [with] good attitude and effort" and showed a "love of math," yet the teacher mentioned a "lack" of "basic math facts" and "inconsistent test performance" in spelling. Bekah "usually" stayed on task, yet "books are always out when we do other subjects," and her handwriting was "careless in daily work." Her speed-reading scores were "off the chart," and as a fourth-grader she read at the ninth-grade level.

I began to attend newly organized district-level parent/teacher meetings on gifted and talented programming. I wrote letters to district personnel and local politicians in support of gifted curricula. I discovered books on gifted education published by Free Spirit Publishing and read Barbara Kerr's *Smart Girls, Gifted Women.*

Fifth grade. I don't want to think about it. Three instructors, three classes of students. Some shifting back and forth of kids between classrooms, so all three teachers engaged with each student. Bekah began to have trouble getting out of the car in the morning to enter the school. She started to gain weight. The school psychologist—the man we met again at the junior high—offered to administer IQ and achievement tests, although he had a specific mandate to serve low-achieving students and not the bright ones. Under severe emotional stress from the classroom situation, Bekah tested in the top 0.13 percent (point-one-three percent) on the WISC®-R. The psychologist recommended private school, because public school "could not meet her needs." He suggested that if she had to reenter the public system later, we should request assignment to "his" junior high. He would look forward to seeing her there.

The school counselor took Bekah under her wing, and recommended outside therapists.

A newly opened private school was running ads in the paper. The finances seemed impossible.

In December, Bekah, her father, her stepmother, and I met with all three fifth-grade teachers to see if we could negotiate a few changes that would make school more palatable. Neither the psychologist nor the school counselor attended.

Perhaps, we suggested, Bekah could do free reading after lunch, instead of having to stay ready to read out loud when asked? (She read too fast and had to flip back through the pages, looking for the right sentence.) No.

Perhaps she could have more challenging assignments? Only if she could propose them herself. (Bekah was ten.)

In that meeting, Bekah's homeroom teacher stated her opinion of Bekah's problem with school: "Bekah is a social zero."

This was the year of Desert Storm. Bekah read the papers and worried. The teachers helped the students assemble care packages of chewing gum and letters to send to the soldiers, but did not want to discuss the political or emotional aspects of the war. Bekah was uncomfortable reciting the pledge of allegiance before school; her own allegiance could not be contained by a flag, any more than her concern about the conflict could be expressed by a pack of gum or a bland note.

Bekah's teacher had a suggestion. "Perhaps in the evening Bekah could call up the other girls and ask what they're wearing to school the next day," she said. "Perhaps she could try to fit in a little better and pretend to be interested."

Then the teachers asked Bekah how she would characterize her own problem.

"I'm bored," Bekah said, somewhat embarrassed.

"We don't believe in bored," came the emphatic answer from the teacher we considered the most sympathetic.

During that one fifth-grade semester Bekah spent in public school, Bekah scored six absences and twenty-five tardy days. We started getting seriously stuck in the red zone at the school's front curb. When I pulled the car up, Bekah would stiffen and look straight forward. My goal became convincing Bekah to go as far as the counselor's office. Then the counselor would help her make the transition to the classroom. Bekah also developed end-of-weekend stomachaches. There was no physical cause.

School #7 (private, reasonably successful), ages 10 to 12: Bekah began her second semester of fifth grade at the start-up private school. She also started a long-term relationship with a private psychologist who helped her deal with the emotional and social aftereffects of her previous school. One of her new teachers commented that "Bekah . . . seems a little melancholy. I think she would be a lot happier if she tried to be a little more gregarious. . . ."

During that first year, this private school operated at half its student capacity. Its well-considered curriculum and academic standards ran so smoothly that few rules were required. The fifth and sixth grades worked together. The few students were all so different—artsy, social, athletic, theatrical, math genius—that they didn't form cliques. Bekah liked mythology and music and reading. In one week, she went from "I *hate* fractions" to "Hey, Mom, look what I can do with common denominators!" She drew a large picture of the Muses and included a Latin quote about laughter. She attended birthday parties. She played with younger kids in the after-school program and helped the math teacher grade papers. She began to boulder (as in "climb rocks"—my nonathletic daughter) and to play soccer and to enjoy the playground. Another teacher wrote, "Last week she gained confidence in the group . . . and outwardly began to trust them." At the end of sixth grade, she went on a weeklong camping trip in the snow and survived. She smiled more often than not. We had no problems in the car on the curb.

She graduated. For a while, this school considered adding a seventh-grade class, but decided against it. One of Bekah's favorite teachers also explored the idea of supervising an independent classroom for a half-dozen of the rising seventh-graders, but illness canceled her plans.

School #8 (public, the worst meltdown), age 12: When we arrived at the public junior high to register, Bekah's dad, stepmother, and I asked questions about placement. Although the counselors knew little about what was taught, it sounded as though Bekah had already covered the seventh-grade material. She had completed pre-algebra and could recite Shakespeare. The counselors asked if Bekah would like to enter eighth grade. That sounded okay to her; at least she might not be bored.

From there, school went downhill fast. On the first day of classes, Bekah's schedule had a handwritten note: "Rebeka [sic], please see me during 3rd hour. Thanks. Mrs. L— in the Counselors Office." Instead of eighth-grade algebra and science, Bekah was directed to a ninth-grade accelerated math/science combination. Many of the other students were fifteen. Bekah didn't look twelve, and none of her teachers was ever notified that she was being skipped one or (for reasons we never discovered) two grades, depending on the subject. Bekah's lunch hour was not the period that combined seventh- and eighth-graders, where she would have been among many new students and might have seen old friends from fifth grade, but the one that served only eighth- and ninth-graders, with established groups and rambunctious hormones.

We began to be stuck in the red zone. When not on the curb, I spent hours waiting for the counselors or the psychologist.

For about a month, Bekah went where she was told: to eighth grade, to parts of ninth grade, and finally—in a proposed retreat—to seventh grade, with a "shortened" schedule because of her "emotional disturbance." At home, the "emotional disturbance" took the form of crying, nightmares, and tantrums. Bekah reached the point where she couldn't enter the school. Even to pick up her gym clothes and take them home.

A note from Bekah's school file, dated September 29, says, "R Robson-May Dad called—they will call w/ test results. All 3 are concerned about emotional statis [sic]. They will contact us next week." The psychologist gave us a directory of private tutors, a bibliography on homeschooling, a list of independent study programs, and the suggestion that we sign papers moving her to official homeschool status.

Legally, the school system was required both to comprehensively test Bekah and to provide her, like every other child in the district, with a "free, appropriate public education." If I had signed the papers they offered me several times, I would have absolved them of that responsibility. I wonder how they thought a single parent with a full-time job, necessary to support the two of us, could reasonably home-educate her disturbed child?

Yet I would not let that same system destroy her, which in my opinion it was doing. Even if I didn't know what else I would do.

Bekah's last day as a full-time registered student in the public schools was October 5, 1993. She was twelve years old and seriously depressed.

Testing, Testing

Schooling situation #9 (out-of-school), ages 12 to 16: In the following weeks, we drove to the Gifted Development Center in Denver several times for testing and advice. The evaluators used the words *profoundly gifted* after Bekah reached the ceiling on two IQ tests. We discovered her learning disabilities. She writes four times more slowly than "normal," while her brain races ahead. The discrepancy between mental and manual speeds must have been excruciating. She scored extremely low on measures of social acceptance, physical appearance, and athletic competence, which contributed to worrisome scores on self-esteem. Bekah's good feelings about her academic abilities, still bolstered by the private-school experience, kept her from landing entirely in the basement on the emotional tests.

The center recommended a gifted program, enrichment, interaction with other gifted girls, program modifications to accommodate Bekah's introversion, more counseling, untimed testing, vision therapy, work/study instead of strict academics, acceleration in math and science (with a calculator), use of a computer to compensate for visual-motor weakness, and an individual education program (IEP) combining independent study, advanced abstract content, and mentorships in math and architecture with assistance to compensate for her slow eye-hand and processing speeds.

In a physical exam to rule out medical complications, specifically bio-chemical depression and attention deficit disorder, the doctor announced that the reason Bekah was having problems in school and didn't have friends was because she was fat. He used window-dressing words that he thought she would not understand. Bekah kept herself under control until we left the office, but I had to hold and comfort her for forty-five minutes in the car before she could stop sobbing.

We changed doctors. We even changed clinics. I wrote the director. Of course, he backed up his staff.

I began to work directly with the district's coordinator of special education. We received lip service—at meetings with many high-level administrators, expensive-to-the-district lip service. Bekah spent the next four years basically out of school. I refused to sign the papers accepting responsibility for homeschooling, continued to pressure the district to provide her with an education, and helped Bekah try different educational settings.

Two months after Bekah left school, her depression was still evident. Her sadness was one thing. Her painful furies when she cried and banged her head on the wall and scratched her arms and legs until she raised welts were another. My own therapist—whose most forceful comment during this time was "you don't need therapy, you need social work"—helped me gather in one room many of the private psychologists and consultants we had been working with. When the school district does this type of meeting, it's called a *staffing*. In this case, I paid the professional hourly rates myself, because most often I had to try to make one coherent picture from their varying perspectives on my own. We compared notes, located a psychiatrist only one town away who was taking new adolescent patients, and got Bekah on antidepressants. We agreed that the alternative was the adolescent psych unit, ASAP.

But the medications worked. It became possible for Bekah to live with herself, and for me to live with her.

A year later, her attention deficit disorder was diagnosed. She began to take Ritalin and to make consistent, rather than scattered, progress in learning.

Sort-of-schools #10, #11, #12, #13: As part of her agreement with me that she would "stay connected with the community," Bekah began working at the children's science museum immediately upon her withdrawal from school. She also volunteered for four years as a teacher's aide in four public elementary schools, assisting two teachers and working in two languages (English and, for a while, rudimentary Spanish). She was particularly helpful to kids who were having trouble adjusting to school.

Sort-of-schools #14, #15, and #16: At thirteen, Bekah tried taking a few classes at a public high school. By Thanksgiving, she had completed the semester's work and was having trouble backing up enough to participate in class. She was technically registered at another high school into which she never set foot; that school appears on her district transcript as her "base." At fourteen, Bekah studied logic during a three-week summer session at the Center for Talented Youth, at Johns Hopkins University in Baltimore. She and her ADD roommate took monitor-approved breaks from evening study to run off energy in the halls. Bekah loved symbolic logic, and came home exuberant about learning.

Sort-of-schools #17 and #18: At fourteen and fifteen, Bekah completed classes at the community college and the state university in our town, although neither institution challenged her. In one case, she didn't consider her fellow students to be serious enough, so she didn't value the A she received. In the other, the instructor arrived with a limited view of Bekah's capacities and humored her, giving her a B+ because that was all she was prepared to imagine Bekah capable of.

Bekah also spent two years reading and discussing de Tocqueville and John Adams in a private tutorial with a university professor. She loved their lunchtime free-for-alls.

School #19, ages 16 to 18: As Bekah reached fifteen and then approached sixteen, this cobbled-together educational approach outran its usefulness. She began to regress. She needed to feel the rewards of substantial accomplishment.

We consulted an educational adviser—again in Denver, again expensive. He helped find a school that she liked that was willing to take a chance on her, medications and all. She spent her sixteenth and seventeenth years at a Quaker boarding school 2,000 miles from home. It was far from perfect, but she adjusted and then excelled in regular and advanced placement classes, as well as theater and volleyball. Because of her patchy record, she applied to six colleges. All six responded positively, and with substantial scholarship offers. Bekah made her own choice of which to accept.

At Last

Over almost twenty years, Bekah's mental health has risen and fallen in direct correlation to her schooling situation. In her case, the private schools consistently helped and the public schools did not. Yet I believe that some public schools hold answers for students like Bekah, while some private schools can inflict great damage.

She made it to high school graduation with her mental health intact (or, more accurately, restored), without a permanent and restrictive label of "emotionally disabled" on her record, with good grades and the start of a social life.

School #20 (private, college, successful): Bekah now attends a very challenging college on a full academic scholarship and she's doing exceptionally well. Ironically, she now has help for her learning disabilities—for the first time, direct and useful resources that she can access on her own terms. Of course, she no longer desperately needs assistance. Yet over the past few weeks she has enjoyed working with the school's new voice-recognition software so much that she has been offered a work-study job training other students in its use. She recently wrote, "Just for fun, I'm doing this email using the voice software. My spelling should be fine, but I'm not completely sure how well it works on the whole deleting issue. In fact, I'm pretty sure it doesn't work at all in PINE. Nope, it doesn't. Oh well. It's still pretty neat." And yes, for once she didn't have to worry about her spelling. That was a new experience.

She joined the fencing club, and this year serves as its co-treasurer (she uses a calculator, as she did for advanced calculus last year). Phone conversations often turn into three-way exchanges between Bekah, her roommate, and me. There's lots of angst and lots of laughter. She's appropriately nineteen.

At last. She has found one place where she fits as well as any of us do.

That's plenty.

And when she arrives home at the Denver airport and she walks down the concourse toward me, I find tears in my eyes because she moves with such grace, inside and out.

22

The Problem of Pain

BY STEPHANIE S. TOLAN

Stephanie S. Tolan, poet, playwright, and Newbery Honor author of novels for children and young adults, is also a consultant on the needs of the highly gifted. A prolific writer and speaker about extreme giftedness, she is coauthor of *Guiding the Gifted Child* (1982), a contributing editor of *The Roeper Review*, and a senior fellow of the Institute for Educational Advancement. She wrote the article "Is It a Cheetah?" a metaphoric look at the reality of the gifted that has been reprinted in numerous publications throughout the United States and translated into many languages.

Stephanie Tolan recognizes the pain experienced by families of gifted children. She helps both parents and children discover the inevitability and meaning of pain, and helps them develop a set of simple, flexible tools for coping with it.

When *Guiding the Gifted Child* was published twenty-five years ago, parents of exceptionally and profoundly gifted children began to call me, pouring out their stories and asking for my advice. At that time, little information was available about the needs of children at the highest ranges of human intelligence. Although our book hadn't focused on that population specifically, the last chapter told the stories of my own exceptionally gifted son and of the profoundly gifted son of my closest friend. This chapter served as a kind of lifeline to parents who had been struggling with the issues of parenting these children alone. When parents called, they usually cried or cursed as they told their stories—often both. They were desperate.

Today much has changed. Parents have access to a great deal of information (e.g., Miraca Gross's excellent book, *Exceptionally Gifted Children*, and the newsletter of the Hollingworth Center, called *Highly Gifted Children*) and a number of Internet lists connect parents (and children) with others facing the same issues. Parents are no longer alone. Thanks to the Internet lists, I get fewer phone calls.

Unfortunately, the calls I do get make it clear that neither more information nor a greater sense of community has eradicated parents' desperation. Life for highly gifted children and their families can still be enormously difficult. What the parents who call me are dealing with is pain—often intense pain: their children's and their own.

Pain isn't a subject that we often address directly, and that may be one reason why we don't cope with it very well. Our culture's attitude is anything but helpful. Watch a little commercial television and you'll see the two most common responses to pain.

The first is, "Have a pain? Take a pill." That response used to apply to physical pain, but lately it has grown to include emotional or psychic pain. In a culture that claims to want to keep children off drugs, drugs are pushed to adults at every turn. Pharmaceutical remedies are now promoted not just for headaches, stomachaches, sore muscles, and heartburn, but for depression (often loosely defined), extreme sensitivity, and shyness (now dubbed *social anxiety disorder*). Worse, these pharmaceutical remedies are more and more being offered to adolescents, children, and even toddlers, without studies to prove either their safety or their effectiveness for young people.

The second response is, "Do something to fix the situation that causes pain, and if it can't be fixed, hire a lawyer and sue someone." If pain can't be fixed, the reasoning seems to be, the perpetrators should be identified and punished and we should be monetarily compensated.

While these responses might be appropriate in certain situations, the idea that all pain can or should be addressed by one or the other suggests that pain is an aberration, that we somehow have a right to a pain-free existence. If we encounter pain, there is something wrong, someone to blame, and a critical need to stop the pain immediately.

But the truth is that life includes pain. For everyone. And the truth for the families of highly gifted children is that a considerable amount of pain may be caused by the degree of giftedness itself. Pain comes with the territory.

The Pain of High-Range Giftedness

The first and most obvious source of pain for the highly gifted is that they don't fit our culture's expectations, norms, and institutions. They are different in a culture that dislikes and fears difference, in a culture that increasingly defines difference as pathology. The term *normal* is often used to mean *average*. This leads to the belief that what is *not average* is *abnormal*. In this climate, a child who is not average will experience pain, regardless of whether she chooses to be true to herself and risk ostracism or to deny important aspects of herself and adopt protective camouflage in order to fit in.

We are a communal species; we need each other. But it can be difficult or even impossible for exceptionally gifted children to find other children with whom they can share their deepest thoughts and most passionate interests. They can come to feel like aliens.

In addition, their differences can lead to attacks from others. Sometimes what feels to the child like an attack was meant to be ordinary childhood teasing, but the child's unusual sensitivity makes it feel much more serious. Often, though, the attack has been quite purposeful. It may come from other children, or from an adult threatened by a child whose vocabulary, knowledge, or understanding of a particular topic is more extensive than his or her own.

The unusual sensitivity that is common to the highly gifted population may cause pain in a variety of ways. Children bright enough to see at an early age the way the world *is* and also to create for themselves an image of the way things *ought to be* must come to terms with the need to live in the gulf between these two visions, and so may be subject to a degree of existential depression or despair. Some children have such strong empathy with other people, with animals, or even with the planet itself that they internalize pain from outside themselves.

Parents, too, experience an unusual amount of pain from the giftedness itself. Some comes from seeing their children's pain, and some comes from their own childhood pain, reactivated when their children have experiences similar to their own. Injustice makes most of us crazy, and the gifted must regularly contend with injustice (often with no remedy). In fact, extreme giftedness in a family can create a level of pain equal to that of dealing with a severe handicap.

When There's No Solution

In call after call over the last two decades, parents have described situations (often truly appalling ones) that for one reason or another cannot be "fixed." There may be no way to change the person or the situation creating the problem, and no way to remove the child or substitute a safer environment. Sometimes there are strategies that may relieve the current pain, but are likely to create different pain, equal to or even greater than the original. Our cultural preference for finding a solution to every problem ignores the fact that some situations are not mere problems but dilemmas, in which all of the available choices have negative consequences. Sometimes we can't choose the best answer; we can only look for the least harmful one. Time and time again, I have hung up the phone after a conversation with a parent and cried, feeling the intensity of the family's pain and knowing I haven't been able to help because there is no way, at least in the immediate future, to take it away.

I have come at last to realize that what many parents need—even more than answers to an immediately painful situation—is a way of seeing life's inevitable pain that is healthier than our standard cultural view, and a set of strategies (what one mother called a "nifty tool kit") for handling pain. Parents need these things both for themselves and to teach to their children.

Pain Thresholds

First, it's important to recognize that pain, whether physical or emotional, is an individual matter. What causes one person enormous pain may give someone else minor discomfort. We need to be aware of individual differences in the perception of pain, the reaction to pain, and the expression of pain.

Some parents have called me in trauma over something that is happening to their child, concerned that the child seems not to be reacting. There are several possible explanations for this. The child may genuinely not feel as traumatized as the parent; the child may feel pain but either denies or refuses to focus on it; or the child may feel pain and react strongly, but hides his feelings rather than expressing them. It's important to observe a child carefully to learn his or her typical pattern. This isn't always easy, especially when parents and children have different pain thresholds and different ways of responding to pain.

When my own son was in a class of older children in which classmates often bullied him and the teacher frequently reminded everyone of how much younger he was, I took him to see a psychologist because I was afraid that his generally cheerful appearance was hiding a level of pain and stress that should be addressed. The psychologist assured me that RJ was just fine; RJ thought the bullying said more about the bullies than about himself, he rather liked the teacher and so allowed the belittling comments to roll off his back, and his cheerful appearance reflected the fact that he was a very cheerful kid! What I would have found painful, RJ was able to take in stride.

A friend of mine has a rule for similar situations: "Never disturb a happy child."

On the other hand, an extremely sensitive child who hasn't been taught to distinguish between levels of pain may go into paroxysms of agony over every tiny bump in the emotional road, so that parents become desensitized to the constant expression of pain. They may then ignore serious alarm bells. Or they may become so impatient with the whole issue that they give the child the message that unusual sensitivity is shameful.

My father, of stoical German heritage, must have been stumped by the problem of raising the "skinless" and highly emotional child that I was. Having done his best to outlaw feelings, he made it clear to me that strong people not only don't *show* pain, they don't have it in the first place. Pain in our family was proof of poor character, weakness, failure. I've often thought how much easier it would have been on my father to have raised my cheerful son instead of me!

It is important to mention that there are a few children, whom some would call "old souls," who come into the world able to handle pain in a unique way. They apparently come equipped with abilities some others develop through Buddhist compassion meditation—they absorb the pain of the world, process it through the heart with compassion, and send it out into the world again as love. If you are lucky enough to have one of these rare children, you may learn more than you will teach.

Perceptions, Definitions, and Meaning

How do you perceive and define pain? What does it *mean* to you? The answers to these questions determine your ability to cope with it.

As parents, it is our responsibility to keep our children from harm. If we equate *pain* with *harm*, then we will think it's our job to keep our children from experiencing pain—an impossibility that will create even more pain, for us and for them, when pain comes in spite of our best efforts to keep it at bay.

If we think pain is a kind of punishment or an unfair visitation of unnecessary distress, then our ability to contend with it will be marginal. Pain can then extend beyond the immediate experience and take on implications of guilt, injustice, or the hostility of a vengeful god or a malign universe, which can be overwhelming. If this is how we view pain, we are likely to teach our children to ignore, deny, run from, or blame themselves or others for pain that can't be immediately stopped, fixed, or avoided. In the worst-case scenarios, this perception of pain can lead to addictions, bitterness, withdrawal, or suicide.

All religious traditions address the issue of pain in one way or another, and a family's religion or spiritual heritage is likely to have important effects on the family members' understanding of what pain means. These effects can be positive or negative, depending on the tradition and on the family's interpretation of its teachings. Whether or not you have a religious or spiritual tradition, you do have a *cosmology*, a belief system about what the universe is like and what your place in it is, and you will teach this cosmology to your children, if not by word, then by modeling. Einstein is quoted as saying that the most important question each person must answer is whether the universe is a hostile or a friendly place. You will find it far easier to handle your own pain and to model good strategies for your children if you believe in a friendly universe!

Practice

The following tools are readily available to anyone of any age, but they require practice. That's why some of the people most able to handle pain are those who have had the most pain in their lives. The more we use the tools, the better we get at using them and the better they work.

Pain is an excellent motivator, and for some people pain alone is quite enough to get them to practice using the tools. Others would rather moan and groan and whine—or grit their teeth and stoically endure, or shriek and rage—than put out personal effort to cope with pain. Using the tools may require going against a good deal of conditioning, or against our natural tendencies. If we tend to run from pain, for instance, it isn't going to be easy at first to get ourselves to turn around and face it.

But the tools work. They don't take pain out of the world, but they can literally turn lives around and bring light into darkness.

Ten Tools for the "Nifty Tool Kit"

1. Acceptance

Accept that pain is part of life, neither unfair nor intended to ruin your day or your children's childhood. Accepting pain allows you to move through it and out the other side, while denying it shoves it inside, where it does not vanish but remains and often festers. When someone hurts your child, old, denied pain can sometimes burst like a boil and turn you into a raving maniac, unable to address the current issue reasonably.

Accepting pain (instead of denying or covering it up) allows us to feel it, experience it for as long as it lasts, and then let it go. Accepting it lets us discover that it *can* and naturally *will* go. On the other side of a painful experience, we are likely to discover that we have learned something important that could have been learned no other way.

2. "One Day at a Time" or "Day-Tight Compartments"

The Bible says, "Sufficient unto the day are the evils thereof." If we can keep our attention confined to a small space, the pain that fills that space will be easier to handle. In times of moderate pain, that space may be a day; in times of intense pain, that space may be a minute or even a second. It's possible to endure something briefly that we can't imagine enduring for a long time. If we focus on the moment, we can get through just this one, then just this one, then just this one. If we look back at all the other bad moments there have been, and extrapolate from that an infinite number of future bad moments, they all run together into a single eternal pain that we're likely *not* to be able to handle.

3. The Blanket

Many children, like Linus, have "security blankets" that provide more than security. They provide comfort. It is important to find out what soothes and comforts us, and what soothes and comforts each of our children, and then provide these elements whenever possible during painful times. What comforts may be a warm bubble bath, or a long walk, or a cuddle and a story. It's important not to think of this as indulgence, but as healing medicine.

My parents' generation disallowed thumb-sucking and bemoaned the introduction of pacifiers. The excuse was teeth: thumb-sucking led to braces. But the underlying reason was that the cultural traditions of their time suggested that comforting a child would make him weak.

There is nothing inherently weakening in comfort during a rough time. As long as the mode of comfort doesn't cause immediate or future pain of its own (like alcohol and drugs, or too much sugar or chocolate), the dosage may be increased as the need increases.

My parents' generation was not entirely wrong, however. As important as it is to provide comfort, we also need to expect and encourage healing and moving on. Carried too far, offered too often or for too long, comfort can become an end in itself. Providing plenty of love and attention when pain *isn't* in the picture can help avoid this problem.

4. Other People

We need each other. One of the most important uses of community is support during bad times. Because families with exceptionally gifted children are a minority, we can find it difficult to establish as many human-to-human ties as we need. Our first step is to seek out companions, either in person or through electronic connection. Our second step is to take very good care of the friends we do find.

It's easy for people with lots of interests to get so busy that we forget to nurture our relationships. We need to be sure to call or visit friends and to arrange for our children to do the same. We need to write letters and exchange email. We need to spend time with the people we care about. Time is vital to building relationships.

And don't forget the value of pets, for both children and adults. Animals provide enormous support, sympathy, and love, and we can gain balance and perspective from the care and love we offer them.

5. Help Somebody Else

Every year during the holidays, newspapers are full of advice to those who find the holidays depressing—get out and volunteer to make a pleasant holiday for someone else. Helping somebody else is an excellent way to keep us from being overwhelmed by our own troubles. Sometimes, in the process, we find people whose pain is far greater than our own and we realize that our lives aren't as bad as we thought. Other times, we simply substitute helping (and the good feeling it brings) for hurting.

6. This, Too, Shall Pass

Nothing remains. Nothing stays the same. One of my own favorite sayings is, "There are no caves, only tunnels." It reminds me that no matter how dark and small a space I may be in, there's a way not just out, but *through*. And outside there's light.

Telling ourselves that nothing lasts reminds us that no pain is forever. But there's another benefit as well. Knowing that good things also pass encourages us to appreciate them while they last.

7. Breathe

Focusing on the breath is a technique that the Lamaze method teaches for dealing with pain during childbirth, and it is the foundation of many meditation practices that work to reduce levels of stress and pain. We all breathe, but seldom do we notice. Conscious breathing is a tool that's easy to learn, works quickly, and can be used virtually any time, anywhere, under any circumstances. The more you practice it, the more quickly it will calm and center you.

Begin by simply noticing your breath—not trying to control it, just noticing each intake and each exhalation. Gradually let your breathing slow and deepen while you concentrate on the sensations as the breath moves into and through you.

Most of us breathe from our chests rather than our diaphragms, and changing to diaphragmatic breathing can increase the effectiveness of the technique. Take a deep breath and watch to see whether it is your chest or your stomach that moves. If it's your chest, see if you can change the way you are breathing so that the movement happens below your rib cage. To teach a child this, have her lie on the floor and place a book on her stomach. Have her breathe so that the book moves up and down. Then let her experiment with moving first her chest and then the book so that she begins to *feel* the difference.

A quick way to switch from chest-breathing to diaphragmatic breathing is to take a very deep breath and then let it out in a hard, fast sigh. Doing this once or twice usually accomplishes the switch.

As simple as the breathing technique sounds, it is amazingly effective. Regular practice can make conscious breathing an important part of daily life, useful not only for times of pain and stress, but for increasing our awareness of positive feelings, bringing us into the moment to experience them more fully.

8. Make a "Terrific Things" List

Bernie Siegel, an M.D. who has worked extensively with cancer patients, often advises people who are dealing with life-and-death issues to make a list of the terrific things that have happened to them in the last week and then share it with someone. It is very easy to notice what hurts, so that in really rough times we may quickly come to believe that pain dominates. Making a conscious effort to find something "terrific" in every day changes our focus. When we consciously look for terrific things, there turn out to be many more than we thought. Most of us have had the experience of learning a new word and then hearing or seeing it used all around us, or buying a car and noticing how many others of the same model are on the road. When we aren't looking for something, we may not see it, even if it's right in front of us.

Since everything is relative, what counts as terrific during a smooth part of our life's journey might need to be spectacular (like winning the lottery), while what counts as terrific in a bad time might be a glimpse of sunset reflected on the surface of a river when we're stuck in a traffic jam. The important issue here is not what the terrific thing is, but that we identify it as terrific!

9. A Gratitude List

Finding things to be grateful for is a common tool in twelve-step programs. At first, it can be difficult to be grateful for *anything* during a time of great pain. But if we take the task seriously and start with the goal of finding five or ten things we are grateful for, and if we do this every day for a week or a month, our feelings can begin to change. Sometimes we find that there are more things to be grateful for than to be hurting about, whether the painful situation that drove us to using this tool has changed or not.

Sometimes a kind of spiritual miracle can occur from this exercise. We can come close to feeling, if not fully understanding, the mystery of pain. If we concentrate hard enough on gratitude, we may eventually find ourselves able to be grateful not just for the things outside of or around the pain (like being able to see, or to walk, or to think, or not having been hit by a bus today) but also to be grateful for the event or the person causing us pain, and eventually for the pain itself. We may discover that pain sharpens our whole experience of life.

10. Joy

How can joy be a tool for dealing with pain, when pain and joy seem to be opposites? Because joy can be a fundamental aspect of life that exists for us at all times, in all places, whether pain exists simultaneously or not.

Many of us are looking for happiness—its pursuit is a right guaranteed to Americans. We expect happiness to be a big thing, long-lasting, we hope even permanent. The idea is that when we find happiness, all the negatives will be superseded in its constant glow.

Joy is different. It is incredibly bright, but may seem brief, fleeting. Joy is what we need to teach ourselves to notice. There is paradox in the fact that being able to notice joy, being *determined* to notice it, turns it from a fleeting moment to the foundation of all our experience, available to us even when pain brings darkness.

If you aren't familiar with the picture book by Leo Lionni titled *Frederick*, it's worth finding, for yourself as well as for children of any age. *Frederick* tells the story of a mouse who, while the other mice industriously store up seeds for the winter, merely stands and looks—at the sun, at the trees, at the sky. The other mice think Frederick is wasting time, but he tells them he is working just as they are. Later, during the long hard winter, the mice gradually eat up their store of seeds and find themselves cold and hungry. It is then that Frederick shares what *he* has stored up. He turns his memories of summer beauty into words and fills the cold, dark place with light and warmth and beauty.

Frederick is one of those simple, classic stories that work on many levels. It can be seen as a celebration of art and artists. But it is also a story about the truth and strength of joy. Each of us can store images of beauty and moments of joy from our daily lives, if we choose to. The greater our store of bright moments, the more aware we will be of their constant presence, and of their instant availability no matter how dark the world seems at the moment.

Perspective and Choice

Some of you will have noticed that the last three tools are so closely related they amount to different ways of saying the same thing. At the bottom of the nifty tool kit, there is what might be called the Swiss-army knife of tools. It does everything. It's *perspective*.

Everything in our life view depends on perspective, viewpoint, the place we're standing at the moment. Photographers know that standing in one spot and shooting a picture five times can produce five entirely different photos, depending on the angle of the camera or the focus. An inch this way, an inch that way, and the whole picture changes. Focus close or focus far, and the picture changes. Face into the light or away from it, and the picture changes. We are always in control of our perspective. We can change focus, back off, take a larger view.

In his powerful book, *Man's Search for Meaning*, Viktor Frankl says, "We must never forget that we may . . . find meaning in life even when confronted with a hopeless situation, when facing a fate that cannot be changed. For what then matters is to bear witness to the uniquely human potential at its best, which is to transform a personal tragedy into a triumph, to turn one's predicament into a human achievement. When we are no longer able to change a situation—just think of an incurable disease such as inoperable cancer—we are challenged to change ourselves."[1]

Changing our perspective, changing ourselves, is a choice. Perhaps the most important thing to remember is that, whatever the life situation, whatever the pain, each of us *always* has that choice.

Notes

1. Frankl, *Man's Search for Meaning*, 116.

References

Frankl, Viktor. *Man's Search for Meaning*. New York: Simon and Schuster, 1984.

Gross, Miraca U. M. *Exceptionally Gifted Children*. New York: Routledge, 1993.

Hollingworth Center. *Highly Gifted Children*. www.hollingworth.org.

Webb, J., E. Meckstroth, and S. Tolan. *Guiding the Gifted Child: A Practical Source for Parents and Teachers*. Scottsdale, AZ: Great Potential Press, 1982.

23

When the Pop Bottle Overflows

BY JUDY FORT BRENNEMAN

Judy Fort Brenneman is a writer, editor, business owner, and advocate for children "who look normal but aren't." Her essays have appeared in *Weber Studies, Puerto del Sol,* and other publications. She hasn't had a violent outburst since 1976, not counting one really bad day in 1985, when she kicked a hole in the kitchen wall. But it's fixed now.

What if, in addition to being too bright for regular school programs, your kid expresses his differences in part by striking out at the places and people who try to confine him? For many profoundly gifted children, emotional volatility combines with frustration to produce explosions. Judy Fort Brenneman tells how she dealt with her son's physical and emotional outbursts of violence, which were dramatic until he reached college age. In the long years before he matured, she had to devise ways to protect him and at the same time, let him experience appropriate consequences while he learned to constructively deal with situations he found intolerable.

The first one was when he was only two days old. The worst one was the summer he was sixteen, when he broke the camp counselor's nose.

In between, there have been meltdowns, rages, eruptions, tantrums, storms, outbursts, and, during one particularly bad week when he was seven, talk of suicide.

He has learned to spackle and paint at the same time that he's learned to program the computer. He's cleaned out the storage room at the local United Way office and sorted canned goods at the Food Bank as part of court-ordered community service, and then he continued volunteering his time to these and other causes because he believed it was the right thing to do.

He's struggled to learn coping skills for chaos, written about restorative justice, and found social success with nonviolent adult friends and mentors. He still punches holes in walls, but now he can usually restrict the pounding to his own room. He still screams in fury and rage, but is able to apologize the same day, sometimes the same hour. And these storms, these rages that wash over and through him, crashing into everything around him, have finally become the exception, not the rule.

This is a cautionary tale, but a tale of power and hope, too.

By the time Kyle was three, I knew two things with absolute certainty: he was smart, and he could throw temper tantrums worse than any other kid I knew. "Smart" wasn't a big deal; sure, it was fun, but as my mom always told us, "It isn't how smart you are, it's what you do with it that's important." The temper tantrums were bothersome and sometimes embarrassing—the acoustics in our small-town mall create amazing amplifications of the shrieks of an enraged toddler—but I initially didn't realize that these tantrums were as different from the norm as his intellectual abilities.

I remember being surprised the first time he threw himself facedown on the living room carpet, screaming, pounding fists and feet on the floor, his bright red face rocking back and forth. I thought only kids in old TV sitcoms did that. I'd never actually seen this behavior in real life. I was pretty sure I'd never done it, though I did throw temper tantrums long past the age when most kids stop. It didn't occur to me that screaming and kicking for half an hour at a stretch was abnormal; TV sitcoms have commercial breaks, but moms don't.

I tried holding him in a bear hug, which made things much worse. I tried singing lullabies. I tried covering him with a soft blanket. I tried yelling.

I finally began treating each episode like a seizure: remove all dangerous objects, stay within line of sight, and wait for the storm to pass, prepared to offer a warm hug and a quiet story when he was ready. The pediatrician said I seemed to be handling it well.

Only after a long time did I begin to understand that these two traits—extremely high intelligence and extreme volatility—were both inextricably part of the unique human who is my son.

By the time Kyle was seven, he had been expelled from two preschools and from the private school he'd attended since pre-kindergarten. He'd also been diagnosed with ADHD and Tourette's syndrome. He was evaluated by a speech therapist, who recognized that something unusual was going on but wasn't sure what, and by an occupational therapist, who told us about tactile defensiveness, the hypersensitivity to touch that intense emotion can trigger. His first evaluation for intelligence and learning differences—done by a family friend in private practice instead of the public school, which refused to do any testing because they had "children with real problems" to serve—indicated that he was in the 97th to 99th percentiles in everything. When we reported the results to the teachers and the school counselor, they said, "Well, we always knew he was smart," a refrain we were to hear every year, at every IEP (individualized education program) review, at every conference. The message—implied and sometimes stated explicitly—was that his intelligence was irrelevant at best, was unrelated to the behavioral difficulties, and was, in fact, a problem itself that needed to be fixed. Tactile defensiveness and other "hyper-responses" to stimuli were abnormal and pathological. And if we were good parents, Kyle would eventually be "normal."

We were told time and again that as soon as his behavior was good, they'd get back to teaching him actual academics. They reassured us: he's so bright, he'll pick up the academics next year or the year after that. They said: the material is repeated two, maybe three, times; there's plenty of time to learn it by high school.

Nowhere in these discussions, these frantic meetings about disruptive behavior or long work sessions trying to develop behavioral strategies that would work for more than a week, did anyone bring up the simple fact that highly and profoundly (H/P) gifted kids (and adults) often have hyper-reactive systems. Combine this with asynchronous development—the condition of being advanced in some areas, lagging in others—and the frustration of not fitting in the world the way the world expects you to, add a dollop of slightly impaired impulse control or sensory-integration difficulties, and what might have been an irritable or fussy personality in an average child becomes a highly reactive, prone-to-raging and acting-out, H/P gifted child.

For five years, from third grade through the first semester of eighth grade, the school focused almost totally on "fixing" Kyle's behavior.

We agreed to transfer him into the special-ed class for children with severe emotional disturbances (SED), even though everyone agreed that he didn't have a severe emotional disturbance. But because the behavior was a good match, perhaps the program would be, too. It was not.

I do not mean—or want—to minimize my son's behavioral difficulties. The actions that resulted in his SED placement—from throwing chairs and ripping displays off bulletin boards to torrents of ear-splitting, rage-driven profanities and occasional head-banging—were serious. They posed a threat to others and sometimes to himself, and they were fearsome to watch.

He needed *something*, and the best teachers we had—and there were several—were as frustrated as we were in our hunt for solutions. Over time, we realized that Kyle had significantly fewer meltdowns at home than at school (in either mainstream or SED classrooms). Ultimately, we replaced in-school instruction with more challenging curriculum and the personalized attention from home-bound tutors, computer-based correspondence classes, home-directed enrichment activities, and other more appropriate learning opportunities. But between that frustration and this solution, Kyle crossed the boundary to violence several times.

Our first introduction to law enforcement occurred during the second semester of fourth grade, about a month after he'd transferred to the SED program. The school called; Kyle had slapped the teacher's face.

The teacher was apologetic. She had lots of experience working with this kind of thing and usually dodged in time, but, she explained, she was distracted for a minute and *smack!* his hand came around and connected.

In our state, a ten-year-old (regardless of disability) is considered old enough for legal action in cases of assault. The teacher was required to file a report. We would need to talk to the police officer assigned to the school.

The pattern established at this first go-round repeated with minor variations several times over the years: give a statement to the police officer, including information about disabilities, hypersensitivity, special-ed status, and the medical care (i.e., current meds and therapy) already in place; speak with the counselor at the Youth Services Bureau (and sometimes the district attorney), providing the same information; agree with the counselor that our child's extreme intelligence makes things much more difficult now, but will ultimately be his saving grace; reassure the counselor that we, as parents, are taking an active part in helping our son overcome this problem; reinforce the fact that incarceration is not an appropriate consequence and would in fact aggravate the problem and undermine the work done to date; supervise community service or other restorative justice; and, throughout it all, continue daily practice with Kyle on developing better strategies for predicting and then appropriately dealing with situations that are likely to trigger meltdowns.

There are three very tough aspects to this routine.

The first is that your child is in serious trouble, even though he's a good kid at heart.

The second is that you, as a parent, have to guide him through the resulting maze in a way that both protects him and allows him to grow and learn more appropriate behavior.

The third, and most important, is that you can never, ever give up, no matter how hard it is, no matter how scared and angry and embarrassed you are, no matter how exhausted or how hopeless or out-of-new-ideas you feel at the moment. Your job as a parent is to help your child learn who he is, how he reacts, and what to do with that knowledge and those feelings.

In *Why They Kill: The Discoveries of a Maverick Criminologist*, author Richard Rhodes presents the hypothesis that four steps lead to severe and irremediable violent behavior: brutalization by authority figure(s), which includes experiencing violence and struggling to come to terms with it; belligerency, when the victim decides to resort to violence in order to prevent further victimization of himself or others; successful violent performances, when the victim discovers that his own violence produces the results he desires, including a decrease in victimization and an increase in the respect and fear others show toward him (i.e., power); and virulency, when he decides to use serious violence as a standard means of dealing with people, because it has worked to decrease his *own* pain and sense of powerlessness. An individual who passes through each step successfully is much more likely to use violence routinely in personal interactions.

No one knows if the hypersensitivity of H/P gifted children puts them at increased risk for following this path and acquiring the belief that violence is an effective means of interacting with others, but I believe it does.

What feels okay to someone of normal sensitivity can feel violent to the hypersensitive. When a touch feels like pain, when a hug feels like suffocation, when the normal hubbub of a classroom feels like the entire world is screaming at you, what conclusion can you draw except that the world is a harsh, uncompromising, unforgiving place? When you can envision perfection and justice but are ridiculed and condemned for your idealism, where can you turn except to despair and cynicism?

Nurturing the gifts our H/P gifted children bring to the world must also mean that we nurture their ability to appropriately interpret and react to the situations they experience. By learning coping skills and strategies for handling situations that trigger intense emotional reactions, they learn that they do not need to resort to violence to be effective.

A school principal once asked me if I thought Kyle was capable of behaving within the limits specified by our district's code of conduct. Without hesitation, I said, "Yes, absolutely."

"Why so confident?" my husband later asked.

"Because of Becky Harris," I told him.

Becky Harris was my best friend in the third grade, right up to the moment I heaved a metal trashcan at her. She was just trying to help, to tell me that things would be okay, but I couldn't hear her then.

That was my last big temper tantrum, one so bad that the teacher fled and took the rest of the class with her.

I'd had others during my first three years of school, and to this day I have no idea what triggered them or what made the last one so severe. But I eventually learned to control and direct my rage—which I discovered in later years to be at least equal parts passion and fury.

So I have faith that if I could learn how to direct that energy to more productive and powerful uses than trashcan tossing, so can my son.

The other reason I'm confident is because of Kyle himself. I was a grown-up before I began to understand what I was feeling or what to do about it. Kyle described his meltdowns when he was ten, not long after his introduction to the legal system.

"It's like a pop bottle," he said. "I fill up with everything—the frustration, the noise, the other kids—and when I'm full, they put a thumb on top and shake the bottle. Then the next thing that goes wrong makes me overflow." This helped explain why, to the teachers, Kyle's meltdowns seemed completely out of proportion to (and sometimes entirely unrelated to) anything going on at the moment. It didn't have to be a "big thing" that triggered the rage; it just had to be the *last* thing.

Kyle's pop bottle image was the tool we needed to help him learn self-control skills: when the bottle is starting to fill, he needs to use his hard-won skills to relieve the pressure or empty the bottle. The first skill was learning to recognize how full the bottle was.

He's learned breathing techniques to calm and center himself. He's learned to "reset" his autonomic nervous system by pressing his fist into the palm of the other hand. He's learned about escape routes and safe places to decompress. He's learning how to step back, how to analyze situations and social interactions, how to let go of the expectation that others will be held to the same high standards he sets for himself. It's taken him much longer to learn these skills than any others, and sometimes we forget that just because he's a "smart kid" doesn't mean that all learning is equally easy.

But with practice and maturity, he is learning that he can control his volatility without losing his passion, his energy, or his commitment. He knows that we, his parents, will not give up on him. Our confidence in his ability to grow from an amazing child into an extraordinary adult, capable of and willing to make positive contributions to society, is gradually transforming into his confidence in himself.

He's not all the way there yet, but he's close. And he will get there, with our unwavering help.

References

Rhodes, Richard. *Why They Kill: The Discoveries of a Maverick Criminologist.* New York: Alfred A. Knopf, 1999.

24 Giftedness Is Heart and Soul

BY ANNEMARIE ROEPER

Annemarie Roeper is an educational consultant with over fifty years' experience, specializing in the emotional needs of gifted children. In 1941, she and her husband, George Roeper, cofounded Roeper School for gifted children. They also founded the *Roeper Review,* a national journal on gifted education and Annemarie continues to be a member of the Editorial Review Board of the journal. She has published hundreds of articles on giftedness and has received numerous awards and honors, including the 1999 NAGC President's Award.

Annemarie Roeper pioneered, and is still pioneering, gifted education that treasures the whole child, not just the important (but insufficient) area of cognitive ability. In this essay she describes ways in which a change in the fundamental educational model will benefit highly gifted children, but will also—ultimately—improve schooling for all children.

The traditional model of education tends to look at human beings as basically driven by cognition. It focuses more on that which is testable, on that which can be learned and reproduced. It sees the human being primarily as rational and logical. It sees education as a linear process that leads to achievement. It sees giftedness as high achievement, and the highly gifted as the highest achievers.

An alternative model of education, called *Self-Actualization and Inter-dependence* (SAI), sees education as a global, all-encompassing process of growth.[1] It sees giftedness in an emotional context in which the cognitive is included. This perspective changes every aspect of education, including its goal, assessment, curriculum, and community structure, and these changes are also reflected in the view of the highly gifted.

The SAI Model

The SAI model views human beings as independent decision-makers, driven by a necessity to be true to themselves. It embraces the core of who they are and their striving to actualize themselves emotionally, cognitively, consciously, and unconsciously, as well as physically. All of these aspects clamor for a place in the world and stem from each person's unique Self. The Self is the *I*, the *I of the beholder*. It is the place from which we see and interpret the world and ourselves.

To understand any human being, any child, and certainly any gifted child, we need to focus on the Self, the inner core. The Self has no choice but to pursue its inner goal, the way a flower must follow its inner destiny.

The Selves of human beings are the most intricate organisms in the world, mosaics of interlocking parts and systems—some conscious and more unconscious—all forming a whole that fluidly connects with other Selves. There is so much that is mysterious, so much that is unconscious, that determines behavior and feelings.

Through the ages, humankind has been intrigued with the Self, the soul, the psyche. This mystery has inspired a variety of thought, is eulogized in poetry, is researched in different branches of psychology, and is hotly debated. Education, however, has a tendency to ignore the Self, and doesn't acknowledge its existence as a primary factor or even a reality. It therefore misses much of what is significant in any child, and especially in the gifted child. Giftedness includes heart and soul and is not limited to intelligence and achievement.

I would like to describe the Self of the gifted child. What is true for all human beings is even more apparent in gifted children. The specific characteristics of the gifted lead them to be in conflict with their environment more often than others are. They bump up against outside expectations because their deepened cognitive understanding leads to emotional urgency.

We learn about a child's giftedness not only through cognitive testing, but also through observation, communication, and our own emotional receptiveness. Giftedness is revealed in who children are, how they feel, how they approach the environment, and what they share in trusting relationships with empathetic adults. Only another human being is an instrument refined enough to recognize the inner world of a human being, and to experience the texture of that innerness. A test can only assess areas that are testable.

The traditional method of assessment uses standardized testing. Its purpose is to find out how much children know and how they learn, in order to predict how they may succeed and to determine their strengths and weaknesses, measured against the accepted norm. It essentially asks the question, *How will these children adjust to the expectations of society?*

The SAI model uses an elaborate, careful method of observation. The purpose is not to evaluate against a norm, but rather to understand each Self individually, with no strings attached. We look at the Self to discover its passions, its inner-directions, its cognitive ability, and only then how it relates to society.

With this accomplished, we can begin to create or find the appropriate learning environment, or to make changes according to the inner needs of this child. We ask the question, *How will this child grow?*

In comparison to other children, gifted children have greater awareness, larger horizons, and more intense emotional reactions to that which they know and experience. For instance, young children who understand that the universe keeps on expanding feel compelled to think about eternity and infinity. They often can't fall asleep, because this knowledge fills them with emotions of awe and terror.

This strong preoccupation is often a sign of giftedness in very young children. Johnny (a composite of many typically gifted children) agonizes about the meaning of death, and the meaning of life. The thoughts haunt him. He feels overwhelmed, dizzy, and somehow dislocated relative to his own insignificance. He says, "I feel so scared about dying."

Johnny tells me that he has a whole world in his head, as big as the world outside. It is a world where there are no labels, either in his clothes to irritate and scratch his sensitive skin or in his environment to define him; a world that accepts him as he is.

In the outside world, he feels exposed; everything touches him directly. He looks at a flower growing out of a tiny seed. His eyes are full of wonder, but his friends look at him with impatience. "Race you to the corner," says one friend, but Johnny has not heard him, for now he wonders about the DNA of the flower and he is overcome with the beauty of this miraculous growth. The sense of beauty fills him with such deep emotions that he cannot keep his whole body from moving with excitement.

This sense of wonder might occur anywhere. That is why, in the classroom, Johnny has not heard a word the teacher has said. When he is not in his inner world, Johnny measures himself against outside expectations and finds himself wanting.

His eyes fill with tears when he says to me, "I am stupid. I try hard, but I cannot spell, my handwriting is horrible, and my room is a mess." When this happens, parents and teachers become concerned, and the system defines his behavior as pathological.

However, the child's way of being proclaims giftedness loud and clear. A contradiction occurs: the child has been tested as highly gifted, but the very actions that exhibit giftedness are interpreted as pathological. This is why it is so important that children be understood within the norm of their emotional giftedness.

Gifted children find themselves in a system that is harmful because it only recognizes the narrow road of expected achievement. They do not fit this system and find themselves in alien territory. They may be bored by what is expected, and also puzzled by it. They are often conscious of being deprived, because the world is so filled with excitement yet they are not allowed to explore and develop their inner agenda.

Seemingly Problematic Behavior

Here are descriptions of some behaviors that are often interpreted as pathological because they are not seen within the context of giftedness.

Fierce Drive to Learn

Daniel, a four-year-old boy, is a terror in nursery school. He fights, disrupts, and knows how to push everyone's buttons. The general belief is that he has a behavior problem and the school is not equipped to handle him.

In desperation, the teacher asks him, "Why do you have to act in a way that makes everyone angry at you?" He answers, in great anger, "You fooled me; I thought school was for learning, and no one is teaching me how to read."

The teacher proposes a bargain: "You stop fighting, and I will teach you how to read." While the others play, she finds time to teach him. It truly works like a miracle. This is clearly a gifted child, driven to learn.

Procrastination

This often occurs when the needs of the Self clash with the expectations of society. An eleven-year-old girl, Angelica, and I were in a deep conversation; she was totally concentrating and carefully choosing her words. Her need to be understood reflected her desperation, and was a cry for help. We were striving to understand her problem of procrastination. It worried her greatly, and together we tried to figure out the reason. She said, "When this happens, I am not exactly bored. It's like you must go down a one-way street the teacher wants you to be on. You come to a crossroad. You really want to turn and go where it looks exciting, but you know you are not supposed to go there. This is why I sit in front of my homework, and cannot do it. It is like one rope pulling one way and another rope pulling the other way."

Such a child feels helpless and cannot listen to either voice—outside demand or inner pressure. This results in stagnation. Her understanding of math concepts is outstanding, and even though she is driven to learn, she can't. Procrastination within this context is a sign of giftedness.

Perfectionism

Many gifted children are like a little Plato; their giftedness allows them to envision the perfect teapot and so they feel the inner pressure to create it. They have to be perfect because they know what perfection is. Many young gifted children shy away from drawing because they can envision the perfect picture, the perfect house, and they haven't developed the fine-motor skills to accurately reproduce it. Perfectionism inhibits the child from performing or practicing, for fear of failure.

Also, it is almost unbearable for the gifted child to see imperfections unrecognized—for instance, when the teacher makes mistakes that are obvious to the child, but unacknowledged by the teacher. Frequently, for example, a child has a better solution for a math problem and innocently confronts the teacher. This often makes the teacher defensive, and conflict ensues. The need for perfection is a sign of giftedness.

Sense of Justice

This is also the result of perfectionism. It stems from depth of insight and empathy. It leads to numerous clashes. Here's an example. A very shy, very gifted seven-year-old boy told me that he didn't like school because the teacher tore up his friend's drawing of a dragon because it didn't look the way the teacher thought it should. He explained with the most sophisticated vocabulary that his friend was an expert on dragons. He was overcome with anger and was so concerned for his friend that he forgot his shyness, unexpectedly stood up, and in a loud voice told the teacher how unfair she was.

Gifted children become the judges of adult behavior and are puzzled and hurt when we fail them. They then react with frustration or anger, and are seen as the problem.

The misunderstanding of these behaviors can create a vicious cycle. Adults begin to worry about the child who disrupts the proceedings and become convinced that there is something wrong with the child. The child feels devastated and afraid of disappointing the parents. The expert diagnoses begin to appear: learning disabilities, ADD, socialization problems, immaturity, even Asperger's syndrome. Giftedness becomes a liability. Gifted children whom I see in my consultation service tell me that they wish they could just be normal. Giftedness comes all too often with a burden of assumed abnormality.

There are, of course, true learning disabilities. It's important to differentiate between giftedness and pathology. It is always an experience for me when I can explain this distinction to parents. I explain that it is the environment that imposes goals and standards that are inappropriate. We must change the expectations of the environment, not change the child. The parents seem to feel relieved and empowered; it's as though they have been given permission to love their child unconditionally.

Parents, a crucial factor in the free evolution of the child's movement through the developmental phases, are caught in the middle and do not know whom to trust. Should they follow the child's inner agenda, or the expectations of the environment?

Parents often feel an obligation to protect their children by insisting that the children embrace the point of view of the system. Unfortunately, the children often feel more isolated as a result, because they have to engage in a struggle with the parents. However, those children who feel unconditional love from their parents, and feel that the parents are on their side, can weather the negative effects of not being understood by the system and can still blossom. Parents are the true lifeline, especially for the gifted. No child can grow without being positively recognized. It is no exaggeration that unconditional love is the most important means of education.

A New Trend

Recently I have noticed an encouraging new trend. I am astounded by the subtle but important changes I observe in the attitudes of parents. Parents used to wonder what they could do to help their children adjust to our competitive society. More and more, however, they ask questions like these:

- Who is my child, really?

- How can I better understand my child?

- Where do I find a learning environment that will be both accepting and understanding?

- How can I change the system to fit my child?

An example: Mary, age eight, feels unconnected at school, a loner. Her parents brought her to consult with me about finding an appropriate learning environment. Her giftedness was exhibited in her sophisticated conversation and detailed knowledge of animal behavior. She arrived clutching a little box. We played and talked, and all the while I waited for her to open the box. When I asked her when she planned to open it, she told me that it was nailed shut. My curiosity grew. Finally I learned that she had been heartbroken over the death of her cat. Her loneliness had increased. Her parents, who are empathetic and spiritually very connected with her, had the cat cremated and allowed her to keep the ashes in the box, always with her. This child seemed content and her spirit remains unhindered because her parents acted upon her needs. Her parents' insightful, unconventional support is like a shield for this gentle child against the harshness she feels from her school environment.

If we begin to allow ourselves to be guided by the agenda of the Self, a door opens to finding alternatives. Society's judgment is no longer seen as absolute. We find that it is possible to meet individual needs and society's needs in many alternative ways, not yet explored.

Children who are seen as having difficulties at school and who chafe under the teacher's expectation may no longer be seen as the problem. Sometimes they cannot cooperate, not because they have attention deficit, but because of attention focused elsewhere. If we listen to our inner voice, it may tell us that such problems are more complex.

Many highly gifted children and adolescents may want to write a book or a symphony, build a car, follow their dreams. I have seen several nine- and ten-year-olds who, with their parents' help, are happily piecing together their own educational structure. For instance, they may take a few subjects at their regular school. They may pursue an area in which they excel, such as math, in a community college. They may spend the rest of the day studying violin, skating, science, or whatever they are passionate about.

When we honor our children's inner agendas, they feel a sense of freedom and power. They feel more accepted. They are no longer bumping up against external roadblocks and they no longer feel bored and worthless. It is evident that they develop fewer behavioral problems, such as procrastination, and are more likely to find enjoyment in their learning environment.

I believe that the contribution these children make to society will be greater than if they had followed the usual course. This does not mean they will be protected from the vicissitudes of life. What I am describing here is clearly the beginning of a movement that has not yet penetrated to the core of society's attitudes.

There is evidence of pressure for change, mostly coming from the children, themselves—and they are forcing us to listen. They are showing us alternative structures for growth and learning. This constitutes a major change in attitude.

In the wake of these evolving perspectives, the goal of education must change from a model of adjusting, fixing, shaping, and remolding the child into our expectations. Education must take the lead in creating a new model based upon supporting the growth of the child, creating a comfortable niche for the highly gifted. This would allow those children to reach for the stars. The first step in bringing about this change is to recognize that giftedness shows in the emotions of the child.

Emotional Evaluation

By understanding emotional characteristics as clues for identifying gifted children, our evaluation methods allow us to tell the degree of giftedness. For example, the more highly gifted children are, the greater are their command of language and symbolic thinking, memory, ability to find creative solutions to vexing problems, and such things as knowing how to handle the computer by the age of two. We understand that the more highly gifted children are, the more their emotions differ from the emotions of others—they are more sensitive and intense. The nature of their experience is different. The more highly gifted, the greater the dissonance between these children and others. They are the most finely tuned instruments and could play the most beautiful music, if we allowed their music to be heard.

What is missing from traditional assessment of giftedness is an understanding of the complex structure of emotions and of the Self of the gifted. Only if we include this consciousness will we be able to do justice to the needs of the gifted and the highly gifted. Only then will they have the chance to develop their Self and their inner agenda. Assessing the emotions must become an important part of any evaluation.

In empathetic assessment of the emotions, we experience the child through a variety of verbal and nonverbal clues, we listen and interact with both child and parent, and our nonjudgmental receptivity brings forth a desire to communicate on the part of the child. The child shares his interests, knowledge, and feelings.

It is equally important to describe what we are not doing. We bring no agenda, no prepared list of questions, no preconceived expectations, and no judgment. Each session is a surprise, and no two are alike.

The evaluator becomes the instrument for evaluation and receives the child as a whole being and listens to the child's impressions. The evaluator must try to be aware of the inner obstacles to a free reception of the child's Self. At our center, we use two evaluators, who together can provide even better understanding. The amount of information gained in this nonjudgmental way is often amazing.

In fact, we gain such specific information that we are able to predict the IQ score without the use of standardized testing. We have literally hundreds of cases where our assessment closely coincided with the recorded IQ, and through our method much additional insight is gained.

In the SAI model, we realize the evaluation itself is an intrusion into the life of another human being and may impact self-image. We are aware that our conclusions may influence attitudes and decisions that have important bearing on the future, as well as the present. The family may see the child in a different light, depending on the result of the evaluation. The IQ score is never forgotten.

The evaluator must therefore take great responsibility for the manner in which the results are communicated. It's not enough to send a form letter. Either a detailed comprehensive letter or a post-assessment consultation is required to do justice to the richness and sensitivity of the information. Results that differ from the expectations must be handled carefully and gently.

In Sum

Educational perspectives have been based on behaviorism, and most of the research about gifted children has been in the area of cognition. In shifting our attitude to appropriately include the affective dimensions, individuals who are assessing, teaching, and parenting gifted children are seeing a whole new vista open up. Psychology, education, and spirituality are merging into a new perspective. There is much we can learn from each other that can enrich our view of the world and can profit the future of gifted children, and of all children.

Notes

|||||||||||||||||||||||||||||||||||||||||||||||||||||||||||||||||||||||||||||||||||||||||||||||||||||||||||||||||||||||||||||||||||||||||||||||||||||||||||||||||||||

1. Roeper, "Self-Actualization and Interdependence."

Reference

|||||||||||||||||||||||||||||||||||||||||||||||||||||||||||||||||||||||||||||||||||||||||||||||||||||||||||||||||||||||||||||||||||||||||||||||||||||||||||||||||||||

Roeper, Annemarie. "Self-Actualization and Interdependence: SAI, A Fundamentally Different Concept of Education." Unpublished article, 1999.

25 A Mixed Blessing

BY ILONA VON KÁROLYI-ROSS

Ilona is currently working full time while she explores a career in journalism.

Often, young profoundly gifted people, like the one who tells her story here, need to leave home and the familiar to find a place where, even briefly, they "fit in," academically and socially. Taking the risk of such an experience requires nerve, at the very least. And, while the sense of belonging they discover rarely lasts, many of them carry with them a new sense of themselves that helps buffer the difficulties of daily life.

Every summer I attend a camp called CTY, standing for the Center for Talented Youth. It is a Johns Hopkins program in which the participants take a college course in three weeks. I have attended CTY for three years now, taking Logic, Introduction to Psychology, and Paleobiology. These have been learning experiences that I will never forget. The things I have learned from CTY—scholastically, emotionally, and philosophically—have been extremely influential in my life.

The first time I attended was after my seventh-grade year. I had found junior high incredibly difficult. I got honor-roll grades, but I was not very convinced of my intelligence. I felt insecure in general. The social pressures were unbelievable. I believe that at that time I also started hiding my true self more than I had before. Every day I presented a complete façade, and although I was satisfied with my outwardly popular and happy life, I am sure that I was not pleased with all the pretending that I had to do to achieve it.

I didn't think much about CTY until right before we had to leave. I packed all of my stuff, trying to bring my more conservative clothes because I was absolutely positive that I would be surrounded by "glasses-wearing, nose-picking, computer geeks," with whom I would never get along. During the five-hour car ride to Clinton, New York, I was nearly in hysterics. At every exit, I begged to turn around and go home, so I could escape from the impending three weeks of torture that I imagined.

By the time we turned onto College Hill Road, leading to Hamilton College, I had resigned myself to my fate. I would go, and deal with it, and just not socialize with anybody. However, while we were trying to find a parking place, I saw a sight that I definitely wasn't expecting: a significantly overweight boy—wearing black lipstick, a T-shirt for a band I liked, and a skirt over his jeans—was turning cartwheels in the grass. I laughed out loud, and decided that perhaps my preconceptions were incorrect. While walking into the breezeway for registration, I felt myself getting unexplainably excited and giddy.

When I actually started meeting people, I was very surprised. Although many of them did fit my stereotypical "nerd" description, they were interesting and thoughtful. I immediately became friends with everyone in my suite.

At CTY, I made many new friends and learned that there actually are other people like me. I learned my boundaries and strengths and weaknesses. I learned that there was a place where I could learn interesting things freely, without criticism or ridicule from my peers. I was pushed to my academic limit and I enjoyed the experience. Previously, I hadn't really put forth much effort—or needed to—on most of the things I did. While taking a college-level course on logic in three weeks, I was expected to do more work than I ever had before. I know it sounds weird, but for the first time I actually had to think while doing my work.

One of the reasons I liked CTY was that I met all sorts of different people. They thought in ways similar to me, as well as completely opposite. I lived in a suite with nine other girls and an R.A. (residential adviser). We all had varied tastes in just about everything. All of us thought in creative and intelligent ways, unlike any group of people I had known before. I found out that there are other people in the world who feel and see things as I do. I felt free to learn and do my best, academically and otherwise, and to share my opinions and thoughts without being squashed for my nonconformity.

Collectively, we had to make great efforts in the college-level work, in the incredibly emotional social situations, and in facing the unbelievable stress of leaving the campus again so soon after we arrived.

On the last Friday, we had tears pouring out of our eyes all day, and we spent that night, at the last dance, in shock at the prospect of having to leave something so utopian. It seemed like the greatest injustice ever. While at CTY, I opened my eyes to more than I ever thought possible. I made friends with anyone and everyone. In my small, Caucasian, Christian town in Maine, I had had no real opportunity to experience diversity, and the people are rather old-fashioned in their thinking. I found it wonderful to be around varied types of people, not just in terms of race, but in ways of thinking. I myself grew more in those three weeks than I had in the previous two years, and gained about ten new best friends who loved me for being someone I didn't even know I could be. I was funny, outgoing, free, and—most of all—happy.

When I returned to school for eighth grade the following fall, much had changed.

At CTY, I learned to do work well, without a struggle, while learning new things. Then at public school, for some reason that I cannot explain, I had a hard time even making myself do the work. So, unfortunately, my work began to suffer, and I fell farther behind than I ever had before.

My old clique of popular friends no longer interested me. I found their priorities unimportant, and their dilemmas trivial. I started associating with older people, some in high school, some graduated or dropped out. I spent hours and hours at a time sitting on the floor at my friends' apartment just talking about everything with a large group of friends. However, I also became depressed. I missed my CTY friends unbearably, and phone calls and emails weren't quite cutting it. I also found it difficult to deal with the more mature issues that my older friends were dealing with. I considered CTY a mixed blessing; I wondered how some greater power could give me a taste of perfection, then take it all away.

On the other hand, the skills and concepts I learned at CTY also gave me the ability to cope. I started visiting my CTY friends, and became happier in general. I felt confident in myself, and had the strength to leave situations that my older friends put themselves in without missing out on the important conversations that we had. I was respected by others for who I was, and—eventually and more importantly—I also began to respect *myself* for who I was. Although it was a rough trail, I recognize the value of what I learned at CTY. I appreciate my own intelligence, sense of humor, and general personality. I am a very happy and self-actualized person, and I hold CTY partially responsible.

26 Out of the Ordinary

BY ELIZABETH LOVANCE

Elizabeth Lovance currently works as a computer programmer within a research group. She started school a year early and did a combination of subject acceleration, grade skips, correspondence courses, and community college which led to her graduation from high school at 14. She graduated from Smith College with a double major in Computer Science and American Studies.

Although Elizabeth Lovance was aware from a very young age that she was different from other children, her understanding of the nature of her differences developed gradually. She carefully chose the environments in which she dealt with her feelings of "differentness," as well as the pace at which she processed them. Initially, these feelings concerned the emotional and social impact of her high IQ. As a college student in her early teens, she came out as a lesbian. She discovered that, as difficult as it was to acknowledge and reveal her sexual orientation, it had been harder to come to terms with her giftedness. Despite the challenging and sometimes painful process of understanding and accepting herself as a unique individual, she developed a strong sense of herself and of how to be in the world.

Ever since I was small, I knew I was different. Different from whom or in what ways was not always clear or consistent, but I learned early that I did not blend in with the crowd.

To be able to do so looked tempting, and I tried. In fourth grade, I made my mother buy me leggings and long sweaters to wear to school. In sixth grade, I got a permanent and was careful about the books I brought to school for free reading. *Gone with the Wind* was acceptable, if odd; *Anna Karenina* was too far out there. By high school, I brought to school the books I wanted, although I was still unnerved when I spotted a classmate in the county's largest library one Saturday. When the entire school reveled in the recent abandonment of a dress code, I settled into the comfortable clothing of jeans and T-shirts or sweaters.

I spent many hours figuring out what compromises to strike, in order to preserve myself without incurring extra criticism. My goal was not to be stylish or to fit in, just to be invisible enough that I would be spared teasing for my other peculiarities. The fact that I was different from the people I spent most of my time with formed the center of many decisions I made. Growing up, I worked to minimize the effects of preconceptions on how others treated me. The glaring difference that I strove to minimize was my giftedness, and the resulting discrepancy between my age and my grade.

After my final acceleration into a class with other highly gifted students, my thoughts and skills did not set me too far apart from my classmates; the fact that I was four years younger did. In my United States history course, I was the only student who would not be able to vote in the upcoming presidential elections. Like many of my classmates, I did not have a firm curfew, but because of my embarrassment and my dependence on my parents for transportation, I rarely had any place to go. At the time, this seemed to be caused by the mismatch between my age and my grade, and by the giftedness that had caused it. This was the difference I had grown up with, and I expected to grow out of it.

As I grew older and my age became less of a factor, I began to notice glimmerings of another difference that I would not grow out of. The brainy, four-years-accelerated, bookworm girl of between twelve and fourteen was not expected to be interested in boys or dating. I maintained that image, because I knew that if I started to examine—especially publicly—the meanings of my feelings and lack of feelings, I would have much more to deal with.

As I spent much of my days immersed in history, most of my female role models had never married and certainly were not romantically involved before their sixteenth birthdays. Although my extended family contained cousins who were lesbians and still very much part of the family, messages at school and on the news made it clear that being gay was not a way for me to enter adulthood free from the preconceptions like those I faced as a gifted child. I waited for a more hospitable environment in which to confront these other matters, and tried to focus on other aspects of life.

At my small private high school, ignoring those feelings was fairly easy. At summer camp, it was more difficult.

One summer, nearly everyone in my circle of friends paired off. I was left trying to figure out why I had pangs of severe jealousy when a boy and a girl from my group started to date. They did not shut me out, and I knew I did not want to date the boy. I tried to attribute my feelings to the fact that our conversations were sometimes interrupted by their cuddling. That same summer, a rumor broke out, later confirmed, that one counselor was gay. People said very supportive things, but there were also many hateful comments. I spent sleepless nights trying to suppress the facts that my feelings about girls and my jealousy toward the couple might be something more. I knew that I could not continue to hold myself together if I had to deal with anything additional that marked me as different.

So I suppressed those feelings again. At the mandatory dances, I snuck outside. I either went back to my cabin or lay in the courtyard looking up at the stars, crying. Concerned counselors could not cajole me back inside.

With the exception of that summer before my senior year of high school, I was able to put off the issue of my sexuality until I got to college. I was in my early teens and had the nerd stereotype to help me along. I still remember the moment when I came back from camp and, holding an orange, decided to wait until I was in a better place. Even a private acknowledgment of yet another difference seemed like one more strike against me and, it seemed, would make it even harder for me to break into the real world.

I was lucky to get to college when I was fourteen, not only because I could continue a good academic and social fit but because of the good timing for coming to terms with my sexual orientation. If I had had to spend four more years in my suburban community, I think I would only have twisted myself into tighter knots and dug myself into a deeper pit of depression.

Yet, unlike many of my lesbian and bisexual college peers, it was harder for me to come to terms with my giftedness than my sexuality. Even as I was on the cusp of deciding to come out to my friends and my parents, my diary entries filled with thoughts about who I might be as a gifted adult. I had to come to terms with the difference I had been running from and hiding for my whole life. Only after that could I move on and fully examine my sexual orientation.

For me, the coming-out process was compounded by worries about accepting an identity that would mark me as different for the rest of my life. As a college student, even at fourteen, I was finally able to live without being continually reminded that I was different. I kept my age to myself as much as possible, so that I could be sure that I was respected or denigrated for who I was, not on the basis of age-related preconceptions.

I had the good fortune to attend a liberal and intellectual women's college that was accepting of diversity. After a year, I was finally comfortable being myself and felt that I belonged and was on a path to what seemed like a normal life. Yet I was frightened by the prospect of dealing with the same sorts of ignorance that had trailed me throughout school while I figured out a path to keep myself whole and also not a target for the rest of my life. I also worried that I was so used to sticking out like a sore thumb that this might be a way to maintain a mark of difference, or else a way to join one of the most vibrant communities on campus. However, my biggest worry concerned accepting a part of myself that would both mark me as different and make me subject to even less societal approval than I endured as a child.

The nearly complete absence of anti-gay sentiment on campus made it easier for me to step forward than it would have been at summer camp three years before. I had friends around me, close friends who were also in the process of coming out, of taking the step forward to weave their lives around a newly public aspect of identity. Few of our discussions concerned the topics one normally thinks a group of women figuring out their sexuality might consider. Most were about dealing with difference—how to explain to others; whether to be publicly defiant, bold, and political; whether to buck stereotypes and keep our hair long; how we would manage our current and future families; and what sorts of jobs we might plan for.

As I have grown older, so many different aspects have become incorporated into my sense of self that I no longer feel a glaring need to ration the amount of difference I am willing to deal with. Just as my college conversations began to deal with larger issues than simply managing and containing the effects of difference, I even more rarely now think about how one aspect of who I am will affect any decision.

Certainly, my sexual orientation and my giftedness play large roles in the direction my life has taken. But neither occupies the forefront of my mind as I go about my life. Other people may see me as primarily either gifted or lesbian, but having come through childhood so focused on *how I am different,* I try instead to focus on just *being in the world,* without concern for the multiplicity of differences I may contain.

Birds and Bees

Sex and the High-IQ Adolescent

BY ANNETTE REVEL SHEELY

Annette Revel Sheely counsels gifted children and their families at the Rocky Mountain School for the Gifted and Creative in Boulder, Colorado.

While their minds leap ahead, young gifted adolescents' emotional maturity frequently scrambles to catch up as they struggle with a heightened sensitivity to everyone and everything. Throw in hormones and surround these young people with either older adolescents (if they've been academically advanced) or age-peers with whom they have few interests in common. Adolescence was complicated without *all these extras! Growing into healthy sexual maturity never looked harder. In this article, Annette Revel Sheely provides a few cautionary notes and lots of practical advice for guiding your high-IQ adolescent through the emotional, physical, and intellectual maze of puberty.*

Many parents find it difficult to acknowledge their adolescent's emerging sexuality. Yet parents are the people who can be most influential in guiding their teen toward a positive adult sexuality. In any family, this can be quite a challenge. For families with highly gifted adolescents, however, the process can be especially confusing.

Some characteristics innate to the highly gifted can complicate an adolescent's developing sexuality. These include asynchrony (either early or late sexual development), social isolation, sensual overexcitability, and androgyny. There are some good resources for parents about sexual education, but none specifically considers issues that will be faced by parents of the highly gifted. This chapter looks at these issues and offers suggestions to help parents guide a highly gifted adolescent toward a sexually healthy adulthood.

Asynchrony: Too Early or Too Late

Asynchronous, or out-of-sync, development—so commonly seen in highly gifted children—wreaks havoc not only with educational needs, but also with the milestones of growth and maturity. Many parents of highly gifted children have reported that the physical changes of puberty and the emotional adjustments of adolescence began years earlier than expected for their children. While parents of highly gifted teens may understand and support advanced cognitive development, they may be uncertain how to react when their child begins to express sexual feelings, either openly or covertly.

Setting appropriate limits for any teenager is difficult. But what rules and guidelines should parents set when a child is chronologically sixteen years old and has the cognitive reasoning of a twenty-five-year-old adult? For many of these highly gifted teens, sexuality is yet another aspect of their developing self that occurs early.

The mother of a sixteen-year-old girl recently shared with me, "When she was little, asynchrony was one thing. We had to battle with the schools to get the right level of books for her to read in school. But now it's about more serious things. She's dating men ten years older than she is. I found out she's already been sexually active. I've always allowed her more freedom due to her maturity. But now I don't know what to do."

A fifteen-year-old boy said this: "It's hard for my parents and me right now. They like how gifted I am when I get awards and stuff, but they want me to slow down with my girlfriend. They say I'm moving too fast. It's the same speed I've always moved at."

Parents' worry and confusion may not always be about very advanced development. Some highly gifted adolescents develop noticeably later than their peers. They may be sixteen or seventeen years old before they experience puberty. Teens who are late developers are often highly self-conscious about their bodies, afraid that they will never develop normally. For highly gifted teens in particular, this can add anxiety to the ongoing stress of always being so different from classmates. Parents can reassure their children that their bodies are changing on an appropriate, individual schedule. If the teen becomes consumed by anxiety about slow development, consulting with a pediatrician can help rule out any medical problems.

Some highly gifted teens need extra time to move toward adulthood. They observe the often overwhelming responsibilities of their parents and choose instead to cling as long as possible to the relative freedom of childhood. These students are most comfortable focusing on schoolwork and friends. They say they feel perfectly satisfied with low-key dating, perhaps even sleeping over with other teens and cuddling.

Social Isolation: Holding Some Back and Pushing Others Forward

Occasionally—when a teen seems hesitant to begin dating or trying new social experiences—parents are concerned that their child won't ever master adult social skills. The father of a nineteen-year-old college student said, "When I was his age, you couldn't keep me away from the girls. But not him—he sits in front of his computer all weekend and doesn't seem interested in even meeting real people, let alone dating." It's possible that this young man hasn't found a safe or appropriate peer group with whom to make the transition to this new type of relationship. While he may not appear to be interested in sex, he is more likely in the midst of an introspective exploration of self and sexuality.

Some teens are unsure of their sexuality and may need to imagine, search out, and try a variety of experiences to discover their personal boundaries. If they don't feel that they can share this exploration with their family, they will be likely to hide it and make it appear that they aren't interested in sex at all.

A candidate for a Ph.D. in mathematics shared that he was the classic "nerd" throughout middle school and high school. The girls to whom he was attracted ignored him. He felt cut off from the dating scene of his classmates. His parents encouraged him to date, but he felt humiliated by their gestures. Their concern about his lack of dates made him more self-conscious. He spent his weekends pursuing his hobbies—remote-control airplanes and computer-game programming. From the outside, he seemed to have no interest in dating or sex. In reality, he says, sex was all he could think about in those years. He just had no outlet to explore or express it. For him, the delay was more about geography than development. When he went to college and met girls who were interested in him, he felt that he was finally catching up, and finally on track with his sense of himself.

Highly gifted high school students who felt socially isolated in elementary and middle school have talked about discovering sex as a new, intense way to finally connect with other people. A twenty-year-old highly gifted young man said that when he went away to an early-entrance college program at fifteen, he finally knew what it was really like to have true peers, and sex was one of the ways that students related to each other. A quiet and studious gifted young woman explained to me that through her open sexuality in high school, she attracted classmates who had previously ignored her. She described the experience as validating and empowering.

Sensual Overexcitability

Another dimension of sexual complexity for some highly gifted adolescents is an increased awareness of sensory experiences. Polish psychiatrist and psychologist Kazimierz Dabrowski described five *overexcitabilities* (OE) present in gifted people: psychomotor, sensual, intellectual, imaginational, and emotional. It is thought that those who have a strong sensual OE, a heightened capacity for sensory stimuli, have unusually high neuronal sensitivities. A young child may need the label cut from his shirt so it won't distract him all day. As a teenager or young adult, this same individual may experience sex with his lover as an ecstatic, almost spiritual union. One young man, a senior in an accelerated academic high school program, described his experience of sex as an "incredible sensual exploration. It takes me from the mundane, closed-in world of homework and rules, to this . . . blissful place beyond words, beyond physical limitations." A young woman who graduated from college at the age of eighteen commented that, in her experience, her highly gifted peers seemed to experience sex in a fuller, more multidimensional way than their age-peers.

Androgyny

Another layer of sexual intricacy is added when looking at the highly gifted and gender roles. As parents, you know that it is not necessary to be the prom queen or the star quarterback to lead a happy and fulfilling life. But in the middle school and high school culture, your teen may have difficulty seeing that.

Few highly gifted people act out the gender-role stereotypes of highly feminine women or highly masculine men. Instead, they tend toward a more androgynous style of being in the world. As children, gifted girls and gifted boys are more similar to each other than they are to their nongifted, same-gender counterparts. But in adolescence, when the social importance of gender roles increases among age-peers, androgynous highly gifted teens are often ignored by peers or even subjected to harassment in school. Some teens have described painful emotional struggles that they have endured because they don't fit neatly into the gender norms of our culture. Parents can reassure their child that it will all work out, and that the heightened focus on gender norms in middle school and high school does not maintain such an emphasis in the adult life of very gifted people.

Support Needed for Those at Greatest Risk

Approximately one in ten highly gifted adolescents faces even greater challenges than most. Unless these young people hide who they are, their very existence puts them at increased risk for physical assault, unmerciful verbal harassment, and, in some states, even legal consequences. Despite their high academic potential, these students are much more likely than other gifted students to skip school in an effort to avoid being attacked by other students. Some of these students are at a greater risk for HIV and other sexually transmitted diseases. Who are they? Highly gifted teens who are gay, lesbian, or bisexual.

Most highly gifted people are sensitive to the expectations and perceptions of the people in their life. If gay, lesbian, or bisexual adolescents grow up in households where homosexuality is portrayed as an immoral or abnormal choice, they will likely not share who they are, at any deep level, with their family. Without family support, these young people feel isolated and are unusually susceptible to depression and risky behaviors. Adults who work with the highly gifted talk about a higher-than-average risk of suicide. Research has shown that around 30 percent of young gay people (without regard to intelligence) attempt suicide. For *highly gifted* gay students with no support, the risks become immeasurably high. One young woman said that she knew she was a lesbian from a very early age, but that she also knew she wasn't going to "come out" publicly until she had appropriate resources around her.

Parents can create a safe and supportive environment from an early age by giving their child the message that it's okay to be different, to be themselves. When an adolescent does share the information that he or she may be, or is, homosexual or bisexual, the first thing the adult listener needs to do is take a deep breath and thank the young person for having enough trust to share something so personal. Reassure the adolescent of your love and support. If you feel uncomfortable or unprepared to provide support for your gay, lesbian, or bisexual teenager, connect with a family-support group, such as Parents, Families and Friends of Lesbians and Gays (PFLAG).

The Role of the Internet

Many highly gifted teens don't have friends that they feel close to at a deep level, with whom they can share their personal concerns about their changing bodies or their budding romantic interests. With current technology, these teens may find a handful of friends over the Internet. While other teens are out on a Friday night, practicing their dating skills, these young people are socializing in their own way, flirting in a private chat room with like-minded adolescents scattered across the country. Shy teens or teens with few social skills can learn a great deal about human interaction and communication by talking with others online. Many people find that the relative anonymity of online communication allows them to experiment with a bolder persona. This can create positive change: what they learn online can actually help them improve their face-to-face interactions with people. But the Internet can also become a crutch, or even an addiction, for a few who don't have any other social connections. And, of course, teens (as well as younger children) using the Internet must be taught how to keep themselves safe from sexual predators.

Today's parents must also recognize that the Internet can influence young people's sexuality in ways that previous generations never experienced. An email address is all a person needs to become the recipient of emails with links to sexually explicit Web sites. While most adult Web sites require verification of age, many do offer free samples of graphic, hard-core sex. There is also a strong presence on the Internet of Web sites that feature paraphilias such as fetishism and sadism. While few people favor censorship, most agree that pornography is not intended for children and young teens. In some cases, exposure at a vulnerable age can have a lifelong negative influence on the person's sexual makeup. Parents who are concerned about the images their children may be exposed to can purchase filtering software, and parental-control settings are free to the users of most popular online services.

Guiding Your Highly Gifted Adolescent Toward Sexual Health

Sexual health has been described by an expert group to the World Health Organization as "the integration of the somatic, emotional, intellectual, and social aspects of sexual well-being in ways that are positively enriching and that enhance personality, communication, and love."

Given the complicating factors that the highly gifted face, and with all the media and Internet influences, how can parents help their adolescents have a healthy, positive attitude about sex and teach them to make responsible, appropriate choices? Most importantly, don't wait until adolescence to teach them what you want them to know. In adolescence, it's practically the young person's developmental job to reject whatever you have to say. As with all other topics, highly gifted children begin to learn about sexuality from birth on. Teach them your personal values when they're young—not just what you believe, but why you believe it. What do you want to teach them about relationships, intimacy, gender roles, sexual orientation, masturbation, and privacy?

- Infants and toddlers will learn about love and closeness from you when you hold them, respond to them, and care for them. They will learn about trust and communication from you. This may seem simple, but it establishes an important foundation for future adult relationships.

- Preschool children are full of questions. Be approachable. When they ask questions that are sexual in nature, reward them by answering in a respectful and honest way. Say things like, "I'm glad that you came to me with that." Now is the time to assure your children that your home is one where questions and concerns can be shared. If they learn this lesson now, they will be more likely to share critical issues with you in their adolescence.

- Highly gifted elementary-age children want more complex information about topics like reproduction, birth, and death. They have probably heard about HIV and other diseases. When they ask questions, listen carefully to determine what they really want to know. They may be seeking concrete examples, or they may want your point of view about more abstract concepts. As they get closer to middle school age, it's not too early to talk with them about pregnancy, disease, condoms, and birth control. Research has shown that giving young people honest information about sex does not promote early sexual activity.

- When you notice puberty beginning, make a concerted effort to keep the lines of communication open between you and your child. This will likely become increasingly difficult, but it is important that your child feels it is still safe to bring questions and concerns to you. Better that you should have an opportunity to provide helpful and loving input about a difficult situation than hope that your child's peers or the media will offer good advice. If your daughter tells you about a crush on a classmate, don't devalue her experience. Ask about her feelings, find out what she values in the other child, and help her feel safe in sharing with you.

- Talking with adolescents about sex may be challenging for both the parent and the teen, but as long as an adolescent will listen to you, continue sharing your values and giving clear messages about your beliefs and expectations.

- If you have an expectation of abstinence, "just say no" is not enough. Teach your children the skills they will need, including decision-making, effective communication, assertiveness, and negotiation. If you know that your teen is sexually active, talk to him or her about sexual behaviors that minimize the risk of teen pregnancy or HIV transmission.

- If you are unsure about your children's sexual activity or orientation, don't push them to tell you. Don't probe more deeply than they are comfortably willing to share. If you demand answers that they are not ready to give, they will be forced to lie. This will set an uncomfortable, and unfortunate, precedent.

- Use what you see on television and in the movies as opportunities to talk about sex and what you feel is healthy or unhealthy sexual behavior. The media are full of abusive relationships, unsafe sex, teen pregnancy; instead of seeing these as negative influences on your child, see them as chances for you to share with your child how he or she can prevent similar experiences.

- Experimentation with sexual behaviors, roles, and different peer groups is a natural part of this phase of life. Do set boundaries as necessary for safety, but do also allow for a healthy amount of exploration of self and environment. Sometimes we need to push up against societal boundaries to discover where our personal boundaries are.

- Consider creating a memorable and respectful ritual that acknowledges the arrival of puberty and the beginning of sexual maturation. Many adults in our culture received negative feedback from their parents about sexuality or gender roles at the beginning of puberty, which can lead to an ambiguous feeling of embarrassment and discomfort. Instead, this transition offers an opportunity to create a shared, positive memory of moving into a new role, full of rich experiences and important responsibilities.

- If you don't feel that you have enough information to share what you think your teen should know, be open to consulting other resources and gaining that information. Others have successfully weathered these transitions, and respectful and balanced assistance is within reach.

Resources

Recommended book for a younger child
Harris, Robie H. *It's So Amazing! A Book About Eggs, Sperm, Birth, Babies, and Families.* Cambridge, MA: Candlewick, 2004.

Recommended book for an older child
Harris, Robie H. *It's Perfectly Normal! Changing Bodies, Growing Up, Sex, and Sexual Health.* Cambridge, MA: Candlewick, 2004.

For parents
De Becker, Gavin. *Protecting the Gift: Keeping Children and Teenagers Safe (and Parents Sane).* New York: Dial Press, 1999.

Engel, Beverly. *Beyond the Birds and the Bees: Fostering Your Child's Healthy Sexual Development in Today's World.* New York: Pocket Books, 1997.

Miron, Charles D., and Amy G. Miron. *How to Talk with Teens About Love, Relationships, & S-E-X: A Guide for Parents.* Minneapolis: Free Spirit Publishing, 2002.

Richardson, Justin, and Mark A. Schuster. *Everything You Never Wanted Your Kids to Know About Sex (But Were Afraid They'd Ask): The Secrets to Surviving Your Child's Sexual Development from Birth to the Teens.* New York: Crown, 2003.

Roffman, Deborah M. *Sex and Sensibility: The Thinking Parent's Guide to Talking Sense About Sex.* Cambridge, MA: Perseus, 2002.

Web sites

www.iwannaknow.org
For teenagers, this Web site provides a safe, educational, and fun place to learn about sexually transmitted infections (STIs) and sexual health.

www.siecus.org
Sexuality Information and Education Council of the United States (SIECUS) affirms that sexuality is a fundamental part of being human, one that is worthy of dignity and respect. It advocates for the right of all people to accurate information, comprehensive education about sexuality, and sexual health services. SIECUS works to create a world that ensures social justice and sexual rights.

www.advocatesforyouth.org

Advocates for Youth is dedicated to creating programs and advocating for policies that help young people make informed and responsible decisions about their reproductive and sexual health. When parents talk to and affirm the value of their children, young people are more likely to develop positive, healthy attitudes about themselves. This is also true when the subject is sex. Research shows that positive communication between parents and their children can help young people establish individual values and make healthy decisions.

www.familiesaretalking.org

This project of SIECUS works to empower parents and caregivers to communicate with their children about sexuality-related issues, to provide tools to help families communicate about these issues, and to encourage parents, caregivers, and young people to become advocates on the local, state, and national levels for sexuality-related issues, including comprehensive sexuality education programs in the schools.

www.pflag.org

Parents, Families and Friends of Lesbians and Gays (PFLAG) is a nonprofit organization with more than 200,000 members and 500 affiliates throughout the United States. 1726 M Street NW, Suite 400, Washington, DC 20036; (202) 467–8180.

28

Abnormally Brilliant, Brilliantly Normal

BY ELIZABETH MECKSTROTH

Since 1981, **Elizabeth Meckstroth** has coordinated development of SENG (Supporting Emotional Needs of the Gifted). Since 1980, she has focused on assessment, counseling, and support for families of highly and profoundly gifted children. She currently concentrates on personality type and emotional and spiritual issues, and works with healing modes and energies. Her extensive training includes thousands of poignant conversations, clinical social work, Jungian Analytic Psychology, and Reiki Master, and she is a Senior Fellow of the Institute for Educational Advancement. Her publications include *Guiding the Gifted Child* and *Teaching Young Gifted Children in the Regular Classroom.*

Finding sufficient intellectual challenges and peers for profoundly gifted children can be difficult, but the tasks are primarily logistical and political. Creating safe emotional and social spaces within which they can grow requires vision, imagination, and flexibility. Elizabeth Meckstroth emphasizes the uniqueness of each child, and offers ways of thinking about and guiding their individual spirits.

"What do you look for every day and sometimes you think you found it, but then the next day you have to start looking again? I'll give you a hint. It's about school." Her riddle is not a funny one. She has been telling me she doesn't like third grade. "Let's see. Is it when you answer a math problem and then the next day you have to do it again?" . . . "I'll tell you the riddle. . . . Every day you look for someone who likes you and sometimes you think you found a friend, but the next day you have to start again."

—Vivian G. Paley[1]

Introduction

If we approach our children with wonder and awe and if we convey that what they care about and think is precious and fascinating, they may begin to reveal their intense experiences of meaning, joy, isolation, suffering, and awareness of exquisite details. Then, as we discover them and as they begin to trust us, we can begin to guide them. My goal is to offer ideas that will help us facilitate gratifying social relationships for our children—the highly, exceptionally, and profoundly gifted beings with whose care we have been entrusted. I have been inspired in this work by Annemarie Roeper and by Linda Silverman, who has said, "My belief is that the trajectory of giftedness is inner development."[2]

A simple, linear, cause-and-effect analysis will not reveal the interweaving of ideas, feelings, and situations that creates our children's complex physical, intellectual, and emotional lives. While children in the generic gifted range tend to be *quantitatively* different from the norm, our children are *qualitatively* different.

Gratifying social relationships provide the context, meaning, support, and vitality for most of our experience. We cannot generalize a child's social and emotional conditions from intellectual and academic achievement, because our social life also depends on personality, economic status, available technology, geographic location, local mores, dominant culture, physical health and limitations, interests, family religion and traditions, discretionary time, and more. Our children are often more confident in their academic abilities than in their social acceptance.[3]

The depth and intensity of our children's responses to thoughts and situations distinguish their social, emotional, and intellectual experiences. These have positive and negative aspects. The *degree* of difference from the norm often creates vulnerability; as intelligence increases, so does the potential for misunderstanding. Experiencing satisfying social relationships is our children's enormous task.

The more intelligent a person is, regardless of age, the less often can he find a truly congenial companion. . . .

A lesson which many gifted persons never learn as long as they live is that human beings in general are inherently very different from themselves in thought, in action, in general intention, and in interests. Many a reformer has died at the hands of a mob which he was trying to improve in the belief that other human beings can and should enjoy what he enjoys. This is one of the most painful and difficult lessons that each gifted child must learn, if personal development is to proceed successfully. It is more necessary that this be learned than that any school subject be mastered. Failure to learn how to tolerate in a reasonable fashion the foolishness of others leads to bitterness, disillusionment, and misanthropy. . . .

But those of 170 IQ and beyond are too intelligent to be understood by the general run of persons with whom they make contact. They are too infrequent to find congenial companions. They have to contend with loneliness and personal isolation from their contemporaries throughout the period of their immaturity. To what extent these patterns become fixed, we cannot yet tell.

—Leta S. Hollingworth[4]

Uniqueness

Finding what is best for our children involves us in controversy. Although I will describe the results of research with groups of highly gifted children, the statements will not apply to any one child. The composite child who appears to emerge from the data does not exist. In a pile of stones with average weights of three ounces, you might not find a single stone that weighs three ounces! There is more diversity in the gifted range than there is in the rest of the intelligence continuum; the *highly gifted* segment alone spans more than 100 IQ points.

Our children are statistically insignificant. In addition, the definitions under which they are grouped and analyzed vary. One study included students who scored above 132 on the Otis-Lennon School Ability Test®, while other studies are based on information about groups with an average IQ of below 140.[5]

Here is one generalization we can make about these children: they differ from each other more than they resemble each other. A characteristic true for one will be opposite in another. Using a plan that worked for another child can sabotage nurturing.

These children are an enigma. We need to let go of the idea that we can determine *the best* plan for our children, or for even one of them. Usually, no one really knows what to do. Each comment or observation may not apply to your child. We can only *consider* possibilities and *try* options.

Lit Scan, and the Composite Child

The small amount of research on the social experiences of highly, exceptionally, and profoundly gifted children reveals recurrent themes. These define a "composite child" who represents the group, but never an individual.

One comprehensive review found our children more susceptible to social-emotional difficulties than children with more average intelligence.[6] The researchers discovered many reasons that our children have difficulty developing friendships, especially with their age-mates. Our children feel that they cannot communicate effectively and that they therefore confuse their peers; they then feel isolated and alienated. With older friends who are more intellectually equal, our children feel physically inferior and have different interests. Mutually rewarding play is rare. Our children generally want more friends and feel that being smart gets in their way.

Another research team learned that at least 20 to 25 percent of highly gifted children suffer from psychosocial problems, compared to 5 to 7 percent of moderately gifted children and 6 to 16 percent of average children.[7] Our children "view themselves as less socially adept, more inhibited, less popular, and less socially active. . . . and may be more at risk for developing problems in emotional and social adjustment than their less gifted counterparts."[8]

Yet despite these observed problems, most of our children relate quite well to peers and adults, and tend to have friends older than themselves.

Extraordinary vulnerabilities, rising from intense sensitivity and awareness, appear to accompany exceptional intelligence. Our children internalize their experiences; require personally *meaningful* relationships; and attribute great significance to ideas and situations. All these qualities affect their exaggerated depth of response.[9]

An article by Grady M. Towers provides a poignant analysis of Lewis Terman's classic research data.[10] Terman's longitudinal study assessed mental and social health or maladjustment relative to intelligence, placing subjects in three categories: *satisfactory adjustment, some maladjustment,* and *serious maladjustment.* Incidence of increase in both categories of maladjustment correlated with verbal intelligence into the highest ranges.[11]

This raises burning questions for me about the ways in which our children are measured, and about where the fulcrum of "adjustment" lies. Paring oneself down in order to "fit in" constitutes a living suicide. I wonder how we can inspire our children to maintain their selves while they learn to interact successfully with other people. I think we need to look at "adjustment" from their point of view, honoring their abilities both to accommodate and to maintain integrity.

Thankfully, recent research by Karen Rogers and Linda Silverman answers some of my questions and portrays our children's phenomenal strengths and bewildering needs.[12] Ninety percent of the children they evaluated are sensitive and are concerned with justice and fairness. Between 84 and 88 percent are perfectionistic, are persistent in their areas of interest, and question authority.

Our children's personality characteristics amplify their life experiences, and their differences from the norm exacerbate their sense of dissonance with others. In the remainder of this paper, I'll summarize how some of their qualities can affect social relationships. I will also provide suggestions for reading about and for interacting with our children that will help us guide them in developing rewarding social relationships.

> Precocity unavoidably complicates the problem of social adjustment. The child of eight years with a mentality of twelve or fourteen is faced with a situation almost inconceivably difficult. In order to adjust normally such a child has to have an exceptionally well-balanced personality and to be well nigh a social genius. The higher the IQ, the more acute the problem.
>
> —Lewis M. Terman[13]

Capacity of Consciousness

I generally define *giftedness* as *capacity of consciousness,* the depth and breadth to which a person processes experience and information. A favorite analogy to television sets illustrates this sense of capacity: where most people get about five channels and some are wired for cable, profoundly gifted people receive as much input as a satellite dish. They pick up signals and make connections other people cannot even imagine.

Any one child's mental satellite dish might have discerning ranges that amplify certain aspects of life, for example, musical nuances, science, or human relationships. In particular areas, this child perceives, receives, experiences, understands, and reacts to *more* than most other people do. If you use this analogy with your children, you may help them accept that there is nothing wrong with them, but that other children simply do not see or understand in the same way.

Mega-awareness does affect social relationships. Addressing a Hollingworth conference, Stephanie Tolan suggested that our classifications of giftedness need to be changed to highly burdened, exceptionally burdened, and profoundly burdened!

Intuition

Our children are often aware of their intuition—a realm of consciousness beyond that perceived by the senses—yet they might not recognize or honor this source of essential information. As intelligence increases, so does the use of hunches. As Isabel Briggs Myers and Mary McCaulley observe, "The fact that introverts with intuition have the highest mean intelligence scores makes it easy to accept that they also have the highest grades. . . ."[14] In a group of male Rhodes Scholars, ninety-four percent were intuitive thinkers.[15]

About 75 percent of American children take in information primarily through their senses. Our intuitive children fall into the 25-percent minority who comfortably perceive ideas and events using insight. They focus on possibilities, meanings, and relationships.

Of course, the two modes of intuitive and sensory perception are not exclusive! Our children integrate sensory information with concepts. Intuition enables them to seek and find solutions. They discover ideas from a global context and perceive achievable events. Because their minds can imagine so many possibilities, our children sometimes have feelings of omnipotence because in their mind they can imagine so many possibilities. In fact, they may become so intent on pursuing possibilities that they overlook or discount reality. For many gifted people, intuitiveness *is* their reality. Their awareness encompasses a realm greater than the immediate material focus.

On intuition: reading suggestions

For ways to honor and connect with intuition, Sonia Choquette's *The Wise Child: A Spiritual Guide to Nurturing Your Child's Intuition* is a great place to start. Explore *Spiritual Intelligence* by Marsha Sinetar, and nestle into *The Joyful Child* by Peggy Jenkins, which includes many sensitive, useful ideas on making and keeping friends. These pages offer techniques for creative visualization, setting personal boundaries, stimulating imagination, and daring to be different. *Welcome to the Ark* by Stephanie Tolan is a story about how intuition lives and breathes in our children. Some of us think this should be required reading for those who work with profoundly gifted children!

On intuition: nurturing suggestions

To build your children's confidence in social situations, you need to validate what they know intuitively. As entrusted caretakers, perhaps the most vital support we can give our children is to take them seriously. Children report that they wish to discuss their unique ideas with their parents or teachers, but that they anticipate that their ideas would be rejected as absurd, impractical, or somehow threatening.

Instinctively, they know they need you to survive! You can be a safe haven for these children, and can help them learn to reap the bounty from their intuition.

Sensitivity

Most of our children have a low sensory threshold. They are affected by sounds, smells, ideas, and situations that others might not notice. It's as if they are permeable—receptive and responsive to experience. They can be hyper-aware of their own feelings and also extend their empathy to others ("I understand others better than they understand me"). They may take things personally and feel directly responsible for other people and events. They may include other people's experiences as extensions of themselves, and they may personify objects and places.

Their compassion can be a magnet for people who seek solace and acceptance. The world needs understanding people, and this sensitivity can be a source of great joy, comfort, and inspiration to our children themselves and to others.

Yet these compassionate children may also be emotionally overloaded and may consequently perceive themselves as exceptionally vulnerable. They may wonder why things seem to bother them more than other children. Hypersensitivity can dampen their courage to risk rejection in social situations.

In addition, profoundly gifted children have more allergies than most children. A pediatrician at a SENG conference discussed this in 1983.[16] In 1997, Karen Rogers and Linda Silverman documented in their research that 44 percent of the young people they examined had allergies.

Many, or most, of the allergic reactions produced behavioral changes. If your child is at times lethargic, impossible, oppositional, or hyperactive, I beg you to have the possibility of allergies studied (especially if there is a family history of allergies). Eliminating a small thing (like red dye from the diet, or petroleum solvents from the environment) can effect a huge difference in attitude and actions. Although allergy detection and management are cumbersome, the unalleviated symptoms can be devastating.

Whenever I address a group of parents of highly gifted children, I request testimonies about the difference detecting allergies made. It is not unusual to hear about dramatic turnarounds! When the basic body and mind are functionally optimally, a child becomes more attractive to herself and to others in social interactions.

Intensity

The intense brain that drives our children amplifies much that they do and think. They have keen memory and may make sudden mountains out of a series of past molehills. What is passed over unnoticed by others can have huge significance to them. They "over-react."

This deep caring can alienate others who feel overwhelmed by such intense reactions. It's futile to try to placate our children with formulas that discount their feelings and perceptions ("Oh, he didn't really mean that," "Just let it roll off your back," or, "By tomorrow, you won't even think about it"). Instead, try giving a warm hug and an empathetic, "This must be hard for you."

On intensity: reading suggestions
To further understand intensities, read more about Dabrowski's theory of "overexcitabilities." A brief, comprehensive source is my article, "Complexities of Giftedness: Dabrowski's Theory." But if you buy one book to help

you assuage and survive your child's intense feelings, choose Mary Sheedy Kurcinka's *Raising Your Spirited Child: A Guide for Parents Whose Child Is More Intense, Sensitive, Perceptive, Persistent, Energetic.* The author offers hundreds of practical suggestions to help guide your child to moderate feelings and constructively incorporate reactions.

Introversion

Part of the mystery of our profoundly gifted children involves their tendency toward introversion. Introversion and extraversion represent preferred styles for interacting with the world, not abilities. The inherent core qualities of introverts evade scrutiny, and introverts gain energy in solitude. Extraverts express themselves, and they are energized by being with other people.

Introversion is a basic personality trait, and the probability of introversion increases along with intelligence. This is another way in which our children are dissonant with most other children and most teachers.

Although each of us possesses a continuum of both introverted and extraverted tendencies, roughly 75 percent of Americans are predominantly extraverted. About 60 percent of gifted people are more comfortable at the other end of the continuum, as introverts.[17] Although some extremely intelligent people are blazing extraverts, most bright young people can be hard to read.

Here are some generalized distinctions between introverts and extraverts, although each person displays an individual combination of traits from both realms.

Introverts:

- need to be alone to recover inner strength, and have intense privacy needs

- focus on their inner thoughts and ideas

- hesitate to try new things and events

- think before speaking, and resist interruptions

- want a few close friends, and feel beleaguered by being with people too long

Extraverts:

- gain energy and enthusiasm by being with other people, and may be lonely when alone

- focus more on the outer world of people, things, and activities

- avidly try new things and go places

- talk while they think and process ideas, and eagerly want to share ideas

- crave company and want many friends

It can be hard to find true friends when you belong to the introverted minority and have very high intelligence, too. These children cannot be "socialized" to fit someone else's projected need. Introverts seek certain qualities in their relationships. They can feel lonely in a group, comfortably connected with one or two other people, and truly happy when alone! There's a difference between *isolation* and *solitude*. Although the mainstream regards introversion as antisocial, it's as normal and natural for these children as left-handedness is to a southpaw.

It's hard to know what's going on inside introverted kids. Often what they do *not* say or show is essential. Our little introverts may share some of their consecrated riches when we invite them . . . gently.

Parents of profoundly gifted children may have their own introversion legitimized by a personality indicator like the Myers-Briggs. These tools may also help children understand that their social needs differ from those of others.

Even so, we all need some extraverted skills to cope with the world and to express ourselves. Knowing our preference for introversion can give us a foundation on which to build these skills.

On introversion: nurturing suggestions

- If our children practice being comfortable with caring parents and teachers, they learn courage they can take into other social situations.

- If at all possible, correct them when you are by yourselves. They are often humiliated when they know they have done the wrong thing, so any wrath likely acts like salt on their wound.

- Honor their need for privacy; they'll let you in when they feel secure about what they want to share.

- After you ask them a question, wait at least three seconds before you talk again.

- Suggest individual sports (swimming, karate, gymnastics, track, or tennis). Team sports, like soccer, can be too invasive.

- Help them find their one best friend.

- Before requiring them to participate in an activity with other people, let them first observe what is expected, or at least explain the situation.

- Teach them to role-play or mentally walk through situations involving other people.

Perfectionism

Certain behaviors associated with our children's apparent perfectionism can cause social problems. We need to help them let go of the equation that imperfection means failure, in their views of both themselves and others. Perfectionism is a symptom of complex needs and qualities, not a syndrome.

We want to avoid the anger and avoidance and disruptive behaviors that perfectionism can produce. Our children can direct these behaviors toward themselves, when they lack courage to enter social relationships because their superb imaginations produce scenes of rejection. Our children can direct these behaviors toward others, when they are disappointed or frustrated at people who "could do better if they only tried" or who don't care enough.

Our children have a need for precision.[18] We expect more from highly gifted children. Children tend to expect high performance in all areas, while *gifted* does not apply equally to all parts. Highly gifted children are especially vulnerable to feeling valued for what they can produce, for being smart and right. They may think they have to be perfect to be acceptable. High standards for behavior (their own and others) can also be adaptive—an attempt to control their lives and the world.

For a child who is "the best in the class," being on top is a fragile position. The smartest children may never experience their own strengths, overcome challenges, or have intellectual peers. They may resent wasting time waiting and may not learn to struggle intellectually. They may think it is okay to give help but not to receive it ("I should know better"). Others may act as if the intelligent one should succeed on his own and may expect him to tutor other children.

But who will assist our child? He may develop feelings of shame and abandonment and regret, for reasons other children probably would not understand.

The child may earn her identity and place in class as the "smartest one." She may expect to exceed others and may develop a need for self-control that produces lifelong resistance to cooperating with others. The child who performs, feels, and knows differently from most of her classmates may feel frightened and alienated, and will find social acceptance hard to achieve.

How many of you, dear readers who care about your children, can relate to this? What can you do?

Miraca Gross has pioneered research on radical acceleration. She has widely documented the enormous social and emotional advantages—even cures!—that come from placing profoundly gifted children with their intellectual peers. With appropriate educational options, your child can have far better days!

On perfectionism: reading suggestion
The First Honest Book About Lies by Jonni Kincher is a treasure-trove of remedies for the need to be right. Warm and lighthearted examples cover: ideas popularly thought to be true that turned out to be wrong; statistics; politeness and "social lies"; "truth" in advertising; and much more. It's fun to read, and helps our little perfectionists give themselves (and others) a break. (This book is out of print and may be hard to find.)

On perfectionism: nurturing suggestions
To loosen the bonds of excruciatingly high expectations:

- *Reward trying.* Encourage children to try new experiences without being committed to high performance. Sometimes it's worth doing poorly to try an activity! Encourage your hesitant children to risk the attempt, and then talk about what they might try the next time in a similar situation.

- *Honor persistence and progress.* One wise mother defined heroes as people who keep striving when things get hard.

- *Practice; transformation comes by trials.* Anticipate awkward social situations and help children practice social skills. (See also the tips for introversion.)

- *Remind yourself, "Done is better than perfect."* Our introverted, sensitively concerned children may have trouble initiating contact. Let them know it's okay to say "hi" even though you're not sure you remember a person's name, or to ask, "how are you?" when you don't have time for a conversation.

The Risk of Depression and Suicide

For over twenty years, I've had the privilege to learn from intimate relationships with countless families of profoundly gifted children. My closest friends are those who share my interests. From professional consultations, the literature, and clinical experience, it seems that the ability to mask desperation becomes a survival mode as children grow into adolescence. Awareness to this idea was from the family of Dallas Egbert, and the founding of Supporting Emotional Needs of Gifted. Dallas's family publicly explained how his impending suicide was unsuspected.[19]

Susan Jackson has documented her research from counseling highly gifted suicidal adolescents.[20] She found that these children are astute enough to act as if nothing is wrong to keep others from interfering with them.

> . . . the most highly gifted of the children were most likely to hide their deep despair and specific depressive symptoms due to many things:
>
> - Fear of hurting others (the depressive thoughts were often self-destructive and even rich with anger);
>
> - Fear of worrying others;
>
> - Deepest fear is that the person hearing the information would not glean the nuances, the interconnectivity of the thoughts-feelings-somatic expression, and would be unable to provide any insight whatsoever, would think lesser of them for not having this mass of thoughts-feelings sorted out;

- Fear that the person hearing would not be able to connect the immediate expression and experiencing of things to precognition of the state and the feeling that they are responsible for the state;

- These children are often carrying the unexpressed issues of their caretakers and do not want to admit to that, to hold their caretakers responsible, to even think of that consciously;

- In treatment they worry that the helping person won't have the processing speed to keep up with the dynamic of the healing itself. Also they worry that they will actually hurt the person helping them; that the material itself is toxic and they should not be exposing it to another of any ilk for fear of contamination.

Masked angst can stem from their need for perfectionism and from their role of holding up other people's expectations of them. It can ensue from feeling that other people probably wouldn't understand anyway—would tell them how good they really have it. We see the characteristic of strong need for self-control prevalent in these situations, too.

There is evidence of how our adolescent children who may seem to have everything going for them can be desperate in the social-emotional aspects of their lives. A survey of high-achieving teens listed in *Who's Who Among High School Students* found that among a sample of 5,000 students, 31 percent had contemplated suicide and 4 percent had attempted suicide.[21] Many of these adolescents could be our children. The reasons that they gave as most contributing to wanting to end their lives were:

- 86 percent: Feelings of personal worthlessness

- 81 percent: Feelings of isolation and loneliness

- 81 percent: Pressure to achieve

- 61 percent: Fear of failure

The authors' interpretations of these figures include that these students apparently make heroic efforts to measure up to high expectations of themselves and others until this becomes unbearable.

Angst

Our children's vast capacity of consciousness carries concomitant angst. This can burden and complicate social relationships. Here are some ways that their incalculable consciousness can also confuse and hinder.

With their astute awareness and sensitivity, our children are usually more conscious of a situation in its entirety. They may experience additional stress from the ambiguity of understanding multiple facets of an issue. A sense of isolation arises when our children realize that other people do not have the awareness to acknowledge their reality, and that they live in a different world.

They accumulate information and meanings in a sort of geometric progression. They can relate situations and ideas to so much else that they know and feel. They cope with more possibilities than others; they have more meanings to consider. Dealing with more alternatives, they may fear potentially making more mistakes.

Because of their asynchronous development and limited resources, they may be discouraged. There is not enough time or resources to actualize most of the options they envision. Even when they accomplish a lot, they usually do so by compromising their ideal and denying more than they actualize. This leads to frustration and grief for the loss of what they never had.

They may have trouble screening out information and may become overloaded. They process experiences with heightened sensitivity and intensity, and then wonder why things seem to bother them more than other people. They can consequently view themselves as less able to cope than others are.

They tend to perceive others' sometimes inconsistent verbal, body, and attitude messages. Their awareness of incongruities creates confusion about how to respond to other people ("I don't know whether I should talk to her about what she is telling me or about what I know she is thinking").

An astute sense of humor is a hallmark of many of our children. However, cynicism lies on another side of humor. Occasionally the difference between humor and cynicism can only be discerned through intonation, a subtle glance, or a grimace. Profoundly gifted people can become cynical because they can "see through" people. They can empathize at the same time that they perceive the dark side.

On conveying respect and interest to children: nurturing suggestions
Here are some ways to convey interest and respect to your children:

- *Listen, listen, listen.* This may involve making an appointment at another time for focused listening.

- *Listen with your entire body, mind, and spirit,* as if nothing else at that moment matters as much as this child's thoughts and feelings.

- *Listen to understand what a situation means* to the child, rather than to respond.

- *Listen as if this child has something important to give to you.*

- *Take the child seriously.* Possible responses include slight head nods and "Mmmm. . . . Uh huh. . . . I see." Reflect essential bits of this child's thoughts and feelings.

What You Can Do

When our children are hurt because they think that other people don't care or when they interpret other people's indifference as an intended attack on them, the satellite-dish analogy can help them understand that it's not that other kids don't care, but that others just don't see and feel the same way.

Children are susceptible to what they *imagine* might happen. You can discuss probabilities of such occurrences and work along with them to develop some constructive responses: "What are some things you might do if she called you a know-it-all?"

You can help your children discern, "Who owns the problem?" Even when a child cares, this does not mean she needs to assume responsibility for so many people that she loses her own self.

As Dierdre Lovecky explained in a Hollingworth conference presentation, you can help a sensitive child accept that he has qualities that are rare in other people, and you can teach him that children who can see and feel things the same way he does may be hard to find. Just as some may censure him for *over-reacting* and *being too sensitive,* you can honor his sensitivity and assure him that eventually he will find people who will admire this and want to be with him because he is so kind and understanding.

When I first delivered my daughter to nursery school, I appealed to Mrs. Carter to "toughen up" Anne because she was "too sensitive." This wise woman told me, "Don't try to change Anne. When she is older, she will attract people to her who appreciate her and won't want to hurt her."

How true.

Creative Problem-Solving

"How are we going to work this out?" is a good theme for raising children and is crucial to facilitating their social relationships. If you teach children creative problem-solving, they learn a lifelong skill. You can think out loud when you are making a decision, such as how to make amends to your neighbor if your dog has been barking a great deal.

On creative problem-solving: encouraging and nurturing suggestions
Here are some steps you can use when you help your children solve sticky social situations:

- *Recognize the problem.* What is involved? Find the facts.

- *Define the problem.* What would I like to be different? Who owns the problem?

- *Brainstorm alternatives.* How might I make this happen?

- *Evaluate consequences.* How might this work for and against me? How might this work for and against others?

- *Allocate resources.*

- *Make a plan.* What will I do, by when?

- *Do it!*

- *Evaluate.* What did I learn? How did it help? What might I try next time?

The Search for Compatible Peers

Our children can experience stress because they feel estranged. Many elementary-age children report that they feel different from their classmates, and usually think this is their fault. Our children have fewer opportunities than other children to experience understanding and empathy.

Many factors complicate their ability to find friends. They make up intricate game rules and create complex play. They may come across as bossy because they can see how to organize the play, and, being creative, they want to express their new ideas.

The search for one best friend can be extremely disappointing. Our children may fare better if they appreciate different friends as components of friendship. Who is a "peer" to a profoundly gifted child in what setting? We may be concerned that a child does not have any real friends. Keep in mind that friends may not be chronological peers.

For our children to find good friends, they usually need to "go out of the box" of the immediate neighborhood or classroom. In some ways, they are developmentally advanced from their age-mates.

Surrogates isn't the term, but some *supplements* may strengthen a child's peer relationships. How many profoundly gifted people grow up with their cat or dog as their confidant? Our adolescents especially can find acceptance and solace in *their* music. One highly gifted adult told me that music was the first thing he could relate to. Some children can connect to art, their own or others'. Any creative self-expression helps our children define and confirm their selves and, to a degree, facilitates their ability to relate to others.

On compatible peers: reading suggestion
For an overview of radical acceleration, go to www.davidsoninstitute.org. See also Miraca Gross's article in this volume.

On compatible peers: nurturing suggestions

- Open peer possibilities by locating *lessons or interest groups where there are no age or grade limitations*. Look at classes at the science museum.

- *Mentors or tutors might help*. Call a high school and ask if there is a student who shares your child's interest—chess, the Civil War, rock and roll, or any topic (esoteric or not). A good match may allow your child to experience a cooperative relationship, and could give you an alternative source of child care.

- Don't forget that *opportunities to associate with profoundly gifted children* usually pay high dividends in finding peers. Check out the Davidson Institute, university talent development programs, space camp, or other special interest camps.

Helping Those Who Are Intensely Aware of Injustice

Fairness matters a lot to our children. Playdates can flop because our child refuses to participate with someone who doesn't play fair. Consider the concept of expanded consciousness when you interpret our children's intense sense of justice. They can often understand the other person's, team's, side's point of view. You've probably experienced their outrage if someone else is treated unfairly. Other times, they wilt when they are dealt an unfair consequence. How many have been punished because someone else in their class broke a rule?

Was the person who initiated the unfair action tired, desperate, in need of power, or unaware of the possible effects? Even though the child feels initial pain, perhaps (with understanding and help) she might come to accept that other people's behavior does not reflect on who she is. She may even develop compassion for the "unfair" one. She doesn't need to like the behavior, but perhaps her experience can be a lesson in how painful it is to be the victim of unfairness.

On coping with injustice: reading suggestions

Two books by Barbara A. Lewis can help empower your children and assist them in learning to participate in the world's social intervention: *The Kid's Guide to Social Action: How to Solve the Social Problems You Choose* and *Kids with Courage: True Stories About Young People Making a Difference*.

The Challenge of Maintaining Integrity in Social Conflict

Sometimes our children become the target of bullies or other children who want to take advantage of their docile, understanding nature. When they see social injustice on a large scale, they may feel helpless.

Conflicts can be rich and fertile ground for insight and awareness. Plenty of resources on conflict resolution are available. If parents and teachers would provide instruction on conflict resolution, their efforts would have lifelong value. Our children may be very interested in exploring ways in which conflicts can be resolved in human societies: by consensus, town meetings, or votes by elders.

Encourage your child to be a diamond: reflect light, to see other people's points of view. Just because our children can understand other people's ideas does not mean that they need to agree or approve.

On maintaining integrity in social conflict: reading suggestions

Two little books can become comforting companions to children who are taken advantage of and pushed around by other children. If you buy just one, get *Stick Up for Yourself!* by Gershen Kaufman, Lev Raphael, and Pamela Espeland. It appeals to our children because the authors skillfully explain the *reasons* for behaviors and for their suggested responses. There are sections on building positive self-esteem, getting to know yourself, and tips for the shy. There are "do" and "don't" suggestions for defensive responses to bullies. Here are some do's: tell a friend; tell a teacher; stand up straight; look the bully in the eye and say in a firm, confident voice, "Leave me alone!" or "Stop it!"; stay calm and walk away toward a group. *Bullies Are a Pain in the Brain* by Trevor Romain is a briefer, "cuter" concise source of support for a child targeted for insult.

I also like Barbara Kerr and Sanford Cohn's suggestions on dealing with bullies, found in *Smart Boys*. They include learning nonverbal ways of communicating assertiveness; seeking allies; and using responses like, "I'm wondering if you're getting what you want by acting this way."

Helping Integrate Self-Control and Independence

Discovering an article describing gifted people's control characteristics was a comforting relief! I'm grateful to Paul Janos and Nancy Robinson for clearing up why nurturing our children can be so exasperating to themselves and to us. Their research *consistently* supports that gifted children of all ages exhibit the following characteristics, which tend to be more obvious in boys than in girls:

- self-sufficiency

- independence

- autonomy

- dominance

- individualism

- self-direction

- nonconformity

These reflect an internal locus of control, and the need for self-control can exacerbate difficulties in developing congenial social relationships.

Here is additional information that can facilitate social relationships. The researchers found that *at all ages,* gifted people express independence and manifest their need for self-control through curiosity, experimentation, exploration, and risk taking. When working to achieve their goals, gifted people show:

- persistence

- perseverance

- energy

- enthusiasm

- vigor

- striving

- sacrificing

These qualities become stronger as the child gets older, especially for *successful* men and women. The key word in understanding how to use this information is *their:* these qualities come to the fore when our children pursue their own goals.

The crux of control is being aware that you are making choices about yourself. We want our children to have control over themselves! Their astute awareness, vivid imagination, and excellent memory enable you to work *with* these control tendencies, helping them learn to make wise choices so that they feel good about themselves and their relationships.

When young children have problems, they usually respond with some form of acting out or withdrawing. Instead, children need to become aware that they always have choices over their behaviors and attitudes when they face challenges. They need to learn that their choices can work for them or against them. They need to experience and see the connections between what they do and what happens to them.

Caution: As caring adults, we need to be conscious that we do not view our children as paragons of virtue, or *Goodness Personified,* as Leslie Margolin's book on gifted children is titled.[22] Our children sometimes suffer other people's mandate that they should be perfect. (One mother told her son, when a child named Ben was standing nearby, that "Ben is a genius. He gets everything right.") Our support and praise for our children's accomplishments can precariously accumulate to convey the idea that they "should know better."

One of a parent's most important roles is to provide a safe, accepting haven when a child does something wrong, foolish, or angry—even when she expresses hate. We all need to accept and try to understand our own not-nice sides. If your children feel safe enough to express their gnawing feelings of jealousy, greed, resentment, and the like, then problem situations can be identified and discussed. This prevents them from being displaced, or from manifesting neurotic or other hard-to-manage ideas and behaviors. In discussion, you can help your children be proactive in trying other behaviors that might be more effective.

One of my favorite families had "Do It Wrong" days every few Saturday mornings. They had popcorn and sodas for breakfast, wore socks that didn't match—you name it!—and found that none of these things really mattered!

On sense of control: nurturing suggestions
Here are ideas to appeal to children's sense of control:

- *Tell them what to expect.* Allow lead time and give notice before an activity is to be started or terminated.

- *Give explanations* and reasons for processes and jobs.

- *Separate parts of a situation and help them distinguish* between which they have control over and which they do not.

- *Allow choices within defined limits.*

- *Teach and depend on shared control.* Guide negotiation to a consensus on how the children will cooperate and assume shared control. You might need to define limits of possible choices. The consequences of each alternative need to be understood.

Helping Those Who Feel Androgynous

When profoundly gifted children "click" in a relationship, they are usually so engrossed in the delight of sharing ideas and interests that the friend's gender doesn't matter. Researchers have discovered that profoundly gifted girls prefer to play with profoundly gifted boys more than with average girls.[23] They have also found that intellectually gifted adolescent girls seek novel experiences; avoid routine; and enjoy challenging experiences—even more than boys![24]

Introverted boys may have added struggles in accommodating societal expectations. Their more passive, demure manner can make others think they are deficient in their masculinity.

We can help our children prefer their androgynous qualities. Help our children explore gender roles in other—perhaps matriarchal—cultures to expand their concepts of masculinity and femininity and to dissolve some concepts of innate gender roles.[25] We can assure our children (and ourselves) that people who balance their masculine and feminine qualities generally have advantages in flexibility, creativity, social functioning, and psychological health. As Barbara Kerr and Sanford Cohn observe, "The best literature on masculinity . . . advises a society in which males are able to be strong, assertive, and constructive but are also able to be emotionally responsive, nurturing, and compassionate as well."[26]

As caretakers, we need to let go of some of our traditional gender roles and allow our children to reap enjoyment from associations that perhaps we would not have sought.

Learning to Be Your Own Best Friend

A premise for satisfying social relationships is that you can only give what you have to give. It takes time to learn coping mechanisms.

Yet childhood is a crucial window for shaping lifelong emotional habits that, once established, become hard to change later in life. Children need to be able to keep distress from swamping their ability to think. Parents and teachers can reinforce emotional management, that is, help kids find positive ways to soothe their own feelings. We can change the way we feel by what we think!

What means of self-soothing have you suggested for your children? What worked? How about yoga, strenuous exercise, journal writing, music, self-massage, meditation, or making plans for doing something you like to do? You can call a friend; imagine a conversation with a treasured relative; sing; or do something just to be silly, even if for just ten minutes. Ask yourself, "Am I focusing on what I want or what I don't want?"

Ask children to develop a list of things they find comforting, and to write the ideas on little cards. The cards can be stored in a large envelope, to be pulled out when needed.

Components of Social Intelligence

Social Skills, and How to Help the Socially Oblivious

On my daughter's tenth birthday, I asked her, "What is the most important thing you've learned in ten years?" I expected to hear "to read; do math; find my way home."

She blurted, "Manners."

Manners can open or close doors faster than money, toys, or test scores. Knowing how to do what is expected provides confidence in social situations. Get a book on manners for children and go over one situation a week. Encourage children to role-play situations and to practice their skills and manners.

Yeah. . . . We know, too, about children who stay in their own world and resist coming out into social interactions. If your child becomes aware of the effects of apparent indifference on herself and others, motivation for cooperation may perk up.

On social skills: reading suggestions
A book too good to miss is *Teaching Your Children Sensitivity* by Linda and Richard Eyre. While most of our children are "too" sensitive, here are many ideas to help them understand how words and behaviors affect other people. Provocatively, the authors ask us to consider our goals in a relationship. They prompt us to become aware of, and possibly change, our social habits. Another great resource for children who have difficulties or may be oblivious about how they influence social relationships is *Helping the Child Who Doesn't Fit In* by Stephen Nowicki and Marshall Duke. They patiently clue kids in about how to read body language and how stance and grimaces impact others.

On social skills: nurturing suggestions
We all could use a refresher to fine-tune our awareness of nonverbal communication. A very small percentage of communication occurs through

the words we use, compared with the meaning conveyed by how we speak and how we move.

- If children are not aware of how their body language affects others, they have no idea why people treat them as they do. Awareness also gives children some control over themselves and others in social situations. To increase their acuity in interpreting body language, play situational charades.

- Their mind is a place to try out new experiences. Mentally walk children through experiences; review alternative behaviors and anticipate consequences. Instill optimism ("I can manage").

- Read, tell, act out wonderfully rich stories and let children walk in others' moccasins. Changing the story changes their perceptions and ideas. Changing perceptions and ideas changes their lives and the world.

- No blame. Blaming leaves the blamer helpless. Create confidence by asking questions that encourage children to find and try possible solutions.

- Turn off the sound of video segments and try to read body language to interpret the scene.

- Repeat and paraphrase what you hear; do not add your own ideas. Be careful to use the child's own words, instead of interpreting.

- Ask for clarification and amplification: "I'd like to know how you might have felt about that," or, "What were some of the ways you were feeling when he said that?" or, "What are some of the things you are feeling now?"

- Allow children to own their feelings ("I get it that you're furious with Rachael!"). Restrain yourself from expressing your own experiences, advice, evaluations, and theories. Focus your attention on gathering the child's information and feelings, and on understanding what these things signify to the child.

- Respond to the children's feelings. Affirm their feelings, and help the children label those feelings. If children can identify their feelings, they then can do something about what their feelings are telling them. "I'm mad" might mean "feeling left out" or "embarrassed," because they feel shunned on the playground. Later, you can help the child look for constructive solutions to this lonely situation.

"When in Rome . . ."

At all ages, our friendships are enhanced if we are conscious of what we are giving to these relationships. Our children, often lauded for their logic, are apt to protest that there is no *reason* to keep their elbows off the table, shake right hands rather than left, or excuse their burps!

Some children can be convinced to apply courtesies if they understand why social modes help them. You might take a social anthropological journey, learning how manners have survival value—they say, "I'm one of your kind." Going around the world to explore protocol can be a great adventure. Get a book on etiquette for children. Find a class on manners training for children.

Next, practice. Practice with fictional or animal characters: let the child act *through* the character—a less threatening way to learn.

You can suggest that your child try to be open to getting along with other children, even if a big relationship has no appeal. A few social reminders can make lunch and recess go better. When your child is faced with being with someone else for no real purpose, you can ask if he would like to try simple conversational ideas, like smiling and asking the person's name. Suggest alternatives to the trite and parroted "How are you?" like asking, "What are you interested in these days?" or "What have you been doing?" or offering a compliment. Dierdre Lovecky and I developed an analogy of seeing yourself and the other person as chests of drawers. What drawer do you want the other person to open? What could you ask about? Which drawer of your own could you open, to offer an idea or event or question that would interest the other person?

"Let me see kindness": another dimension of being compassionate allows us to see the benevolence in other people. If we look for other people's kindness, they will experience our kindheartedness and we'll feel better, too. The ability to see kindness is a gift you give yourself—that of more congenial relationships.

On making friends: nurturing suggestions

- *Alter your expectations.* Your children's need for friends might not match your hopes of popularity.

- As often as is comfortable, *acknowledge your child's social sensitivity and skill* ("Sammy seemed happy when you asked if he wanted to have the first turn; no wonder he likes to come over and play").

- *Motivate by cooperation, rather than competition.* Most of our children desperately want to fit in. For teachers, "cooperation" includes refraining from showing that Mitzi is "the best," or better than her classmates.

- *Proactively help find components of relationships.* Search for friends who have similar interests. One person can be a favorite for computer games, another for collaborative science experiments.

- *Ask the children:* What qualities do you look for in a friend? How do you show these qualities yourself? What are some things you might do to make friends?

- *Role-play social situations.* Let the children experience the impact of their own behaviors.

Learning to Honor Differences, and the Platinum Rule

"It is essential that our children recognize that people act from different motives and that no one's behaviors are always rational, justified, moral or informed."[27] We can expand our children's capacity for understanding ideas and behaviors that counter what they think is right. Children learn that awareness, and thus compassion, continually evolves as they explore other countries' customs, examine different religious beliefs and practices, and study their own country's history. These explorations give children perspective. They understand that not everyone sees things as they do, and that they are just beginning to formulate what can be considered acceptable.

We want our children to respect other people's differences and to have enough coping options to interact with all types of people. Our children can learn much from participating in and observing various situations. Different experiences refine what they value, and give them ideas of how they want and don't want to be. Instead of applying the Golden Rule (treating others as we would like to be treated), it is often more appropriate to consider the Platinum Rule (treating others as *they* want to be treated), to caringly try to understand the other person and give what that person wants and needs.

On honoring differences: reading suggestion
David White's *Philosophy for Kids* is an interactive book that delves into philosophical questions around values, reality, and knowledge.

The Critical Component Is You, and You Teach What You Are

Adults who believe in children, encourage their attempts, listen to them, and express interest in *them* (not just their achievements) pass on courage and hope. You can become a child's appreciated, cherished friend. This chapter is about *you* investing yourself to make an important difference by inspiring children's lives. It's about teaching your children to live peacefully, wisely, joyfully, kindly, healthily.

"What you are speaks so loudly, I can't hear what you are saying": We cannot avoid learning our mother tongue. If you live in a home where English is spoken, you will learn to speak English. The process is sometimes called *imprinting*. In *The Ape and the Sushi Master,* Frans de Waal tells how the sushi apprentice learns by watching his master, and the ape learns by watching his parents.[28] Our astute children absorb our language. They also absorb our gestures, values, and manners.

Our respect for and understanding of our children teaches them how they can be friends to others.

On modeling behavior: activity suggestions

- *Model that it is good to grow up.* Would you want to emulate someone who's not happy?

- *Stop violating yourself!* Listen to yourself; your greatest support can come from within. Give yourself permission to do something to meet your needs, rather than resent a situation. Be your own ally!

- *Consider how much time you invest in facilitating other people's priorities.*

- *Find understanding and support.* Spend time with people who give you energy and inspire you. Develop a relationship with a mentor; help this person help you. Imagine conversations with people you respect and who admire you. This gives you another perspective and source of understanding.

- Read Vivian Paley's *The Kindness of Children* and anything by Daphne Rose Kingma, especially *A Garland of Love: Daily Reflections on the Magic and Meaning of Love.*

- *Have your own goals.* Make a goal plan and do something every day toward actualizing your hopes. Continually look for ways to evolve your plan.

  o What are your most important goals in life right now?

  o What would you do if you only had six months to live?

  o What have you always wanted to do but were afraid to attempt?

  o What have you done that gave you feelings of meaningful satisfaction and importance?

  o What would you do if you were guaranteed success?

- Make a list of things you like to do; do at least one each day.

- Exercise for more energy! Try it and decide for yourself.

- Listen to your body: What does tiredness, shoulder pain, or headache tell you?

- Take very good care of yourself! You teach what you are, and you can only give what you have.

"And now here is my secret, a very simple secret: it is only with the heart that one can see rightly; what is essential is invisible to the eye."

—Antoine de Saint-Exupéry, *The Little Prince*

Notes

1. Paley, *The Kindness of Children*, 120–121.

2. Fletcher, "Touched by an Angel."

3. Sheely and Silverman, "Defining the Few."

4. Hollingworth, *Children Above 180 IQ*, 253, 259, 264.

5. Norman, et al., "Relationship Between Levels of Giftedness."

6. Janos, Marwood, and Robinson, "Friendship Patterns in Highly Intelligent Children."

7. Janos and Robinson, "Psychosocial Development in Intellectually Gifted Children."

8. Norman, et al., 5.

9. Kline and Meckstroth, "Understanding and Encouraging the Exceptionally Gifted."

10. Towers, "The Outsiders." Based on 344 people with IQs 140–149, 100 people with IQs 150–159, 70 people with IQs 160–169, and 48 people with IQs greater than 170.

11. Subjects with *satisfactory adjustment* had desires, emotions, and interests generally compatible with their society and group. They could manage their lives without becoming distraught or disruptive. Terman defined subjects with *some maladjustment* as having " . . . excessive feelings of inadequacy or inferiority, nervous fatigue, mild anxiety neurosis, and the like. The . . . maladjustments . . . , while they presented definite problems, were not beyond the ability of the individual to handle, and there was no marked interference with social or personal life or with achievement." People with *serious maladjustment* presented symptoms of anxiety, mental depression, psychopathic personality, or lesser neurotic conditions. A subcategory defined subjects who had required hospitalization for mental disorder.

12. Rogers and Silverman, "Factors in 160+ IQ Children." They examined 241 children with IQs of 160+.

13. Terman, "The Gifted Child."

14. Myers and McCaulley, *Manual: A Guide to the Myers-Briggs*, 107.

15. Myers and Myers, *Gifts Differing*, 38.

16. Supporting Emotional Needs of the Gifted, www.sengifted.org.

17. Myers and Myers, *Gifts Differing*.

18. Lovecky, "Exceptionally Gifted Children."

19. "Gifted Children and Suicide," *The Phil Donahue Show*.

20. Jackson, "Black Sky, Bright Star."

21. Hepworth, Farley, and Griffiths, "Clinical Work with Suicidal Adolescents."

22. Margolin, *Goodness Personified*.

23. Kerr, *Smart Girls*, 115. She found: "In their interests, gifted girls are more like gifted boys than they are like average girls. . . ."

24. Janos and Robinson, "Psychosocial Development."

25. Boys, especially, might garner self-confidence by reading books about successful, dynamic men who had isolated childhoods.

26. Kerr and Cohn, *Smart Boys*, 96.

27. Mika and Meckstroth, " . . . To Suffer Fools Gladly."

28. de Waal, *The Ape and the Sushi Master.*

References

Choquette, Sonia. *The Wise Child: A Spiritual Guide to Nurturing Your Child's Intuition.* New York: Three Rivers Press, 1999.

Delisle, James R. *Gifted Kids Speak Out: Hundreds of Kids Ages 6–13 Talk About School, Friends, Their Families, and the Future.* Minneapolis: Free Spirit Publishing, 1987.

————. *Guiding the Social and Emotional Development of Gifted Youth: A Practical Guide for Educators and Counselors.* New York: Longman, 1992.

de Waal, Frans B. M. *The Ape and the Sushi Master: Cultural Reflections of a Primatologist.* New York: Basic Books, 2001.

Eyre, Linda, and Richard Eyre. *Teaching Your Children Sensitivity.* New York: Simon and Schuster, 1995.

Fletcher, Harrison. "Touched by an Angel." *Westword,* September 8, 2001: 6.

Goleman, Daniel. *Emotional Intelligence.* New York: Bantam Books, 1995.

Hepworth, D. H., O. W. Farley, and J. K. Griffiths. "Clinical Work with Suicidal Adolescents and Their Families." *Social Casework: The Journal of Contemporary Social Work* 29, no. 3 (April 1988): 195–203.

Hollingworth, Leta Stetter. *Children Above 180 IQ: Stanford-Binet Origin and Development.* New York: World Book, 1942.

Jackson, P. Susan. "Black Sky, Bright Star: A Phenomenological Inquiry into Depression and the Gifted Adolescent." Master's thesis, 1995.

Janos, P. "The Psychosocial Adjustment of Children of Very Superior Intellectual Ability." Ph.D. diss., Ohio State University, 1983.

Janos, P. M., K. Marwood, and N. Robinson. "Friendship Patterns in Highly Intelligent Children." *Roeper Review* 8, no. 1 (1985): 46–49.

Janos, P. M., and N. M. Robinson. "Psychosocial Development in Intellectually Gifted Children." *The Gifted and Talented: Developmental Perspectives,* edited by Frances Degen Horowitz and Marion O'Brien: 149–195. Washington, DC: The American Psychological Association, 1985.

Jenkins, Peggy Davison. *The Joyful Child: A Sourcebook of Activities and Ideas for Releasing Children's Natural Joy.* Santa Rosa, CA: Aslan Publishing, 1996.

Kaufman, Gershen, Lev Raphael, and Pamela Espeland. *Stick Up for Yourself! Every Kid's Guide to Personal Power and Positive Self-Esteem.* Minneapolis: Free Spirit Publishing, 1999.

Kerr, Barbara A. *Smart Girls: A New Psychology of Girls, Women, and Giftedness.* Scottsdale, AZ: Gifted Psychology Press, 1997.

Kerr, Barbara A., and Sanford J. Cohn. *Smart Boys: Talent, Manhood, and the Search for Meaning.* Scottsdale, AZ: Gifted Psychology Press, 2001.

Kincher, Jonni. *The First Honest Book About Lies.* Minneapolis: Free Spirit Publishing, 1992.

Kingma, Daphne Rose. *A Garland of Love: Daily Reflections on the Magic and Meaning of Love.* Berkeley, CA: Conari Press, 1992.

Kline, B. E., and Elizabeth A. Meckstroth. "Understanding and Encouraging the Exceptionally Gifted." *Roeper Review* 8, no. 1 (1985): 24–30.

Kurcinka, Mary Sheedy. *Raising Your Spirited Child: A Guide for Parents Whose Child Is More Intense, Sensitive, Perceptive, Persistent, Energetic.* New York: HarperCollins, 1991.

Lawrence, Gordon. *People Types and Tiger Stripes.* Gainesville, FL: Center for Applications of Psychological Types, 1993.

Lewis, Barbara A. *The Kid's Guide to Social Action: How to Solve the Social Problems You Choose— and Turn Creative Thinking into Positive Action.* Minneapolis: Free Spirit Publishing, 1998.

———. *Kids with Courage: True Stories About Young People Making a Difference.* Minneapolis: Free Spirit Publishing, 1992.

Lovecky, Deirdre V. "Exceptionally Gifted Children: Different Minds." *Roeper Review* 17, no. 2 (December 1994): 116–120.

Margolin, Leslie. *Goodness Personified: The Emergence of Gifted Children.* New York: Aldine De Gruyter, 1994.

Meckstroth, Elizabeth A. "Complexities of Giftedness: Dabrowski's Theory." *The Young Gifted Child, Potential and Promise: An Anthology,* edited by Joan Franklin Smutny: 295–307. Cresskill, NJ: Hampton Press, 1997.

Mika, E., and Elizabeth A. Meckstroth. " . . . To Suffer Fools Gladly." *Gifted Education Communicator* (California Association for the Gifted) 31, no. 4 (Fall 2000): 34–35, 60–62.

Myers, Isabel Briggs, and Mary H. McCaulley. *Manual: A Guide to the Development and Use of the Myers-Briggs Type Indicator.* Palo Alto, CA: Consulting Psychologists Press, 1985.

Myers, Isabel Briggs, and Peter B. Myers. *Gifts Differing: Understanding Personality Type.* Palo Alto, CA: Davies-Black Publishing, 1995.

Norman, A. D., S. G. Ramsay, C. R. Martray, and J. L. Roberts. "Relationship Between Levels of Giftedness and Psychosocial Adjustment." *Roeper Review* 22, no. 1 (1999): 5–9

Nowicki, Stephen, and Marshall P. Duke. *Helping the Child Who Doesn't Fit In.* Atlanta: Peachtree Publishers, 1992.

Paley, Vivian Gussin. *The Kindness of Children.* Cambridge, MA: Harvard University Press, 1999.

Payne, Lauren Murphy, and Claudia Rohling. *A Leader's Guide to Just Because I Am: A Child's Book of Affirmation.* Minneapolis: Free Spirit Publishing, 1994.

Rogers, Karen, and Linda Kreger Silverman. "Personal, Social, Medical, and Psychological Factors in 160+ IQ Children." Presented at National Association for Gifted Children, 44th Annual Convention, Little Rock, Arkansas, November 1997.

Romain, Trevor. *Bullies Are a Pain in the Brain.* Minneapolis: Free Spirit Publishing, 1997.

Sheely, Annette Revel, and Linda Kreger Silverman. "Defining the Few." *Gifted Education Communicator* (California Association for the Gifted) 31, no. 4 (Fall 2000): 36–37.

Silverman, Linda Kreger. "A Developmental Model for Counseling the Gifted." *Counseling the Gifted and Talented,* edited by Linda Kreger Silverman: 51–78. Denver: Love, 1993.

———."Social and Emotional Education of the Gifted: The Discoveries of Leta Hollingworth." *Roeper Review* 12, no. 3 (1990): 171–178.

Sinetar, Marsha. *Spiritual Intelligence: What We Can Learn from the Early Awakening Child.* Maryknoll, NY: Orbis Books, 2000.

Terman, Lewis M. "The Gifted Child." *A Handbook of Child Psychology,* edited by Carl A. Murchison: 568–584. Worcester, MA: Clark University Press, 1931.

Tolan, Stephanie S. *Welcome to the Ark.* New York: Morrow Junior Books, 1996.

Towers, Grady M. "The Outsiders." *Gift of Fire: Journal of the Prometheus Society,* issue 22 (April 1987). Available online at www.prometheussociety.org/articles/Outsiders.html (May 2007).

Webb, James T., Elizabeth A. Meckstroth, and Stephanie S. Tolan. *Guiding the Gifted Child: A Practical Source for Parents and Teachers.* Scottsdale, AZ: Gifted Psychology Press, 1982.

Zohar, Danah, and Ian Marshall. *Connecting with Our Spiritual Intelligence.* New York: Bloomsbury Press, 2001.

29 Rainbow Spirits

BY ANNAMARIE SUMMERS

This author has requested that no additional biographical information be included.

Annamarie Summers, the first in her family to enter college, graduated summa cum laude and traveled the long road to become a physician. When she married and became mother to five gifted children, she discovered that remaining true to the doctors' Hippocratic oath that she had taken—to "do no harm"—required her to abandon her profession and use her abilities to parent her offspring. In doing this, she ran counter to both her family's and society's expectations. But she knows her choice is essential if her children's "rainbow spirits" are to survive.

When I was working, I went to extremes to avoid telling people that I was a physician. I wanted to be perceived as a regular person; not that doctors aren't "regular people," but it seemed that once people knew what I did, they either asked for medical advice or assumed that I was too intelligent to enjoy their friendship. I'm probably exaggerating, but I always wanted people to feel comfortable around me, and not disclosing my profession was a good start.

Now that I'm a full-time mother, I want to be perceived as someone with a brain and an education who has chosen to stay home with my children.

The journey from full-time physician to part-time physician to full-time parent has had many stages and lots of ups and downs. I've dealt with guilt and feeling torn between a career that I loved and my children's needs, between society's expectations and my obligation to my family. Over time, I have come to realize that the costs to my children's sense of self-worth far outweigh the money spent on my education, my sense of loss regarding my career, and my sense of obligation for having been given the opportunity to become a doctor.

I did try working full time when my oldest child was 2½ and my second child was about one year old. The one-year-old seemed to be doing fine, but my toddler experienced temporary attachment disorder and depression. He became withdrawn and wanted nothing to do with me. He wouldn't even let me tie his shoes, a sign that something was wrong—a sign I at first missed. The problem became painfully obvious later, when I watched a video that my husband took from around the same time. In it, I sat on the sofa calling my son to come for a picture. He not only ignored me but got as far away as he could. I decided to take some time off from work to see if it would help my son's feelings. Much to my surprise, by the end of the week he started to come around and let me into his world.

That's when I realized full-force how much pain he was in for such a small child and how his heart was breaking, and so I decided to resign from my residency.

After I had been home with him for a few weeks, he was much more open and loving with me. During this time, I was also able to take a closer look at some of the experiences he was having at preschool. I know now that these experiences (which several people suggested were ways he was trying to manipulate me) are fairly typical of many profoundly gifted (PG) children, but at the time, I didn't realize the extent of his giftedness or what that might mean.

After leaving work that first time, I waited about six months before returning to work part time. I continued to work part time through an adoption and another pregnancy, during which I went on extended bed rest. I did not return to work after my baby girl was born. My increasing awareness of my oldest son's high abilities contributed to my decision to stay home full time for a while, but I still intended to return to doctoring.

Well, I never did return. My children's needs became more important.

It has taken some time, but I believe that I have come to terms with leaving my career, and I feel overwhelmingly confident that I made the right decision.

My oldest son and his siblings need me here, desperately. Not all the time, not every day, but sometimes for long stretches. They need me to recognize when they are having trouble, and to provide a place of safety for as long as they need it. Barring catastrophe, I will continue to be here, working to have their needs met.

I have come to value my role as their mother, although my change in values took years to come to terms with, in spurts and starts. I was a good doctor; now I hardly remember how to treat diabetes. I'll never be as good a doc as I once was, or could have been. Medicine has changed dramatically in the decade since my residency. I recently told a classmate that I had not renewed my medical license. She said it was a shame that I couldn't find a way to continue to be a doctor, and surprised me by saying that I was one of the better students in our class.

I still underestimate myself, wish I were a better mother, and feel undeserving when someone comments on his or her positive perception of me as a mother. Another friend told me recently that when she feels like yelling at her children, she stops and asks, "What would Annamarie do in this situation?"

I find it both horrifying and funny that what I would do might be seen as a standard.

I will never know what kind of physician I might have been. But I don't care anymore. I have a more important job: to nurture five children, all profoundly and exceptionally and highly gifted. That little voice that used to whisper, "There goes Annamarie—she could have been a very good doctor," has fallen silent. I needed to silence it, or my children would get the message that I made a great sacrifice for them, and that would be too great a burden on them.

It was an honor and a privilege to work as a doctor for the relatively short time that I did, to touch other people's lives in that way, but my responsibility to society is to bring up these five children to be whole adults, able to take their place in this world, to love others, and to give of themselves to whatever they choose.

I'm not the first mother who has given up her work for her children, and I won't be the last. But there is something different about leaving medicine, possibly because it is such a respected profession. When I gave up my career,

I gave up both honor and privilege. And the preparation involved all those years of learning to deal with the most intimate, painful, and heartbreaking details of the lives of my fellow humans, as well as their joys. . . . What I spent on my education is a fraction of what society paid to educate me. But did this mean that I had a debt to repay to society?

When I took my Hippocratic oath, I had no idea that later I would be given these extraordinary children, and that "do no harm" would come to mean leaving my profession for my children.

It wasn't an easy adjustment, especially realizing I couldn't do it all. First I abandoned the idea of keeping the house organized. Then I discovered that I couldn't even work part time and maintain a happy home. One example of how difficult I found it only seems humorous now. For some reason, scrubbing the kitchen floor came to symbolize for me all that I had given up, and I would literally sob over spilt milk.

I learned that childcare and preschool providers couldn't comprehend that by the age of four my children already knew their letters and numbers, wanted to learn long division, preferred not to battle over toy trucks in the sandpit, and ultimately wanted to be at home because "that's where I can use my brain."

I was told that my children didn't know how to play with other children, and that I'd better get professional help fast so that I could learn how to let go and let them be children. I had long talks with professionals and friends about why I felt that very few people, if anyone, understood my children as well as I did. I wondered if I was being grandiose in thinking this, and in thinking that I was the only one who could adequately meet their emotional and academic needs because I was the only person who didn't brush off their concerns.

People told me to let them go, to force them to continue with preschool, so that they could build relationships with others. People said my children were too attached to me, that my need to keep them close was not in their best interests, that I was doing them no favors by bowing to their demands for my time. People insisted the children were just being manipulative.

Several months ago my father surprised me with one of his rare phone calls. After making small talk, he asked if I had gone back to work. I answered, "I can't." He asked why I had gone to medical school, why I had studied so hard and spent so much money, if I wasn't going to use my education.

People often ask why I left my career, why instead of being a doctor I spend my time chauffeuring my children to classes or teaching them myself. I usually answer simply that I have five children. I rarely need to elaborate.

"Ahh, yes," they say, and underneath there is an unspoken, instant understanding: "Good for you. You are doing the honorable thing."

But that is only the easier half of my reason. The real reason comes in the answer I reserve for close friends or sometimes for complete strangers, people I know I won't see again, so there is little risk in telling them. In addition to caring for my five children—ages ten, nine, four, three, and just under one year—I have another full-time job. I educate and advocate for my two oldest children, both profoundly gifted, one of them learning disabled as well.

I'll backtrack here to my childhood. I am the second oldest of five children and was raised in a low-income housing project. During most of my school years, I was the oddball who was repeatedly chastised for daydreaming, playing with my hair, or doodling. I received many Cs and Ds. I still wince at the memory of my fourth-grade report card, where the teacher gave me a grade of B- on the line where I was evaluated "as an individual." We moved several times, so I never quite settled into a social group.

In high school, in spite of my grades, a counselor who saw promise in me encouraged me to apply to an Ivy League school as a candidate for pre-veterinary medicine. However, I lacked confidence in my abilities, as well as the funds for such an education. During my final year of high school, I did become a good student and chose to attend our state university system as a biology major. At college, my academic skills blossomed and I graduated *summa cum laude*. Of course, I attributed this accomplishment to the fact that I was only attending a state college. My parents didn't attend my graduation. But during my final year of college, I began to think that I might be able to realize the dream that I had pushed so far back: my dream of becoming a doctor.

I was accepted to medical school, and thoroughly enjoyed it. I decided on pediatrics as my specialty, and entered a residency in the Northeast. I felt privileged to be working so closely with children and their families.

My most heartwarming recollection from the residency is of a nonEnglish–speaking immigrant family who brought in their beautiful but seriously ill ten-year-old daughter. They were crying and heartbroken, because they believed that she was dying. The senior resident and I diagnosed Rocky Mountain spotted fever, began treatment, and she improved. At her discharge from the hospital, the family thanked me in broken English and hugged me, and their healthy daughter handed me a single rose and thanked me for saving her life.

I will always cherish memories like this, of times that exemplify the joy I felt as a doctor. I felt deeply honored to take this part in people's lives. I looked forward to my own practice, where I could continue using my skills to positively affect people.

But at the same time, I felt undeserving. This was a little feeling, one that would sneak up on me in times of doubt. Was I a good enough doctor? How could I, a little girl from the projects, think that I was smart and capable enough to save lives? How many of my past teachers would believe that the quiet girl with the buck teeth and the hand-me-down clothes, the one who seemed to be nothing special, had become a physician? How many of them imagined my potential, or suspected my gift for healing and for touching hearts?

This leads me to consider the expectations of my family, in which I was the first to enter college, the first to get an advanced degree. An expectation was sometimes voiced, in apparent jest, when someone would remark that I would be the one to bring the family out of poverty. When I reached medical school, I was encouraged to enter a high-paying surgical field, like plastic surgery, so my aging aunts could benefit from my skills. They had little use for a pediatrician. I was continually reminded not to get married until after my training. They were all afraid that I would become a dropout and would not fulfill their expectations.

So here I am, a dropout from medicine, at home with five wonderful children. And my father calls to ask when I'm going back to work so I can help him with his financial difficulties.

Several weeks ago my four-year-old, Natalie, gave me a gift. An extremely sensitive child who loves adults but has no friends her age, she told me the following poignantly beautiful story, which I'm certain is a metaphor for her spirit. She said:

"Once upon a time there was a rainbow that never went away. But one day all the children wanted to eat it. Then another rainbow came and said, 'Let's hide in the clouds! They'll never find us there.'

"One night they peeked out and the children saw them so they ran far, far away. Then the children never bothered them again."

Contrary to popular psychology, I know in my heart that Natalie, like her brothers at the same age, needs to be in a very safe place. Her rainbow spirit feels threatened by being misunderstood by other children. She doesn't have the maturity to know that she will grow and will someday soon feel safe with other children, and that there's nothing wrong with being the way she is.

I know the time will come. I've been through this before with my two oldest children.

With time, I'm hoping to help my little rainbow rewrite the ending of her story, so she doesn't run away forever. I'm hoping the new ending will go like this:

"After staying in the clouds for a long time, the rainbow, now strong and with her colors more vibrant than ever, emerged confidently from her clouds. No longer afraid that the children would eat her, she found her place in the daylight, and she let the beauty of her spirit shine upon all she knew."

Resources and More Information

30 Strength in Numbers

An Introduction to the Resources

BY JUDY FORT BRENNEMAN

Back when we were still trying to shoehorn our son into a mainstream classroom, we spent a lot of time in school meetings. The consensus was that the special ed class wasn't working, but the mainstream class wasn't a good fit either. He could tolerate it for maybe half an hour, then his behavior would deteriorate and the mainstream teacher would have to send him back to the special ed classroom. The mainstream teacher sighed and shook her head. "If only he could slow down so we could teach him." The other teachers nodded sympathetically. It was unfortunate, they agreed, and then they went back to discussing the behavior problems.

The words, "If only he could slow down" hung in the air like a helium-filled balloon tethered to my wrist.

I left the meeting feeling sad and discouraged, the words a floating taunt before me. What was wrong with my son? Why couldn't he slow down?

As the fog of exhaustion and worry that always accompanied these meetings dissipated, I began to see those words for what they were: subtle blame-shifting. "Why can't *they* speed *up*?" I wanted to shout.

It was one of those turning points that in retrospect seems so obvious, a time when something first came into focus.

The school's goal was to make my son match the mainstream kids. They were working hard to make him "normal."

But "normal" in that sense of the word was not who my child was or ever could be. "Normal" was the wrong goal.

Pursuing the wrong goal meant we were asking the wrong questions. Questions like, "How can we make him fit into the regular classroom?" distracted us from questions like, "Why is his behavior fine in the math enrichment class?"

It never occurred to us that the question we should be asking was, "What is the effect of his intellectual giftedness in all this?" No one, not at school, in our families, none of the therapists or doctors, even suggested the possibility that some of his behavioral and emotional challenges stemmed from his high IQ. The prevailing opinion was that intelligence was irrelevant. If we couldn't remedy the behavioral and emotional problems first, it wouldn't matter how smart he was.

This is who my kid is, I remember thinking, and who my kid is, is just fine. If he can't fit into the world defined by the school, then we will find a way to make the world fit him.

To my surprise, our first useful resource when we began asking different questions was the same special ed department that we'd been working with all along. In a meeting with the director, I vented my frustration with the situation. "At home, he dives into whatever he's interested in. A couple of weeks later, he'll switch to a different topic. Why can't he do that in school?"

The director hemmed and hawed a little and then admitted there was an approach called passion learning that a lot of homeschoolers used. He suggested I read some of John Holt's books.

I left that meeting buoyed by hope—not just because I had something different that might help my son, but because for the first time, I knew there were other kids who learned the way my son preferred to learn—there must be. Why else would anyone write an entire book about it? My kid wasn't abnormal or "broken"; he was a passion learner!

A special ed teacher from another school in the district provided the next nugget. She and I were part of a group of special ed teachers, paraprofessionals, and parent volunteer advocates who were developing guidelines for special ed staffing. A discussion about certain programs turned into a heated exchange about managing behavior problems. Most of her students had autism, and most had serious language difficulties. Their cognitive functioning ranged from below average to very bright, but even the smartest kids in her class had a hard time articulating anything. These kids, she said, had taught her to look at behavior as communication.

Behavior as communication: not a bad kid, a problem child, but a kid trying to communicate.

These were new thoughts, new places to begin. Of course they weren't enough—but each clue connected us to another resource that provided another hint, or suggestion, or crucial bit.

Sometimes when I sit at my computer late into the night, I forget that it has only been within my son's lifetime that the amazing resource we know as the World Wide Web has come into existence. When he toddled through Aunt Chris's house naming everything, the words *cyberspace, Listserv, online,* and *blog* weren't part of our vocabulary.

Sometimes I wonder what our lives would have been like if we'd had access to that wealth. Would we have found answers sooner? Felt less isolated? Would we have discovered the programs at Johns Hopkins and Stanford? Would we have been better advocates? (Would we have challenged the school's decision to expel him from the summer enrichment program because he locked the teacher out of the classroom?) Would we have worried less about our child's "problems" and taken more joy in his gifts?

I'd like to think the answer to all these questions is "yes," but the truth is, I don't know. We had to find our way to the right questions first.

If I were beginning this search today, I would make use of everything the Internet and Web have to offer, from sites with general information to parent Listservs, from research reports posted online months before they reach print to blogs (and whatever comes next) written by high-IQ kids.

And I'd still seek out and use resources close to home: the special ed department, local (or regional) colleges and universities, therapists and support groups, conferences (even if you have to organize them yourself), bookstores and public libraries—because you never know where that crucial bit of info will come from.

Raising high-IQ kids takes commitment—intellectual, emotional, physical, and financial. It takes understanding and acceptance—of our kids, of ourselves. It takes support—from our families, friends, and community. For most families with high-IQ kids, there isn't enough help locally. We need to reach out, not once, but routinely, receiving and giving help and support within a community that is far-flung geographically and tightly knit in purpose and need.

Thanks to the Internet and Web, there are more resources for gifted children and the adults in their lives than ever before. New research, programs, information, and networks are coming online every day; the sites listed here are only a starting point. All of them are packed with good information and have links to other sites of interest. Many have Listservs or newsletters to connect with high-IQ kids and the adults who care about and for them.

Welcome to the neighborhood!

Organizations

The American Homeschool Association (AHA)
www.americanhomeschoolassociation.org
P.O. Box 3142
Palmer, AK 99645
800-236-3278
AHA is a service organization sponsored in part by the publishers of *Home Education Magazine*. The AHA was created in 1995 to network homeschoolers on a national level. Current AHA services include an online news and discussion list which provides news, information, and resources for homeschoolers, media contacts, and education officials.

The Center for Talented Youth at Johns Hopkins University (CTY)
cty.jhu.edu
McAuley Hall
5801 Smith Ave, Suite 400
Baltimore, MD 21209
410-735-4100
CTY seeks students of the highest academic ability through its talent search and offers them challenging educational opportunities that develop the intellect, encourage achievement, and nurture social development; conducts research and evaluation studies that advance knowledge about gifted education; develops best practices in educating highly able children; disseminates its findings to parents, the education community, and policymakers; supports educators in their efforts to meet the needs of highly able students; assists parents in advocating for their gifted children; and participates actively in community service.

Council for Exceptional Children (CEC)
www.cec.sped.org
1110 North Glebe Road, Suite 300
Arlington, VA 22201
703-620-3660
The CEC is a professional organization dedicated to improving educational outcomes for individuals with exceptionalities, students with disabilities, and/or the gifted. CEC advocates for appropriate governmental policies, sets professional standards, provides continual professional development, advocates for newly and historically underserved individuals with exceptionalities, and helps professionals obtain conditions and resources necessary for effective professional practice.

Davidson Institute for Talent Development

ditd.org
9665 Gateway Drive, Suite B
Reno, NV 89521
775-852-3483

The Davidson Institute's mission is to recognize, nurture, and support profoundly intelligent young people and to provide opportunities for them to develop their talents to make a positive difference. The Davidson Young Scholars Program includes consulting, an online community, annual get-togethers, and other resources for profoundly gifted children and their families. The institute's GT-CyberSource includes a searchable database of events, news, article archives, and discussion forums for and about gifted and talented children and teens.

Education Program for Gifted Youth (EPGY), Stanford University

epgy.stanford.edu
Ventura Hall
220 Panama Street
Stanford, CA 94305-4101
800-372-EPGY (800-372-3749)

EPGY at Stanford University is a continuing project dedicated to developing and offering multimedia computer-based distance-learning courses. EPGY provides an individualized educational experience, optimized in both pace and content, for high-ability students of all ages. Through EPGY, students have access to courses in a variety of subjects at levels ranging from kindergarten through advanced-undergraduate. EPGY offers online courses year round and also recently launched the EPGY Online High School at Stanford University.

Gifted Development Center (GDC)

gifteddevelopment.com
1452 Marion Street
Denver, CO 80218
303-837-8378

GDC is a resource center for developmentally advanced children and their parents and for gifted individuals of all ages. The center provides comprehensive testing of giftedness and visual-spatial learners; diagnosis of learning disabilities, particularly twice-exceptional learners; assessment of learning style, personality type, self-concept, and levels of achievement; counseling of gifted children and adults; consulting services for parents, school districts, private schools, and homeschooling families; worldwide referrals to professional diagnosticians; and innovative books, journals, articles, and other materials.

Hoagies' Gifted Education Page

hoagiesgifted.com

Hoagies' Gifted Education Page offers resources, articles, books, and links for parents, educators, counselors, administrators and other professionals, and for kids and teens about all aspects and levels of giftedness. The site includes a wide range of information as well as message boards and blogs.

The Hollingworth Center for Highly Gifted Children

hollingworth.org
The Hollingworth Center is a national volunteer resource and support network for highly gifted children, their families, schools, and communities. It primarily serves as a clearinghouse of information and events concerning the needs of highly gifted children. The Center was named in honor of Dr. Leta Hollingworth, who conducted one of the first pioneering studies of exceptionally gifted children, their social-emotional needs, and how best to educate them.

National Association for Gifted Children (NAGC)

nagc.org
1707 L Street, NW, Suite 550
Washington, DC 20036
202-785-4268
NAGC is an organization of parents, teachers, educators, other professionals, and community leaders who unite to address the unique needs of children and youth with demonstrated gifts and talents as well as those children who may be able to develop their talent potential with appropriate educational experiences. NAGC supports and develops policies and practices that encourage and respond to the diverse expressions of gifts and talents in children and youth from all cultures, racial and ethnic backgrounds, and socioeconomic groups. The organization also supports and engages in research and development, staff development, advocacy, communication, and collaboration with other organizations and agencies who strive to improve the quality of education for all students.

SENG (Supporting Emotional Needs of the Gifted)

www.sengifted.org
P.O. Box 6074
Scottsdale, AZ 85261
480-370-2193
SENG is dedicated to fostering environments in which gifted adults and children, in all their diversity, understand and accept themselves and are understood, valued, nurtured, and supported by their families, schools, workplaces and communities. SENG empowers families and communities by informing gifted individuals, their families, and the professionals who work with them about the unique social and emotional needs of gifted persons, and by supporting programs that foster the mental health and social competence necessary for gifted individuals to be free to choose ways to fully develop and express their abilities and talents.

Uniquely Gifted

uniquelygifted.org
This site, which is named after the book *Uniquely Gifted: Identifying and Meeting the Needs of the Twice-Exceptional Student*, is a collection of resources for families with gifted and special needs children and the professionals who work with them. The site includes articles, links, and resources about and for gifted children who also have special needs that may interfere with the expression of their giftedness.

Books

〰〰〰

Armstrong, Thomas. *In Their Own Way: Discovering and Encouraging Your Child's Personal Learning Style.* **New York: G. P. Putnam's Sons, 1987.** Armstrong suggests ways parents can help children to learn any subject according to their own style (based on Howard Gardner's theory of multiple intelligences) and to develop self-esteem.

Chapman, Randy. *The Everyday Guide to Special Education Law: A Handbook for Parents, Teachers, and Other Professionals.* **Denver: The Legal Center for People with Disabilities and Older People, 2005.** This book helps parents advocate to get the best education for their children with disabilities. It's also a good reference for teachers and administrators. A Spanish-language version is also available.

Davidson, Jan, Bob Davidson, and Laura Vanderkam. *Genius Denied: How to Stop Wasting Our Brightest Young Minds.* **New York: Simon & Schuster, 2005.** This book, from the founders of the Davidson Institute for Talent Development, a nonprofit foundation that helps educate gifted children, shows how the United States is neglecting gifted students and offers advice to parents on how they can help their children and advocate on their behalf.

Delisle, James R., and Judy Galbraith. *When Gifted Kids Don't Have All the Answers: How to Meet Their Social and Emotional Needs.* **Minneapolis: Free Spirit Publishing, 2002.** Delisle and Galbraith provide real-life strategies and solutions for meeting gifted kids' social and emotional needs and creating gifted-friendly classrooms.

Dobson, Linda. *The First Year of Homeschooling Your Child: Your Complete Guide to Getting Off to the Right Start.* **New York: Three Rivers Press, 2001.** This guide helps first-time homeschoolers determine the appropriate first steps, build their own educational philosophies, and discover the best ways to cater to their children's specific learning styles.

Elias, Stephen, and Susan Levinkind. *Legal Research: How to Find and Understand the Law.* **Berkeley, CA: Nolo Press, 2005.** This book provides a systematic research method to find answers and get results. Readers learn how to read and understand statutes, regulations, and cases; evaluate cases for their value as precedent; and use all the basic tools of legal research.

Fisher, Gary, and Rhoda Cummings. *The Survival Guide for Kids with LD (Learning Differences).* **Minneapolis: Free Spirit Publishing, 2002.** Proven strategies and sound advice help teens with LD succeed in school and prepare for life as adults.

Galbraith, Judy. *You Know Your Child Is Gifted When . . . A Beginner's Guide to Life on the Bright Side.* **Minneapolis: Free Spirit Publishing, 2000.** A lighthearted introduction to life with a gifted child, this book blends humorous cartoons and lively illustrations with solid information on giftedness.

Galbraith, Judy, and Jim Delisle. *The Gifted Kids' Survival Guide: A Teen Handbook.* **Minneapolis: Free Spirit Publishing, 1996.** Teens will find vital information on giftedness, IQ, school success, college planning, stress, perfectionism, and much more in this helpful resource.

Gilman, Barbara Jackson. *Empowering Gifted Minds: Educational Advocacy That Works.* **Denver: DeLeon Publishing, 2003.** This book provides parents and teachers the information they need to effectively advocate for gifted kids.

Heward, William L. *Exceptional Children: An Introductory Survey of Special Education.* **Upper Saddle River, NJ: Pearson Education/Merrill/Prentice Hall, 2006.** Using stories of teachers and children in special ed, as well as research-based practices and strategies, this book helps readers become exceptional teachers of special education.

Holt, John. *How Children Learn.* **Reading, MA: Perseus Books, 1995.** The revised edition of a classic offers insight into early learning, including how we learn to talk, read, count, and reason, and how to nurture these abilities in children.

Karnes, Frances A., and Ronald G. Marquardt. *Gifted Children and Legal Issues: An Update.* **Scottsdale, AZ: Gifted Psychology Press, 2000.** This book provides information about legal issues and school policies of gifted education.

Kay, Kiesa, ed. *Uniquely Gifted: Identifying and Meeting the Needs of the Twice-Exceptional Student.* **Gilsum, NH: Avocus, 2000.** This book explains the needs of twice-exceptional students and provides ideas for adapting education to deal with them.

Llewellyn, Grace. *The Teenage Liberation Handbook: How to Quit School and Get a Real Life and Education.* **Rockport, MA: Element, 1997.** In this classic, Llewellyn encourages teens to drop out of school in favor of "unschooling," a process by which they educate themselves using libraries, museums, the Internet, books, and other resources. She devotes many chapters to teaching oneself subjects and provides advice on jobs and getting into college.

Llewellyn, Grace, and Amy Silvers. *Guerrilla Learning: How to Give Your Kids a Real Education With or Without School.* **New York: John Wiley & Sons, 2001.** Parents learn how to become more involved in their children's education, whether through homeschooling or by supplementing traditional instruction.

Main, Frank. *Perfect Parenting and Other Myths.* **Minneapolis: CompCare Publishers, 1986.** Parents are encouraged to abandon unrealistic expectations, and examples and techniques help them take a more common-sense approach to parenting. (This book is out of print and may be hard to find.)

Mooney, Jonathan, and David Cole. *Learning Outside the Lines: Two Ivy League Students with Learning Disabilities and ADHD Give You the Tools for Academic Success and Educational Revolution.* **New York: Simon & Schuster, 2000.** The authors, who have LD and ADHD and graduated at the top of their class at Brown University, tell how they succeeded and show readers how to achieve whatever larger, postschool goals they may have.

Palmer, David. *Parents' Guide to IQ Testing and Gifted Education: All You Need to Know to Make the Right Decisions for Your Child, with a Special Section on Bright Kids with Learning Problems.* **Long Beach, CA: Parent Guide Books, 2006.** This book gives parents an insider's look at how the selection process for special programs works. It explains how schools identify gifted students and sheds light on who gets tested and why.

Rupp, Rebecca. *The Complete Home Learning Source Book: The Essential Resource Guide for Homeschoolers, Parents, and Educators Covering Every Subject from Arithmetic to Zoology.* **New York: Three Rivers Press, 1998.** Rupp provides a thorough reference guide for homeschoolers.

Silverman, Linda Kreger. *Upside-Down Brilliance: The Visual-Spatial Learner.* **Denver: DeLeon Publishing, 2002.** Silverman's book is a great guide for parenting, teaching, and living with visual-spatial learners.

Silverman, Linda Kreger, ed. *Counseling the Gifted and Talented.* **Denver: Love Publishing, 1993.** Silverman examines the cognitive complexity and emotional intensity of gifted children and discusses the need for modification of counseling techniques. Specific strategies for individual and group counseling are provided.

Taylor, Ronald L. *Assessment of Exceptional Students: Educational and Psychological Procedures.* **Boston: Pearson Allyn and Bacon, 2006.** This book offers a practical approach that emphasizes how both informal and formal procedures fit into the overall assessment process.

Turnbull, H. Rutherford, III. *Free Appropriate Public Education: The Law and Children with Disabilities.* **Denver: Love Publishing, 2007.** A revised edition of a classic, this book provides current information about the law governing the education of children with disabilities.

Walker, Sally Yahnke. *The Survival Guide for Parents of Gifted Kids.* **Minneapolis: Free Spirit Publishing, 2002.** In this book, parents learn what giftedness is (and isn't), how kids are identified as gifted, how to live with their gifted children, how to prevent perfectionism, when to get help, and how to advocate for their children's education.

Webb, James T., Elizabeth A. Meckstroth, and Stephanie S. Tolan. *Guiding the Gifted Child: A Practical Source for Parents and Teachers.* **Columbus, OH: Great Potential Press, 1999.** This book provides the guidance that parents need to support the unique social and emotional needs of gifted children.

West, Thomas G. *In the Mind's Eye: Visual Thinkers, Gifted People with Learning Difficulties, Computer Images, and the Ironies of Creativity.* **Buffalo, NY: Prometheus Books, 1997.** West profiles gifted individuals who used nontraditional methods in their work, debunking many myths about conventional intelligence. He asserts that modern computer visualization technologies signify a shift toward the increased use of visual approaches throughout the economy.

Wilmshurst, Linda. *A Parent's Guide to Special Education: Insider Advice on How to Navigate the System and Help Your Child Succeed.* **New York: AMACOM, 2005.** Wilmshurst offers guidance to parents and their children, and to teachers, counselors, and administrators on navigating special education programs.

Wodrich, David L. *Children's Psychological Testing: A Guide for Non-Psychologists.* **Baltimore: P. H. Brookes, 1997.** This classic reference for administrators, educators, and counselors demystifies the specialized information embodied in the results of children's psychological tests.

Wright, Pamela Darr, and Peter W. D. Wright. *Wrightslaw: From Emotions to Advocacy, The Special Education Survival Guide.* **Hartfield, VA: Harbor House Law Press, 2006.** This book for parents explains how to plan, prepare, organize, and get quality special education services.

Index

About the Editors

Kiesa Kay, who initiated this project, is the mother of two high-IQ kids. She has published articles and essays about profoundly gifted students and other topics and edited the anthology *Uniquely Gifted*. Kiesa has been guest editor of *Highly Gifted Children* special issues on adolescence and twice exceptionality and has been a featured speaker at conferences addressing the concerns of gifted children. She served as the program coordinator of Universal High School, a public school program in Colorado designed for highly capable autonomous learners. Kiesa is also a poet and playwright, and she recently founded Oleander Cottage, a writers' retreat in the south of France.

Deborah Robson is the parent of a profoundly gifted, learning-different daughter who has successfully reached adulthood. She and her daughter teamed up to make that happen. In the process, they both learned a lot. Deborah is also a writer, editor, visual and textile artist, and book designer, as well as the owner of Nomad Press, a small publishing company specializing in traditional and ethnic knitting books. She loves to work with her dogs on obedience and agility, has recently rediscovered the fun of bike riding, almost always has knitting in hand, keeps building new bookshelves but still needs more, and does yoga daily. She was cofounder with Judy Fort Brenneman of Greenfire Creative.

Judy Fort Brenneman is mom to a now-grown twice-exceptional son. She's a long-time volunteer advocate for "kids who look normal but aren't" and has served as an organizer, board member, and program director for support groups and conferences addressing the needs of these children. She is the owner of Greenfire Creative, a small business that helps individuals, agencies, and institutions tell their stories. Judy is an award-winning writer and editor whose works have appeared in a wide variety of publications. She's also a speaker and has developed and presented workshops on writing, creativity, and the power of story in forming identity and showing us who we can become.

Other Great Books from Free Spirit!

When Gifted Kids Don't Have All the Answers
How to Meet Their Social and Emotional Needs
by Jim Delisle, Ph.D., and Judy Galbraith, M.A.

Gifted kids are much more than test scores and grades. Topics include self-image and self-esteem, perfectionism, multipotential, depression, feelings of "differentness," and stress. Includes first-person stories, easy-to-use strategies, survey results, activities, reproducibles, and up-to-date research and resources. For teachers, gifted coordinators, guidance counselors, and parents.

$19.95; 288 pp.; softcover; B&W photos; 7¼" x 9¼"

More Than a Test Score
Teens Talk About Being Gifted, Talented, or Otherwise Extra-Ordinary
by Robert A. Schultz, Ph.D., and Jim Delisle, Ph.D.

We often hear about gifted kids, but seldom from them. Drawing on the voices of thousands of gifted teenagers from around the world, this book is a real-life look at what being gifted means to teens today. Essential reading for gifted teens and the adults who care about them. For ages 13 & up.

$14.95; 160 pp.; softcover; two-color illust.; 6" x 9"

The Gifted Kids' Survival Guide
For Ages 10 & Under
Revised & Updated Edition
by Judy Galbraith, M.A.

First published in 1984, now revised and updated, this book has helped countless young gifted children realize they're not alone, they're not "weird," and being smart, talented, and creative is a bonus, not a burden. Includes advice from hundreds of gifted kids. For ages 10 & under.

$10.95; 104 pp.; softcover; illust.; 6" x 9"

The Gifted Kids' Survival Guide
A Teen Handbook
Revised, Expanded, and Updated Edition
by Judy Galbraith, M.A., and Jim Delisle, Ph.D.

Vital information on giftedness, IQ, school success, college planning, stress, perfectionism, and much more. For ages 11–18.

$15.95; 304 pp.; softcover; illust.; 7¼" x 9⅛"

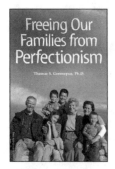

Freeing Our Families from Perfectionism
by Thomas S. Greenspon, Ph.D.

Parents have a powerful influence on their children's emotional development. Their attitudes about love, acceptance, success, and failure can create an environment that promotes perfectionism. In this encouraging, insightful book, Tom Greenspon explains perfectionism, where it comes from (including influences outside the family), and what to do about it. His healing process can work for anyone who is concerned about perfectionism and its harmful effects on children and adults alike. For parents.

$14.95; 128 pp.; softcover; illust.; 6" x 9"

What to Do When Good Enough Isn't Good Enough
The Real Deal on Perfectionism: A Guide for Kids
Thomas S. Greenspon, Ph.D.

Perfectionism may seem like a worthy goal, but it's actually a burden. When you believe you must be perfect, you live in constant fear of making mistakes. Most children don't know what perfectionism is, yet many suffer from it. Nothing they do is ever good enough. School assignments are hard to start or hand in. Relationships are challenging, and self-esteem is low. This book helps kids understand how perfectionism hurts them and how to free themselves. Includes true-to-life vignettes, exercises, and a note to grown-ups. For ages 9–13.

$9.95; 128 pp.; softcover; two-color illust.; 5⅜" x 8⅜"

The Survival Guide for Parents of Gifted Kids
How to Understand, Live With, and Stick Up for Your Gifted Child
by Sally Yahnke Walker, Ph.D.

How can parents make sure that their gifted children get the learning opportunities they need? And how can parents cope with the unique challenges gifted kids present? Since 1991, parents have looked to this survival guide for answers to questions like these. Now revised and updated, it's the first place to turn for facts, insights, strategies, and sound advice. Parents learn what giftedness is (and isn't), how kids are identified, how to live with their gifted children, how to prevent perfectionism, when to get help, how to advocate for their children's education, and more. For parents of children ages 5 & up.

$14.95; 176 pp.; softcover; illust.; 6" x 9"

The Survival Guide for Teachers of Gifted Kids
How to Plan, Manage, and Evaluate Programs for Gifted Youth K–12
by Jim Delisle, Ph.D., and Barbara A. Lewis

Two veteran educators of the gifted share strategies, insights, practical tips, and survival skills gleaned from years in the field. Includes advice on how to set the foundation for a gifted program; how to evaluate, identify, and select students; how to differentiate the regular curriculum for gifted kids; how to extend or enrich the content areas; and much more. For teachers of gifted students, all grades.

$24.95; 176 pp.; softcover; 8½" x 11"

To place an order or to request a free catalog of Self-Help for Kids® and Self-Help for Teens® materials, please write, call, email, or visit our Web site:

Free Spirit Publishing Inc.
217 Fifth Avenue North • Suite 200 • Minneapolis, MN 55401-1299
toll-free 800.735.7323 • local 612.338.2068 • fax 612.337.5050
help4kids@freespirit.com • www.freespirit.com

Fast, Friendly, and Easy to Use

www.freespirit.com

Browse the catalog

Info & extras

Many ways to search

Quick check-out

Stop in and see!

Our Web site makes it easy to find the positive, reliable resources you need to empower teens and kids of all ages.

The Catalog.
Start browsing with just one click.

Beyond the Home Page.
Information and extras such as links and downloads.

The Search Box.
Find anything superfast.

Your Voice.
See testimonials from customers like you.

Request the Catalog.
Browse our catalog on paper, too!

The Nitty-Gritty.
Toll-free numbers, online ordering information, and more.

The 411.
News, reviews, awards, and special events.

 Our Web site is a secure commerce site. All of the personal information you enter at our site—including your name, address, and credit card number—is secure. So you can order with confidence when you order online from Free Spirit!

1.800.735.7323 • fax 612.337.5050 • help4kids@freespirit.com